STARMAN
SINS OF THE FATHER

JAMES ROBINSON
WRITER

TONY HARRIS
PENCILLER

WADE VON GRAWBADGER
INKER

GREGORY WRIGHT
COLORIST

JOHN WORKMAN
LETTERER

TONY HARRIS
COVERS

INTRODUCTION BY
MIKE ALLRED

STARMAN: SINS OF THE FATHER

Published by DC Comics. Cover and compilation
copyright © 1996 DC Comics.
All Rights Reserved.

Originally published in single magazine form
as STARMAN 0, 1-5. Copyright © 1994, 1995
DC Comics. All Rights Reserved. All
characters, their distinctive likenesses and
related indicia featured in this publication are
trademarks of DC Comics.
The stories, characters, and incidents featured in
this publication are entirely fictional.

DC Comics, 1700 Broadway, New York, NY 10019
A division of Warner Bros. - A Time Warner
Entertainment Company
Printed in Canada. First Printing.
ISBN: 1-56389-248-0
Cover illustration by Tony Harris and Brian Frey

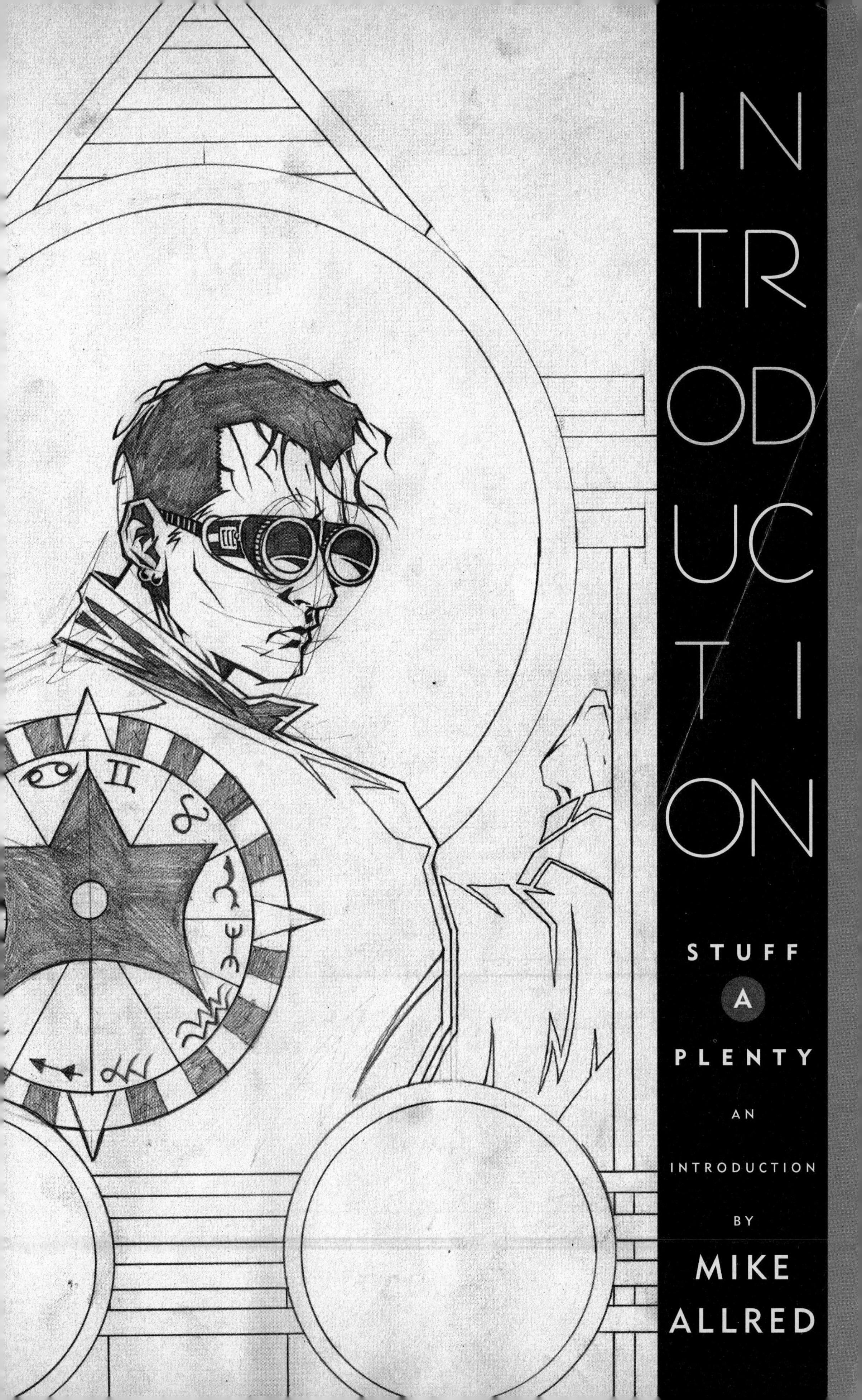

INTRODUCTION

STUFF A PLENTY

AN INTRODUCTION BY

MIKE ALLRED

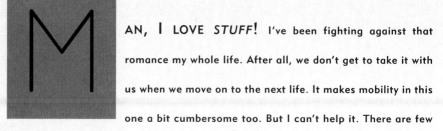

AN, I LOVE *STUFF*! I've been fighting against that romance my whole life. After all, we don't get to take it with us when we move on to the next life. It makes mobility in this one a bit cumbersome too. But I can't help it. There are few things more *exciting* than *looking* for cool *stuff* (the treasure hunt). There are few things more *satisfying* than *finding* cool *stuff* (digging up the X). And it's always the greatest victory finding something with value for next to nothing. It's shameful to pay the collector's market price for any item. Still, sometimes you just gotta.

This collection costs relatively next to nothing considering what it holds. Read it. Savor it. Hang on to it. If you don't have the original issues, hunt them down if you so desire (I highly recommend STARMAN #1 since James says something very nice about me in the back of the issue) but the victory lies in how you find them and what you end up paying for them. Since Tony Harris's stunning covers are included in this collection, do you REALLY need those individual issues? Probably.

"SHADE"

You won't find the letter column here. Where else can you discuss comics and hunt down a much-desired Fredric Brown paperback at the same time?

If good comics are among your favorite *stuff*, and you're truly on the ball, your hunter's nose should have found these treasures when they were still cover price on the stands. But forget that, speculator collecting is a sucker's game. The *stuff* I cherish most is worthless from a financial point of view and the "but it's priceless to me" attitude is the one I suggest for acquiring all cherished items.

You should know the biggest compliment you can give a comics creator when asking them to sign your book is if that book looks like it's been through a garbage disposal. Hermetically sealing your comics implies you've never read them. OUCH! Of course you can always claim the "I buy one to read, one to save" story. Good. Collect on your own terms. If it's the good comic you want, you're holding it. You've won the game — at least the way I play it. Forget its dollar value. What is it REALLY worth? That's the important question. Comic-book collections rarely go up in price, even when they're out of print. Someday, like in all things, a collector's market may develop for trade paperbacks. So what? You've got it. Protect it. Every once in a while bring it back out and read it again. Smile as you put it back on its narrow cherished spot on the shelf. Plan an evacuation of your *stuff* in the event of fire or flood. Be prepared. The game isn't over until you're dead. Protect. Defend. Instruct your descendants. Pass on.

If you're new to this game, it's not too late. Start now. Mourning of things past is part of the fun. If you are one of the greats who held on to your original MAJOR MATT MASONs, AURORA MODEL KITS, FAMOUS MONSTERS OF FILMLAND, VIEW-MASTER REELS, CAPTAIN ACTION, HOT WHEELS, BOB'S BIG BOY BANKS (and, of course, GLOW-IN-THE-DARK MADMAN FLIPPY FLYERS), good for you. I hate you. You're not my friend unless you give me some of **your** *stuff*. Heck, you probably didn't spend one thin dime on

TANK DRIVER GOGGLES
HAIR PULLED BACK IN A "TOP KNOT"
EARS DOUBLE PIERCED
ALWAYS STREET CLOTHES
BUT THE JACKET I
A CONSTA
ACK KNIGHT"
STARMAN
TATTO
BACK OF BOMBER JACKET

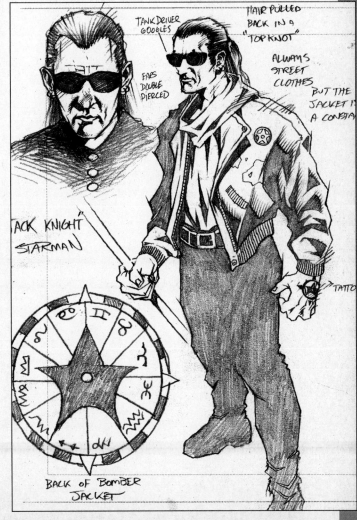

"NASH"
MISI'S DAUGHTER
COLD BITCH

it. I mourn all these things and the lack of vision of my mom and dad who chucked my childhood treasures behind my back. Sure I want them all back, but on my terms. I suggest making your own money like I do (trading "original art"). That's how I've been getting most of my new treasures (although I ponied up some steep dough for my Kent Melton ROCKE-TEER bronzini. GRRRR!). These are the mad ravings of the collector in us all.

To my knowledge, James Robinson is the first comic-book author to attach these oh, so admirable character traits to an actual comic-book hero (Dang! Why didn't I think of that?). Not since SANDMAN has a DC character of old been reborn radiantly unique with the thinnest, most fragile of threads tethering it to its charming (yet flawed) past. You see, I miss the old Starman, the ones drawn by Jack Burnley and Mort Meskin. That is, I think I do. It's been decades since I read the wonderful 100-PAGE DC SUPER-SPECTACULARs that reprinted those Golden Age gems. I'm afraid to dig them out for fear the ADULT ME will be embarrassed that the KID ME thought they were so great. The artwork was swell. That's a fact. I'm afraid the stories won't hold up. (Keep in mind that I took the 60's BATMAN TV series VERY seriously when I was a kid.) I rarely read pre-60's comics these days. I just can't take the disillusionment (though EC, TOTH, KIRBY, EISNER and Jack Cole's PLASTIC MAN can do no wrong).

It's cause for celebration when someone like the STARMAN creative team can come along and transform nostalgic affection into modern classic. James's writing, Tony Harris and Wade Von Grawbadger's stark graphic one-two punch, and Gregory Wright's supporting colors (Don't EVER underestimate the contribution of a good colorist!) have done this. They are building new myths

"KYLE" MISTS' SON

KYLES WEAPON
44 MAGNUM
AUTOMATIC 8 ROUND MAGAZINE
WITH OPTIONAL
MINI FLAMETHROWER
16 OZ. CAPACITY
LIQUID PLASMA FLAME

THEODORE KNIGHT
"TED"
ORIGINAL STARMAN
FATHER TO DAVID
AND JACK
SCIENTIST

HARRIS 93

enriched with adult sensibilities and growing characterizations. I still can't get over what a coup the Jack Knight Starman is. Almost every comic-book fan (if not every human in some way) is a rabid collector of some kind and can instantly relate to Jack. His passion for stuff makes him someone I could easily spend hours with happily. James accomplished this utilizing the oldest writing trick in the world. JAMES IS JACK! JACK IS JAMES! Tony Harris has invested much of himself into the star of STARMAN as well. If you ever meet Tony you'll know what I'm talking about. (There's more than a passing resemblance.) Clearly, STARMAN is very special to these guys. With that kind of personal investment, you can be sure the level of quality in the stories will more than sustain. It will improve.

James, like Jack, like me, and most likely, like you, is also a collector. Annoyingly so. I immediately identified with Jack, even more so in the moments when Jack wants big brother David's BIG LITTLE BOOKS. I've "borrowed" my big brother Lee's treasures more than once, always justifying the act since I wanted the goods more than Lee did.

You might guess that I'm not a big fan of "Golden Age Revisionism." I like holding on to things past (another collector quirk). Revisionism rarely works, usually irritating the true believers. My first complaint is usually "Why don't they leave the costume alone?" followed by "It's only complicating things." I usually prefer the SANDMAN MYSTERY THEATRE approach which gives you the old *stuff* done right. STARMAN isn't attempting to rewrite history but to celebrate it, often filling out the story with a SKYMAN reference or a universal emotion like the need for a father's love and respect. It manages to enrich the present instead of cluttering it. Just imagine having a simple hand-me-down like a COSMIC ROD in your collection. Most important, instead of throwing up my hands flustered, it creates, for me, an antici- pation for the character's future.

I have to admit, when I first saw STARMAN my reaction was "The fin! Where's the fin!" Obviously I've been won over. STARMAN is a hit, currently one of the most celebrated and anticipated titles on the stands. A true sleeper. STARMAN's Opal City is populated by thrilling heroes in the Knight and O'Dare families, wicked villains in the Mist clan and the Shade (or is he a good guy?). I'm tempted to dwell on favorite sequences like pages 20 and 21 from issue #4 or the final word in sibling rivalry that terrifically ends this collection. But if you've read the comics, you've already been initiated; and if you haven't, it's time you did.

So what do you think? Should Jack Knight strap a big mean green fin to the top of his head? Now, that would be cool *stuff*!

Mike Allred is the creator, writer and artist of Madman Comics (Legends/Dark Horse and has contributed his talents to Grafik Muzik (Slave Labor Press), Creatures of the ID (Caliber Press), The Everyman (Epic), and for DC/Vertigo BROTHER POWER THE GEEK, VERTIGO JAM and THE SANDMAN (The "Golden Boy" chapter of WORLDS' END). He lives in Oregon with his wife, three kids and lots of cool stuff. He sent cool stuff in with this introduction and hopes to get cool stuff back.

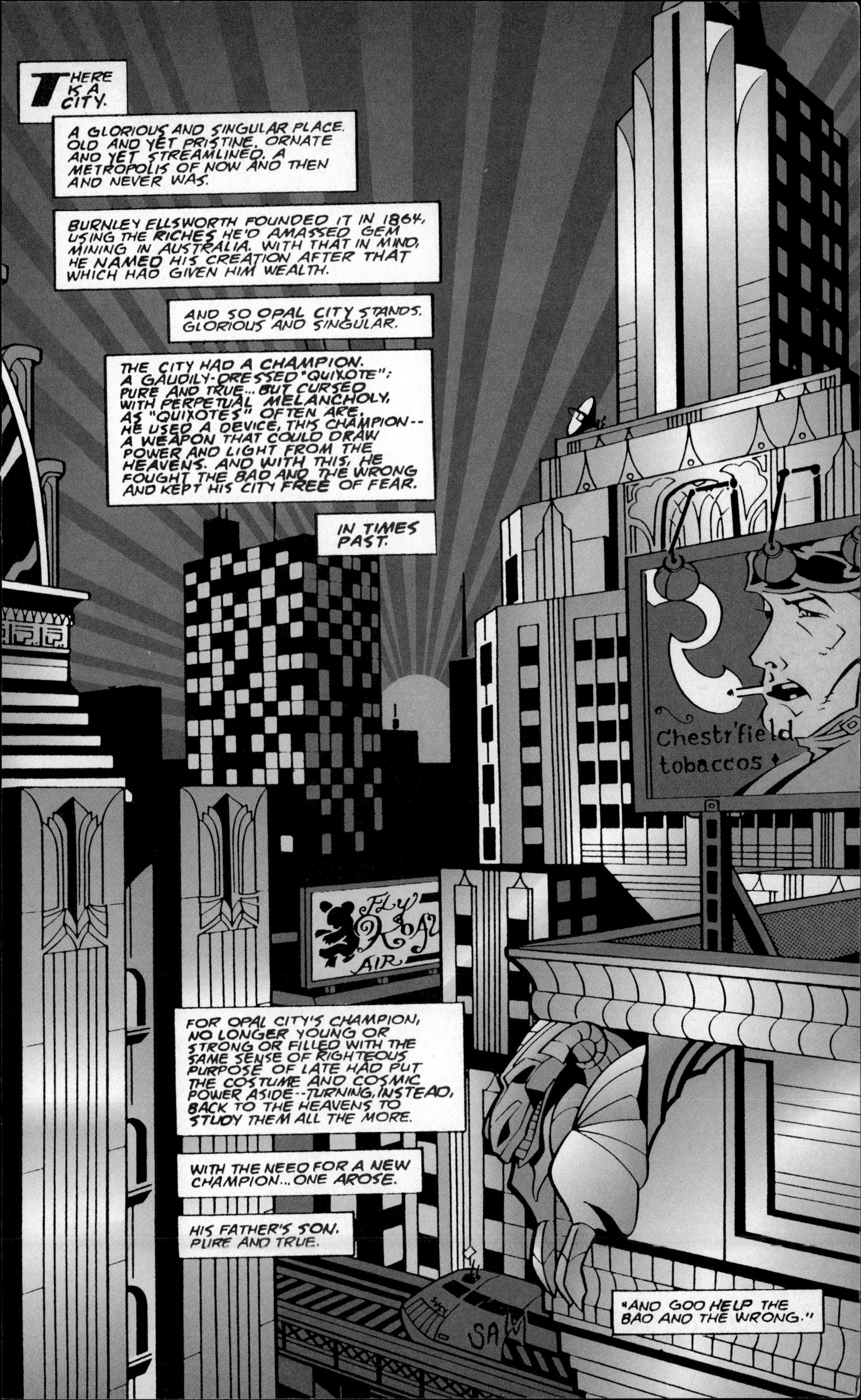
THERE IS A CITY.
A GLORIOUS AND SINGULAR PLACE. OLD AND YET PRISTINE. ORNATE AND YET STREAMLINED. A METROPOLIS OF NOW AND THEN AND NEVER WAS.
BURNLEY ELLSWORTH FOUNDED IT IN 1864, USING THE RICHES HE'D AMASSED GEM MINING IN AUSTRALIA. WITH THAT IN MIND, HE NAMED HIS CREATION AFTER THAT WHICH HAD GIVEN HIM WEALTH.
AND SO OPAL CITY STANDS. GLORIOUS AND SINGULAR.
THE CITY HAD A CHAMPION. A GAUDILY-DRESSED "QUIXOTE": PURE AND TRUE... BUT CURSED WITH PERPETUAL MELANCHOLY, AS "QUIXOTES" OFTEN ARE. HE USED A DEVICE, THIS CHAMPION-- A WEAPON THAT COULD DRAW POWER AND LIGHT FROM THE HEAVENS. AND WITH THIS, HE FOUGHT THE BAD AND THE WRONG AND KEPT HIS CITY FREE OF FEAR.
IN TIMES PAST.
Chestr'field tobaccos
FLY
AIR
FOR OPAL CITY'S CHAMPION, NO LONGER YOUNG OR STRONG OR FILLED WITH THE SAME SENSE OF RIGHTEOUS PURPOSE OF LATE HAD PUT THE COSTUME AND COSMIC POWER ASIDE--TURNING, INSTEAD, BACK TO THE HEAVENS TO STUDY THEM ALL THE MORE.
WITH THE NEED FOR A NEW CHAMPION... ONE AROSE.
HIS FATHER'S SON. PURE AND TRUE.
"AND GOD HELP THE BAD AND THE WRONG."

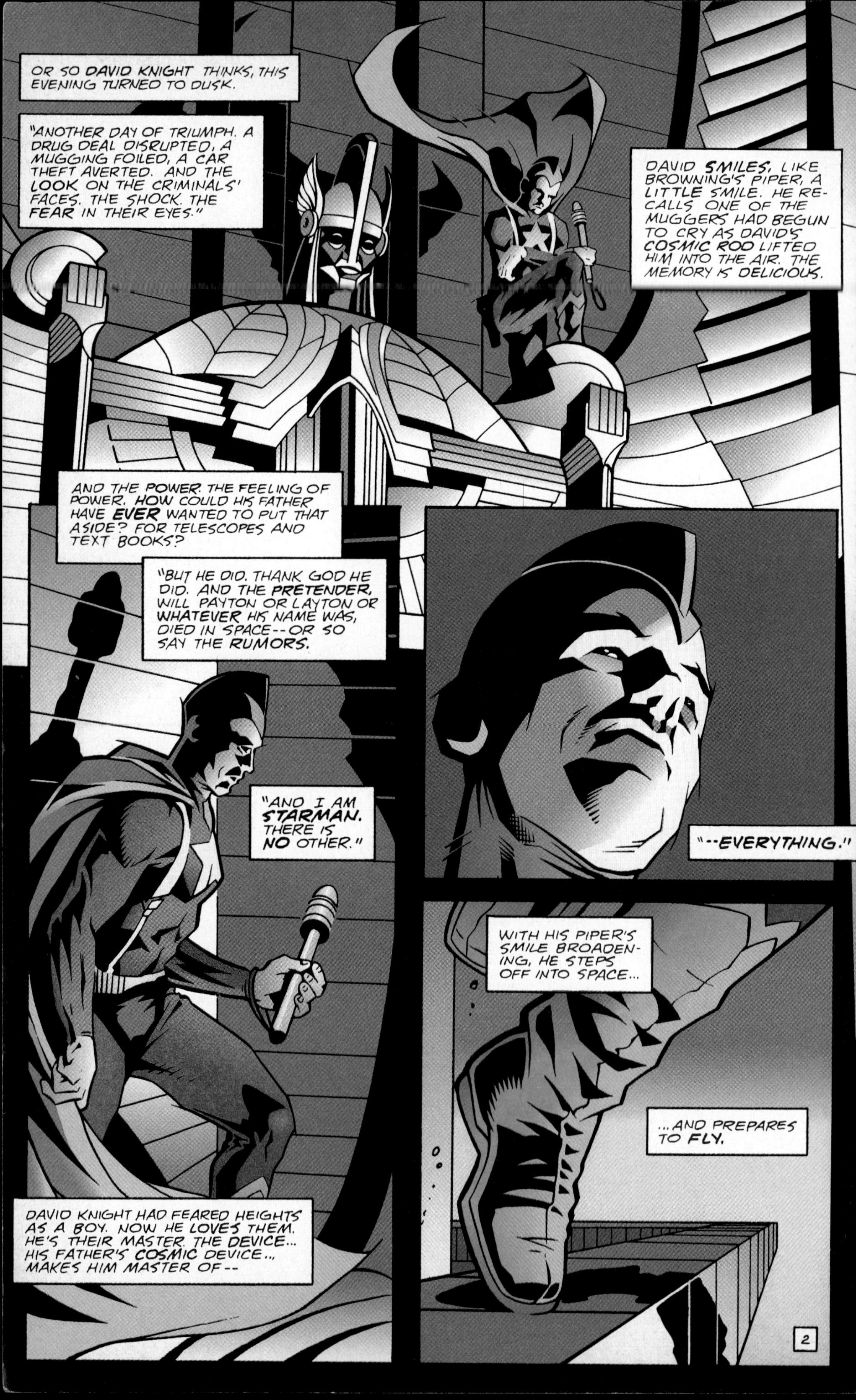
OR SO DAVID KNIGHT THINKS, THIS EVENING TURNED TO DUSK.
"ANOTHER DAY OF TRIUMPH. A DRUG DEAL DISRUPTED, A MUGGING FOILED, A CAR THEFT AVERTED. AND THE LOOK ON THE CRIMINALS' FACES. THE SHOCK. THE FEAR IN THEIR EYES."
DAVID SMILES, LIKE BROWNING'S PIPER, A LITTLE SMILE. HE RECALLS ONE OF THE MUGGERS HAD BEGUN TO CRY AS DAVID'S COSMIC ROD LIFTED HIM INTO THE AIR. THE MEMORY IS DELICIOUS.
AND THE POWER. THE FEELING OF POWER. HOW COULD HIS FATHER HAVE EVER WANTED TO PUT THAT ASIDE? FOR TELESCOPES AND TEXT BOOKS?
"BUT HE DID. THANK GOD HE DID. AND THE PRETENDER, WILL PAYTON OR LAYTON OR WHATEVER HIS NAME WAS, DIED IN SPACE--OR SO SAY THE RUMORS.
"AND I AM STARMAN. THERE IS NO OTHER."
DAVID KNIGHT HAD FEARED HEIGHTS AS A BOY. NOW HE LOVES THEM. HE'S THEIR MASTER. THE DEVICE... HIS FATHER'S COSMIC DEVICE... MAKES HIM MASTER OF--
"--EVERYTHING."
WITH HIS PIPER'S SMILE BROADENING, HE STEPS OFF INTO SPACE...
...AND PREPARES TO FLY.
2

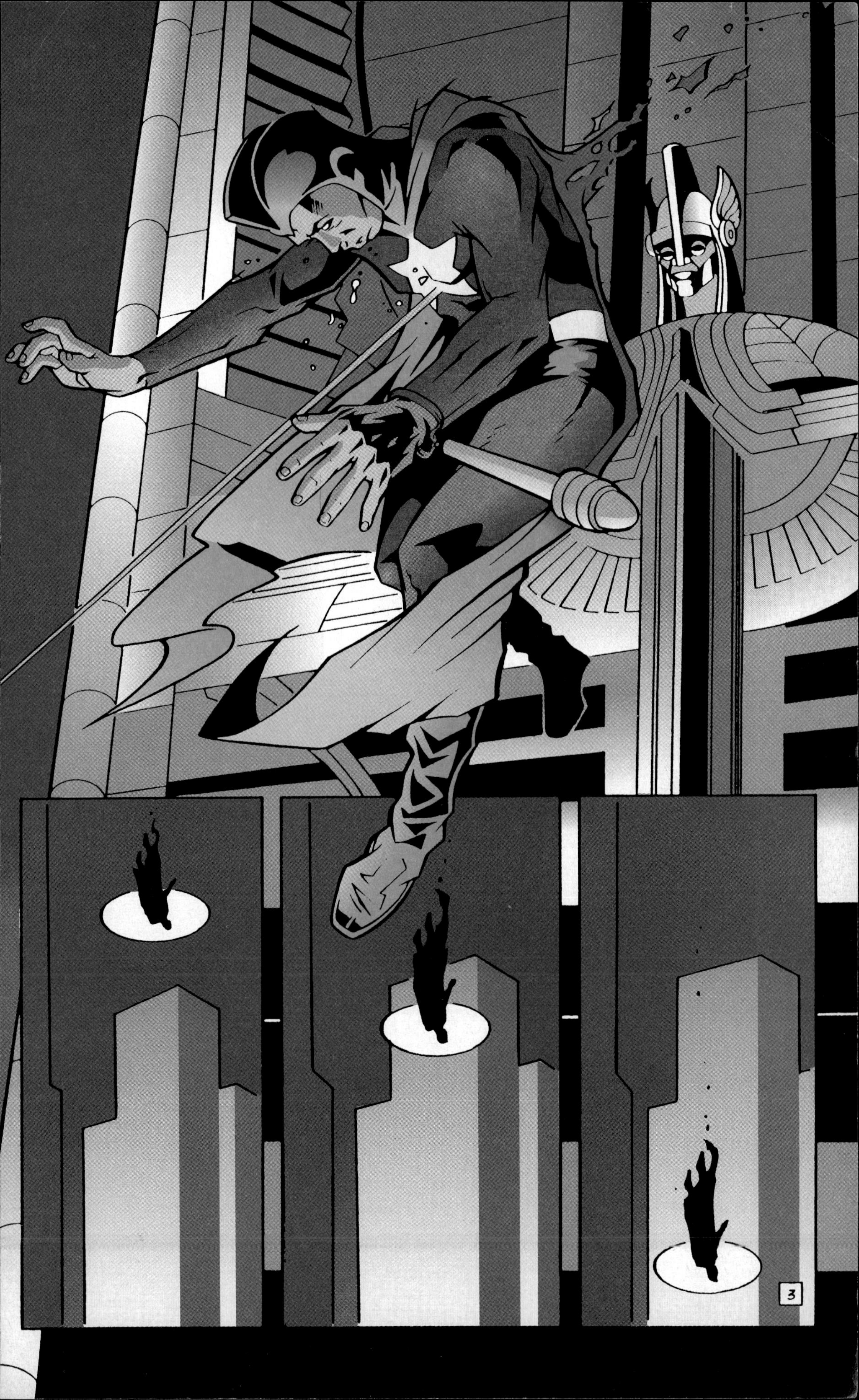
3

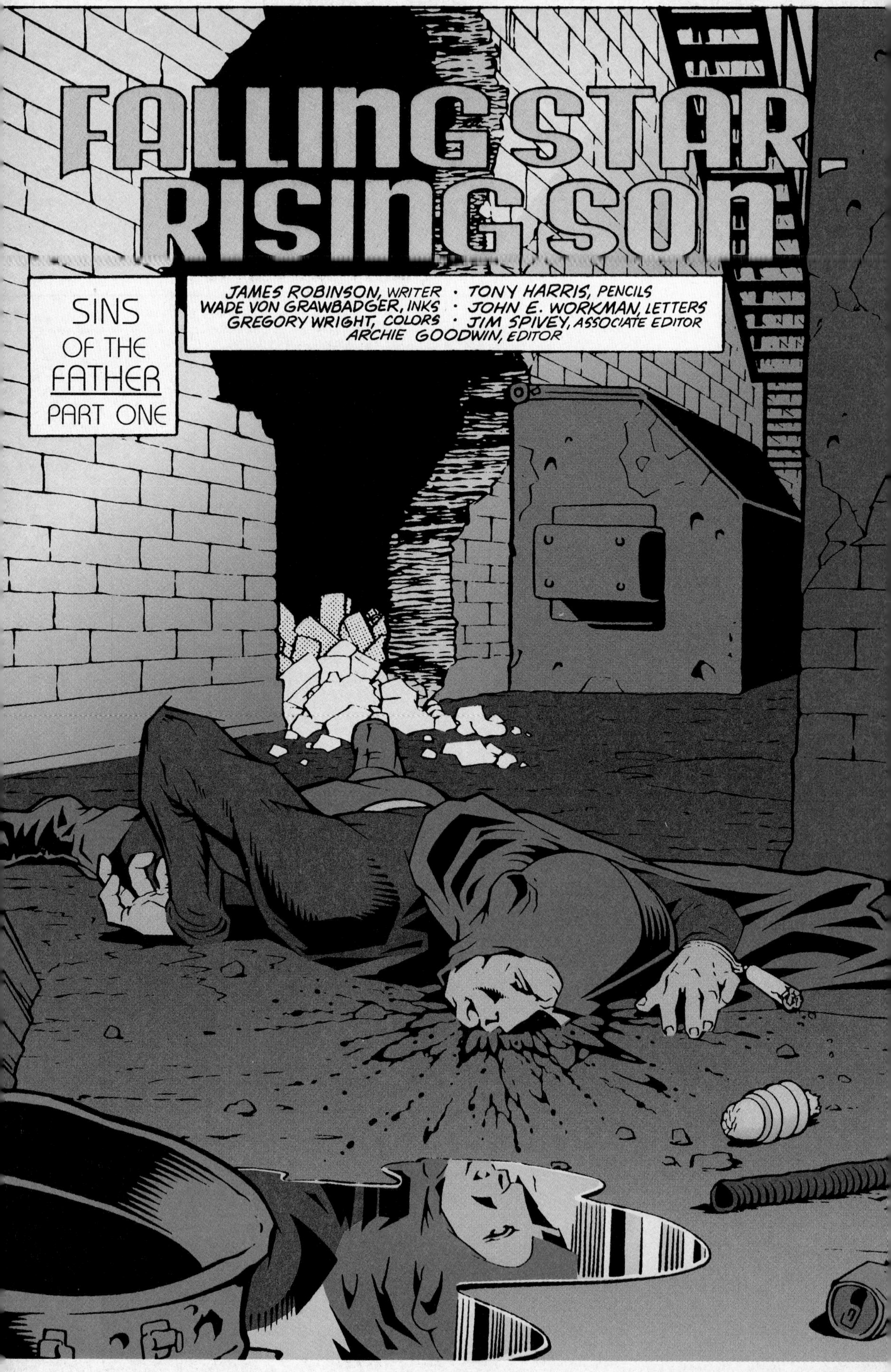
FALLING STAR-RISING SON
SINS OF THE FATHER PART ONE
JAMES ROBINSON, WRITER · TONY HARRIS, PENCILS
WADE VON GRAWBADGER, INKS · JOHN E. WORKMAN, LETTERS
GREGORY WRIGHT, COLORS · JIM SPIVEY, ASSOCIATE EDITOR
ARCHIE GOODWIN, EDITOR

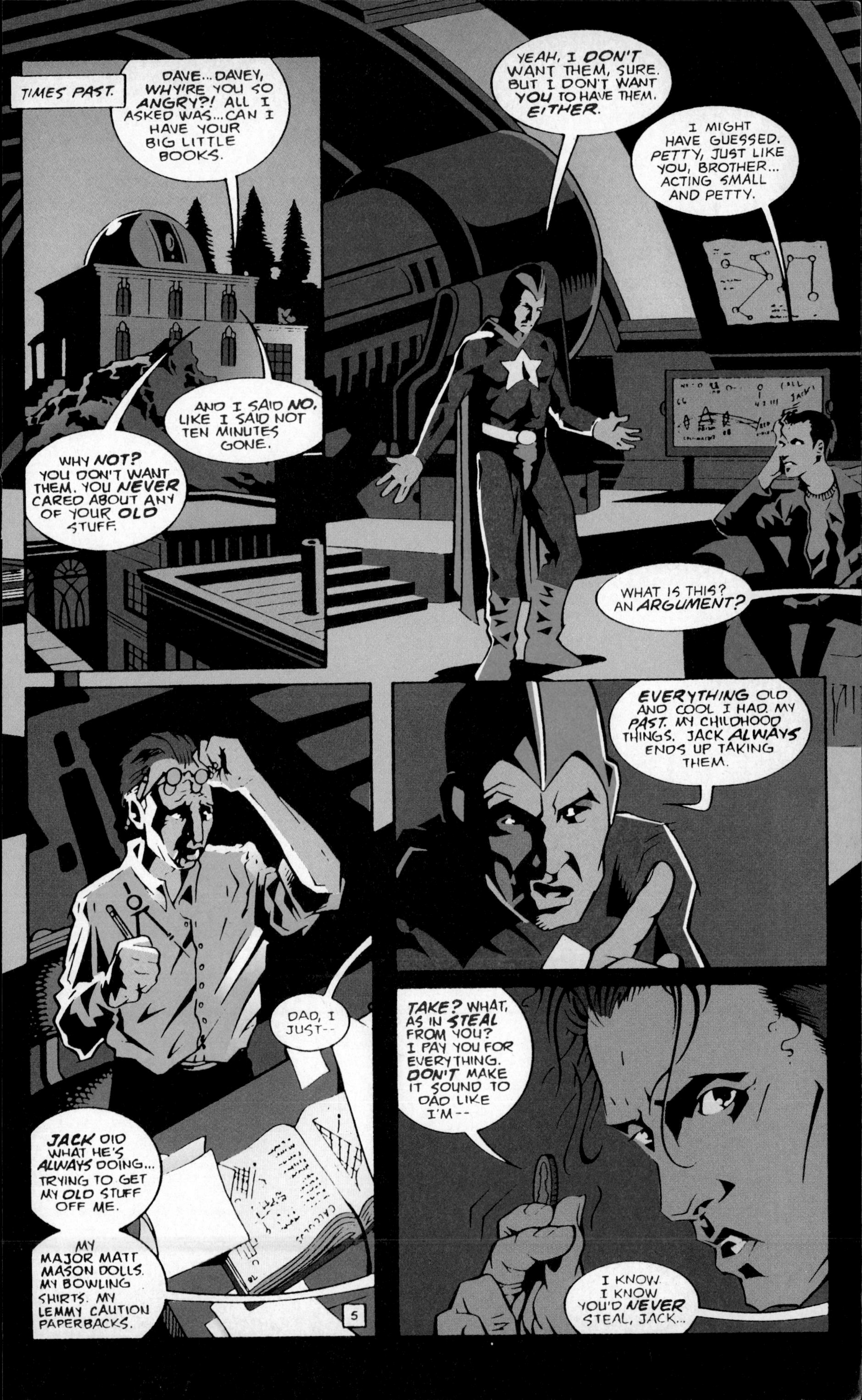
TIMES PAST.
DAVE... DAVEY, WHY'RE YOU SO ANGRY?! ALL I ASKED WAS... CAN I HAVE YOUR BIG LITTLE BOOKS.
AND I SAID NO, LIKE I SAID NOT TEN MINUTES GONE.
WHY NOT? YOU DON'T WANT THEM. YOU NEVER CARED ABOUT ANY OF YOUR OLD STUFF.
YEAH, I DON'T WANT THEM, SURE. BUT I DON'T WANT YOU TO HAVE THEM, EITHER.
I MIGHT HAVE GUESSED. PETTY, JUST LIKE YOU, BROTHER... ACTING SMALL AND PETTY.
WHAT IS THIS? AN ARGUMENT?
DAD, I JUST--
JACK DID WHAT HE'S ALWAYS DOING... TRYING TO GET MY OLD STUFF OFF ME.
MY MAJOR MATT MASON DOLLS. MY BOWLING SHIRTS. MY LEMMY CAUTION PAPERBACKS.
EVERYTHING OLD AND COOL I HAD. MY PAST. MY CHILDHOOD THINGS. JACK ALWAYS ENDS UP TAKING THEM.
TAKE? WHAT, AS IN STEAL FROM YOU? I PAY YOU FOR EVERYTHING. DON'T MAKE IT SOUND TO DAD LIKE I'M--
I KNOW. I KNOW YOU'D NEVER STEAL, JACK...

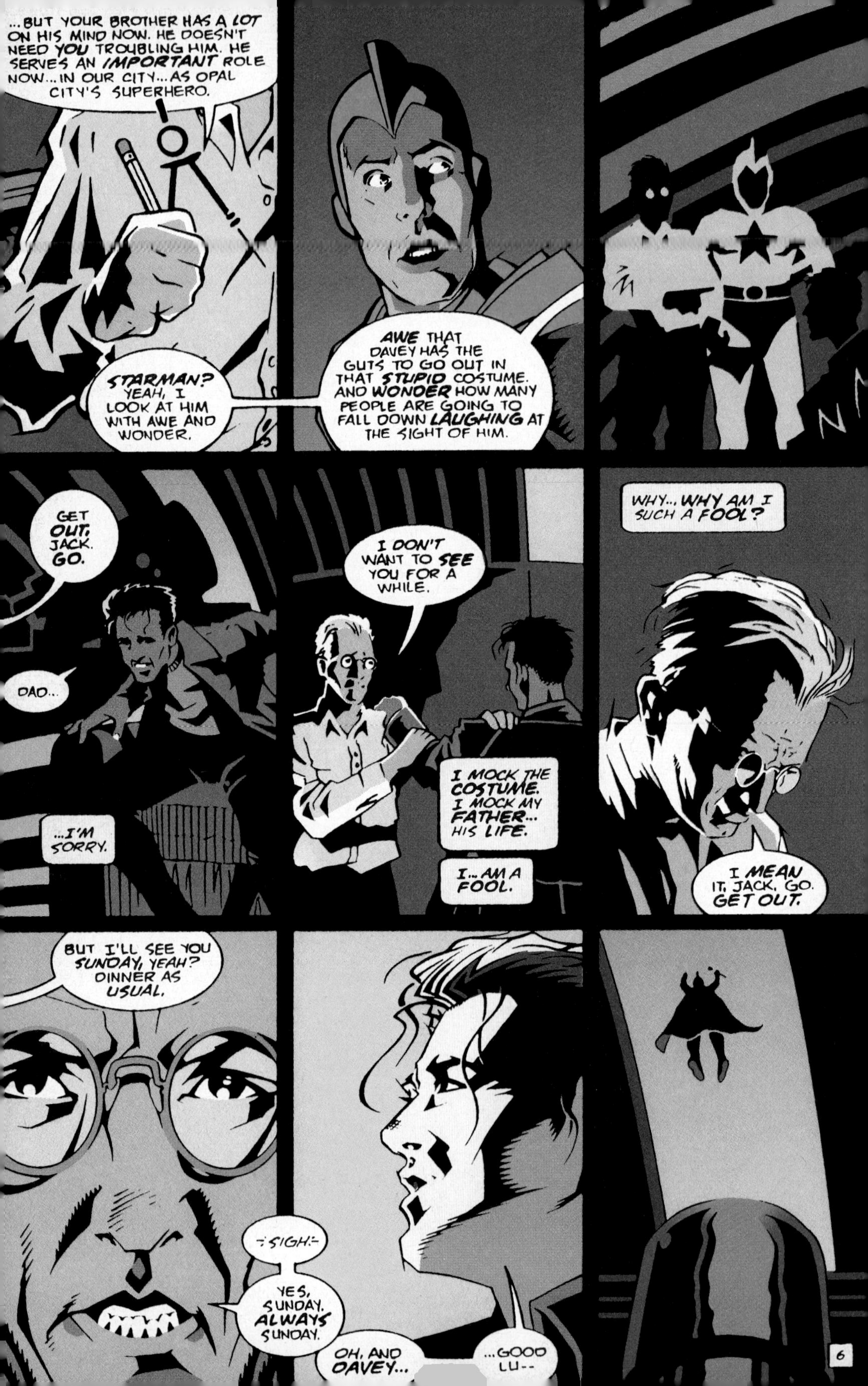
...BUT YOUR BROTHER HAS A LOT ON HIS MIND NOW. HE DOESN'T NEED YOU TROUBLING HIM. HE SERVES AN IMPORTANT ROLE NOW... IN OUR CITY... AS OPAL CITY'S SUPERHERO.
STARMAN? YEAH, I LOOK AT HIM WITH AWE AND WONDER.
AWE THAT DAVEY HAS THE GUTS TO GO OUT IN THAT STUPID COSTUME. AND WONDER HOW MANY PEOPLE ARE GOING TO FALL DOWN LAUGHING AT THE SIGHT OF HIM.
GET OUT, JACK. GO.
DAD...
...I'M SORRY.
I DON'T WANT TO SEE YOU FOR A WHILE.
I MOCK THE COSTUME. I MOCK MY FATHER... HIS LIFE.
I... AM A FOOL.
WHY... WHY AM I SUCH A FOOL?
I MEAN IT, JACK. GO. GET OUT.
BUT I'LL SEE YOU SUNDAY, YEAH? DINNER AS USUAL.
-:SIGH:-
YES, SUNDAY. ALWAYS SUNDAY.
OH, AND DAVEY...
...GOOD LU--

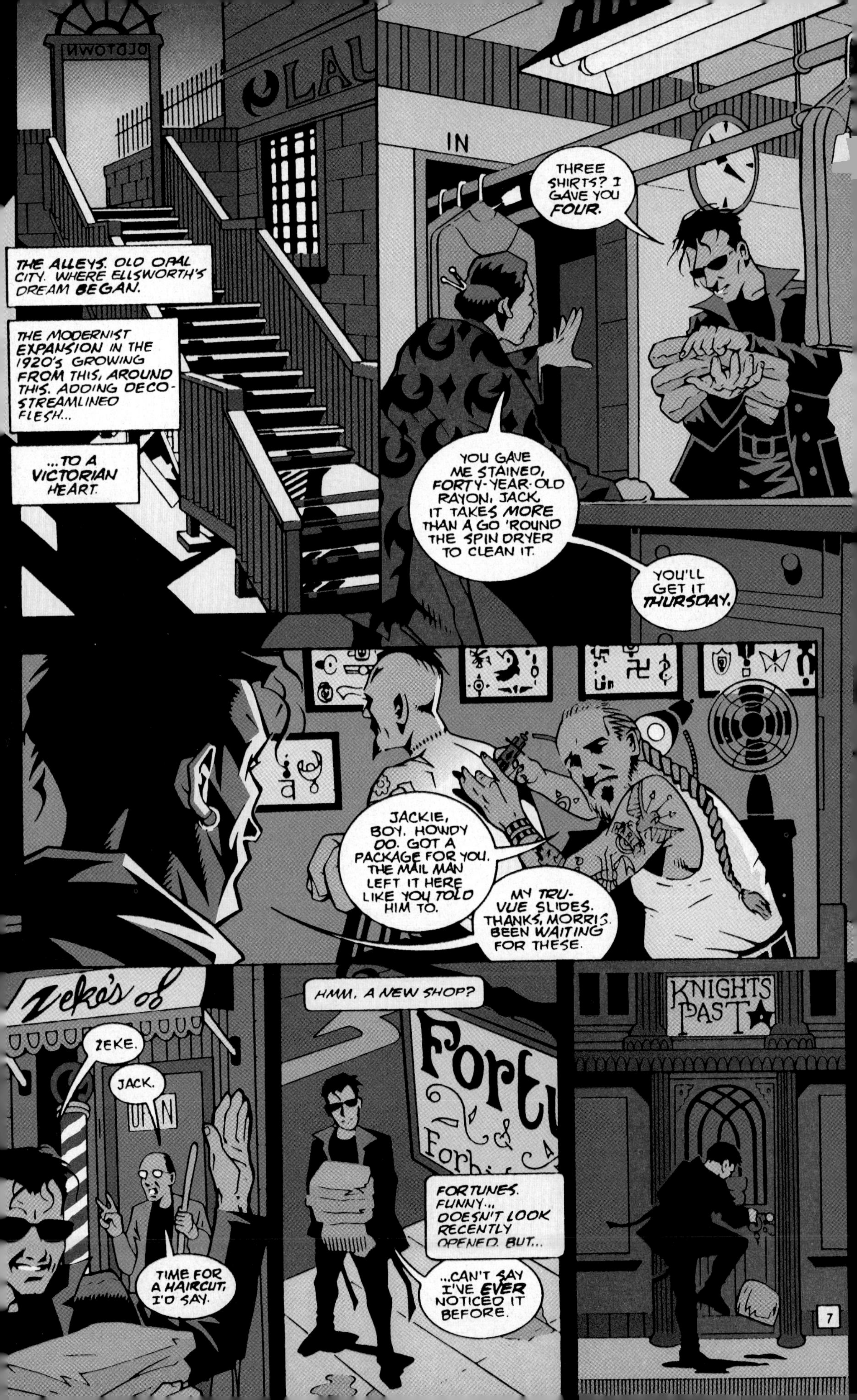
OLDTOWN
LAU
IN
THE ALLEYS. OLD OPAL CITY. WHERE ELLSWORTH'S DREAM BEGAN.
THE MODERNIST EXPANSION IN THE 1920'S GROWING FROM THIS, AROUND THIS. ADDING DECO-STREAMLINED FLESH...
...TO A VICTORIAN HEART.
THREE SHIRTS? I GAVE YOU FOUR.
YOU GAVE ME STAINED, FORTY-YEAR-OLD RAYON, JACK. IT TAKES MORE THAN A GO 'ROUND THE SPIN DRYER TO CLEAN IT.
YOU'LL GET IT THURSDAY.
JACKIE, BOY. HOWDY DO. GOT A PACKAGE FOR YOU. THE MAIL MAN LEFT IT HERE LIKE YOU TOLD HIM TO.
MY TRU-VUE SLIDES. THANKS, MORRIS. BEEN WAITING FOR THESE.
Zeke's
ZEKE.
JACK.
TIME FOR A HAIRCUT, I'D SAY.
HMM. A NEW SHOP?
Fortu
FORTUNES. FUNNY... DOESN'T LOOK RECENTLY OPENED. BUT...
...CAN'T SAY I'VE EVER NOTICED IT BEFORE.
KNIGHTS PAST

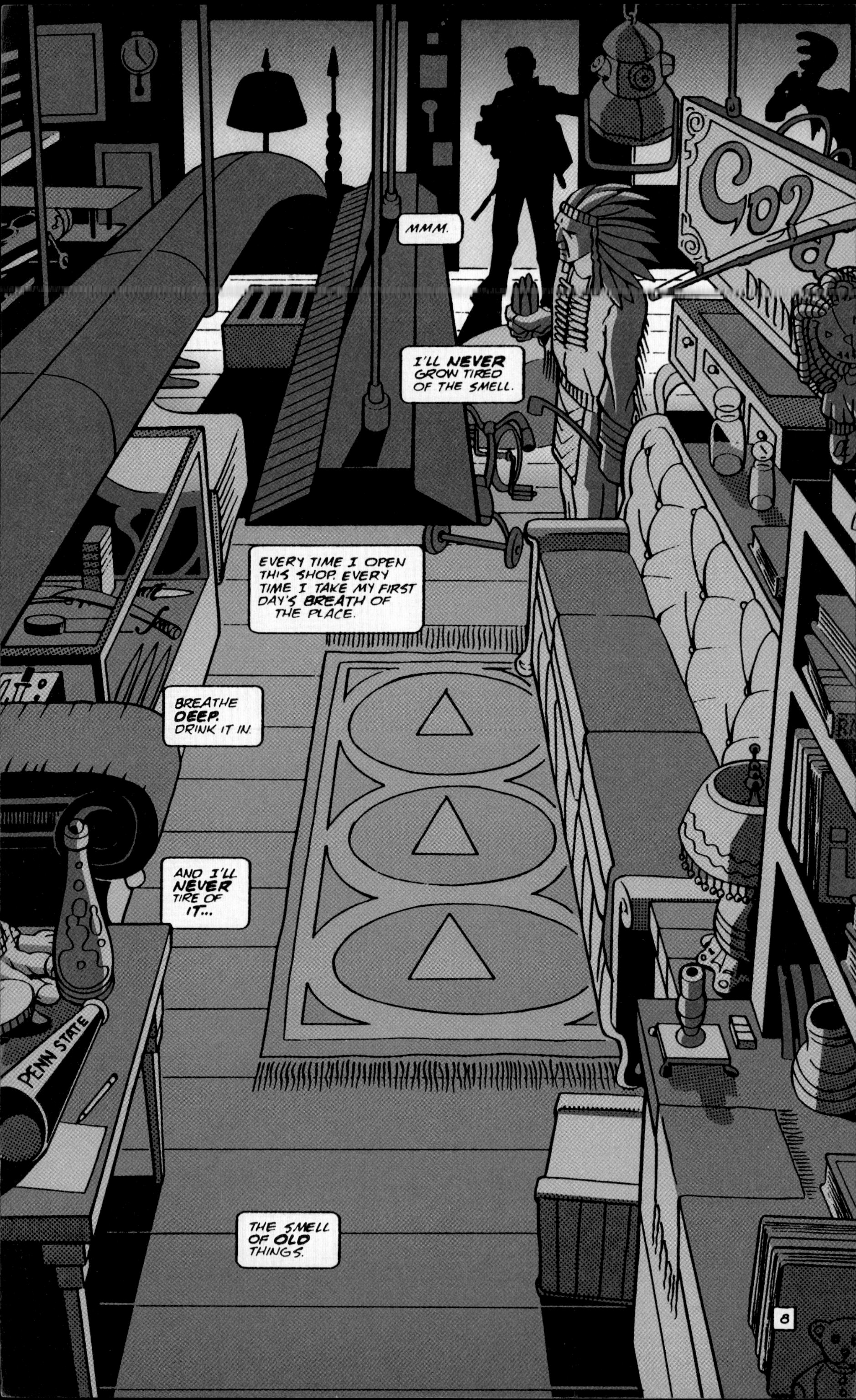

MMM.
I'LL NEVER GROW TIRED OF THE SMELL.
EVERY TIME I OPEN THIS SHOP. EVERY TIME I TAKE MY FIRST DAY'S BREATH OF THE PLACE.
BREATHE DEEP. DRINK IT IN.
AND I'LL NEVER TIRE OF IT...
THE SMELL OF OLD THINGS.
PENN STATE

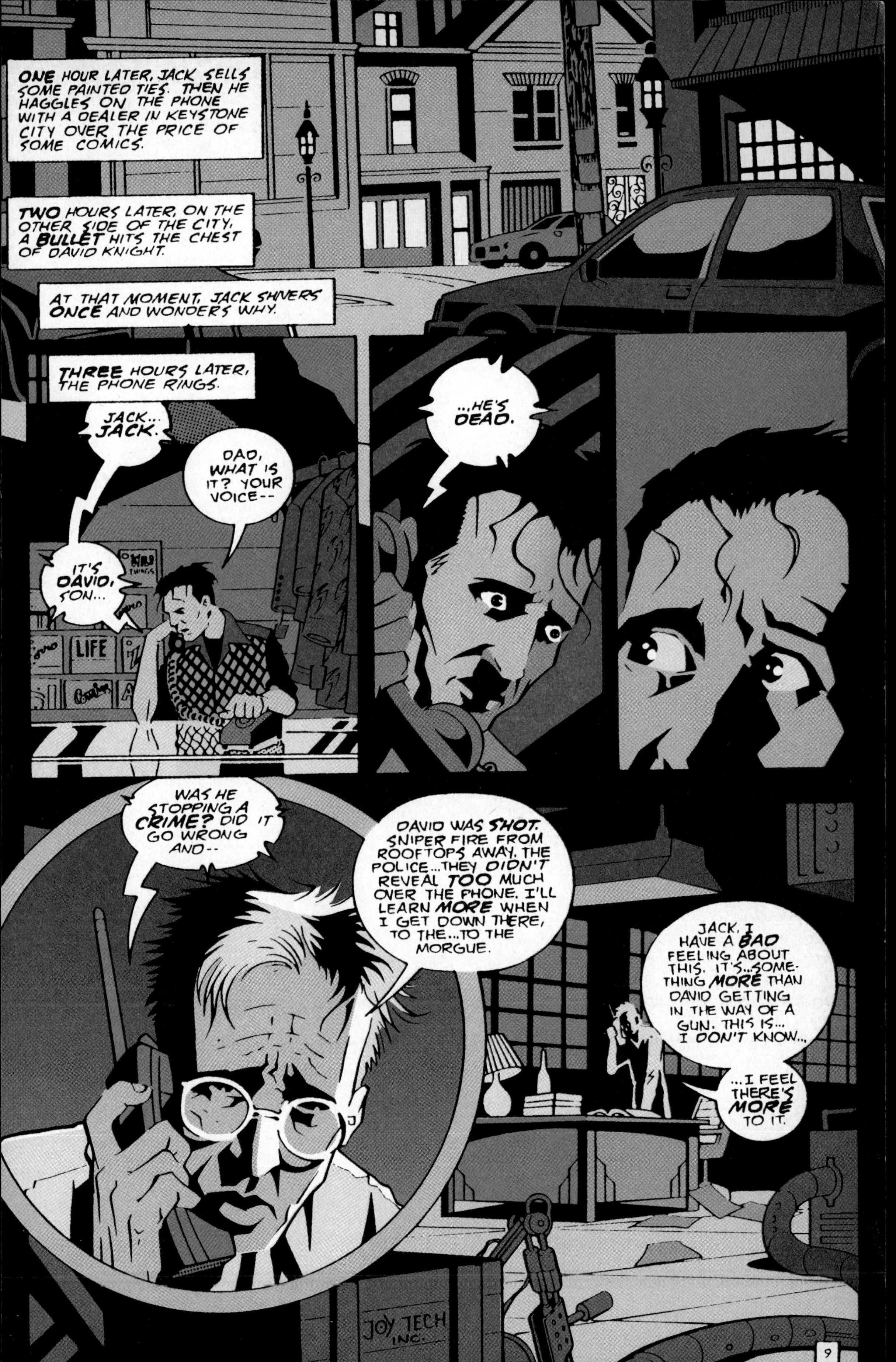
ONE HOUR LATER, JACK SELLS SOME PAINTED TIES. THEN HE HAGGLES ON THE PHONE WITH A DEALER IN KEYSTONE CITY OVER THE PRICE OF SOME COMICS.
TWO HOURS LATER, ON THE OTHER SIDE OF THE CITY, A BULLET HITS THE CHEST OF DAVID KNIGHT.
AT THAT MOMENT, JACK SHIVERS ONCE AND WONDERS WHY.
THREE HOURS LATER, THE PHONE RINGS.
JACK... JACK.
DAD, WHAT IS IT? YOUR VOICE--
IT'S DAVID, SON...
LIFE
...HE'S DEAD.
WAS HE STOPPING A CRIME? DID IT GO WRONG AND--
DAVID WAS SHOT. SNIPER FIRE FROM ROOFTOPS AWAY. THE POLICE...THEY DIDN'T REVEAL TOO MUCH OVER THE PHONE. I'LL LEARN MORE WHEN I GET DOWN THERE, TO THE...TO THE MORGUE.
JACK, I HAVE A BAD FEELING ABOUT THIS. IT'S...SOMETHING MORE THAN DAVID GETTING IN THE WAY OF A GUN. THIS IS... I DON'T KNOW...
...I FEEL THERE'S MORE TO IT.
JOY TECH INC.

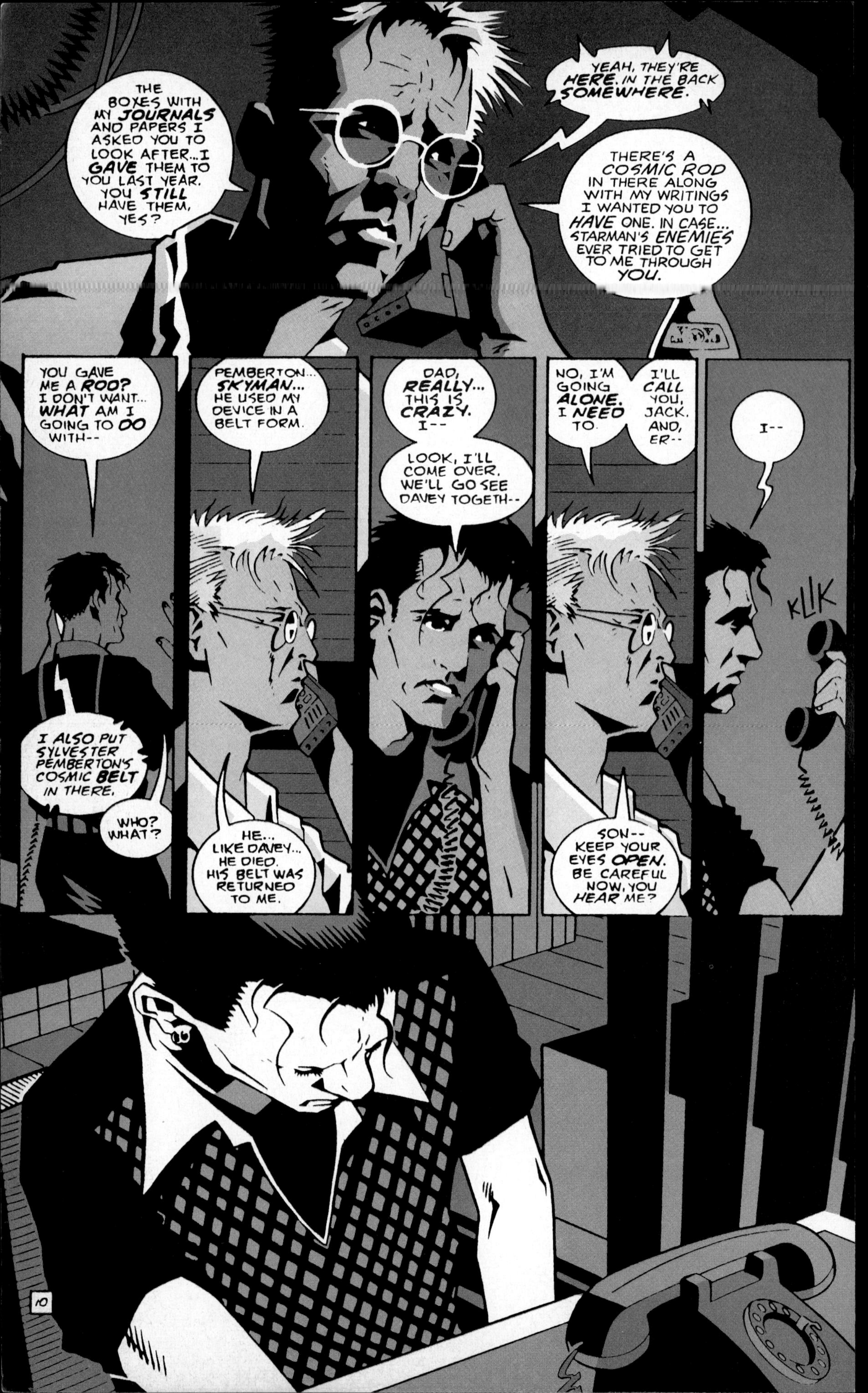
THE BOXES WITH MY JOURNALS AND PAPERS I ASKED YOU TO LOOK AFTER...I GAVE THEM TO YOU LAST YEAR. YOU STILL HAVE THEM, YES?
YEAH, THEY'RE HERE. IN THE BACK SOMEWHERE.
THERE'S A COSMIC ROD IN THERE ALONG WITH MY WRITINGS I WANTED YOU TO HAVE ONE. IN CASE... STARMAN'S ENEMIES EVER TRIED TO GET TO ME THROUGH YOU.
YOU GAVE ME A ROD? I DON'T WANT... WHAT AM I GOING TO DO WITH--
I ALSO PUT SYLVESTER PEMBERTON'S COSMIC BELT IN THERE.
WHO? WHAT?
PEMBERTON... SKYMAN... HE USED MY DEVICE IN A BELT FORM.
HE... LIKE DAVEY... HE DIED. HIS BELT WAS RETURNED TO ME.
DAD, REALLY... THIS IS CRAZY. I--
LOOK, I'LL COME OVER. WE'LL GO SEE DAVEY TOGETH--
NO, I'M GOING ALONE. I NEED TO.
I'LL CALL YOU, JACK. AND, ER--
SON-- KEEP YOUR EYES OPEN. BE CAREFUL NOW, YOU HEAR ME?
I--
KLIK

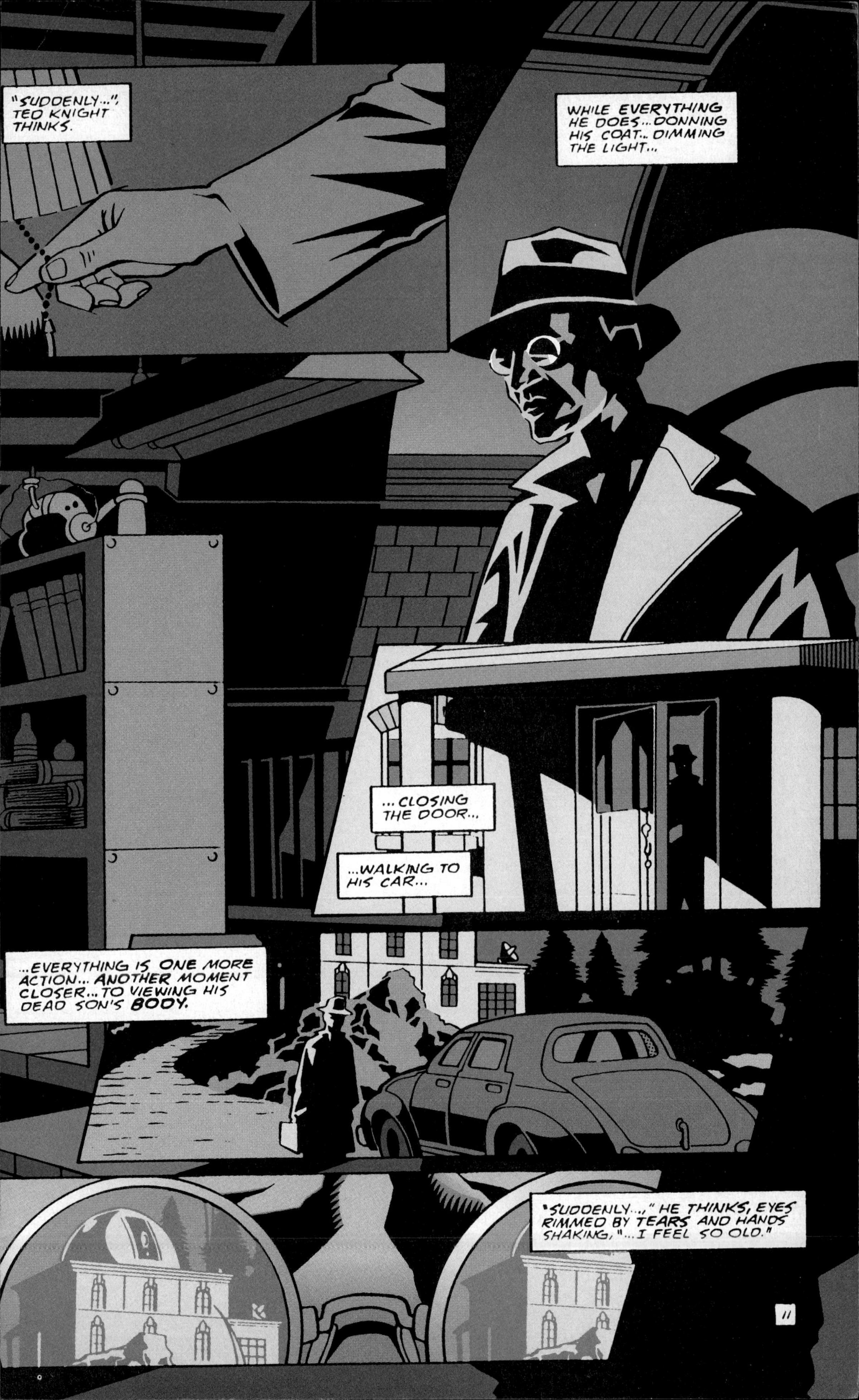
"SUDDENLY...", TED KNIGHT THINKS.
WHILE EVERYTHING HE DOES... DONNING HIS COAT... DIMMING THE LIGHT...
...CLOSING THE DOOR...
...WALKING TO HIS CAR...
...EVERYTHING IS ONE MORE ACTION... ANOTHER MOMENT CLOSER... TO VIEWING HIS DEAD SON'S BODY.
"SUDDENLY...," HE THINKS, EYES RIMMED BY TEARS AND HANDS SHAKING, "...I FEEL SO OLD."

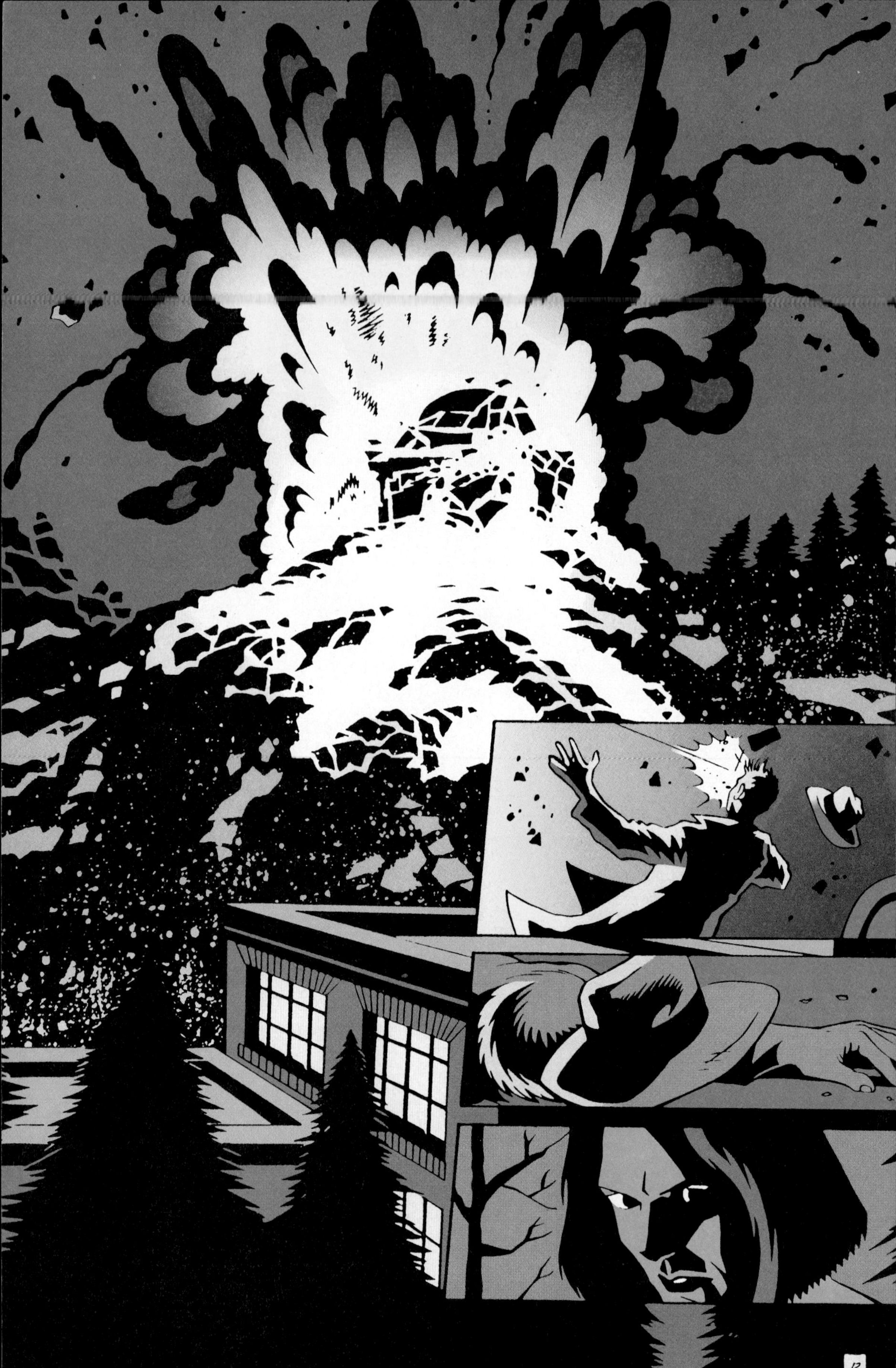

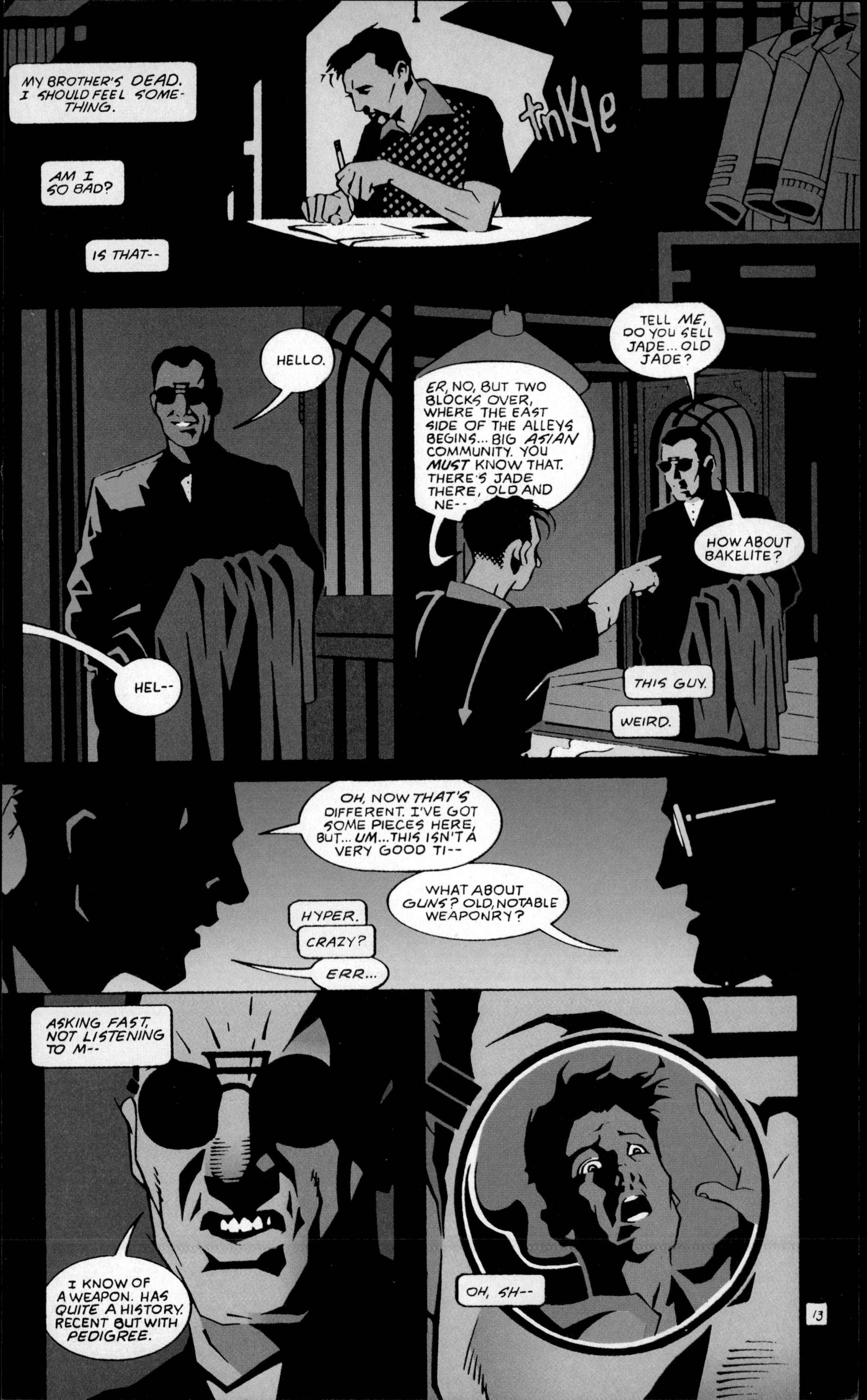
MY BROTHER'S DEAD. I SHOULD FEEL SOMETHING.
AM I SO BAD?
IS THAT--
TNKLE
HELLO.
HEL--
TELL ME, DO YOU SELL JADE... OLD JADE?
ER, NO, BUT TWO BLOCKS OVER, WHERE THE EAST SIDE OF THE ALLEYS BEGINS... BIG ASIAN COMMUNITY. YOU MUST KNOW THAT. THERE'S JADE THERE, OLD AND NE--
HOW ABOUT BAKELITE?
THIS GUY.
WEIRD.
OH, NOW THAT'S DIFFERENT. I'VE GOT SOME PIECES HERE, BUT... UM... THIS ISN'T A VERY GOOD TI--
WHAT ABOUT GUNS? OLD, NOTABLE WEAPONRY?
HYPER.
CRAZY?
ERR...
ASKING FAST. NOT LISTENING TO M--
I KNOW OF A WEAPON. HAS QUITE A HISTORY. RECENT BUT WITH PEDIGREE.
OH, SH--
13

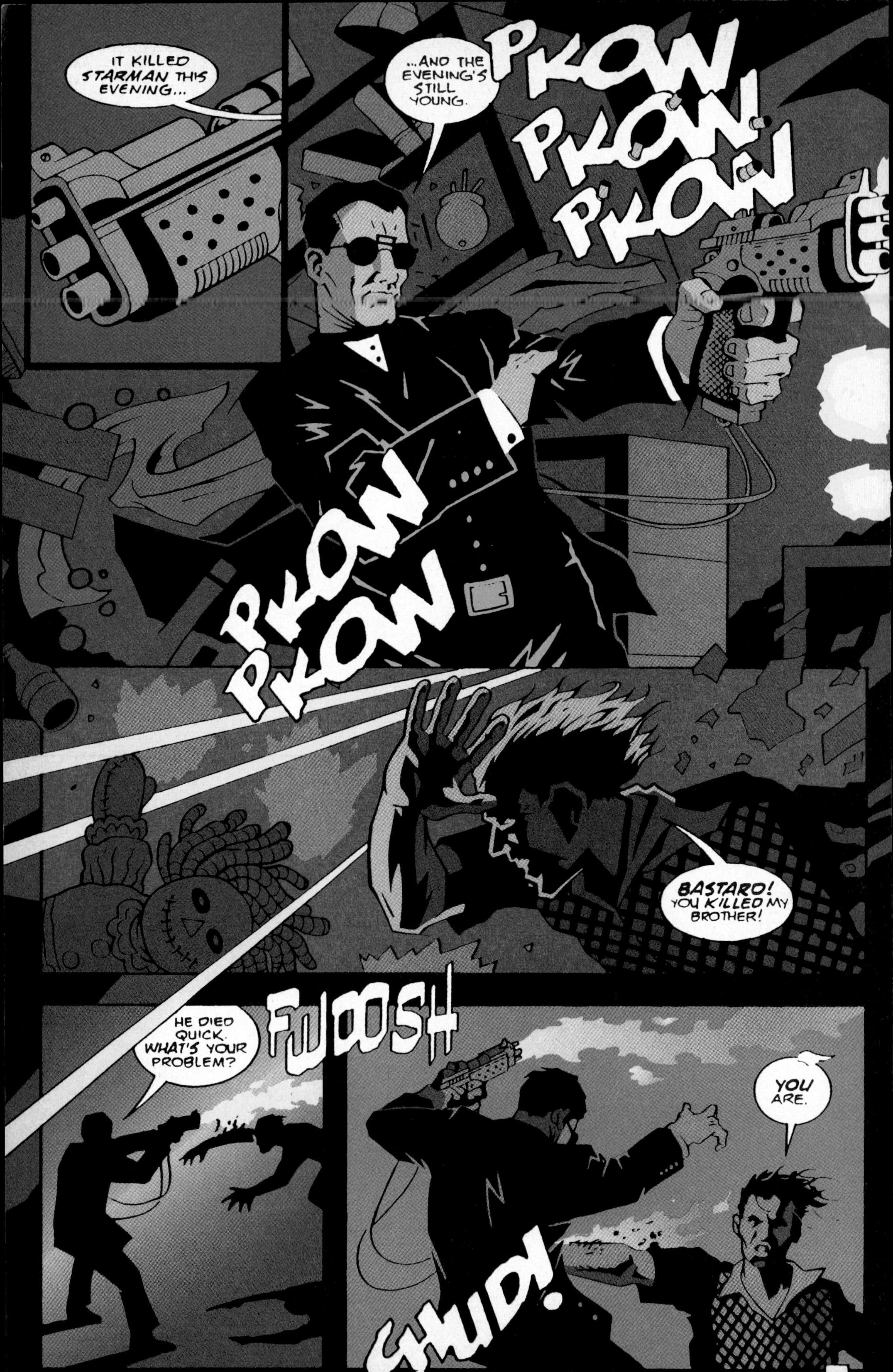
IT KILLED STARMAN THIS EVENING...
...AND THE EVENING'S STILL YOUNG.
PKOW PKOW PKOW
PKOW PKOW
BASTARD! YOU KILLED MY BROTHER!
HE DIED QUICK. WHAT'S YOUR PROBLEM?
FWOOSH
YOU ARE.
CHUD!

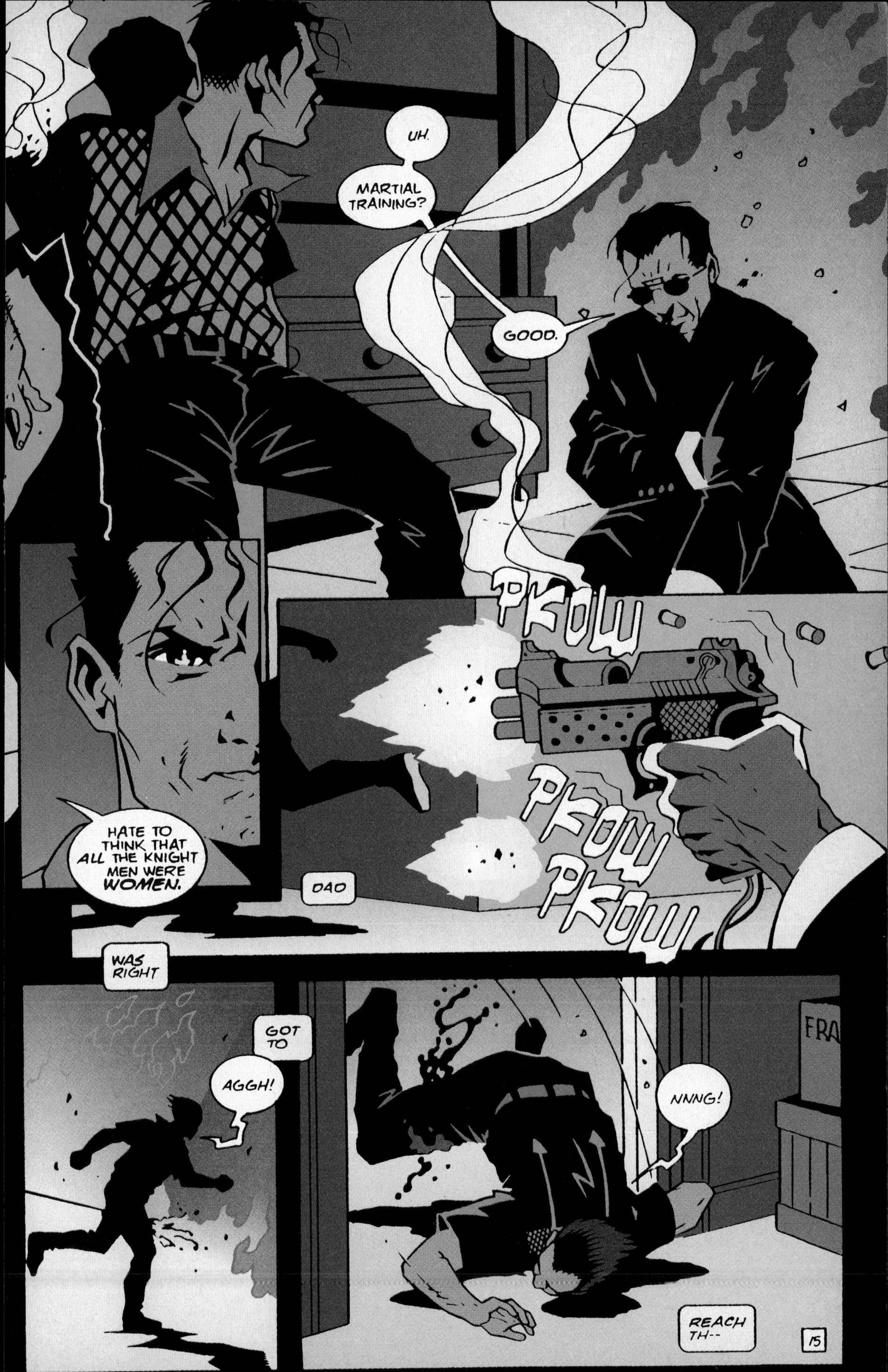
UH.
MARTIAL TRAINING?
GOOD.
HATE TO THINK THAT ALL THE KNIGHT MEN WERE WOMEN.
DAD
PKOW
PKOW
PKOW
PKOW
WAS RIGHT
GOT TO
AGGH!
NNNG!
REACH TH--
15

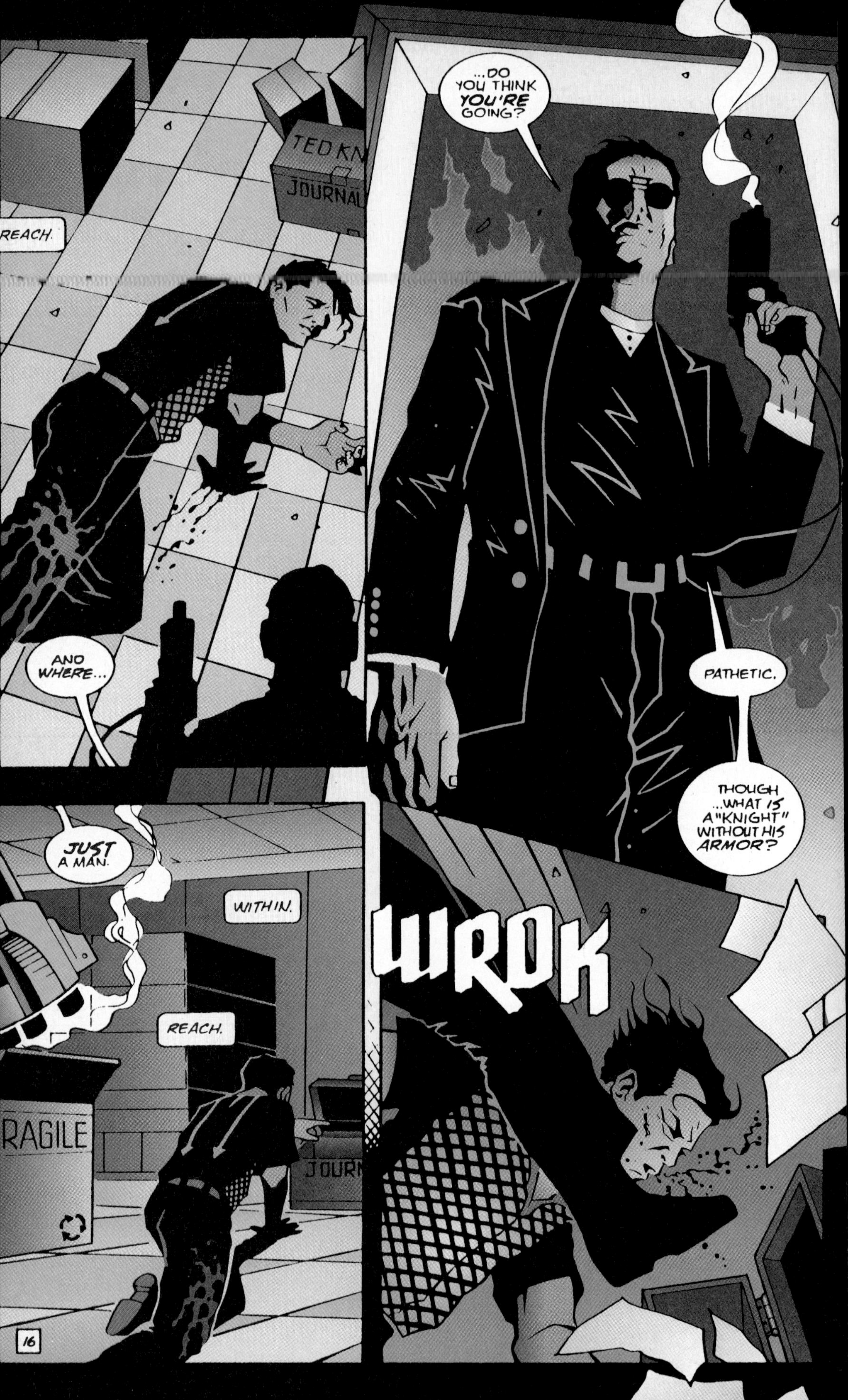
REACH.
AND WHERE...
...DO YOU THINK YOU'RE GOING?
PATHETIC.
THOUGH ...WHAT IS A "KNIGHT" WITHOUT HIS ARMOR?
JUST A MAN.
WITHIN.
REACH.
WROK

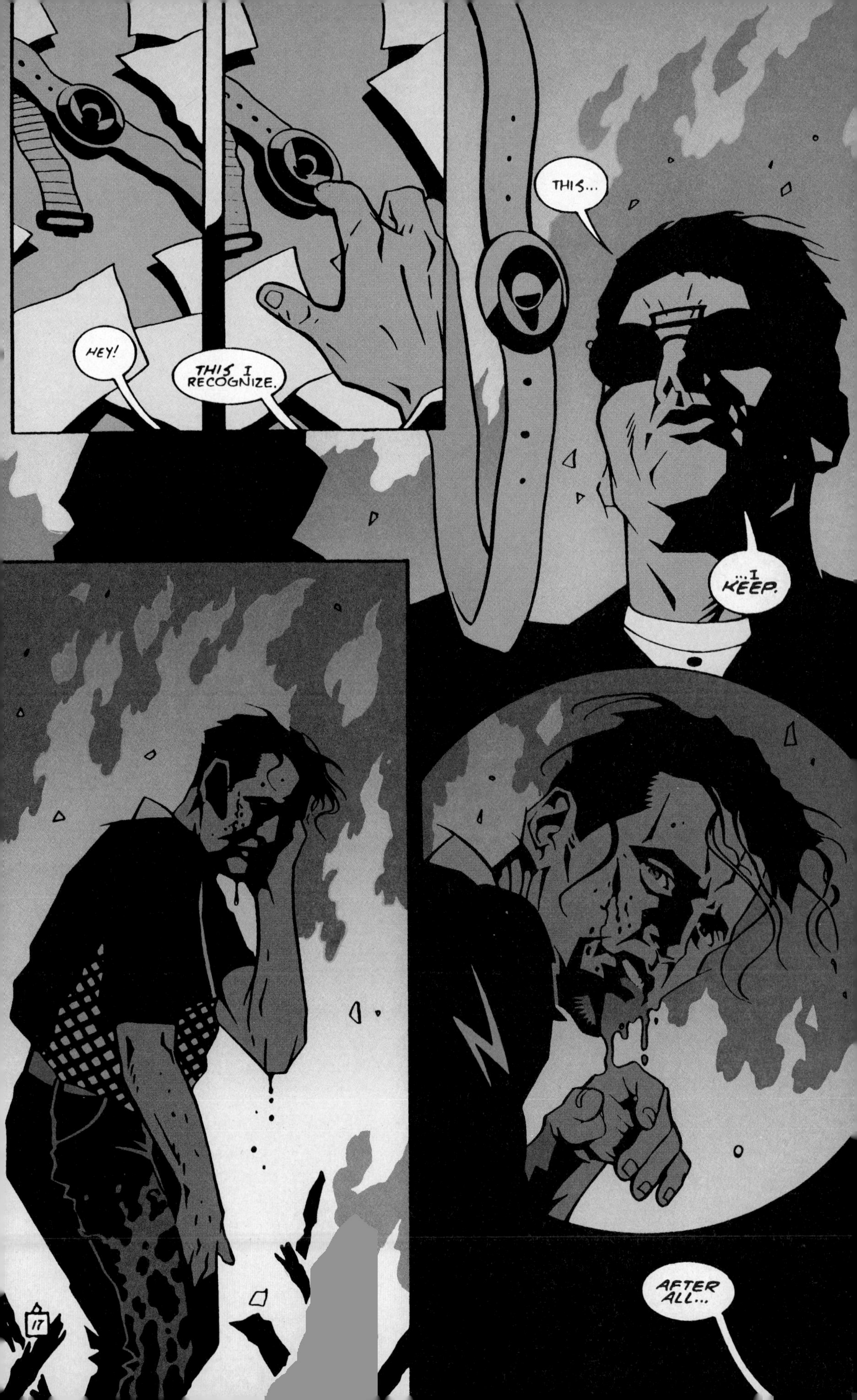
HEY!
THIS I RECOGNIZE.
THIS...
...I KEEP.
AFTER ALL...

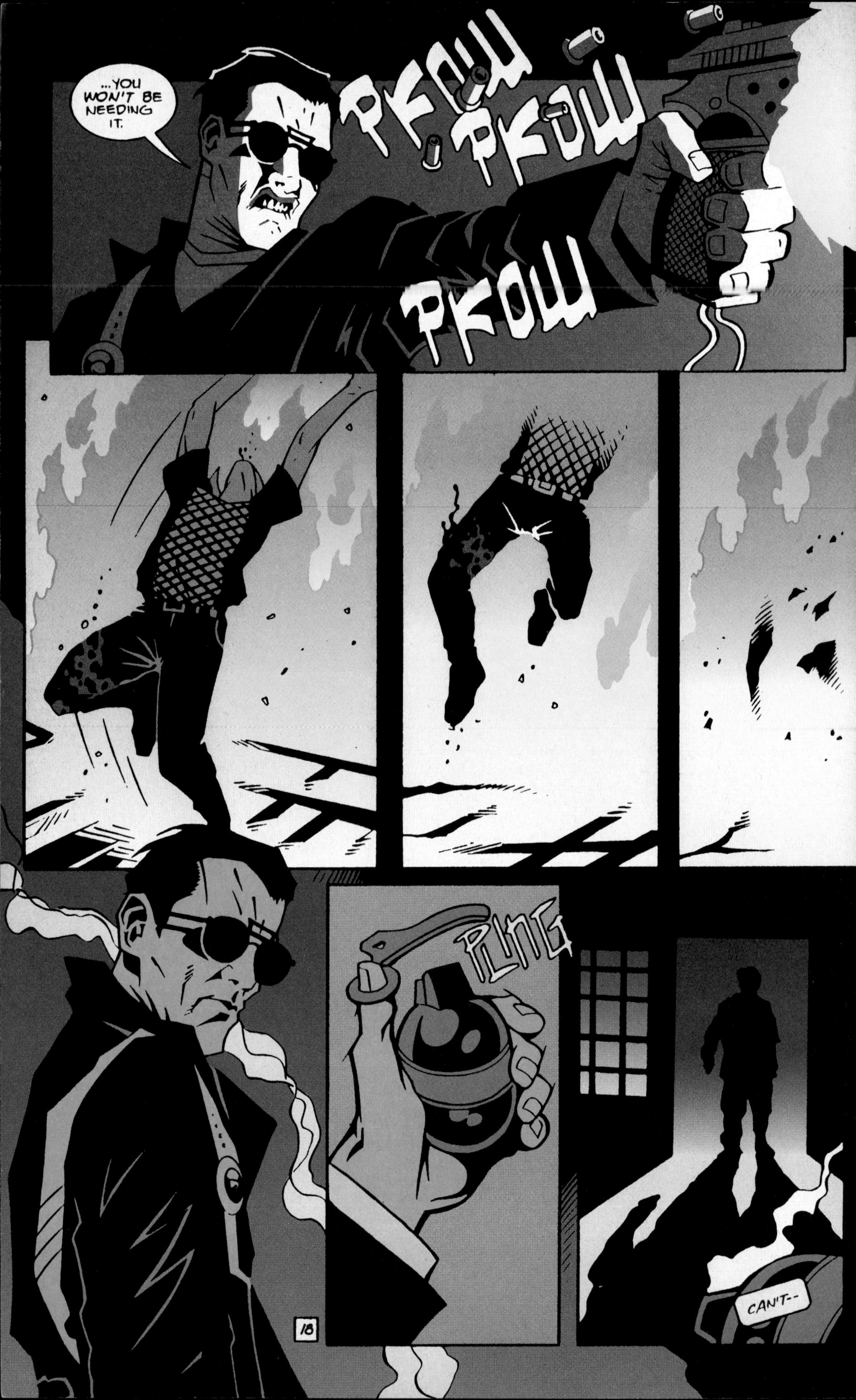
...YOU WON'T BE NEEDING IT.
PKOW PKOW
PKOW
PLING
CAN'T--

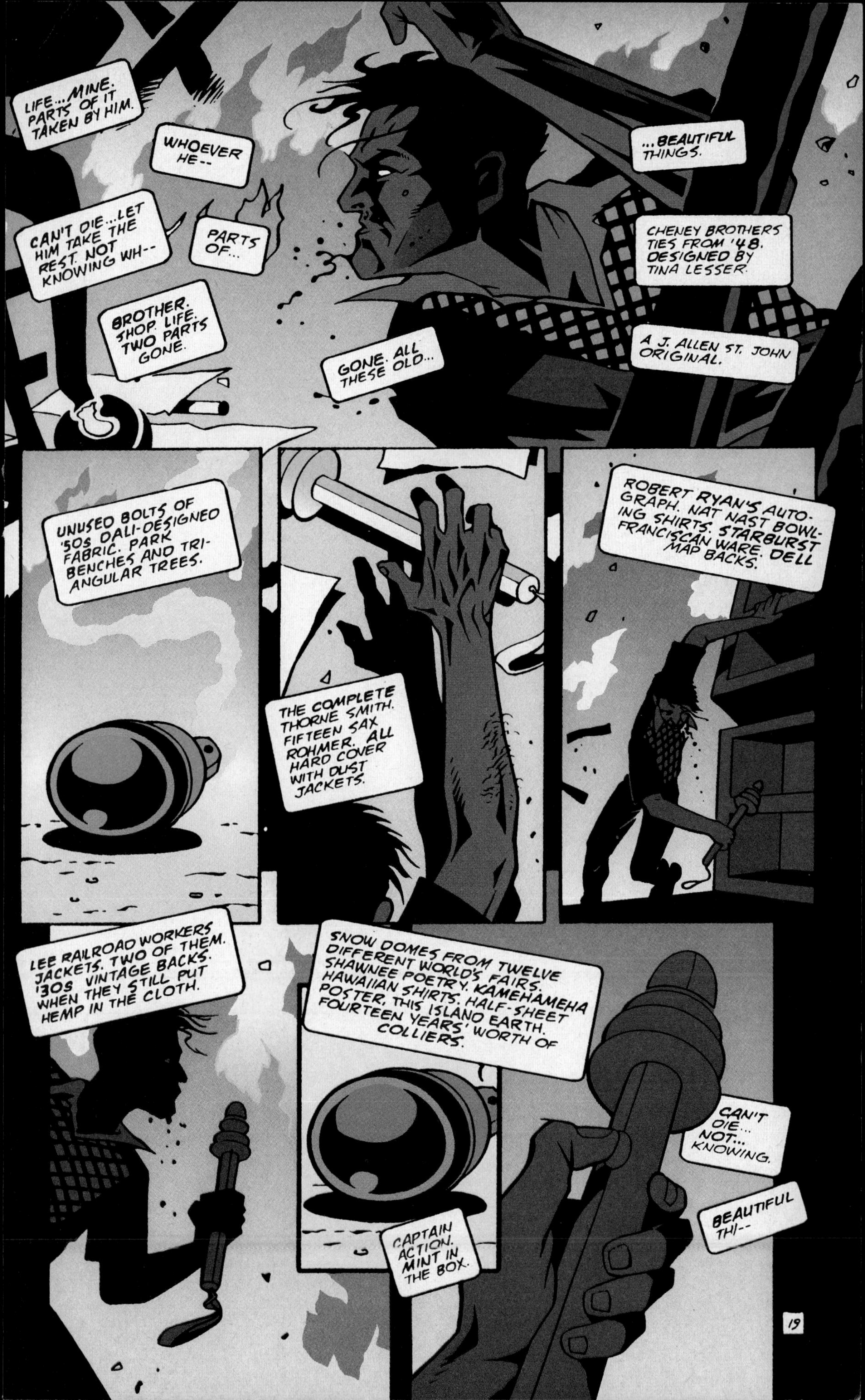
LIFE...MINE. PARTS OF IT TAKEN BY HIM.
WHOEVER HE--
CAN'T DIE...LET HIM TAKE THE REST. NOT KNOWING WH--
PARTS OF...
BROTHER. SHOP. LIFE. TWO PARTS GONE.
GONE. ALL THESE OLD...
...BEAUTIFUL THINGS.
CHENEY BROTHERS TIES FROM '48. DESIGNED BY TINA LESSER.
A J. ALLEN ST. JOHN ORIGINAL.
UNUSED BOLTS OF '50S DALI-DESIGNED FABRIC. PARK BENCHES AND TRI-ANGULAR TREES.
THE COMPLETE THORNE SMITH. FIFTEEN SAX ROHMER. ALL HARD COVER WITH DUST JACKETS.
ROBERT RYAN'S AUTO-GRAPH. NAT NAST BOWL-ING SHIRTS. STARBURST FRANCISCAN WARE. DELL MAP BACKS.
LEE RAILROAD WORKERS JACKETS. TWO OF THEM. '30S VINTAGE BACKS. WHEN THEY STILL PUT HEMP IN THE CLOTH.
SNOW DOMES FROM TWELVE DIFFERENT WORLD'S FAIRS. SHAWNEE POETRY. KAMEHAMEHA HAWAIIAN SHIRTS. HALF-SHEET POSTER, THIS ISLAND EARTH. FOURTEEN YEARS' WORTH OF COLLIERS.
CAPTAIN ACTION. MINT IN THE BOX.
CAN'T DIE... NOT... KNOWING.
BEAUTIFUL THI--

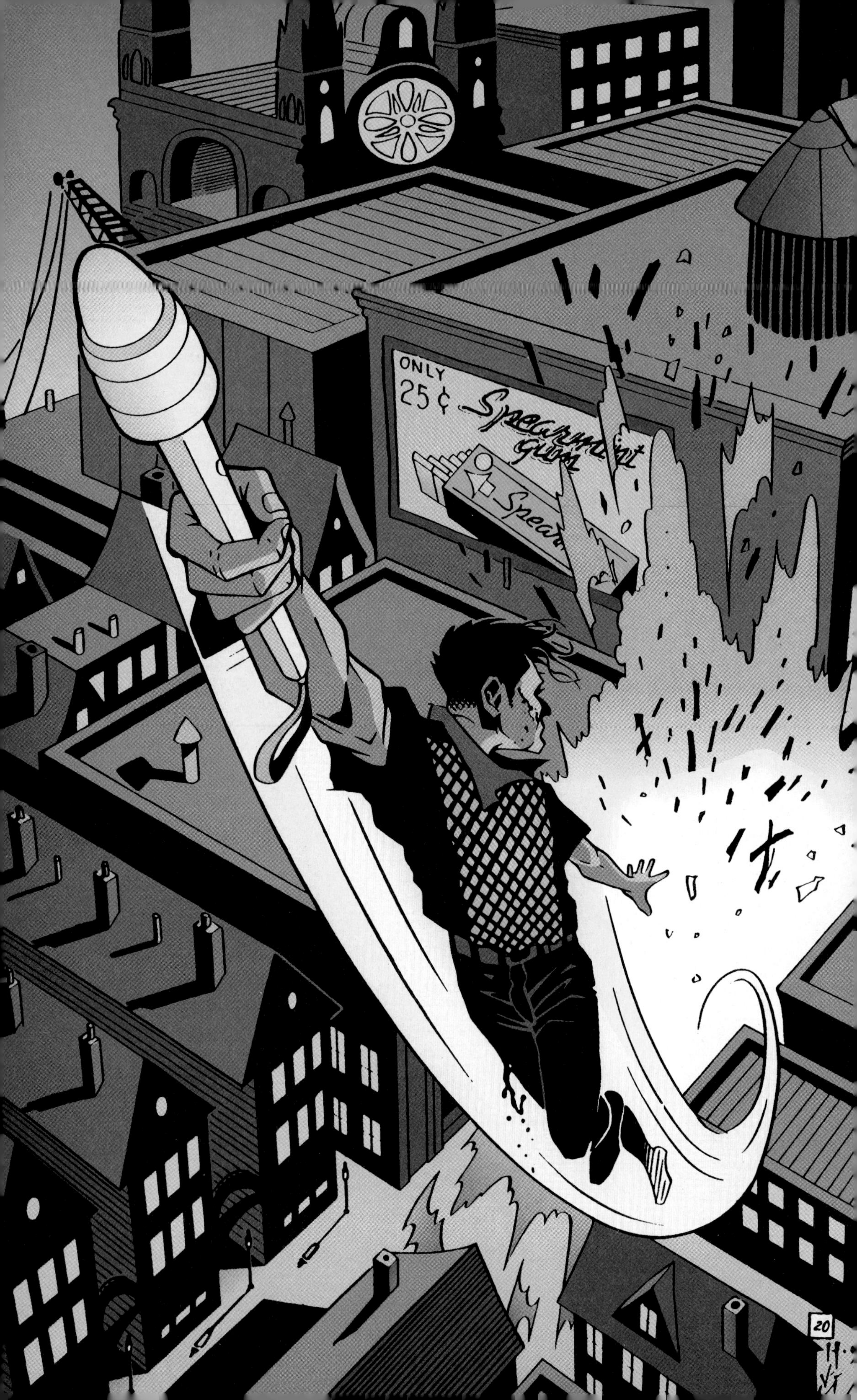
ONLY
25¢
Spearmint gum
20

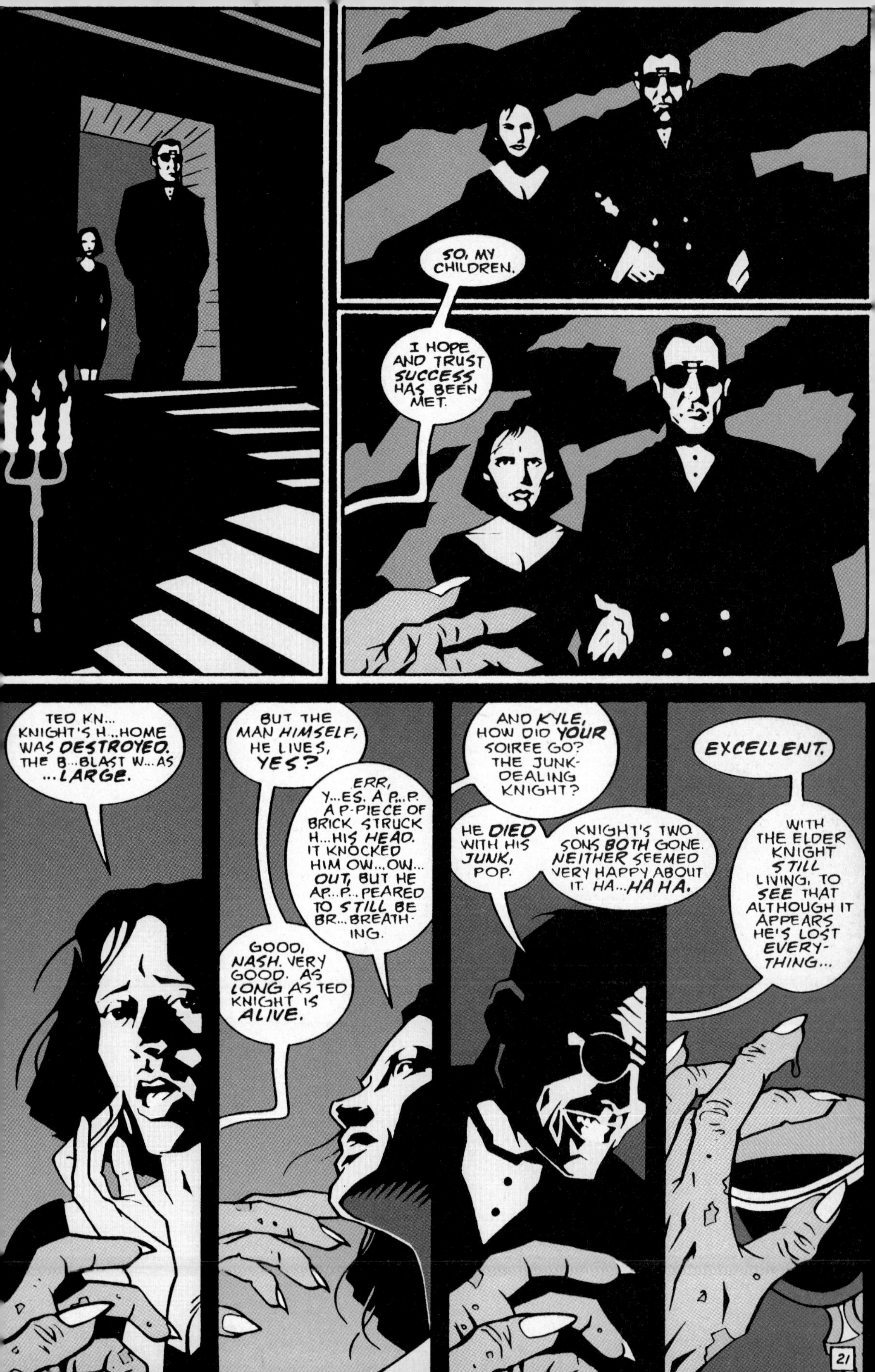
SO, MY CHILDREN.
I HOPE AND TRUST SUCCESS HAS BEEN MET.
TED KN... KNIGHT'S H...HOME WAS DESTROYED. THE B...BLAST W...AS ...LARGE.
BUT THE MAN HIMSELF, HE LIVES, YES?
ERR, Y...ES. A P...P. A P-PIECE OF BRICK STRUCK H...HIS HEAD. IT KNOCKED HIM OW...OW... OUT, BUT HE AP...P...PEARED TO STILL BE BR...BREATH-ING.
GOOD, NASH. VERY GOOD. AS LONG AS TED KNIGHT IS ALIVE.
AND KYLE, HOW DID YOUR SOIREE GO? THE JUNK-DEALING KNIGHT?
HE DIED WITH HIS JUNK, POP.
KNIGHT'S TWO SONS BOTH GONE. NEITHER SEEMED VERY HAPPY ABOUT IT. HA...HA HA.
EXCELLENT.
WITH THE ELDER KNIGHT STILL LIVING, TO SEE THAT ALTHOUGH IT APPEARS HE'S LOST EVERY-THING...

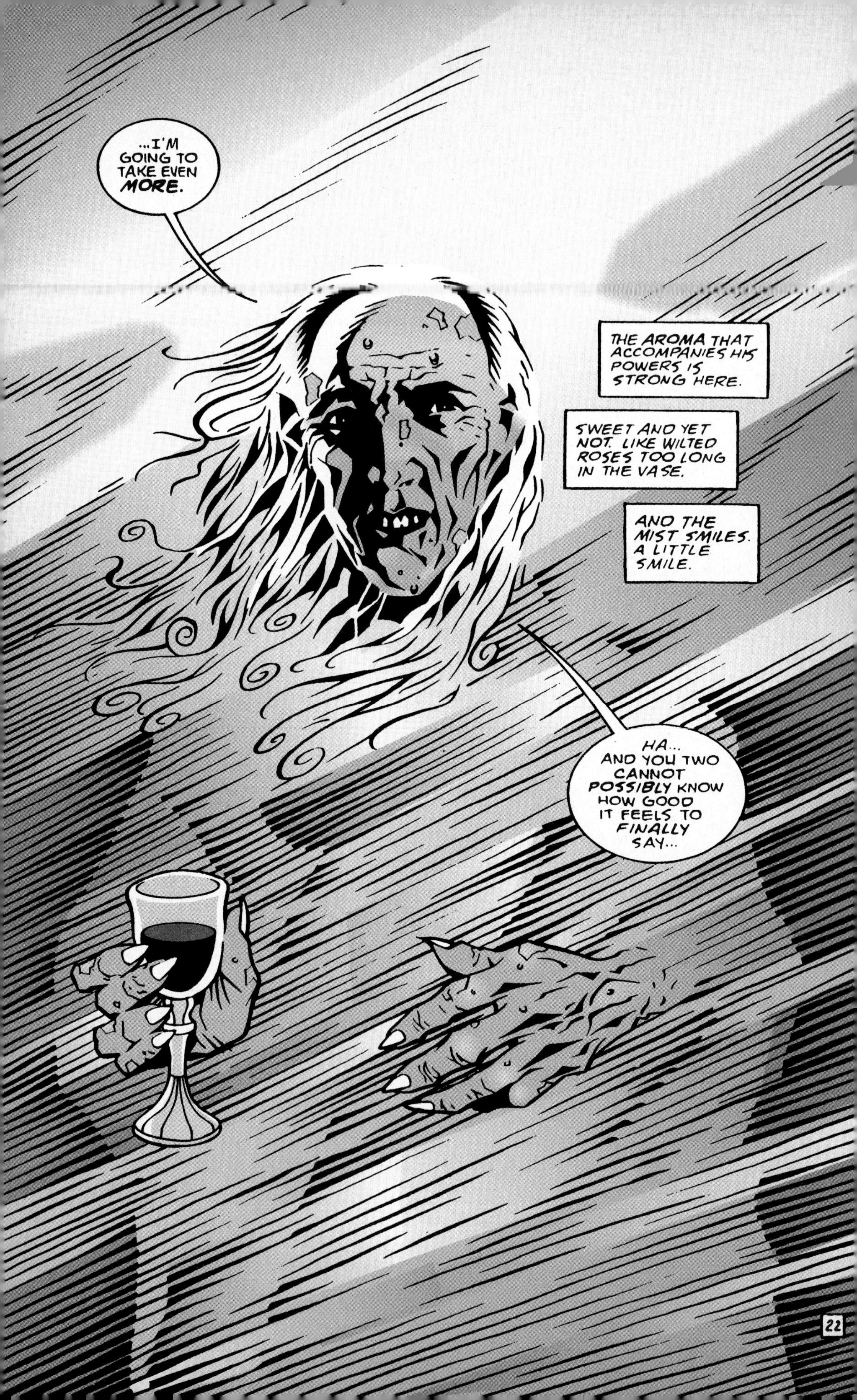
...I'M GOING TO TAKE EVEN MORE.
THE AROMA THAT ACCOMPANIES HIS POWERS IS STRONG HERE.
SWEET AND YET NOT. LIKE WILTED ROSES TOO LONG IN THE VASE.
AND THE MIST SMILES. A LITTLE SMILE.
HA... AND YOU TWO CANNOT POSSIBLY KNOW HOW GOOD IT FEELS TO FINALLY SAY...

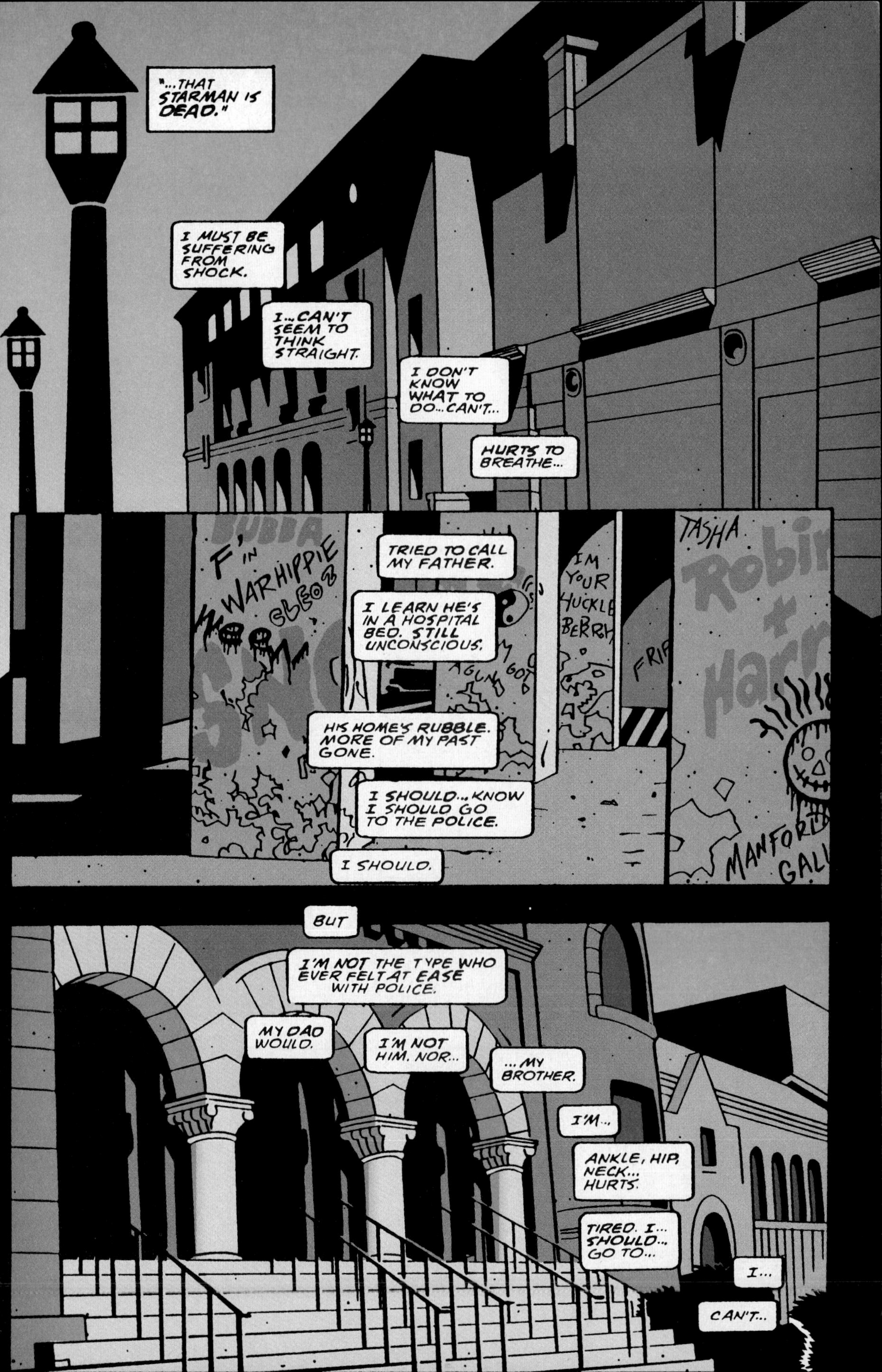
"...THAT STARMAN IS DEAD."
I MUST BE SUFFERING FROM SHOCK.
I...CAN'T SEEM TO THINK STRAIGHT.
I DON'T KNOW WHAT TO DO...CAN'T...
HURTS TO BREATHE...
BUBBA
WARHIPPIE
TASHA
TRIED TO CALL MY FATHER.
I LEARN HE'S IN A HOSPITAL BED. STILL UNCONSCIOUS.
HIS HOME'S RUBBLE. MORE OF MY PAST GONE.
I SHOULD...KNOW I SHOULD GO TO THE POLICE.
I SHOULD.
BUT
I'M NOT THE TYPE WHO EVER FELT AT EASE WITH POLICE.
MY DAD WOULD.
I'M NOT HIM. NOR...
...MY BROTHER.
I'M...
ANKLE, HIP, NECK... HURTS.
TIRED. I... SHOULD... GO TO...
I...
CAN'T...

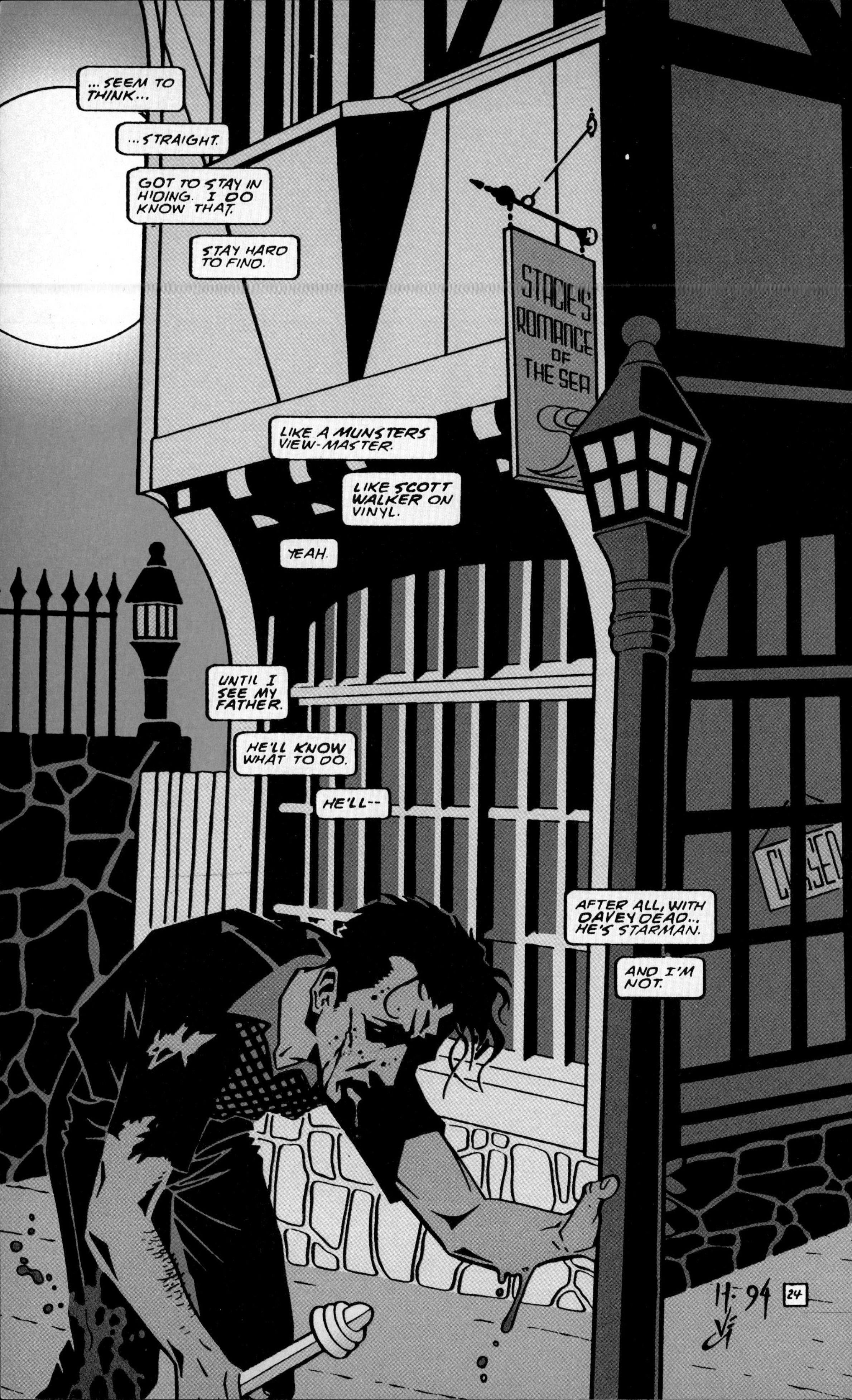
... SEEM TO THINK...
... STRAIGHT.
GOT TO STAY IN HIDING. I DO KNOW THAT.
STAY HARD TO FIND.
STACIE'S ROMANCE OF THE SEA
LIKE A MUNSTERS VIEW-MASTER.
LIKE SCOTT WALKER ON VINYL.
YEAH.
UNTIL I SEE MY FATHER.
HE'LL KNOW WHAT TO DO.
HE'LL--
AFTER ALL, WITH DAVEY DEAD... HE'S STARMAN.
AND I'M NOT.
24

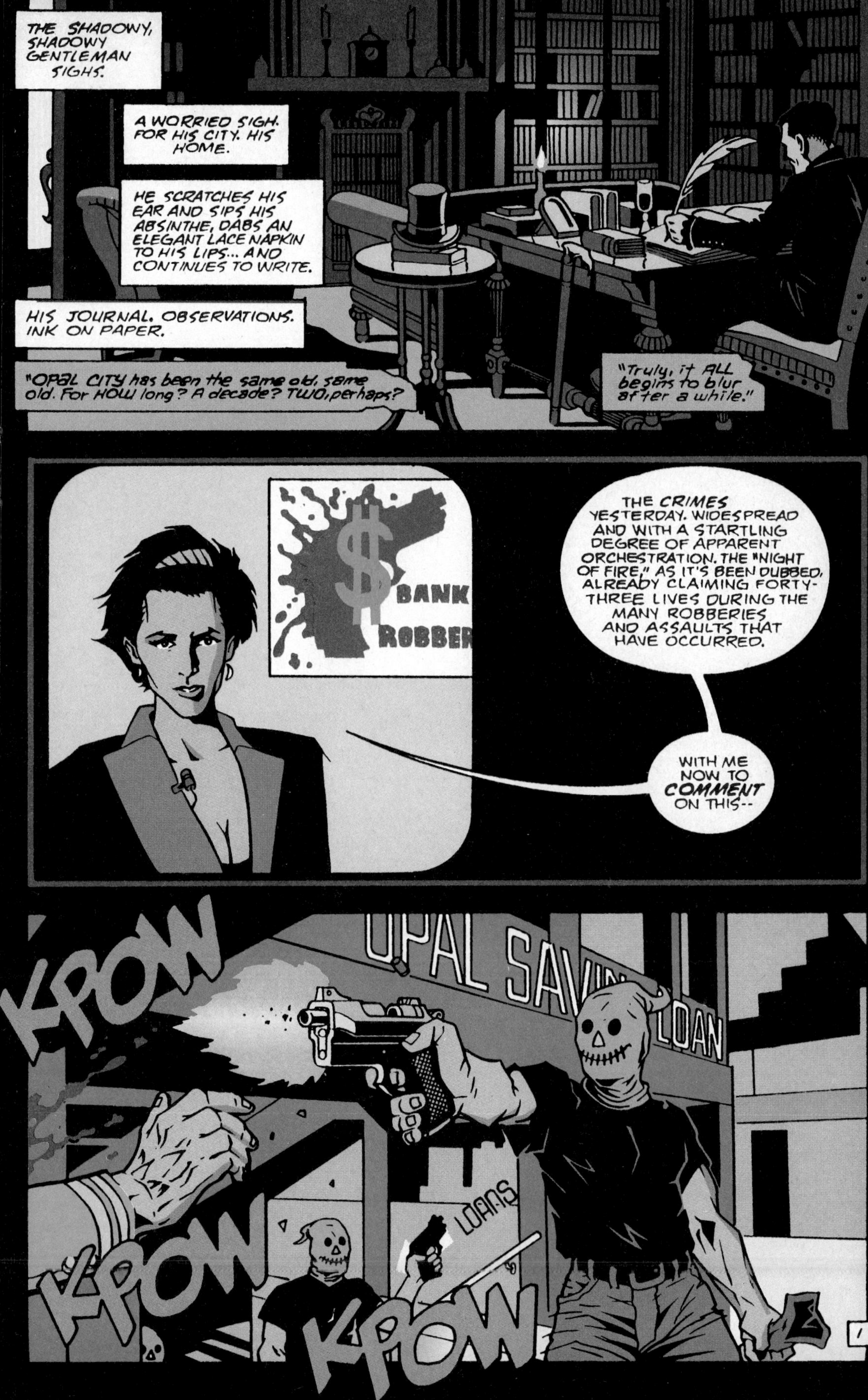
THE SHADOWY, SHADOWY GENTLEMAN SIGHS.
A WORRIED SIGH. FOR HIS CITY. HIS HOME.
HE SCRATCHES HIS EAR AND SIPS HIS ABSINTHE, DABS AN ELEGANT LACE NAPKIN TO HIS LIPS... AND CONTINUES TO WRITE.
HIS JOURNAL. OBSERVATIONS. INK ON PAPER.
"OPAL CITY has been the same old, same old. For HOW long? A decade? TWO, perhaps?
"Truly, it ALL begins to blur after a while."
$ BANK ROBBER
THE CRIMES YESTERDAY. WIDESPREAD AND WITH A STARTLING DEGREE OF APPARENT ORCHESTRATION. THE "NIGHT OF FIRE," AS IT'S BEEN DUBBED, ALREADY CLAIMING FORTY-THREE LIVES DURING THE MANY ROBBERIES AND ASSAULTS THAT HAVE OCCURRED.
WITH ME NOW TO COMMENT ON THIS--
KPOW
OPAL SAVIN LOAN
LOANS
KPOW
KPOW

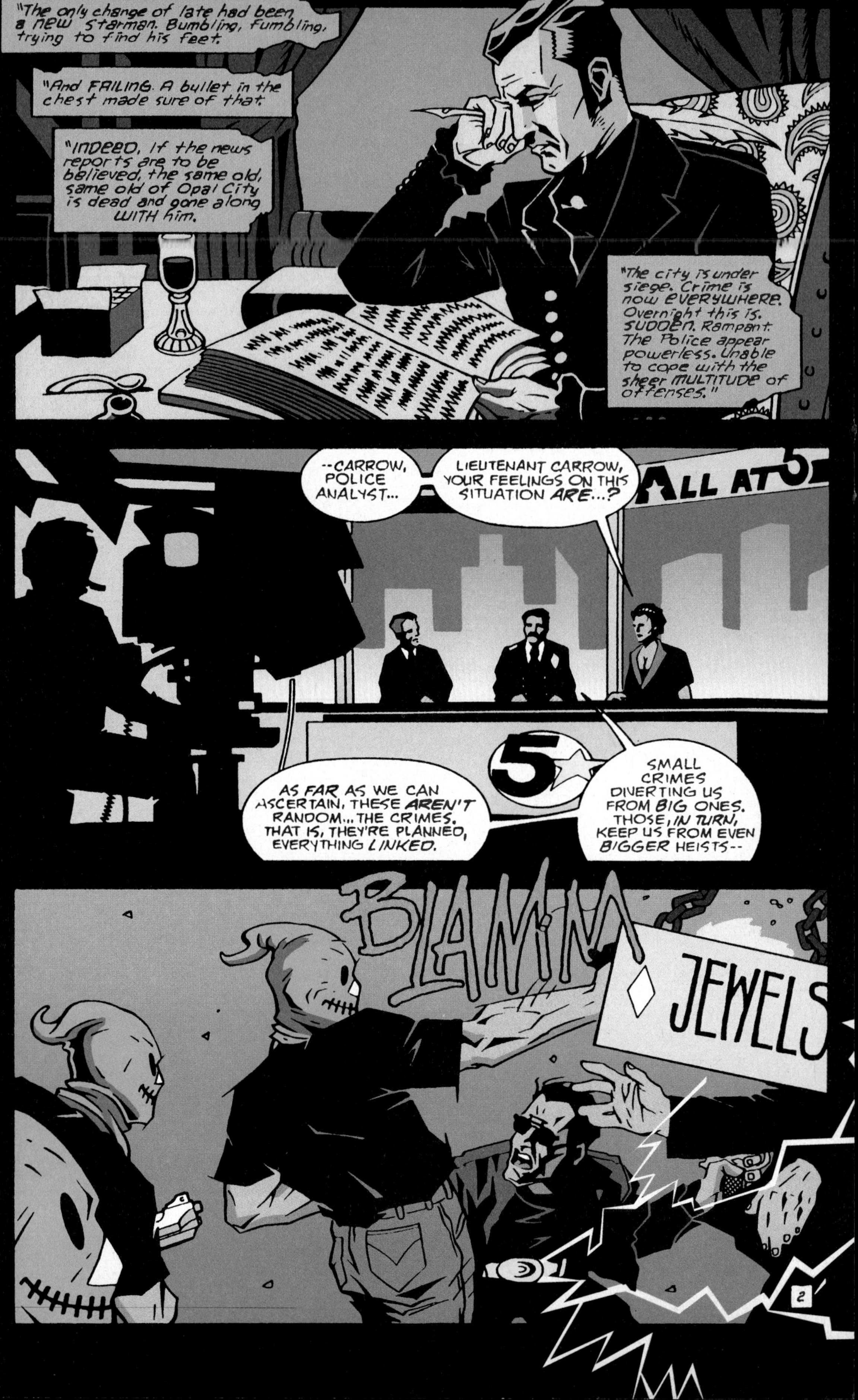
"The only change of late had been a NEW Starman. Bumbling, fumbling, trying to find his feet.
"And FAILING. A bullet in the chest made sure of that.
"INDEED, if the news reports are to be believed, the same old, same old of Opal City is dead and gone along WITH him.
"The city is under siege. Crime is now EVERYWHERE. Overnight this is. SUDDEN. Rampant. The Police appear powerless. Unable to cope with the sheer MULTITUDE of offenses."
--CARROW, POLICE ANALYST...
LIEUTENANT CARROW, YOUR FEELINGS ON THIS SITUATION ARE...?
ALL AT 5
AS FAR AS WE CAN ASCERTAIN, THESE AREN'T RANDOM... THE CRIMES. THAT IS, THEY'RE PLANNED, EVERYTHING LINKED.
SMALL CRIMES DIVERTING US FROM BIG ONES. THOSE, IN TURN, KEEP US FROM EVEN BIGGER HEISTS--
BLAMM
JEWELS
2

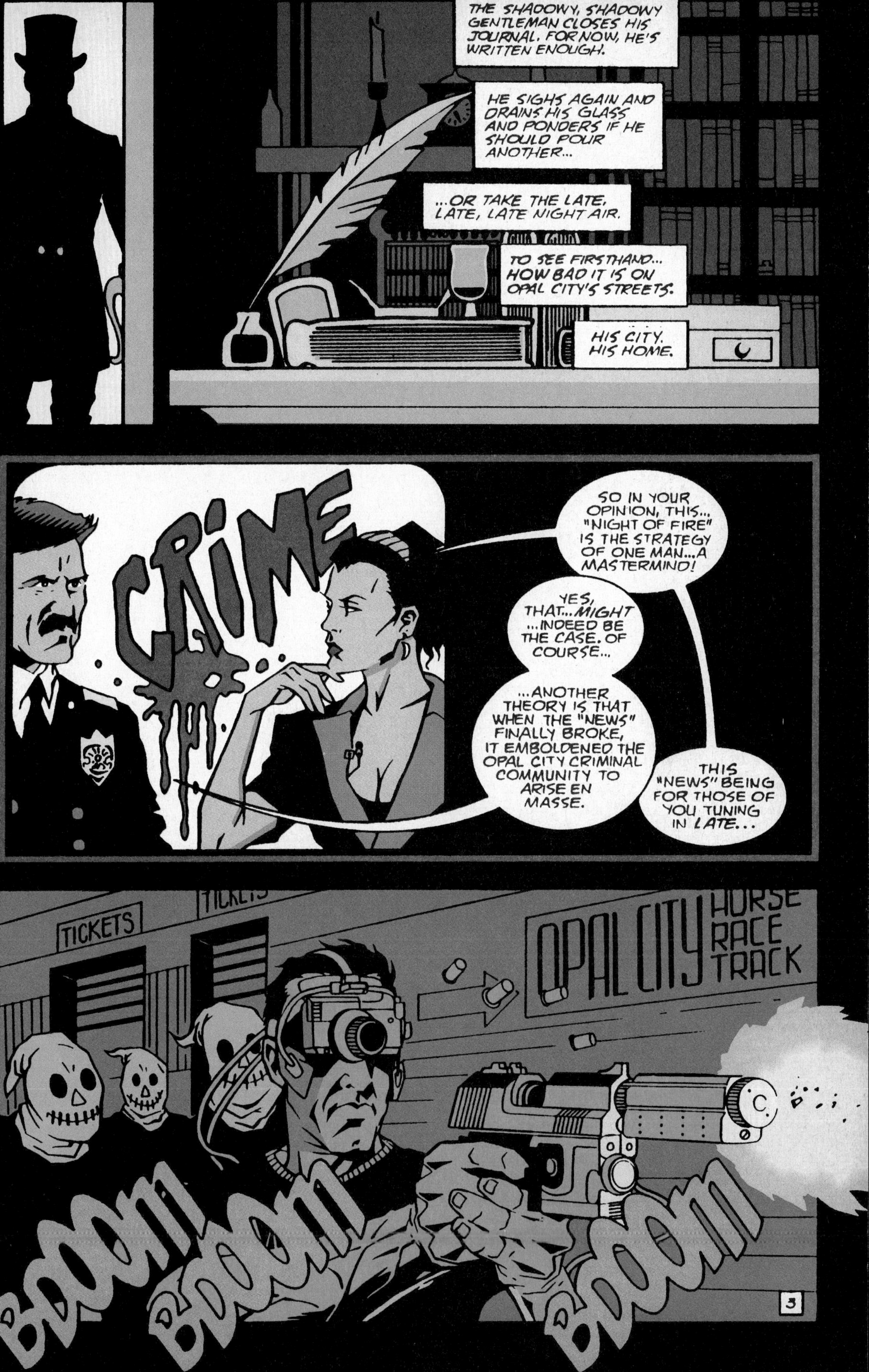
THE SHADOWY, SHADOWY GENTLEMAN CLOSES HIS JOURNAL. FOR NOW, HE'S WRITTEN ENOUGH.
HE SIGHS AGAIN AND DRAINS HIS GLASS AND PONDERS IF HE SHOULD POUR ANOTHER...
...OR TAKE THE LATE, LATE, LATE NIGHT AIR.
TO SEE FIRSTHAND... HOW BAD IT IS ON OPAL CITY'S STREETS.
HIS CITY. HIS HOME.
CRIME
SO IN YOUR OPINION, THIS... "NIGHT OF FIRE" IS THE STRATEGY OF ONE MAN...A MASTERMIND!
YES, THAT...MIGHT ...INDEED BE THE CASE. OF COURSE...
...ANOTHER THEORY IS THAT WHEN THE "NEWS" FINALLY BROKE, IT EMBOLDENED THE OPAL CITY CRIMINAL COMMUNITY TO ARISE EN MASSE.
THIS "NEWS" BEING FOR THOSE OF YOU TUNING IN LATE...
TICKETS
TICKETS
OPAL CITY HORSE RACE TRACK
BOOOM
BOOOM
BOOOM

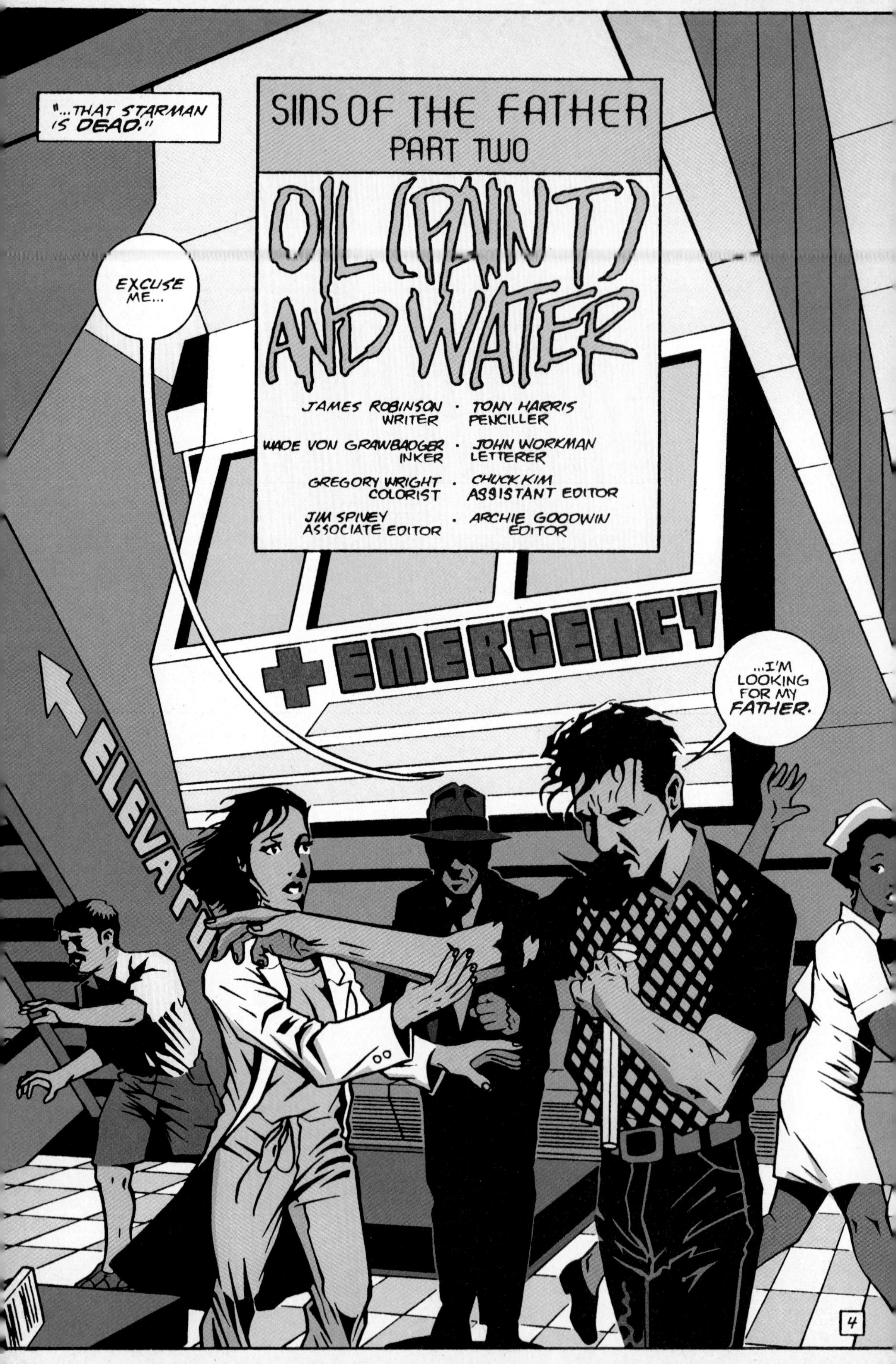
"...THAT STARMAN IS DEAD."
SINS OF THE FATHER
PART TWO
OIL (PAINT) AND WATER
JAMES ROBINSON · WRITER
TONY HARRIS · PENCILLER
WADE VON GRAWBADGER · INKER
JOHN WORKMAN · LETTERER
GREGORY WRIGHT · COLORIST
CHUCK KIM · ASSISTANT EDITOR
JIM SPIVEY · ASSOCIATE EDITOR
ARCHIE GOODWIN · EDITOR
EXCUSE ME...
+ EMERGENCY
...I'M LOOKING FOR MY FATHER.
ELEVATO

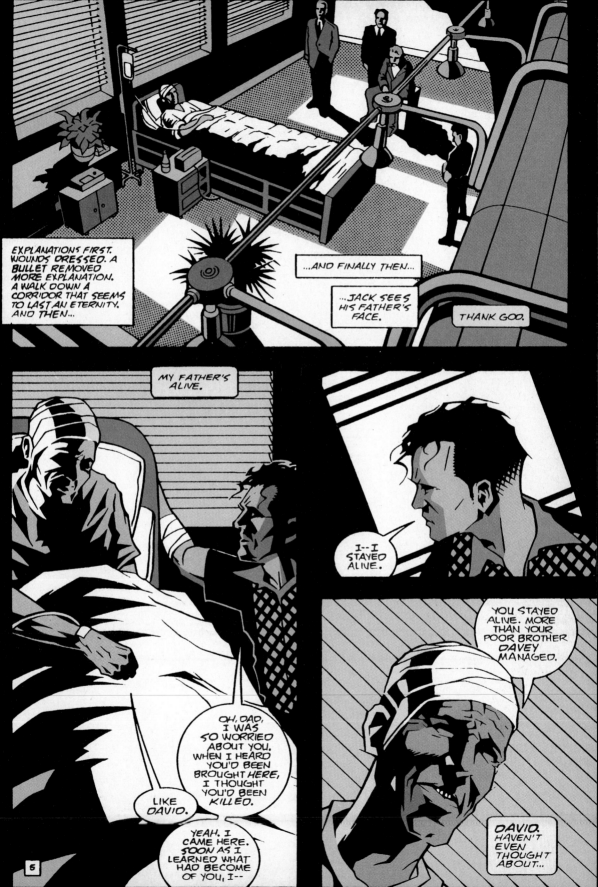

EXPLANATIONS FIRST. WOUNDS DRESSED. A BULLET REMOVED MORE EXPLANATION. A WALK DOWN A CORRIDOR THAT SEEMS TO LAST AN ETERNITY. AND THEN...

...AND FINALLY THEN...

...JACK SEES HIS FATHER'S FACE.

THANK GOO.

MY FATHER'S ALIVE.

I--I STAYED ALIVE.

YOU STAYED ALIVE. MORE THAN YOUR POOR BROTHER DAVEY MANAGED.

OH, DAD, I WAS SO WORRIED ABOUT YOU. WHEN I HEARD YOU'D BEEN BROUGHT HERE, I THOUGHT YOU'D BEEN KILLED.

LIKE DAVID.

YEAH. I CAME HERE. SOON AS I LEARNED WHAT HAD BECOME OF YOU, I--

DAVID. HAVEN'T EVEN THOUGHT ABOUT...

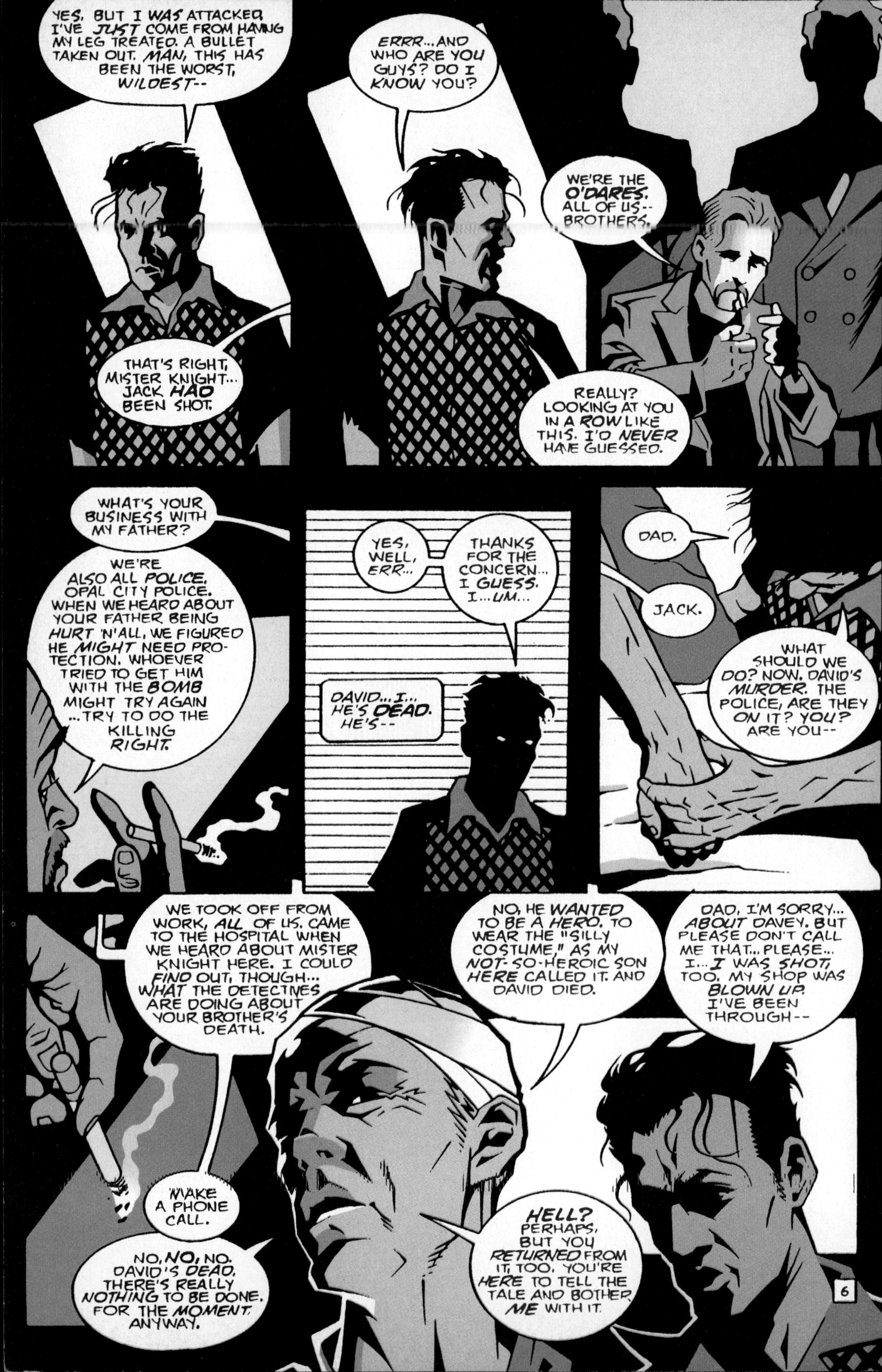
YES, BUT I WAS ATTACKED. I'VE JUST COME FROM HAVING MY LEG TREATED. A BULLET TAKEN OUT. MAN, THIS HAS BEEN THE WORST, WILDEST--
THAT'S RIGHT, MISTER KNIGHT... JACK HAD BEEN SHOT.
ERRR... AND WHO ARE YOU GUYS? DO I KNOW YOU?
WE'RE THE O'DARES. ALL OF US-- BROTHERS.
REALLY? LOOKING AT YOU IN A ROW LIKE THIS, I'D NEVER HAVE GUESSED.
WHAT'S YOUR BUSINESS WITH MY FATHER?
WE'RE ALSO ALL POLICE. OPAL CITY POLICE. WHEN WE HEARD ABOUT YOUR FATHER BEING HURT 'N'ALL, WE FIGURED HE MIGHT NEED PROTECTION. WHOEVER TRIED TO GET HIM WITH THE BOMB MIGHT TRY AGAIN ...TRY TO DO THE KILLING RIGHT.
YES, WELL, ERR...
THANKS FOR THE CONCERN... I GUESS. I...UM...
DAVID... I... HE'S DEAD. HE'S--
DAD.
JACK.
WHAT SHOULD WE DO? NOW. DAVID'S MURDER. THE POLICE, ARE THEY ON IT? YOU? ARE YOU--
WE TOOK OFF FROM WORK, ALL OF US. CAME TO THE HOSPITAL WHEN WE HEARD ABOUT MISTER KNIGHT HERE. I COULD FIND OUT, THOUGH... WHAT THE DETECTIVES ARE DOING ABOUT YOUR BROTHER'S DEATH.
MAKE A PHONE CALL.
NO, NO, NO. DAVID'S DEAD. THERE'S REALLY NOTHING TO BE DONE. FOR THE MOMENT. ANYWAY.
NO, HE WANTED TO BE A HERO. TO WEAR THE "SILLY COSTUME," AS MY NOT-SO-HEROIC SON HERE CALLED IT. AND DAVID DIED.
HELL? PERHAPS, BUT YOU RETURNED FROM IT, TOO. YOU'RE HERE TO TELL THE TALE AND BOTHER ME WITH IT.
DAD, I'M SORRY... ABOUT DAVEY. BUT PLEASE DON'T CALL ME THAT... PLEASE... I... I WAS SHOT, TOO. MY SHOP WAS BLOWN UP. I'VE BEEN THROUGH--
6

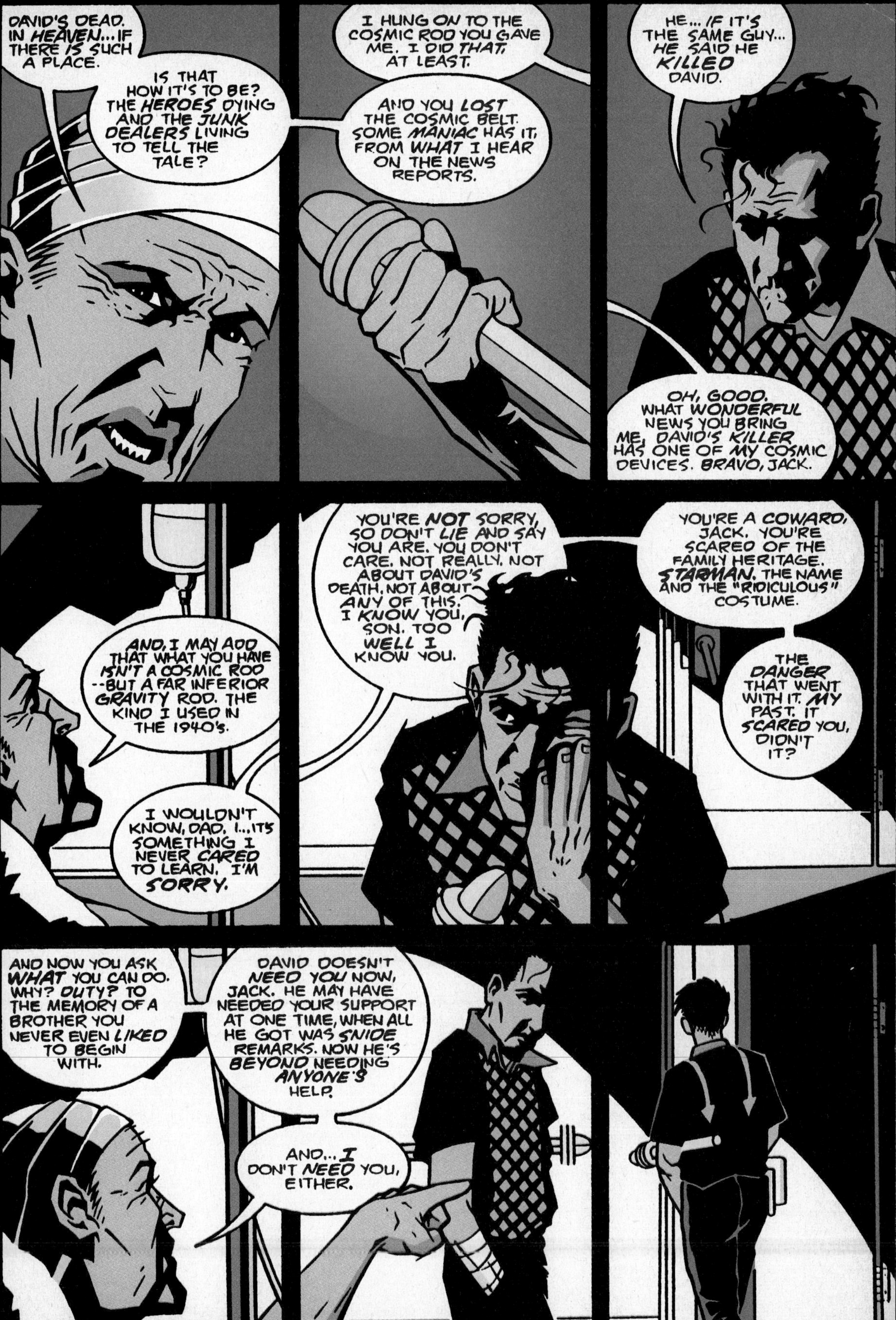
DAVID'S DEAD. IN HEAVEN... IF THERE IS SUCH A PLACE.
IS THAT HOW IT'S TO BE? THE HEROES DYING AND THE JUNK DEALERS LIVING TO TELL THE TALE?
I HUNG ON TO THE COSMIC ROD YOU GAVE ME. I DID THAT, AT LEAST.
AND YOU LOST THE COSMIC BELT. SOME MANIAC HAS IT, FROM WHAT I HEAR ON THE NEWS REPORTS.
HE... IF IT'S THE SAME GUY... HE SAID HE KILLED DAVID.
OH, GOOD. WHAT WONDERFUL NEWS YOU BRING ME. DAVID'S KILLER HAS ONE OF MY COSMIC DEVICES. BRAVO, JACK.
AND, I MAY ADD THAT WHAT YOU HAVE ISN'T A COSMIC ROD --BUT A FAR INFERIOR GRAVITY ROD. THE KIND I USED IN THE 1940'S.
I WOULDN'T KNOW, DAD. I...IT'S SOMETHING I NEVER CARED TO LEARN. I'M SORRY.
YOU'RE NOT SORRY, SO DON'T LIE AND SAY YOU ARE. YOU DON'T CARE. NOT REALLY. NOT ABOUT DAVID'S DEATH. NOT ABOUT ANY OF THIS. I KNOW YOU, SON. TOO WELL I KNOW YOU.
YOU'RE A COWARD, JACK. YOU'RE SCARED OF THE FAMILY HERITAGE. STARMAN. THE NAME AND THE "RIDICULOUS" COSTUME.
THE DANGER THAT WENT WITH IT. MY PAST. IT SCARED YOU, DIDN'T IT?
AND NOW YOU ASK WHAT YOU CAN DO. WHY? DUTY? TO THE MEMORY OF A BROTHER YOU NEVER EVEN LIKED TO BEGIN WITH.
DAVID DOESN'T NEED YOU NOW, JACK. HE MAY HAVE NEEDED YOUR SUPPORT AT ONE TIME, WHEN ALL HE GOT WAS SNIDE REMARKS. NOW HE'S BEYOND NEEDING ANYONE'S HELP.
AND... I DON'T NEED YOU, EITHER.
7

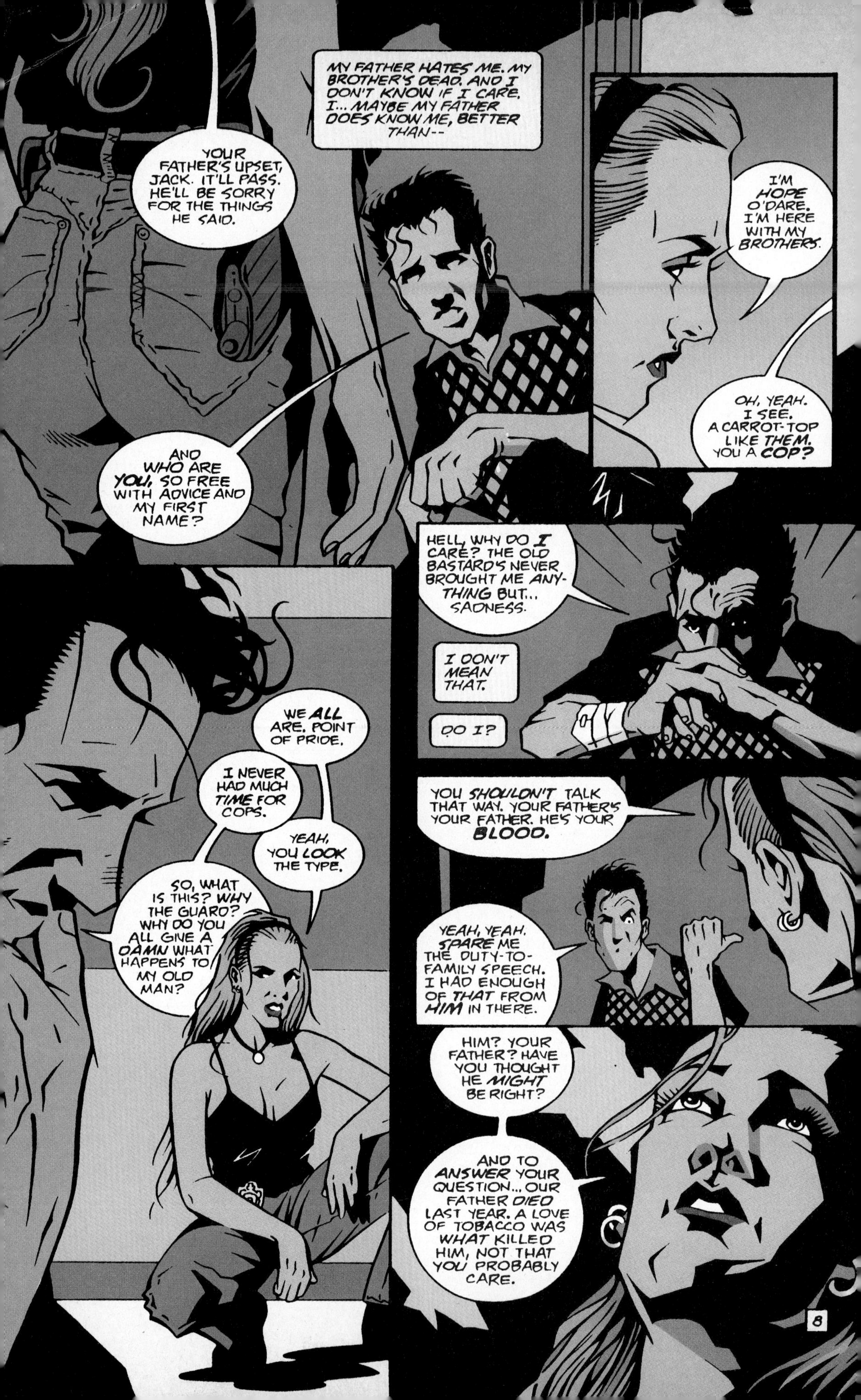
MY FATHER HATES ME. MY BROTHER'S DEAD. AND I DON'T KNOW IF I CARE. I... MAYBE MY FATHER DOES KNOW ME, BETTER THAN--
YOUR FATHER'S UPSET, JACK. IT'LL PASS. HE'LL BE SORRY FOR THE THINGS HE SAID.
AND WHO ARE YOU, SO FREE WITH ADVICE AND MY FIRST NAME?
I'M HOPE O'DARE. I'M HERE WITH MY BROTHERS.
OH, YEAH. I SEE. A CARROT-TOP LIKE THEM. YOU A COP?
HELL, WHY DO I CARE? THE OLD BASTARD'S NEVER BROUGHT ME ANYTHING BUT... SADNESS.
I DON'T MEAN THAT.
DO I?
WE ALL ARE. POINT OF PRIDE.
I NEVER HAD MUCH TIME FOR COPS.
YEAH, YOU LOOK THE TYPE.
SO, WHAT IS THIS? WHY THE GUARD? WHY DO YOU ALL GIVE A DAMN WHAT HAPPENS TO MY OLD MAN?
YOU SHOULDN'T TALK THAT WAY. YOUR FATHER'S YOUR FATHER. HE'S YOUR BLOOD.
YEAH, YEAH. SPARE ME THE DUTY-TO-FAMILY SPEECH. I HAD ENOUGH OF THAT FROM HIM IN THERE.
HIM? YOUR FATHER? HAVE YOU THOUGHT HE MIGHT BE RIGHT?
AND TO ANSWER YOUR QUESTION... OUR FATHER DIED LAST YEAR. A LOVE OF TOBACCO WAS WHAT KILLED HIM, NOT THAT YOU PROBABLY CARE.

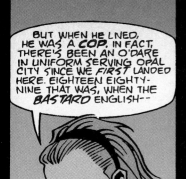

BUT WHEN HE LIVED, HE WAS A *COP.* IN FACT, THERE'S BEEN AN O'DARE IN UNIFORM SERVING OPAL CITY S'INCE WE *FIRST* LANDED HERE. EIGHTEEN EIGHTY-NINE THAT WAS, WHEN THE *BASTARD* ENGLISH--

HEY, HEY, HEY... YOU HAVE *NO IDEA* HOW MUCH I DO *NOT* WANT TO HEAR ABOUT *YOUR* FAMILY HISTORY AND THE POOR, POOR IRISH AND THEIR POTATOES AND THEIR FAMINES AND ALL, NOT AT *THIS* MOMENT, ANYWAY.

I'VE HAD A *BAD* HAIR DAY. A BAD *SHOP-BEEN-BLOWN-UP* DAY. A BAD *BROTHER-BEING-MURDERED,* AND MY-*FATHER-THINKS-I'M-SCUM* DAY. SO... CAN YOU GET TO THE *POINT* AND TELL ME WHY YOU AND YOUR BROTHERS ARE *HERE?*

SIGH... .. MY FATHER WAS A *COP,* YOUNG IN THE 1940'S. *BRASH* IN '43. A SUPER-VILLAIN WAS MENACING THE CITY.

MY FATHER GOT IN HIS WAY. ALMOST *DIED* 'CAUSE OF IT. YOUR FATHER... *STARMAN*... SAVED HIS LIFE.

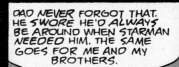

DAD NEVER FORGOT THAT. HE *SWORE* HE'D *ALWAYS* BE AROUND WHEN STARMAN *NEEDED* HIM. THE SAME GOES FOR ME AND MY BROTHERS.

I'M *TOUCHED.* REALLY, I AM.

THOUGH, AT THE SAME TIME, I HAVE TO ASK IF *YOU'RE* TOUCHED, ALL OF YOU, IN THE *HEAD.* I MEAN, ALL THIS TALK OF *DUTY* AND *HONOR* AND *FAMILY* IS--

AND *I* HAVE TO ASK IF *MAYBE* YOUR DAD IS *RIGHT* ABOUT YOU. MAYBE YOU *ARE* A CALLOW, *GUTLESS*--

UH...

UMM..., *JACK,* I THINK YOU'D *BEST* COME IN HERE. YOUR PA... HE JUST RECEIVED A *PHONE CALL* AND... ERR... *SUDDENLY*...

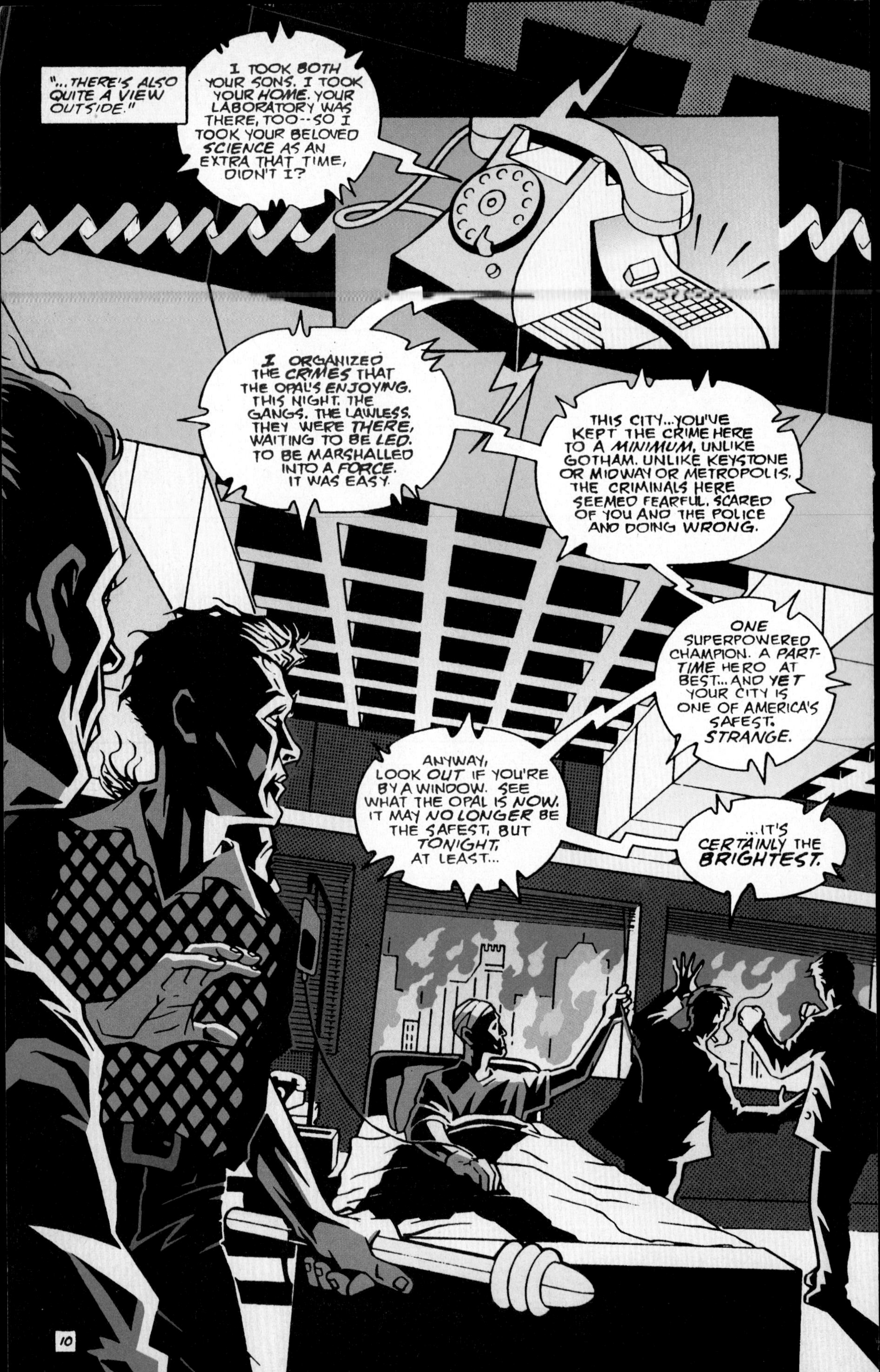
"...THERE'S ALSO QUITE A VIEW OUTSIDE."
I TOOK BOTH YOUR SONS. I TOOK YOUR HOME. YOUR LABORATORY WAS THERE, TOO--SO I TOOK YOUR BELOVED SCIENCE AS AN EXTRA THAT TIME, DIDN'T I?
I ORGANIZED THE CRIMES THAT THE OPAL'S ENJOYING THIS NIGHT. THE GANGS. THE LAWLESS. THEY WERE THERE, WAITING TO BE LED. TO BE MARSHALLED INTO A FORCE. IT WAS EASY.
THIS CITY...YOU'VE KEPT THE CRIME HERE TO A MINIMUM, UNLIKE GOTHAM. UNLIKE KEYSTONE OR MIDWAY OR METROPOLIS. THE CRIMINALS HERE SEEMED FEARFUL. SCARED OF YOU AND THE POLICE AND DOING WRONG.
ONE SUPERPOWERED CHAMPION. A PART-TIME HERO AT BEST...AND YET YOUR CITY IS ONE OF AMERICA'S SAFEST. STRANGE.
ANYWAY, LOOK OUT IF YOU'RE BY A WINDOW. SEE WHAT THE OPAL IS NOW. IT MAY NO LONGER BE THE SAFEST, BUT TONIGHT, AT LEAST...
...IT'S CERTAINLY THE BRIGHTEST.

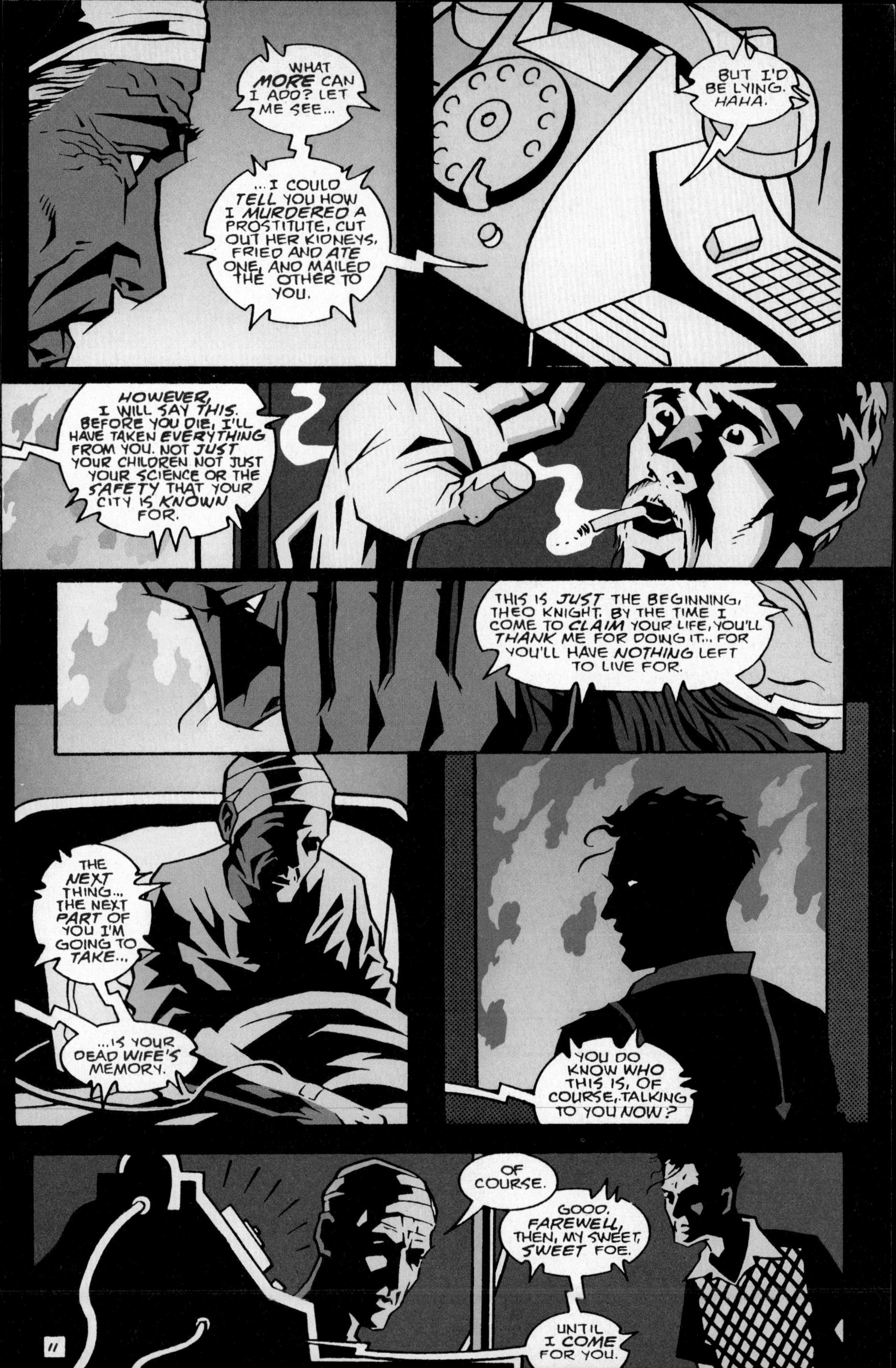
WHAT MORE CAN I ADD? LET ME SEE...
...I COULD TELL YOU HOW I MURDERED A PROSTITUTE, CUT OUT HER KIDNEYS, FRIED AND ATE ONE, AND MAILED THE OTHER TO YOU.
BUT I'D BE LYING. HAHA.
HOWEVER, I WILL SAY THIS. BEFORE YOU DIE, I'LL HAVE TAKEN EVERYTHING FROM YOU. NOT JUST YOUR CHILDREN. NOT JUST YOUR SCIENCE OR THE SAFETY THAT YOUR CITY IS KNOWN FOR.
THIS IS JUST THE BEGINNING, THEO KNIGHT. BY THE TIME I COME TO CLAIM YOUR LIFE, YOU'LL THANK ME FOR DOING IT... FOR YOU'LL HAVE NOTHING LEFT TO LIVE FOR.
THE NEXT THING... THE NEXT PART OF YOU I'M GOING TO TAKE...
...IS YOUR DEAD WIFE'S MEMORY.
YOU DO KNOW WHO THIS IS, OF COURSE, TALKING TO YOU NOW?
OF COURSE.
GOOD. FAREWELL, THEN, MY SWEET, SWEET FOE.
UNTIL I COME FOR YOU.

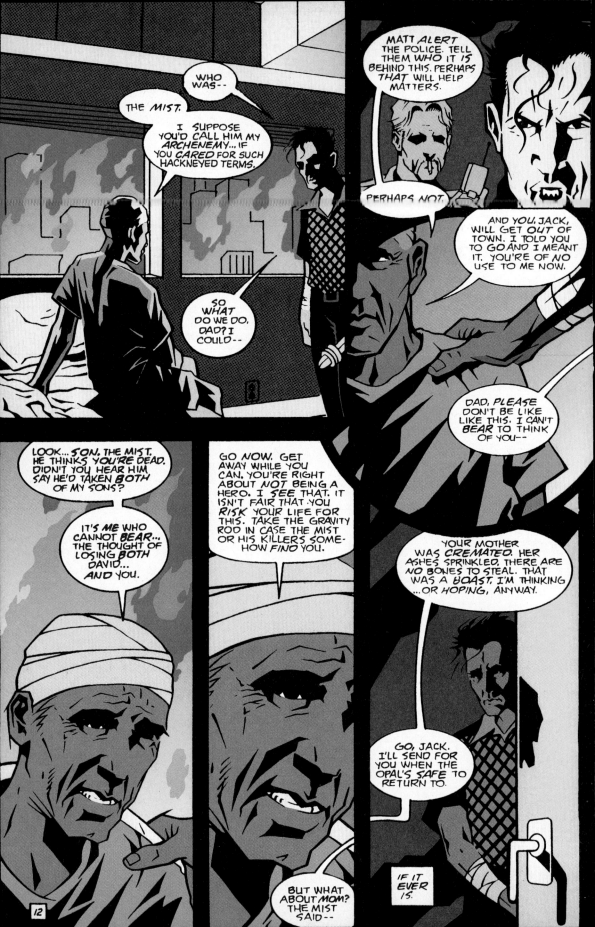

WHO WAS--

THE MIST. I SUPPOSE YOU'D CALL HIM MY ARCHENEMY... IF YOU CARED FOR SUCH HACKNEYED TERMS.

SO WHAT DO WE DO, DAD? I COULD--

MATT ALERT THE POLICE. TELL THEM WHO IT IS BEHIND THIS. PERHAPS THAT WILL HELP MATTERS.

PERHAPS NOT.

AND YOU, JACK, WILL GET OUT OF TOWN. I TOLD YOU TO GO AND I MEANT IT. YOU'RE OF NO USE TO ME NOW.

DAD, PLEASE DON'T BE LIKE LIKE THIS. I CAN'T BEAR TO THINK OF YOU--

LOOK... SON, THE MIST. HE THINKS YOU'RE DEAD. DIDN'T YOU HEAR HIM SAY HE'D TAKEN BOTH OF MY SONS?

IT'S ME WHO CANNOT BEAR... THE THOUGHT OF LOSING BOTH DAVID... AND YOU.

GO NOW. GET AWAY WHILE YOU CAN, YOU'RE RIGHT ABOUT NOT BEING A HERO. I SEE THAT. IT ISN'T FAIR THAT YOU RISK YOUR LIFE FOR THIS. TAKE THE GRAVITY ROD IN CASE THE MIST OR HIS KILLERS SOMEHOW FIND YOU.

YOUR MOTHER WAS CREMATED. HER ASHES SPRINKLED. THERE ARE NO BONES TO STEAL. THAT WAS A BOAST, I'M THINKING ...OR HOPING, ANYWAY.

GO, JACK. I'LL SEND FOR YOU WHEN THE OPAL'S SAFE TO RETURN TO.

BUT WHAT ABOUT MOM? THE MIST SAID--

IF IT EVER IS.

12

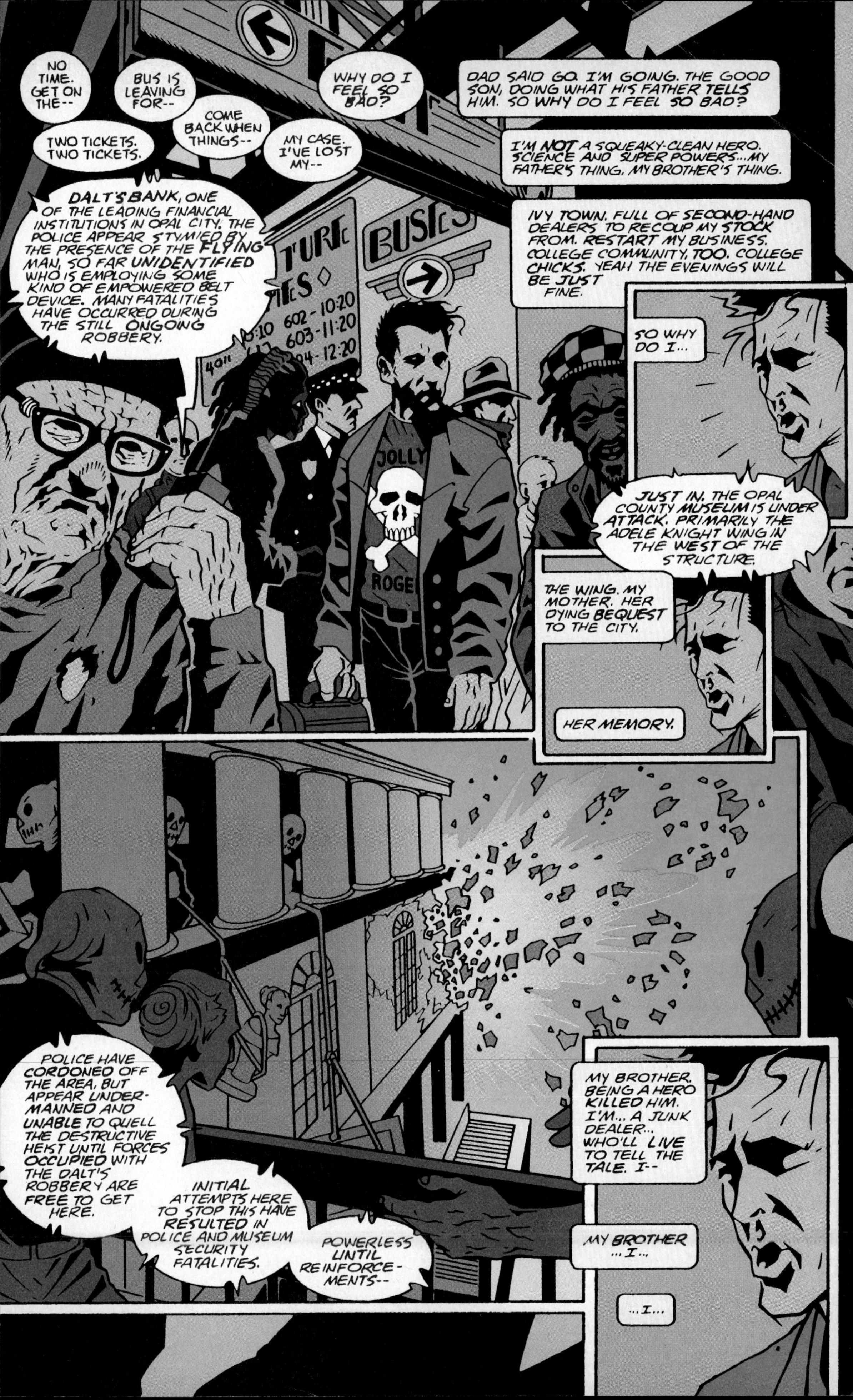
NO TIME. GET ON THE--
BUS IS LEAVING FOR--
COME BACK WHEN THINGS--
WHY DO I FEEL SO BAD?
TWO TICKETS. TWO TICKETS.
MY CASE. I'VE LOST MY--
DAD SAID GO. I'M GOING. THE GOOD SON, DOING WHAT HIS FATHER TELLS HIM. SO WHY DO I FEEL SO BAD?
I'M NOT A SQUEAKY-CLEAN HERO. SCIENCE AND SUPER POWERS... MY FATHER'S THING. MY BROTHER'S THING.
DALT'S BANK, ONE OF THE LEADING FINANCIAL INSTITUTIONS IN OPAL CITY. THE POLICE APPEAR STYMIED BY THE PRESENCE OF THE FLYING MAN, SO FAR UNIDENTIFIED WHO IS EMPLOYING SOME KIND OF EMPOWERED BELT DEVICE. MANY FATALITIES HAVE OCCURRED DURING THE STILL ONGOING ROBBERY.
IVY TOWN. FULL OF SECOND-HAND DEALERS TO RECOUP MY STOCK FROM. RESTART MY BUSINESS. COLLEGE COMMUNITY, TOO. COLLEGE CHICKS. YEAH THE EVENINGS WILL BE JUST FINE.
BUSES
602-10:20
603-11:20
SO WHY DO I...
JOLLY ROGE
JUST IN. THE OPAL COUNTY MUSEUM IS UNDER ATTACK. PRIMARILY THE ADELE KNIGHT WING IN THE WEST OF THE STRUCTURE.
THE WING. MY MOTHER. HER DYING BEQUEST TO THE CITY.
HER MEMORY.
POLICE HAVE CORDONED OFF THE AREA, BUT APPEAR UNDER-MANNED AND UNABLE TO QUELL THE DESTRUCTIVE HEIST UNTIL FORCES OCCUPIED WITH THE DALT'S ROBBERY ARE FREE TO GET HERE.
INITIAL ATTEMPTS HERE TO STOP THIS HAVE RESULTED IN POLICE AND MUSEUM SECURITY FATALITIES.
POWERLESS UNTIL REINFORCE-MENTS--
MY BROTHER. BEING A HERO KILLED HIM. I'M... A JUNK DEALER... WHO'LL LIVE TO TELL THE TALE. I--
MY BROTHER ...I...
...I...

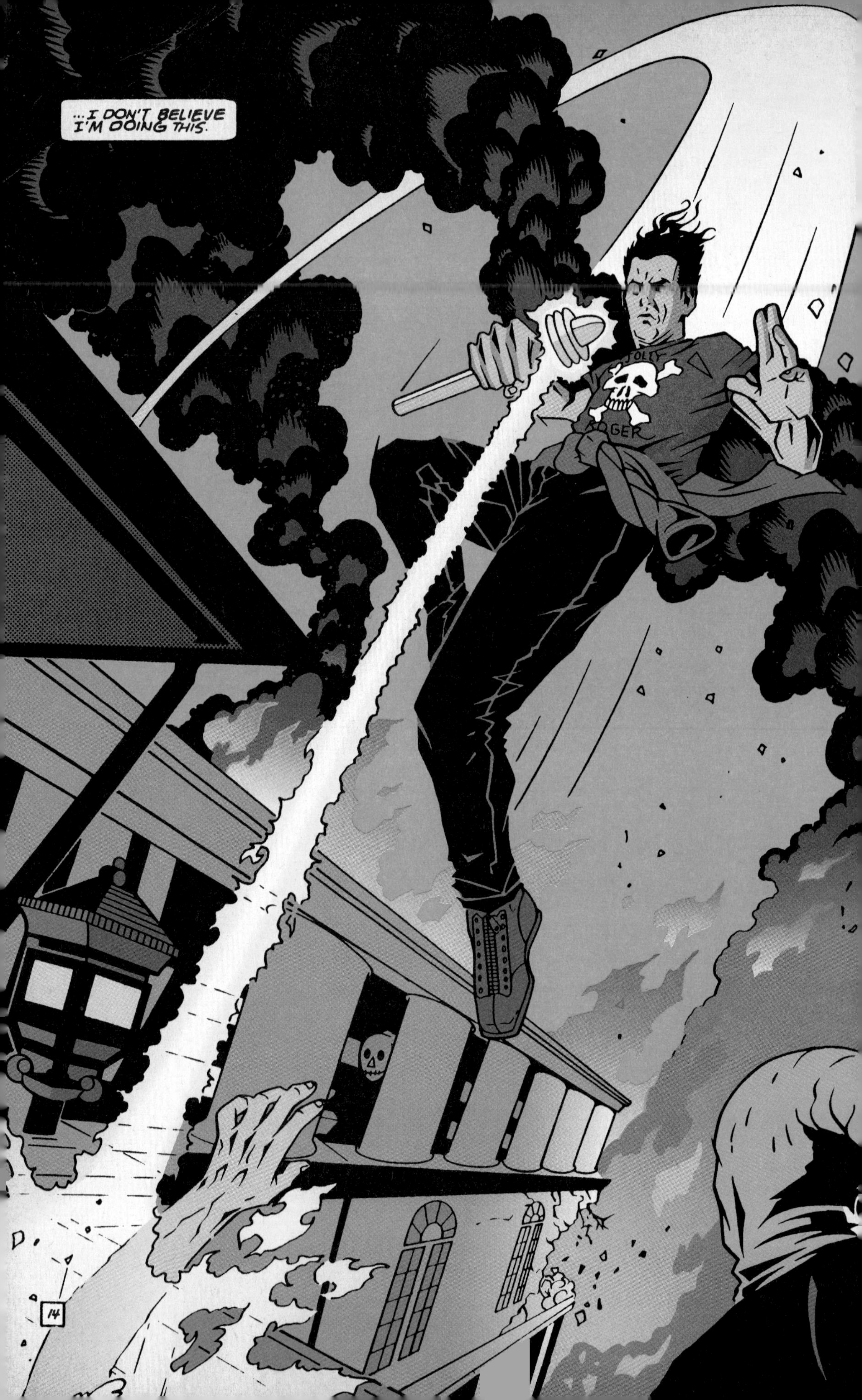
...I DON'T BELIEVE I'M DOING THIS.
JOLLY ROGER
14

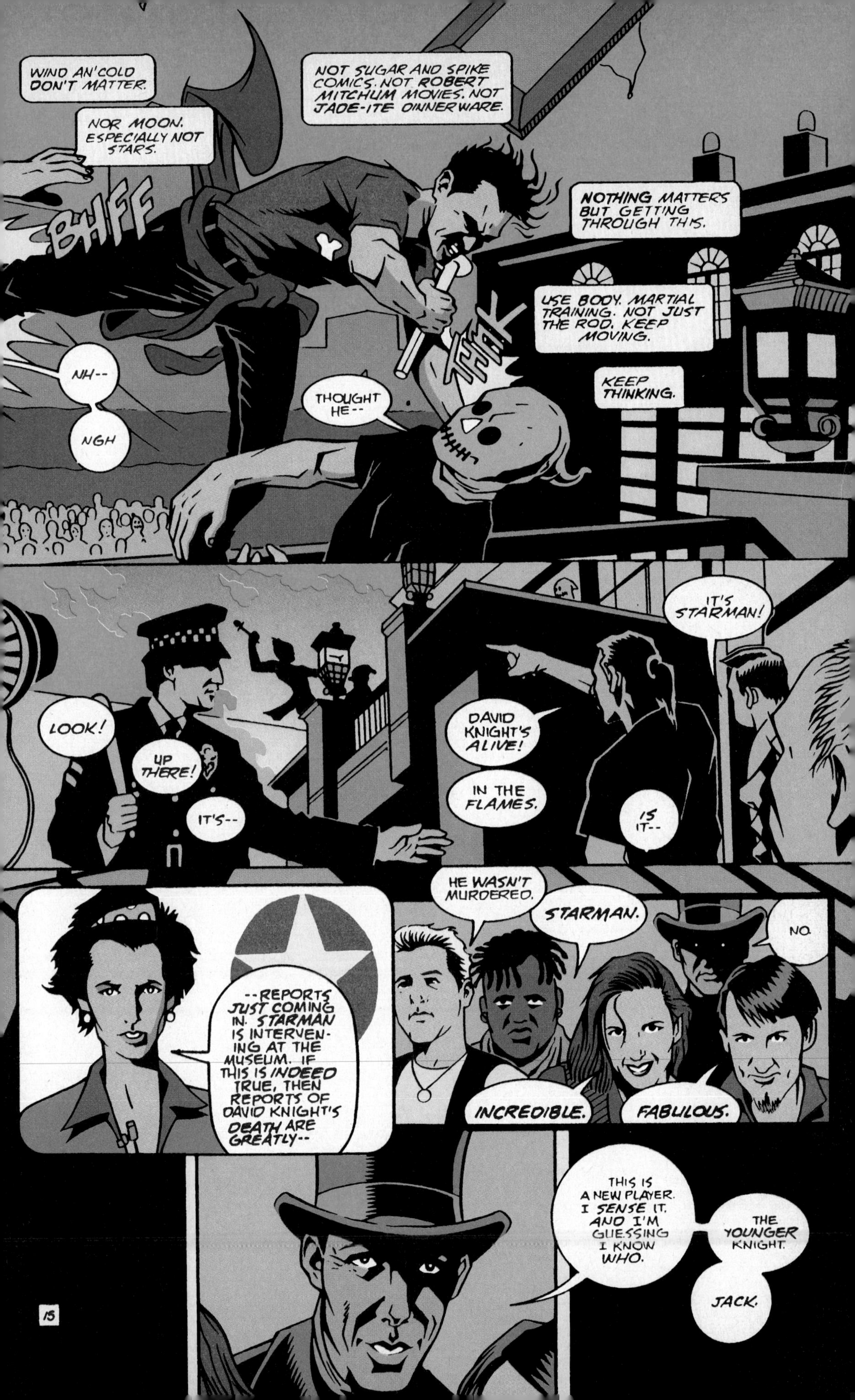

WIND AN'COLD DON'T MATTER.
NOT SUGAR AND SPIKE COMICS. NOT ROBERT MITCHUM MOVIES. NOT JADE-ITE DINNERWARE.
NOR MOON. ESPECIALLY NOT STARS.
BHFF
NOTHING MATTERS BUT GETTING THROUGH THIS.
USE BODY. MARTIAL TRAINING. NOT JUST THE ROD. KEEP MOVING.
THAK
KEEP THINKING.
NH--
NGH
THOUGHT HE--
IT'S STARMAN!
LOOK!
UP THERE!
IT'S--
DAVID KNIGHT'S ALIVE!
IN THE FLAMES.
IS IT--
HE WASN'T MURDERED.
STARMAN.
NO.
--REPORTS JUST COMING IN. STARMAN IS INTERVENING AT THE MUSEUM. IF THIS IS INDEED TRUE, THEN REPORTS OF DAVID KNIGHT'S DEATH ARE GREATLY--
INCREDIBLE.
FABULOUS.
THIS IS A NEW PLAYER. I SENSE IT. AND I'M GUESSING I KNOW WHO.
THE YOUNGER KNIGHT.
JACK.

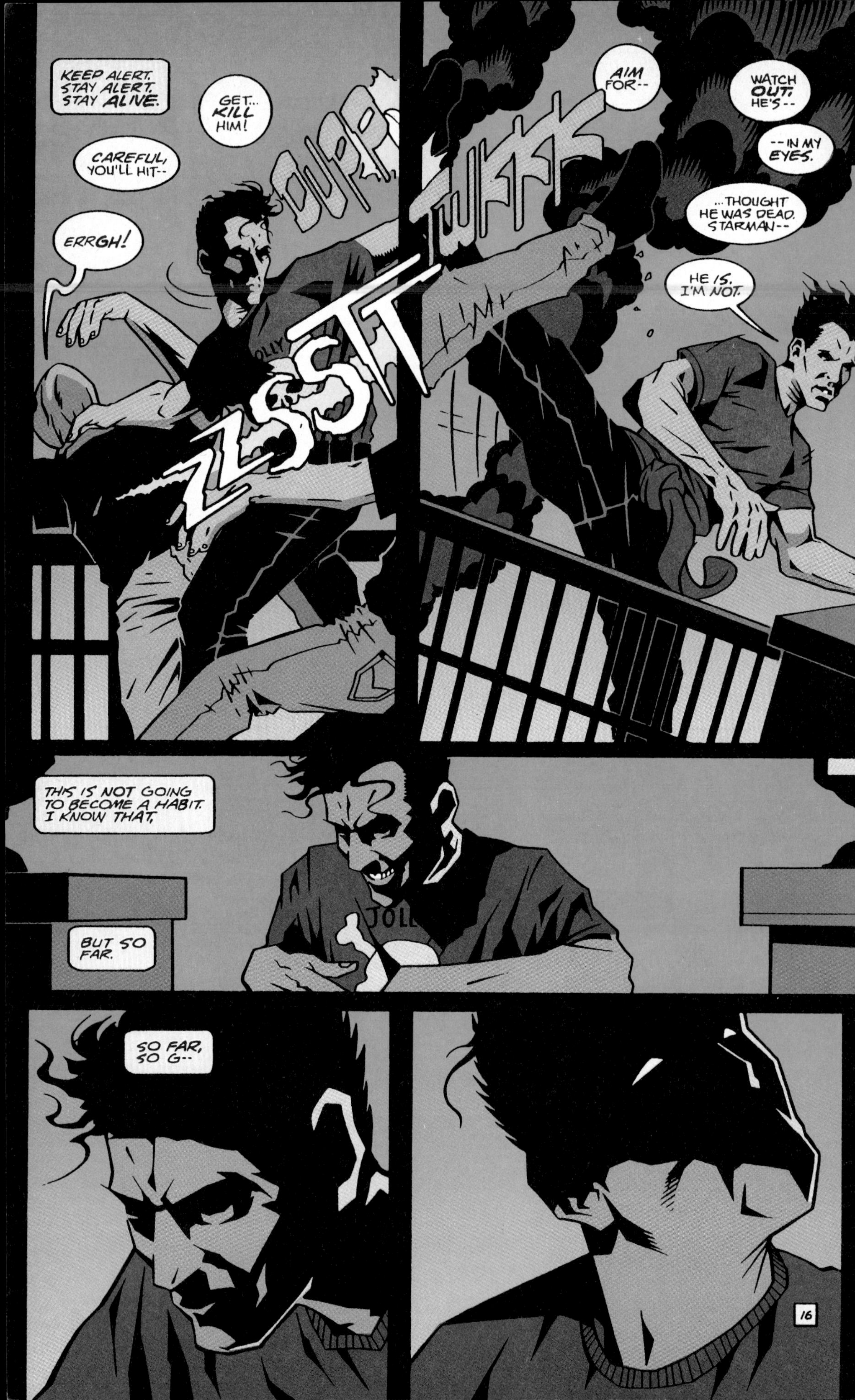
KEEP ALERT. STAY ALERT. STAY ALIVE.
GET... KILL HIM!
CAREFUL, YOU'LL HIT--
DUPP
ERRGH!
ZZSSTT
AIM FOR--
TUKKK
WATCH OUT, HE'S--
--IN MY EYES.
...THOUGHT HE WAS DEAD. STARMAN--
HE IS. I'M NOT.
THIS IS NOT GOING TO BECOME A HABIT. I KNOW THAT,
BUT SO FAR.
SO FAR, SO G--

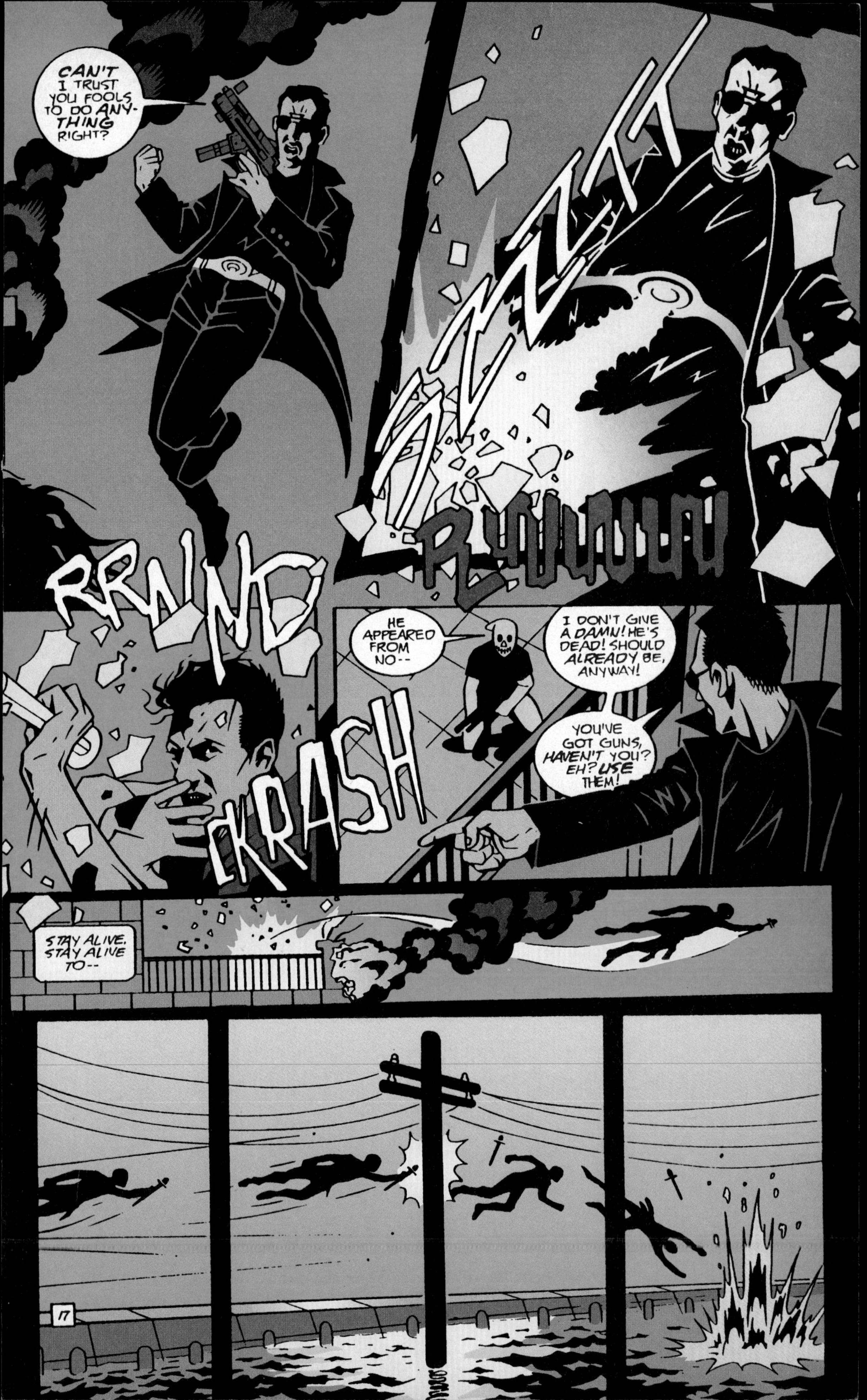
CAN'T I TRUST YOU FOOLS TO DO ANY-THING RIGHT?
SZZZTT
RRUUUUUUUU
RRAWWD
HE APPEARED FROM NO--
I DON'T GIVE A DAMN! HE'S DEAD! SHOULD ALREADY BE, ANYWAY!
YOU'VE GOT GUNS, HAVEN'T YOU? EH? USE THEM!
CKRASH
STAY ALIVE. STAY ALIVE TO--
17

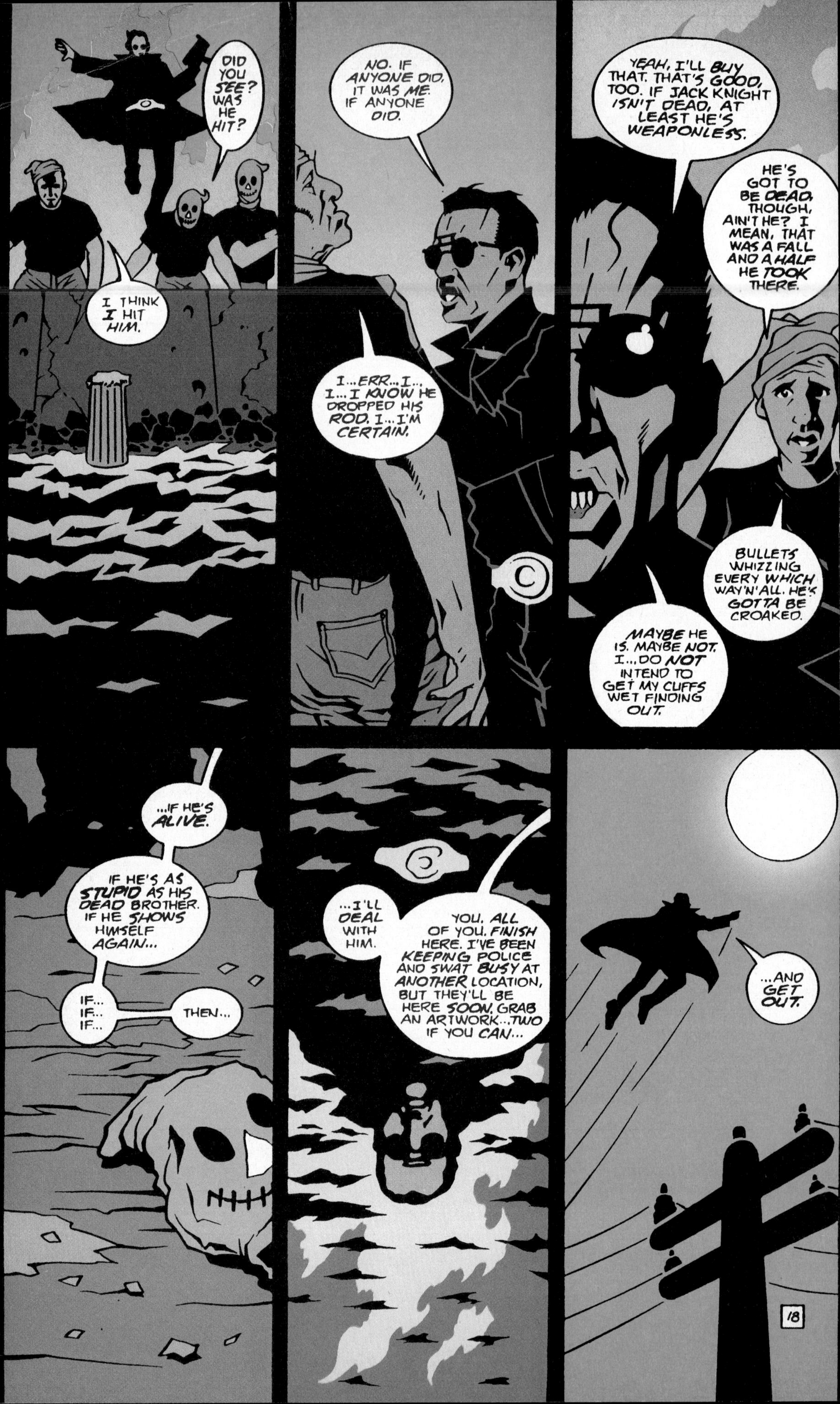
DID YOU SEE? WAS HE HIT?
I THINK I HIT HIM.
NO. IF ANYONE DID, IT WAS ME. IF ANYONE DID.
I...ERR...I... I...I KNOW HE DROPPED HIS ROD. I...I'M CERTAIN.
YEAH, I'LL BUY THAT. THAT'S GOOD, TOO. IF JACK KNIGHT ISN'T DEAD, AT LEAST HE'S WEAPONLESS.
HE'S GOT TO BE DEAD, THOUGH, AIN'T HE? I MEAN, THAT WAS A FALL AND A HALF HE TOOK THERE.
BULLETS WHIZZING EVERY WHICH WAY'N'ALL. HE'S GOTTA BE CROAKED.
MAYBE HE IS. MAYBE NOT. I...DO NOT INTEND TO GET MY CUFFS WET FINDING OUT.
...IF HE'S ALIVE.
IF HE'S AS STUPID AS HIS DEAD BROTHER. IF HE SHOWS HIMSELF AGAIN...
IF... IF... IF...
THEN...
...I'LL DEAL WITH HIM.
YOU. ALL OF YOU. FINISH HERE. I'VE BEEN KEEPING POLICE AND SWAT BUSY AT ANOTHER LOCATION, BUT THEY'LL BE HERE SOON. GRAB AN ARTWORK...TWO IF YOU CAN...
...AND GET OUT.
18

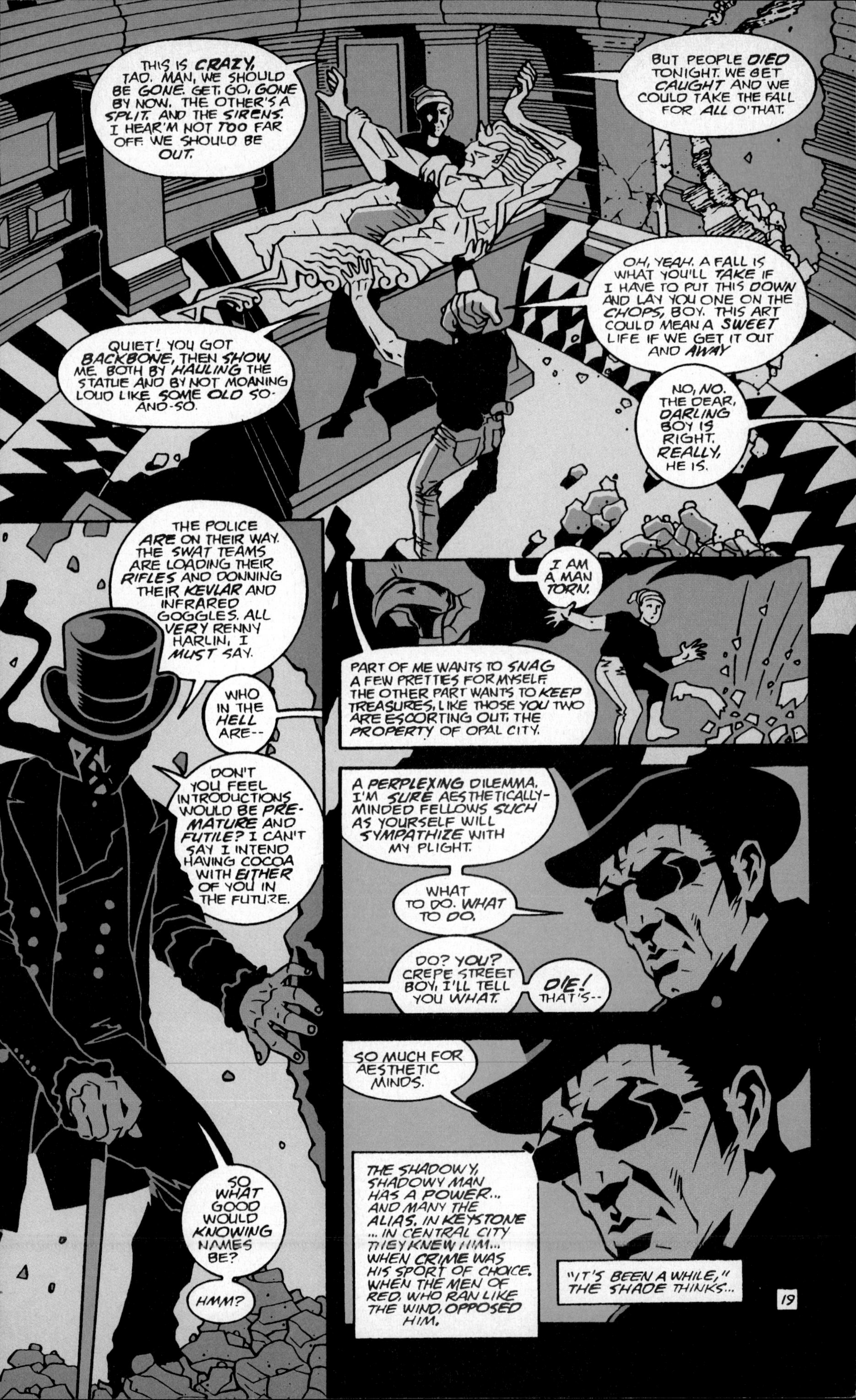
THIS IS CRAZY, TAO. MAN, WE SHOULD BE GONE. GET, GO, GONE BY NOW. THE OTHER'S A SPLIT. AND THE SIRENS. I HEAR'M NOT TOO FAR OFF. WE SHOULD BE OUT.
BUT PEOPLE DIED TONIGHT. WE GET CAUGHT AND WE COULD TAKE THE FALL FOR ALL O'THAT.
OH, YEAH. A FALL IS WHAT YOU'LL TAKE IF I HAVE TO PUT THIS DOWN AND LAY YOU ONE ON THE CHOPS, BOY. THIS ART COULD MEAN A SWEET LIFE IF WE GET IT OUT AND AWAY
QUIET! YOU GOT BACKBONE, THEN SHOW ME. BOTH BY HAULING THE STATUE AND BY NOT MOANING LOUD LIKE SOME OLD SO-AND-SO.
NO, NO. THE DEAR, DARLING BOY IS RIGHT. REALLY, HE IS.
THE POLICE ARE ON THEIR WAY. THE SWAT TEAMS ARE LOADING THEIR RIFLES AND DONNING THEIR KEVLAR AND INFRARED GOGGLES. ALL VERY RENNY HARLIN, I MUST SAY.
WHO IN THE HELL ARE--
DON'T YOU FEEL INTRODUCTIONS WOULD BE PREMATURE AND FUTILE? I CAN'T SAY I INTEND HAVING COCOA WITH EITHER OF YOU IN THE FUTURE.
SO WHAT GOOD WOULD KNOWING NAMES BE?
HMM?
I AM A MAN TORN.
PART OF ME WANTS TO SNAG A FEW PRETTIES FOR MYSELF. THE OTHER PART WANTS TO KEEP TREASURES, LIKE THOSE YOU TWO ARE ESCORTING OUT, THE PROPERTY OF OPAL CITY.
A PERPLEXING DILEMMA. I'M SURE AESTHETICALLY-MINDED FELLOWS SUCH AS YOURSELF WILL SYMPATHIZE WITH MY PLIGHT.
WHAT TO DO. WHAT TO DO.
DO? YOU? CREPE STREET BOY, I'LL TELL YOU WHAT.
DIE! THAT'S--
SO MUCH FOR AESTHETIC MINDS.
THE SHADOWY, SHADOWY MAN HAS A POWER... AND MANY THE ALIAS. IN KEYSTONE ... IN CENTRAL CITY THEY KNEW HIM... WHEN CRIME WAS HIS SPORT OF CHOICE. WHEN THE MEN OF RED, WHO RAN LIKE THE WIND, OPPOSED HIM.
"IT'S BEEN A WHILE," THE SHADE THINKS...

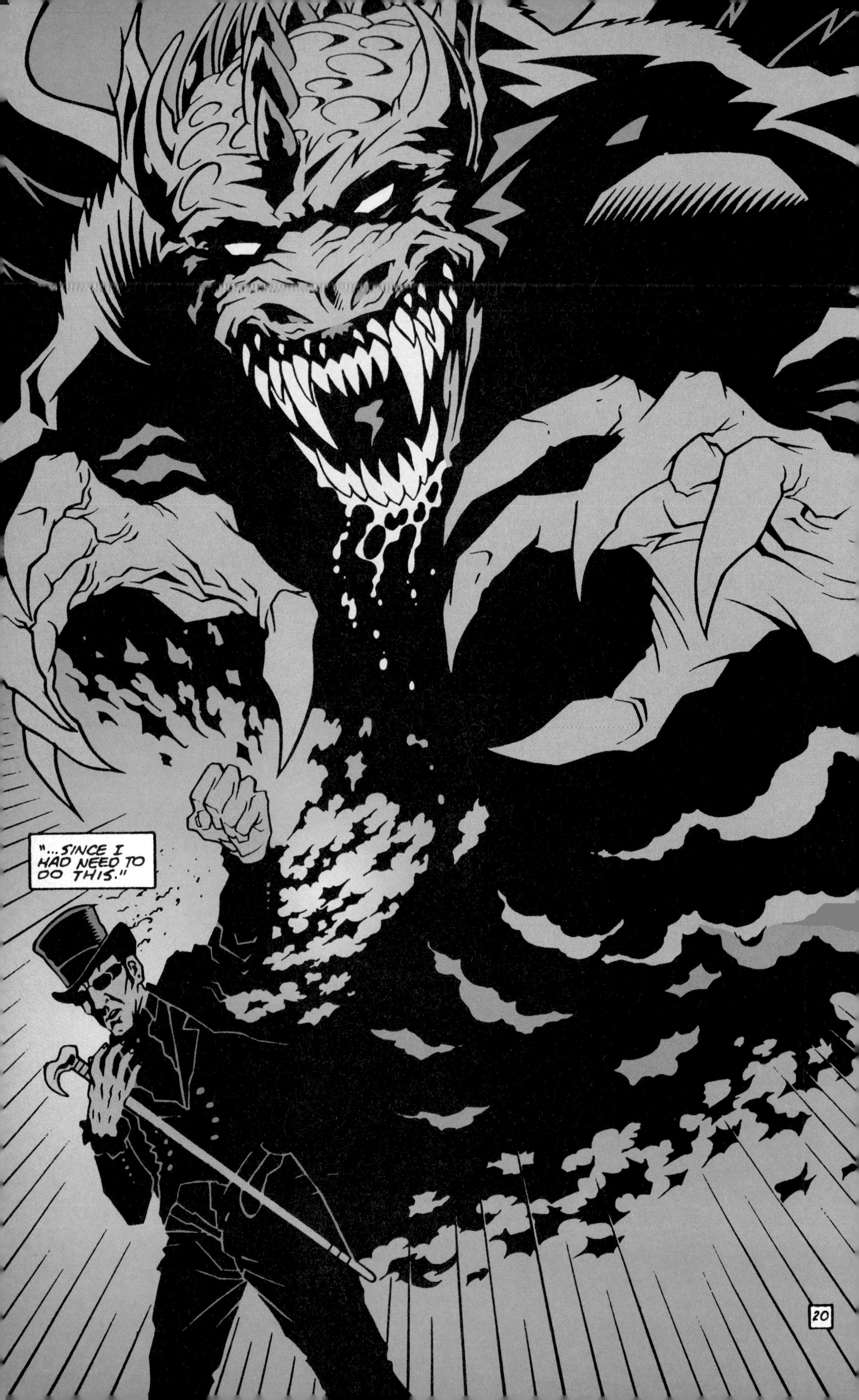
"...SINCE I HAD NEED TO DO THIS."

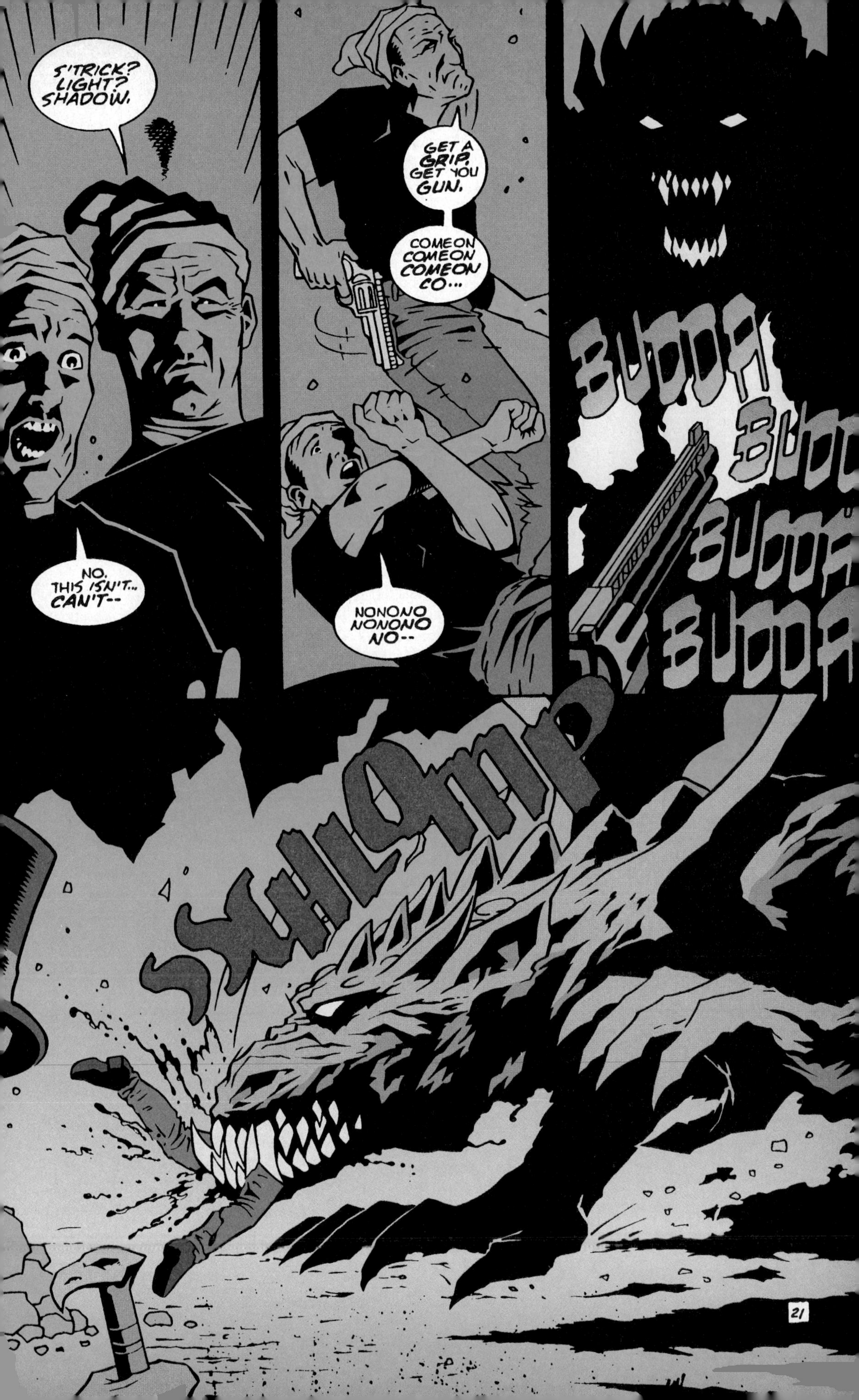
S'TRICK? LIGHT? SHADOW.
NO. THIS ISN'T... CAN'T--
GET A GRIP. GET YOU GUN.
COMEON COMEON COMEON CO...
NONONO NONONO NO--
BUDDA BUDD BUDDA BUDDA
SHHLOMP

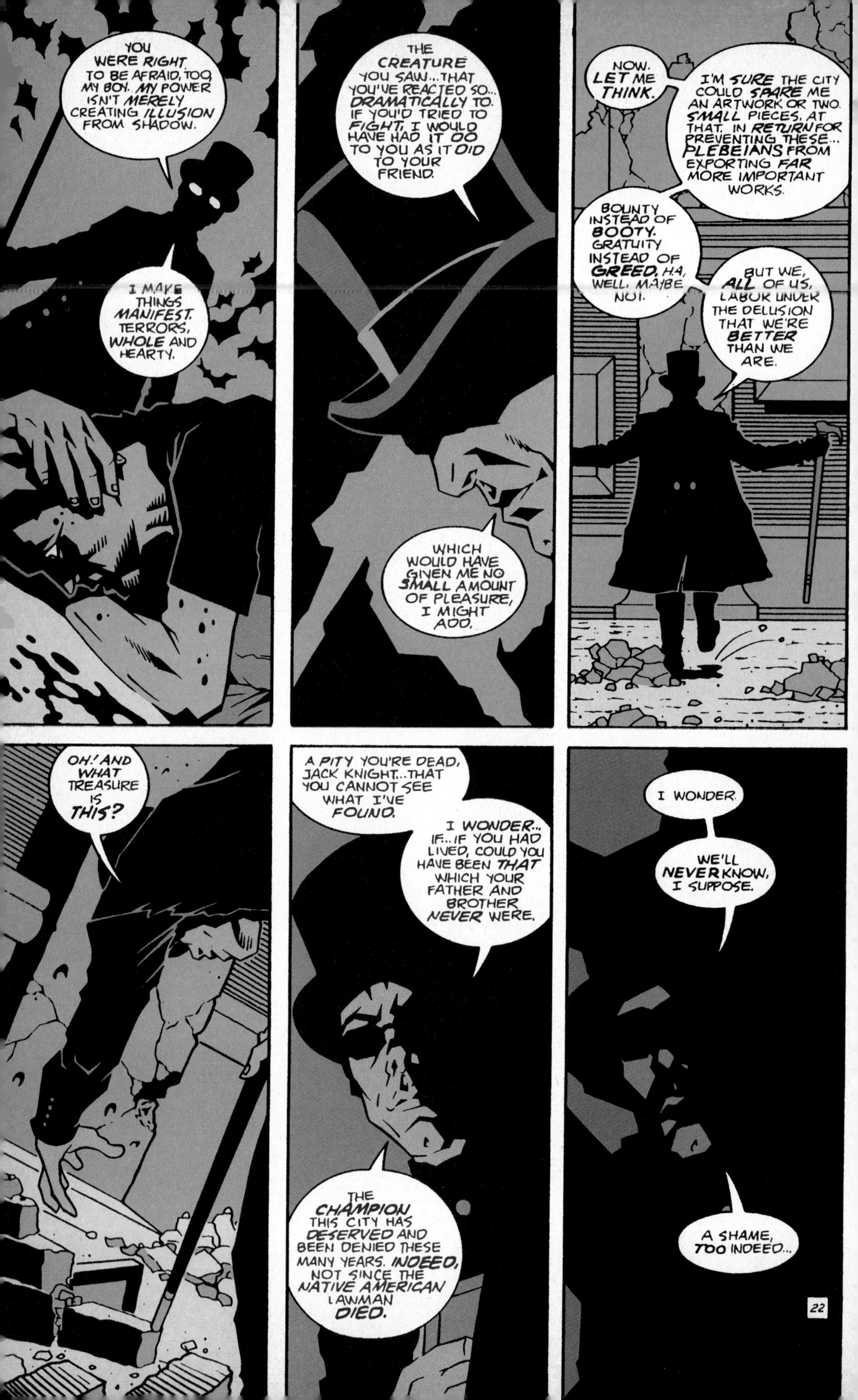
YOU WERE RIGHT TO BE AFRAID, TOO, MY BOY. MY POWER ISN'T MERELY CREATING ILLUSION FROM SHADOW.
I MAKE THINGS MANIFEST. TERRORS, WHOLE AND HEARTY.
THE CREATURE YOU SAW... THAT YOU'VE REACTED SO... DRAMATICALLY TO. IF YOU'D TRIED TO FIGHT, I WOULD HAVE HAD IT DO TO YOU AS IT DID TO YOUR FRIEND.
WHICH WOULD HAVE GIVEN ME NO SMALL AMOUNT OF PLEASURE, I MIGHT ADD.
NOW. LET ME THINK.
I'M SURE THE CITY COULD SPARE ME AN ARTWORK OR TWO. SMALL PIECES, AT THAT, IN RETURN FOR PREVENTING THESE... PLEBEIANS FROM EXPORTING FAR MORE IMPORTANT WORKS.
BOUNTY INSTEAD OF BOOTY. GRATUITY INSTEAD OF GREED. HA, WELL, MAYBE NOT.
BUT WE, ALL OF US, LABOR UNDER THE DELUSION THAT WE'RE BETTER THAN WE ARE.
OH! AND WHAT TREASURE IS THIS?
A PITY YOU'RE DEAD, JACK KNIGHT... THAT YOU CANNOT SEE WHAT I'VE FOUND.
I WONDER... IF... IF YOU HAD LIVED, COULD YOU HAVE BEEN THAT WHICH YOUR FATHER AND BROTHER NEVER WERE.
THE CHAMPION THIS CITY HAS DESERVED AND BEEN DENIED THESE MANY YEARS. INDEED, NOT SINCE THE NATIVE AMERICAN LAWMAN DIED.
I WONDER.
WE'LL NEVER KNOW, I SUPPOSE.
A SHAME, TOO INDEED...
22

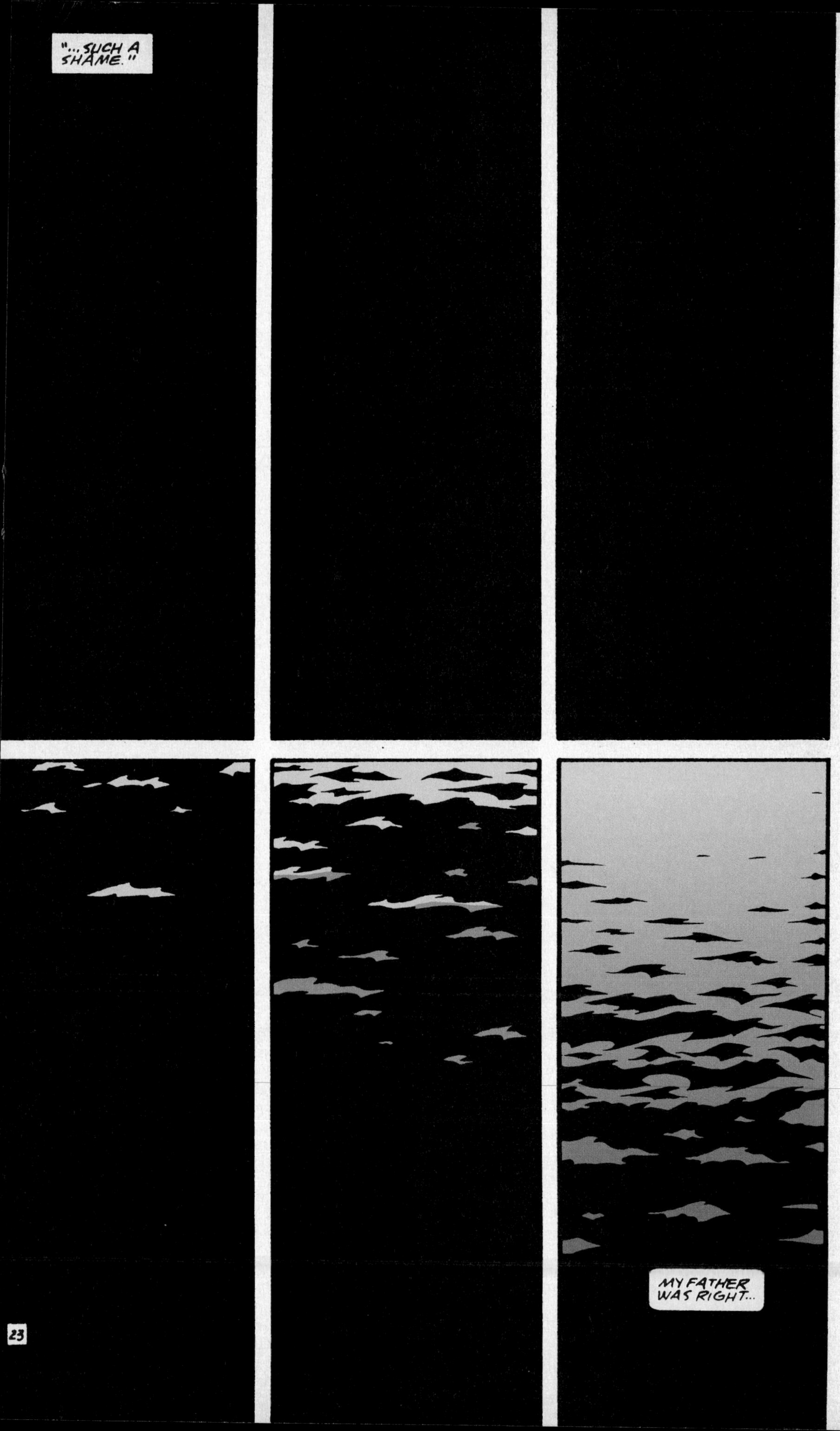
"...SUCH A SHAME."
MY FATHER WAS RIGHT...

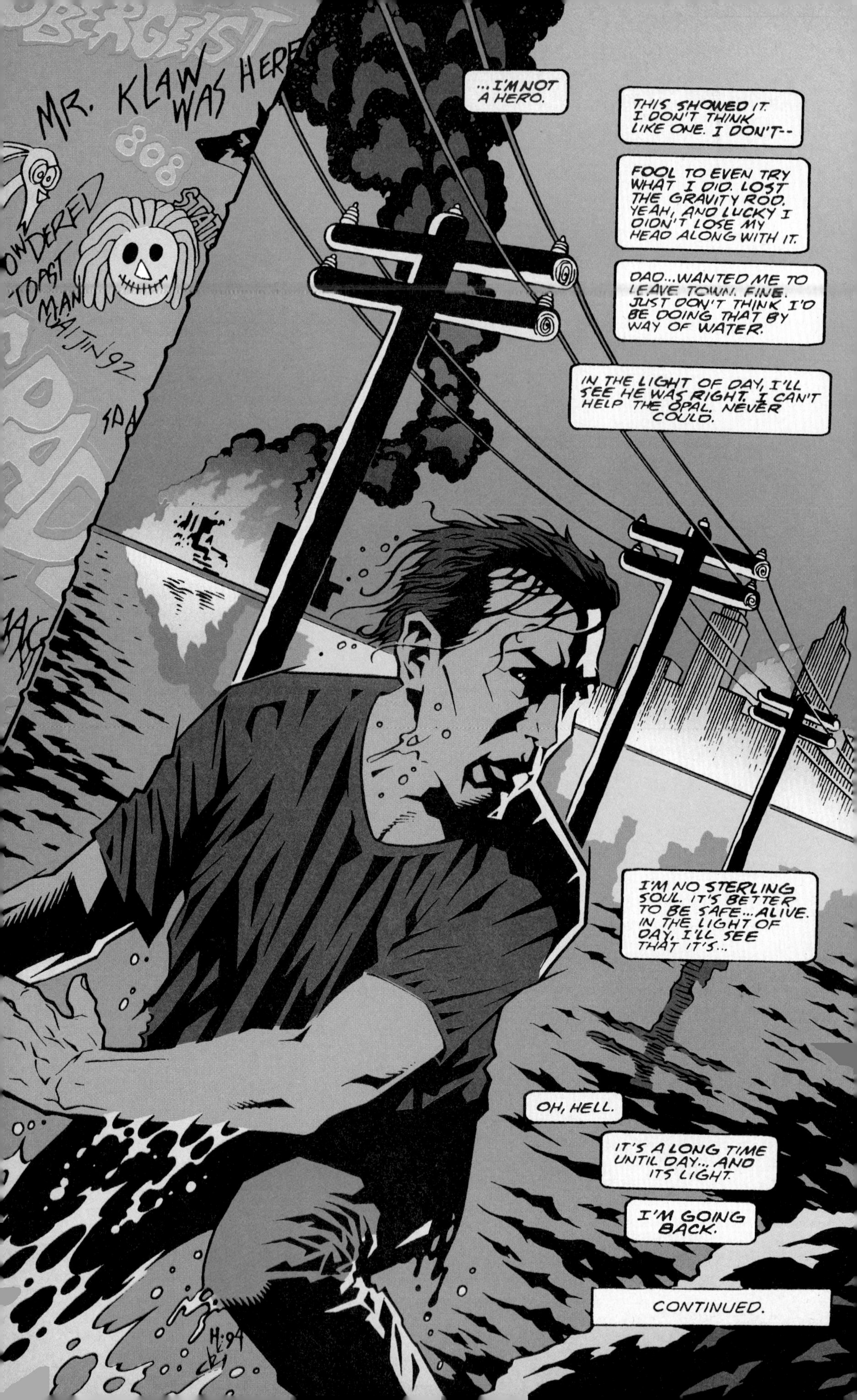
MR. KLAW WAS HERE
808
...I'M NOT A HERO.
THIS SHOWED IT. I DON'T THINK LIKE ONE. I DON'T--
FOOL TO EVEN TRY WHAT I DID. LOST THE GRAVITY ROD. YEAH, AND LUCKY I DIDN'T LOSE MY HEAD ALONG WITH IT.
DAD...WANTED ME TO LEAVE TOWN. FINE. JUST DON'T THINK I'D BE DOING THAT BY WAY OF WATER.
IN THE LIGHT OF DAY, I'LL SEE HE WAS RIGHT. I CAN'T HELP THE OPAL. NEVER COULD.
I'M NO STERLING SOUL. IT'S BETTER TO BE SAFE...ALIVE. IN THE LIGHT OF DAY, I'LL SEE THAT IT'S...
OH, HELL.
IT'S A LONG TIME UNTIL DAY... AND ITS LIGHT.
I'M GOING BACK.
CONTINUED.

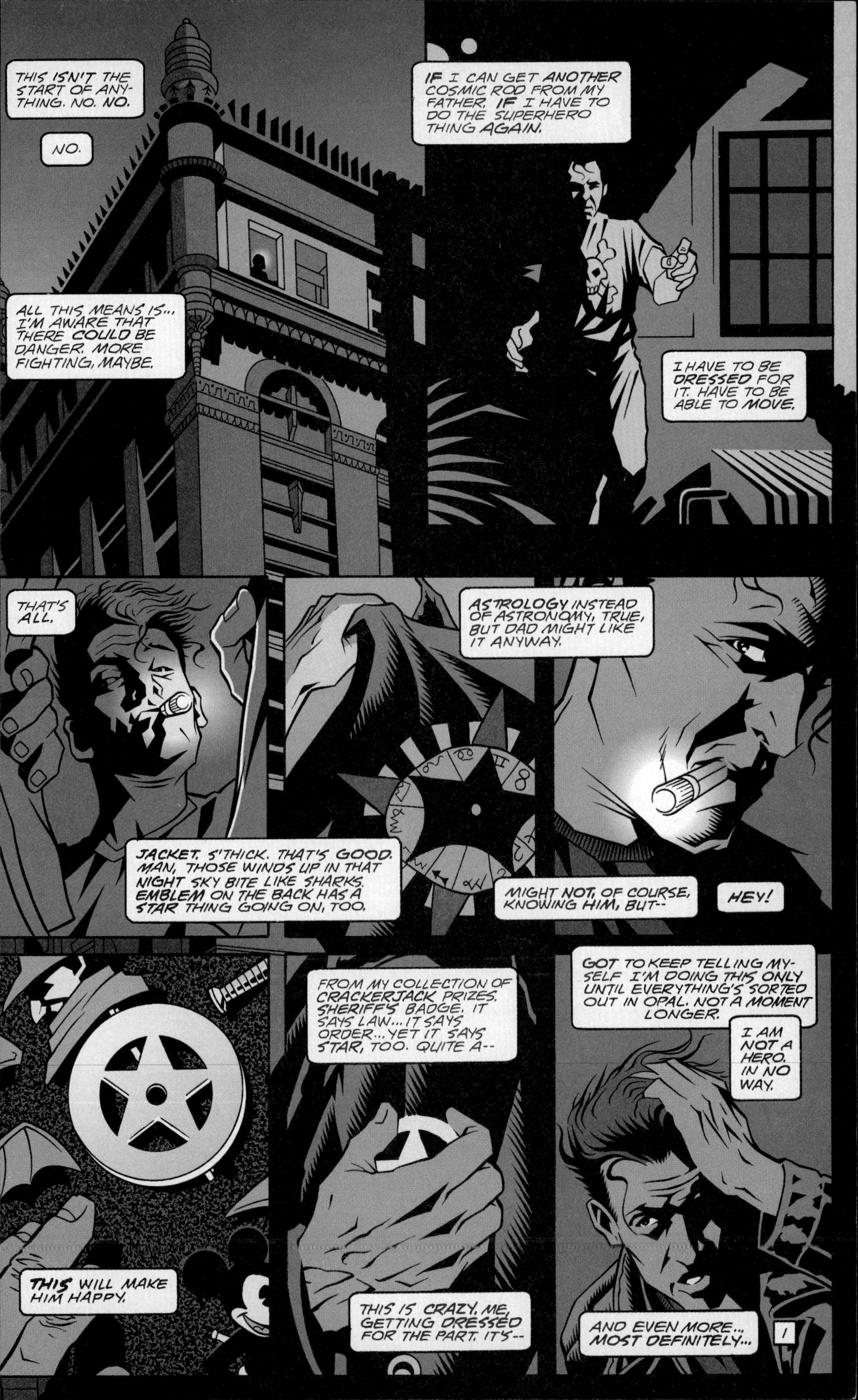
THIS ISN'T THE START OF ANY-THING. NO. NO.
NO.
IF I CAN GET ANOTHER COSMIC ROD FROM MY FATHER. IF I HAVE TO DO THE SUPERHERO THING AGAIN.
ALL THIS MEANS IS... I'M AWARE THAT THERE COULD BE DANGER. MORE FIGHTING, MAYBE.
I HAVE TO BE DRESSED FOR IT. HAVE TO BE ABLE TO MOVE.
THAT'S ALL.
JACKET. S'THICK. THAT'S GOOD. MAN, THOSE WINDS UP IN THAT NIGHT SKY BITE LIKE SHARKS. EMBLEM ON THE BACK HAS A STAR THING GOING ON, TOO.
ASTROLOGY INSTEAD OF ASTRONOMY, TRUE, BUT DAD MIGHT LIKE IT ANYWAY.
MIGHT NOT, OF COURSE, KNOWING HIM, BUT--
HEY!
THIS WILL MAKE HIM HAPPY.
FROM MY COLLECTION OF CRACKERJACK PRIZES. SHERIFF'S BADGE. IT SAYS LAW... IT SAYS ORDER... YET IT SAYS STAR, TOO. QUITE A--
THIS IS CRAZY. ME, GETTING DRESSED FOR THE PART. IT'S--
GOT TO KEEP TELLING MY-SELF I'M DOING THIS ONLY UNTIL EVERYTHING'S SORTED OUT IN OPAL. NOT A MOMENT LONGER.
I AM NOT A HERO. IN NO WAY.
AND EVEN MORE... MOST DEFINITELY...
1

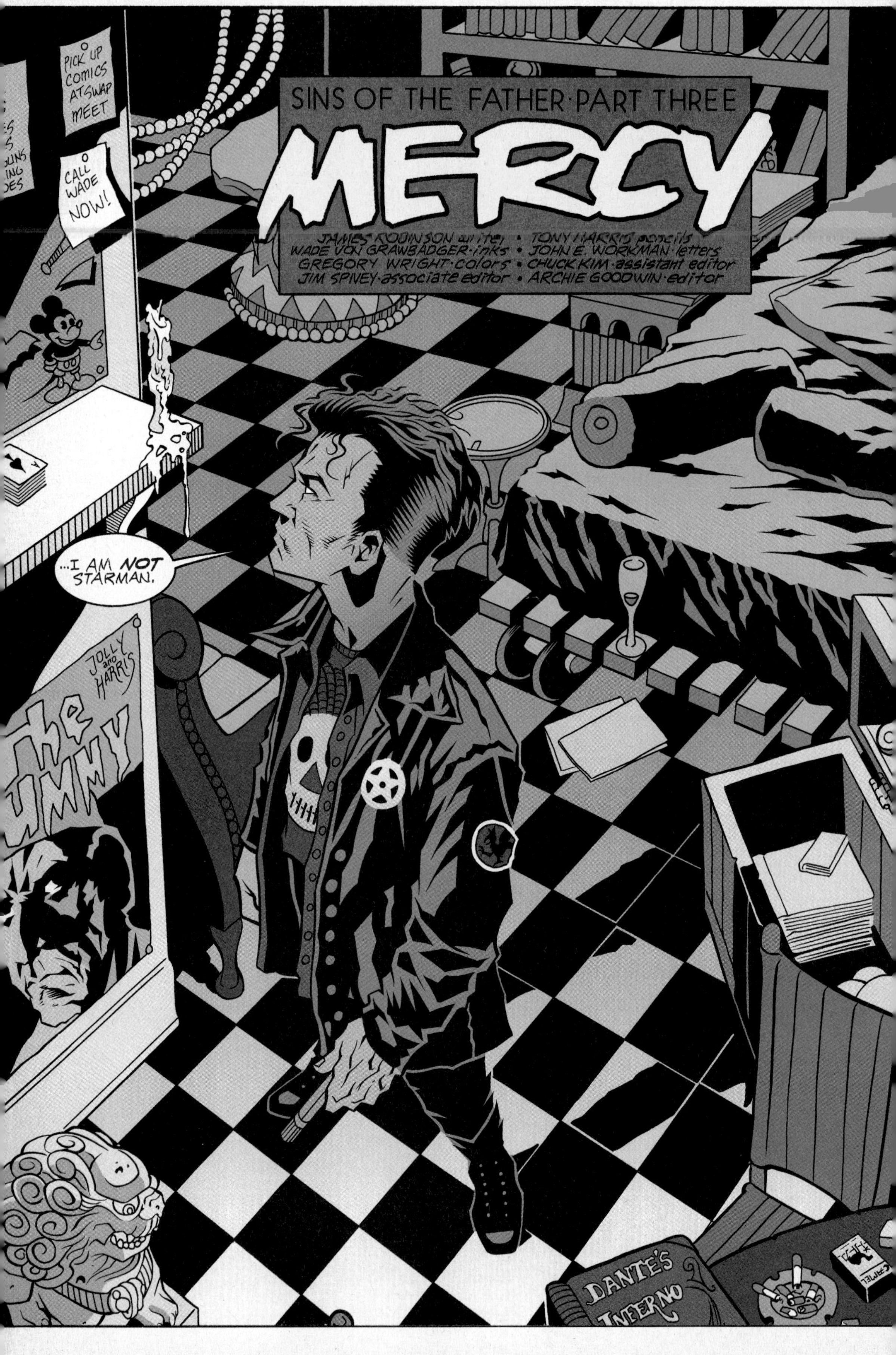

PICK UP COMICS AT SWAP MEET
CALL WADE NOW!
SINS OF THE FATHER · PART THREE
MERCY
JAMES ROBINSON writer • TONY HARRIS pencils
WADE VON GRAWBADGER · inks • JOHN E. WORKMAN · letters
GREGORY WRIGHT · colors • CHUCK KIM · assistant editor
JIM SPIVEY · associate editor • ARCHIE GOODWIN · editor
...I AM NOT STARMAN.
JOLLY and HARRIS
DANTE'S INFERNO

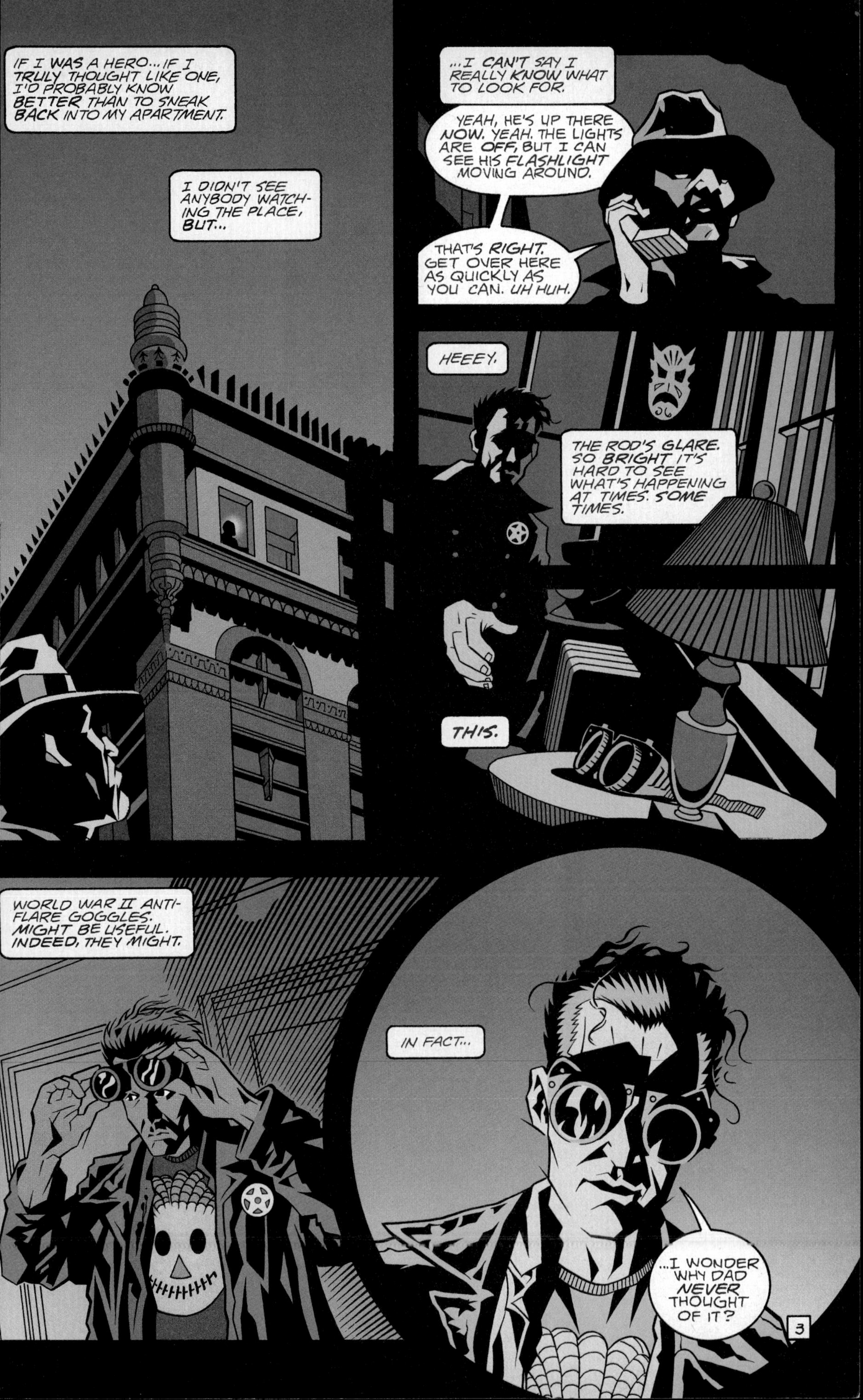

IF I WAS A HERO... IF I TRULY THOUGHT LIKE ONE, I'D PROBABLY KNOW BETTER THAN TO SNEAK BACK INTO MY APARTMENT.
I DIDN'T SEE ANYBODY WATCHING THE PLACE, BUT...
...I CAN'T SAY I REALLY KNOW WHAT TO LOOK FOR.
YEAH, HE'S UP THERE NOW. YEAH. THE LIGHTS ARE OFF, BUT I CAN SEE HIS FLASHLIGHT MOVING AROUND.
THAT'S RIGHT. GET OVER HERE AS QUICKLY AS YOU CAN. UH HUH.
HEEEY.
THE ROD'S GLARE. SO BRIGHT IT'S HARD TO SEE WHAT'S HAPPENING AT TIMES. SOME TIMES.
THIS.
WORLD WAR II ANTI-FLARE GOGGLES. MIGHT BE USEFUL. INDEED, THEY MIGHT.
IN FACT...
...I WONDER WHY DAD NEVER THOUGHT OF IT?

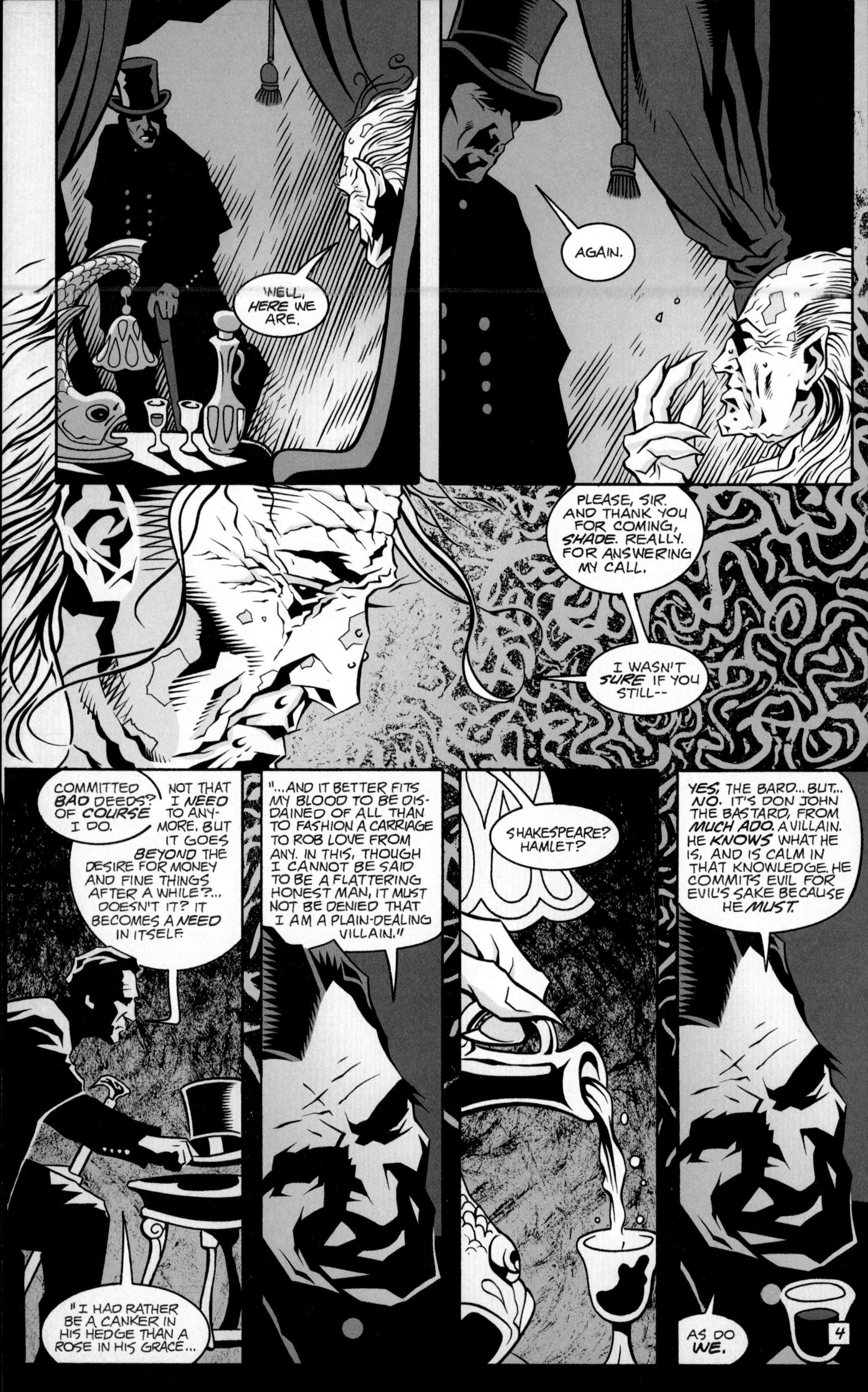
WELL, HERE WE ARE.
AGAIN.
PLEASE, SIR. AND THANK YOU FOR COMING, SHADE. REALLY. FOR ANSWERING MY CALL.
I WASN'T SURE IF YOU STILL--
COMMITTED BAD DEEDS? OF COURSE I DO.
NOT THAT I NEED TO ANYMORE. BUT IT GOES BEYOND THE DESIRE FOR MONEY AND FINE THINGS AFTER A WHILE?... DOESN'T IT? IT BECOMES A NEED IN ITSELF.
"I HAD RATHER BE A CANKER IN HIS HEDGE THAN A ROSE IN HIS GRACE...
"...AND IT BETTER FITS MY BLOOD TO BE DISDAINED OF ALL THAN TO FASHION A CARRIAGE TO ROB LOVE FROM ANY. IN THIS, THOUGH I CANNOT BE SAID TO BE A FLATTERING HONEST MAN, IT MUST NOT BE DENIED THAT I AM A PLAIN-DEALING VILLAIN."
SHAKESPEARE? HAMLET?
YES, THE BARD... BUT... NO. IT'S DON JOHN THE BASTARD, FROM MUCH ADO. A VILLAIN. HE KNOWS WHAT HE IS, AND IS CALM IN THAT KNOWLEDGE. HE COMMITS EVIL FOR EVIL'S SAKE BECAUSE HE MUST.
AS DO WE.
4

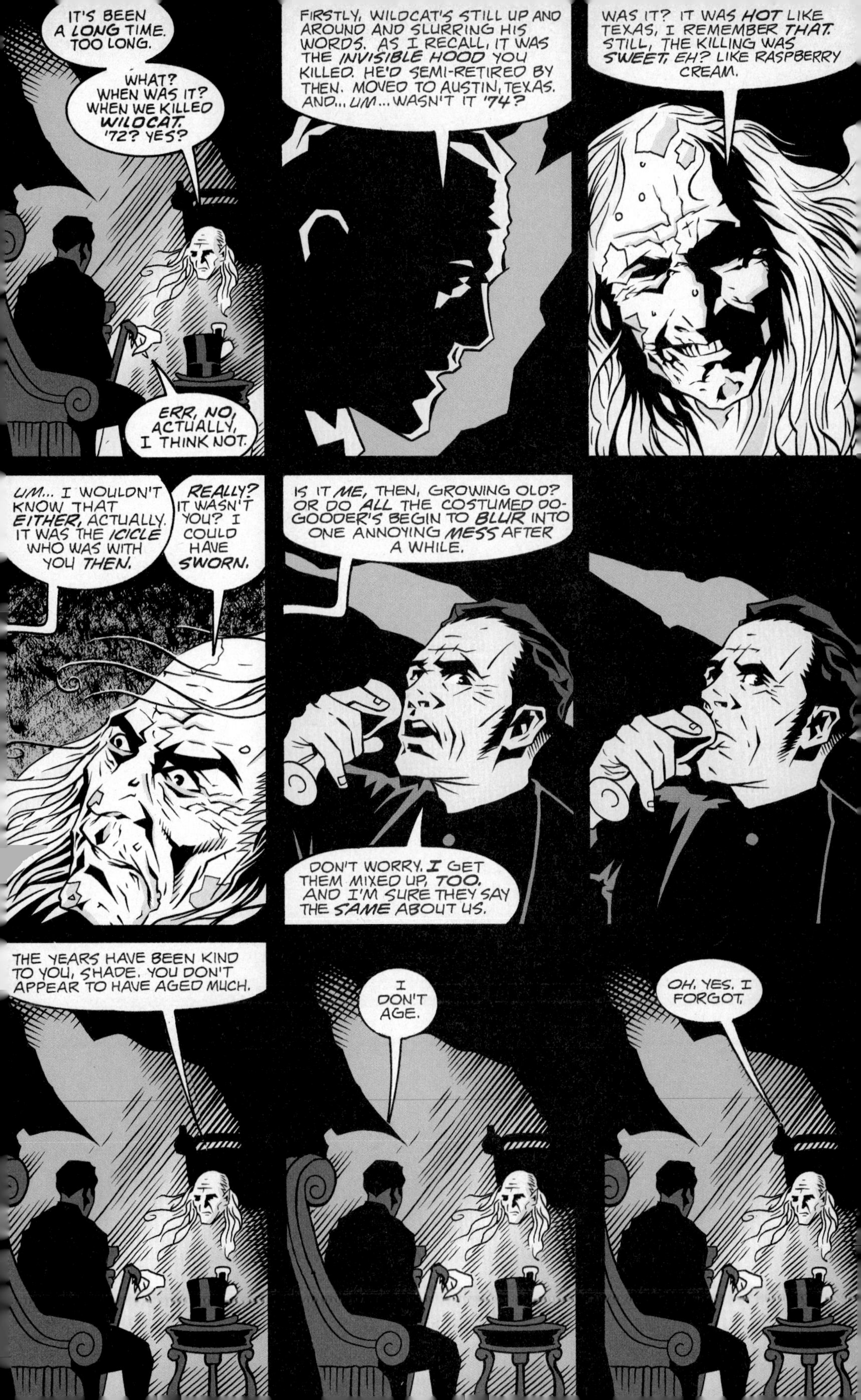
IT'S BEEN A LONG TIME. TOO LONG.
WHAT? WHEN WAS IT? WHEN WE KILLED WILDCAT. '72? YES?
ERR, NO, ACTUALLY, I THINK NOT.
FIRSTLY, WILDCAT'S STILL UP AND AROUND AND SLURRING HIS WORDS. AS I RECALL, IT WAS THE INVISIBLE HOOD YOU KILLED. HE'D SEMI-RETIRED BY THEN. MOVED TO AUSTIN, TEXAS. AND... UM... WASN'T IT '74?
WAS IT? IT WAS HOT LIKE TEXAS, I REMEMBER THAT. STILL, THE KILLING WAS SWEET, EH? LIKE RASPBERRY CREAM.
UM... I WOULDN'T KNOW THAT EITHER, ACTUALLY. IT WAS THE ICICLE WHO WAS WITH YOU THEN.
REALLY? IT WASN'T YOU? I COULD HAVE SWORN.
IS IT ME, THEN, GROWING OLD? OR DO ALL THE COSTUMED DO-GOODER'S BEGIN TO BLUR INTO ONE ANNOYING MESS AFTER A WHILE.
DON'T WORRY. I GET THEM MIXED UP, TOO. AND I'M SURE THEY SAY THE SAME ABOUT US.
THE YEARS HAVE BEEN KIND TO YOU, SHADE. YOU DON'T APPEAR TO HAVE AGED MUCH.
I DON'T AGE.
OH. YES. I FORGOT.

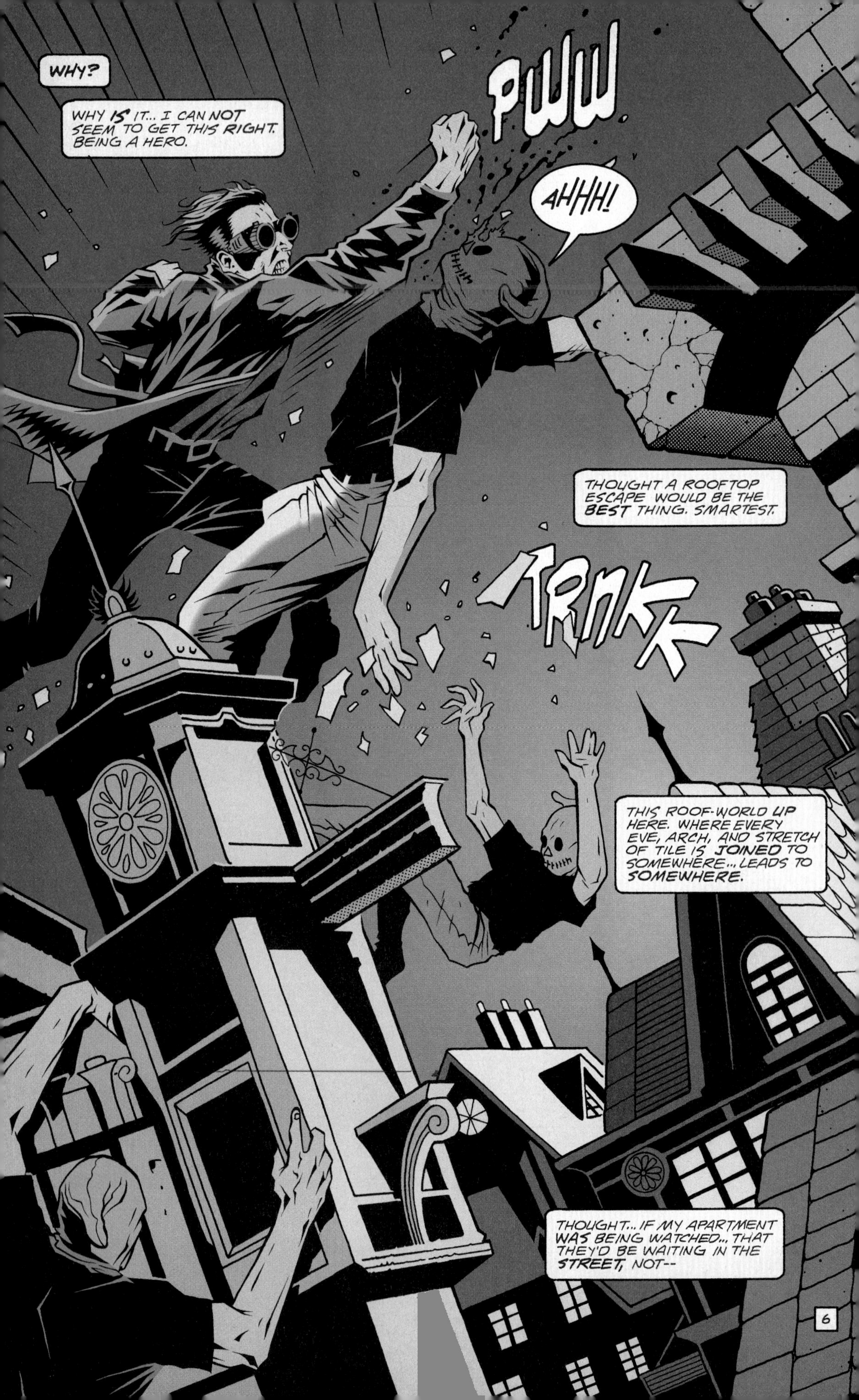
WHY?
WHY IS IT... I CAN NOT SEEM TO GET THIS RIGHT. BEING A HERO.
PWW
AHHH!
THOUGHT A ROOFTOP ESCAPE WOULD BE THE BEST THING. SMARTEST.
KRNKK
THIS ROOF-WORLD UP HERE. WHERE EVERY EVE, ARCH, AND STRETCH OF TILE IS JOINED TO SOMEWHERE... LEADS TO SOMEWHERE.
THOUGHT... IF MY APARTMENT WAS BEING WATCHED... THAT THEY'D BE WAITING IN THE STREET, NOT--

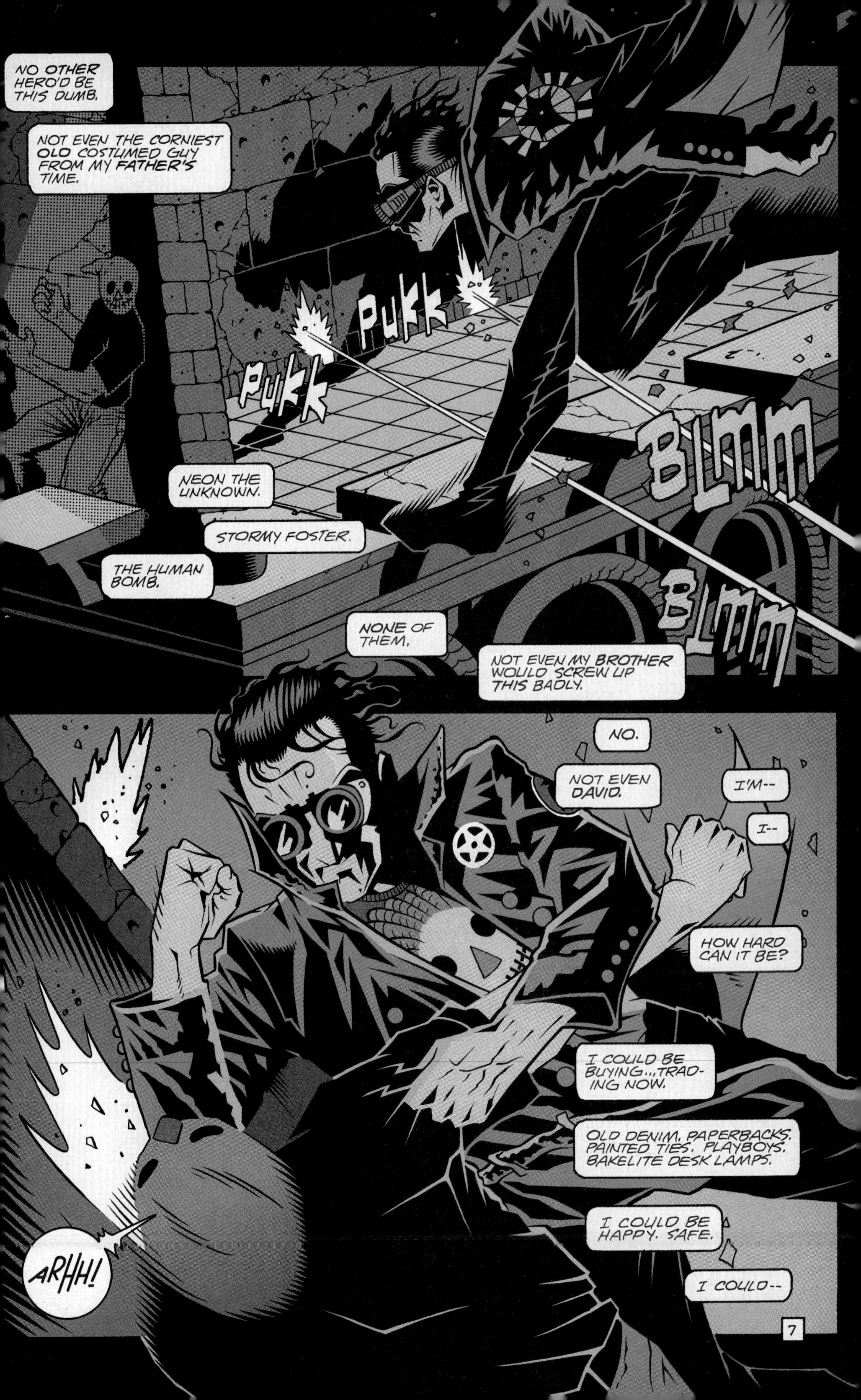

NO OTHER HERO'D BE THIS DUMB.
NOT EVEN THE CORNIEST OLD COSTUMED GUY FROM MY FATHER'S TIME.
PUKK
PUKK
NEON THE UNKNOWN.
STORMY FOSTER.
THE HUMAN BOMB.
BLMM
BLMM
NONE OF THEM.
NOT EVEN MY BROTHER WOULD SCREW UP THIS BADLY.
NO.
NOT EVEN DAVID.
I'M--
I--
HOW HARD CAN IT BE?
I COULD BE BUYING...TRADING NOW.
OLD DENIM. PAPERBACKS. PAINTED TIES. PLAYBOYS. BAKELITE DESK LAMPS.
I COULD BE HAPPY. SAFE.
I COULD--
ARHH!

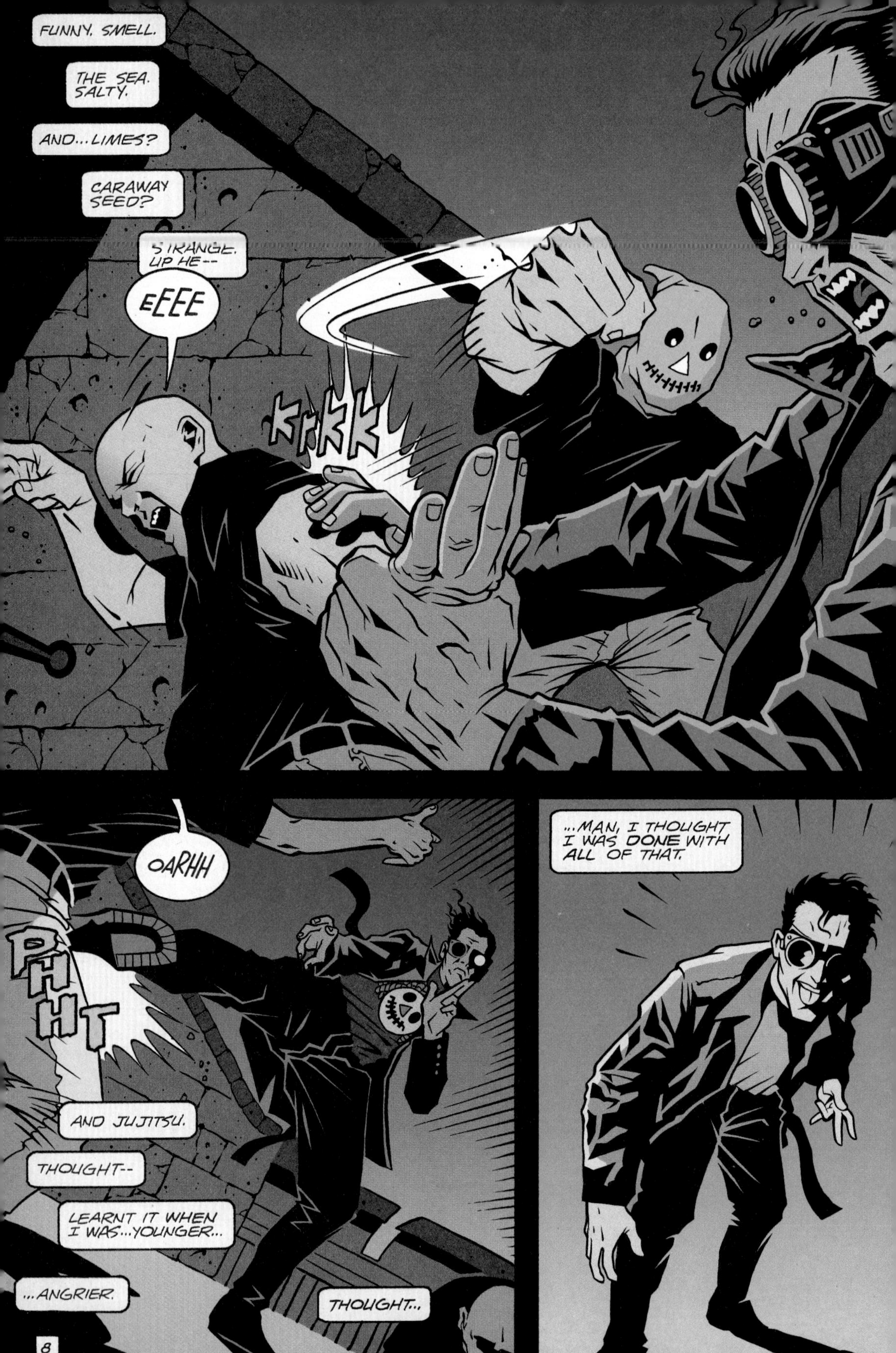
FUNNY. SMELL.
THE SEA. SALTY.
AND...LIMES?
CARAWAY SEED?
STRANGE. UP HE--
EEEE
KRKK
OARHH
PHHT
AND JUJITSU.
THOUGHT--
LEARNT IT WHEN I WAS...YOUNGER...
...ANGRIER.
THOUGHT...
...MAN, I THOUGHT I WAS DONE WITH ALL OF THAT.

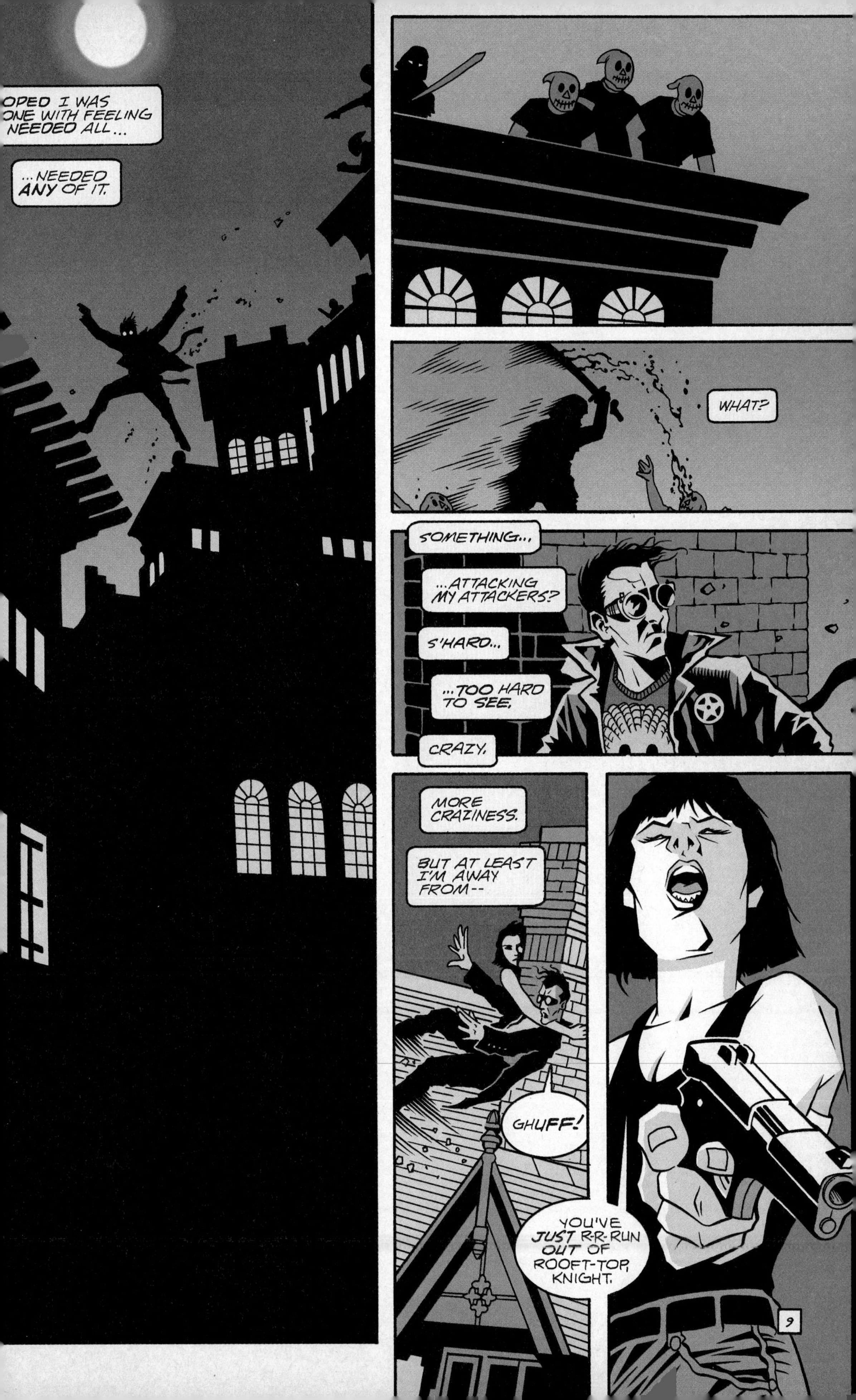
OPED I WAS
ONE WITH FEELING
NEEDED ALL...
...NEEDED ANY OF IT.
WHAT?
SOMETHING...
...ATTACKING MY ATTACKERS?
S'HARD...
...TOO HARD TO SEE.
CRAZY.
MORE CRAZINESS.
BUT AT LEAST I'M AWAY FROM--
GHUFF!
YOU'VE JUST R-R-RUN OUT OF ROOFT-TOP, KNIGHT.
9

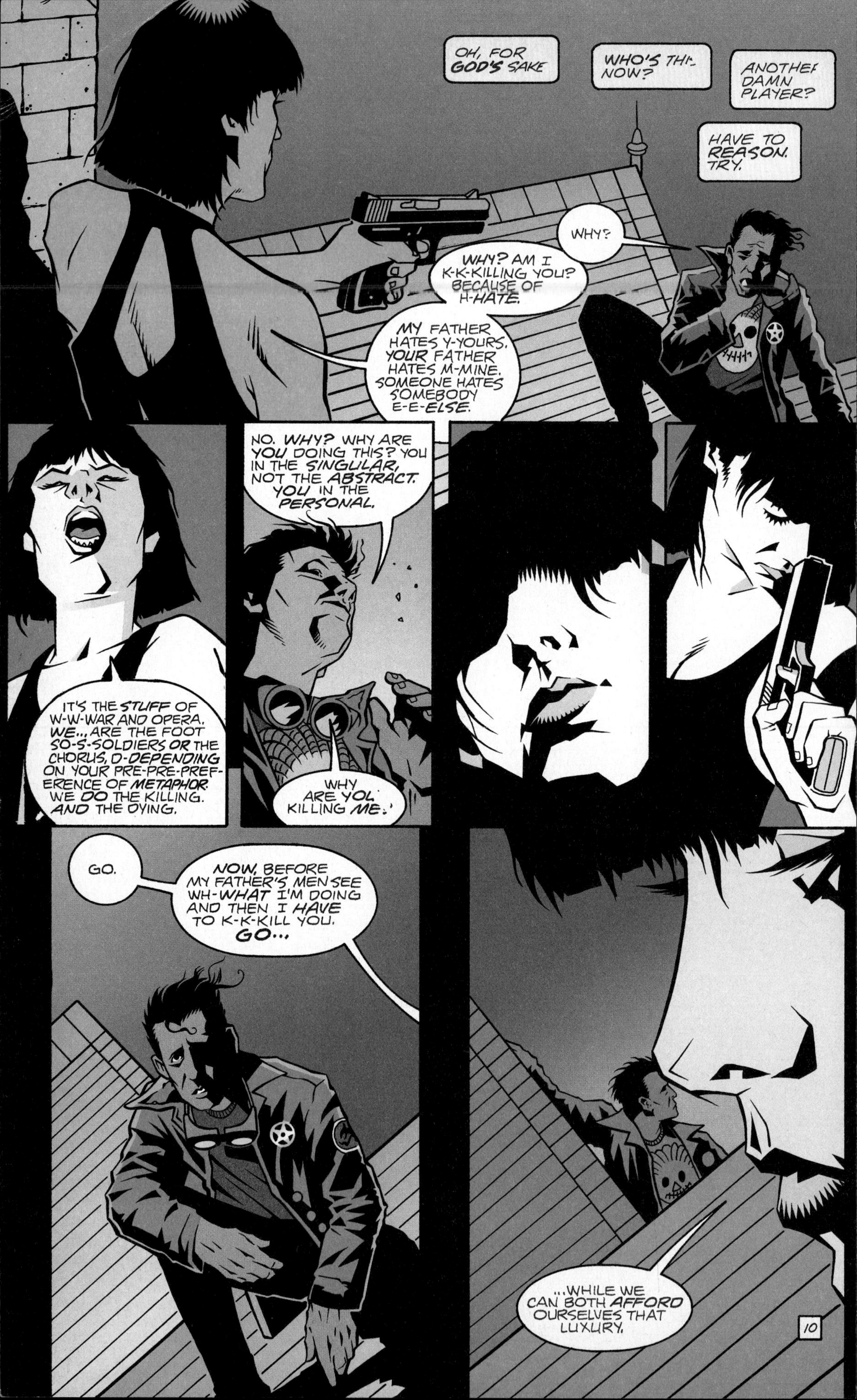
OH, FOR GOD'S SAKE
WHO'S THI- NOW?
ANOTHEF DAMN PLAYER?
HAVE TO REASON. TRY.
WHY?
WHY? AM I K-K-KILLING YOU? BECAUSE OF H-HATE.
MY FATHER HATES Y-YOURS. YOUR FATHER HATES M-MINE. SOMEONE HATES SOMEBODY E-E-ELSE.
NO. WHY? WHY ARE YOU DOING THIS? YOU IN THE SINGULAR, NOT THE ABSTRACT. YOU IN THE PERSONAL.
IT'S THE STUFF OF W-W-WAR AND OPERA. WE... ARE THE FOOT SO-S-SOLDIERS OR THE CHORUS, D-DEPENDING ON YOUR PRE-PRE-PREFERENCE OF METAPHOR. WE DO THE KILLING. AND THE DYING.
WHY ARE YOL KILLING ME
GO.
NOW, BEFORE MY FATHER'S MEN SEE WH-WHAT I'M DOING AND THEN I HAVE TO K-K-KILL YOU. GO...
...WHILE WE CAN BOTH AFFORD OURSELVES THAT LUXURY.
10

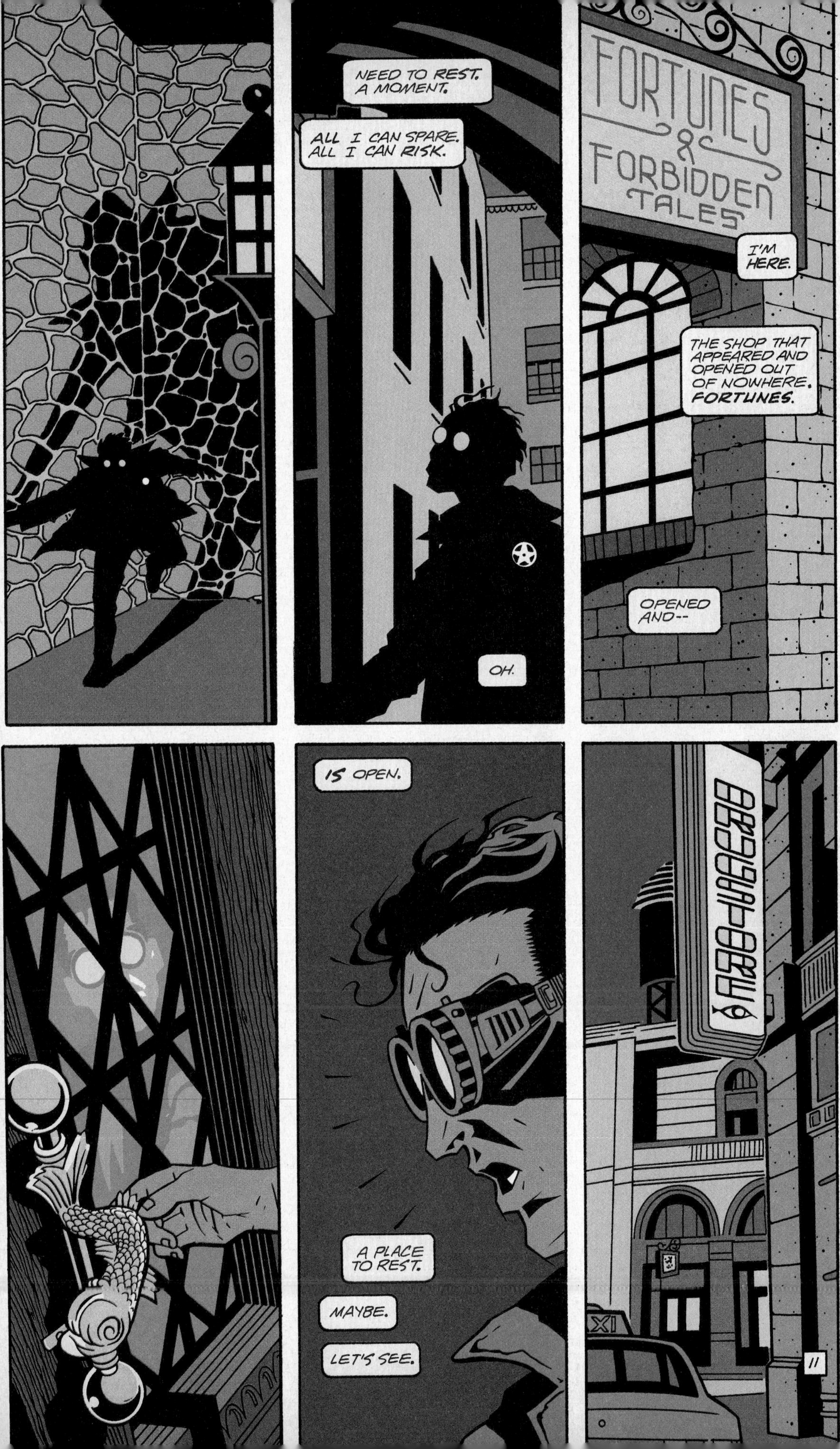
NEED TO REST. A MOMENT.
ALL I CAN SPARE. ALL I CAN RISK.
OH.
FORTUNES & FORBIDDEN TALES
I'M HERE.
THE SHOP THAT APPEARED AND OPENED OUT OF NOWHERE. FORTUNES.
OPENED AND--
IS OPEN.
A PLACE TO REST.
MAYBE.
LET'S SEE.
11

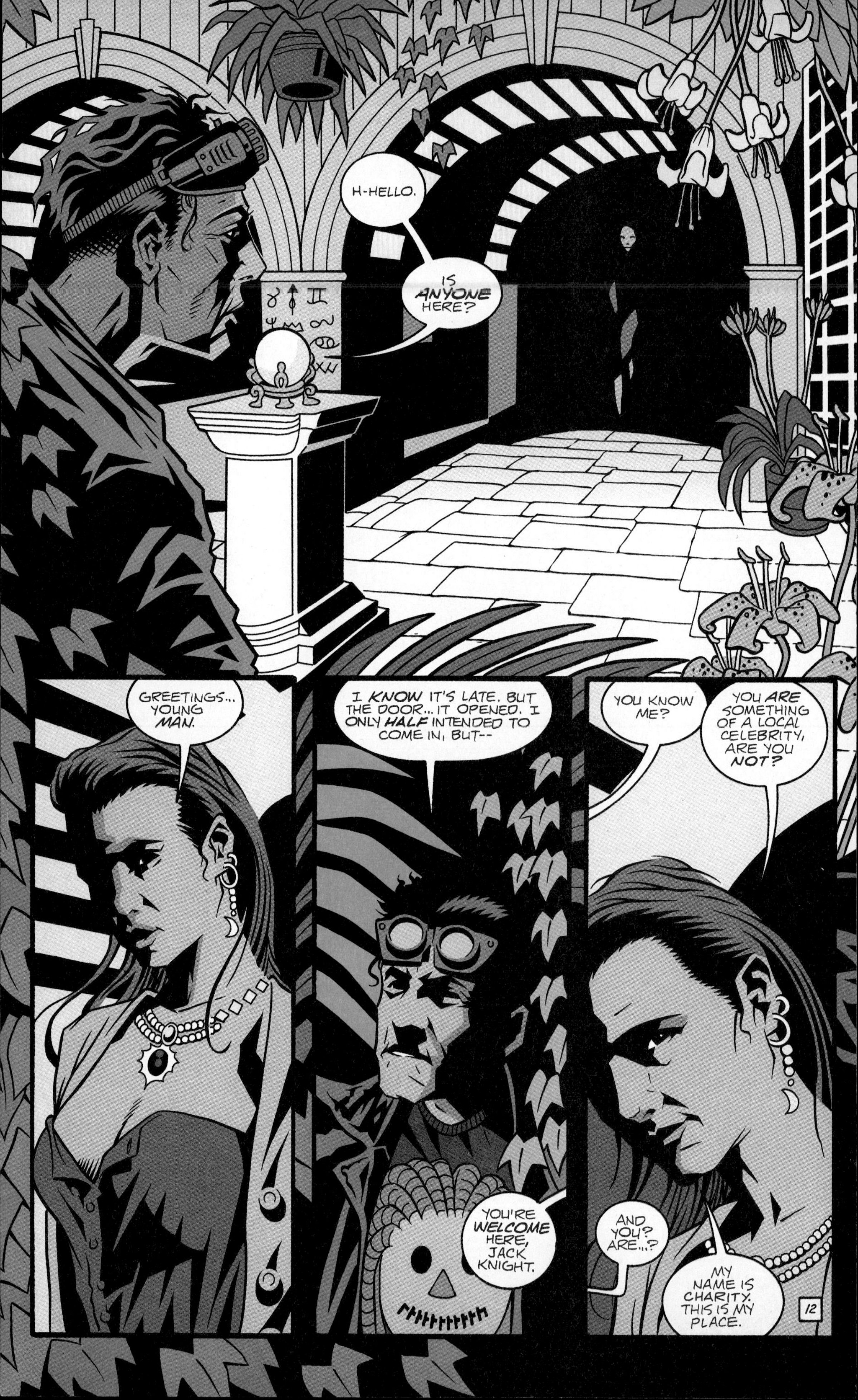
H-HELLO.
IS ANYONE HERE?
GREETINGS... YOUNG MAN.
I KNOW IT'S LATE. BUT THE DOOR... IT OPENED. I ONLY HALF INTENDED TO COME IN, BUT--
YOU'RE WELCOME HERE, JACK KNIGHT.
YOU KNOW ME?
YOU ARE SOMETHING OF A LOCAL CELEBRITY, ARE YOU NOT?
AND YOU? ARE...?
MY NAME IS CHARITY. THIS IS MY PLACE.
12

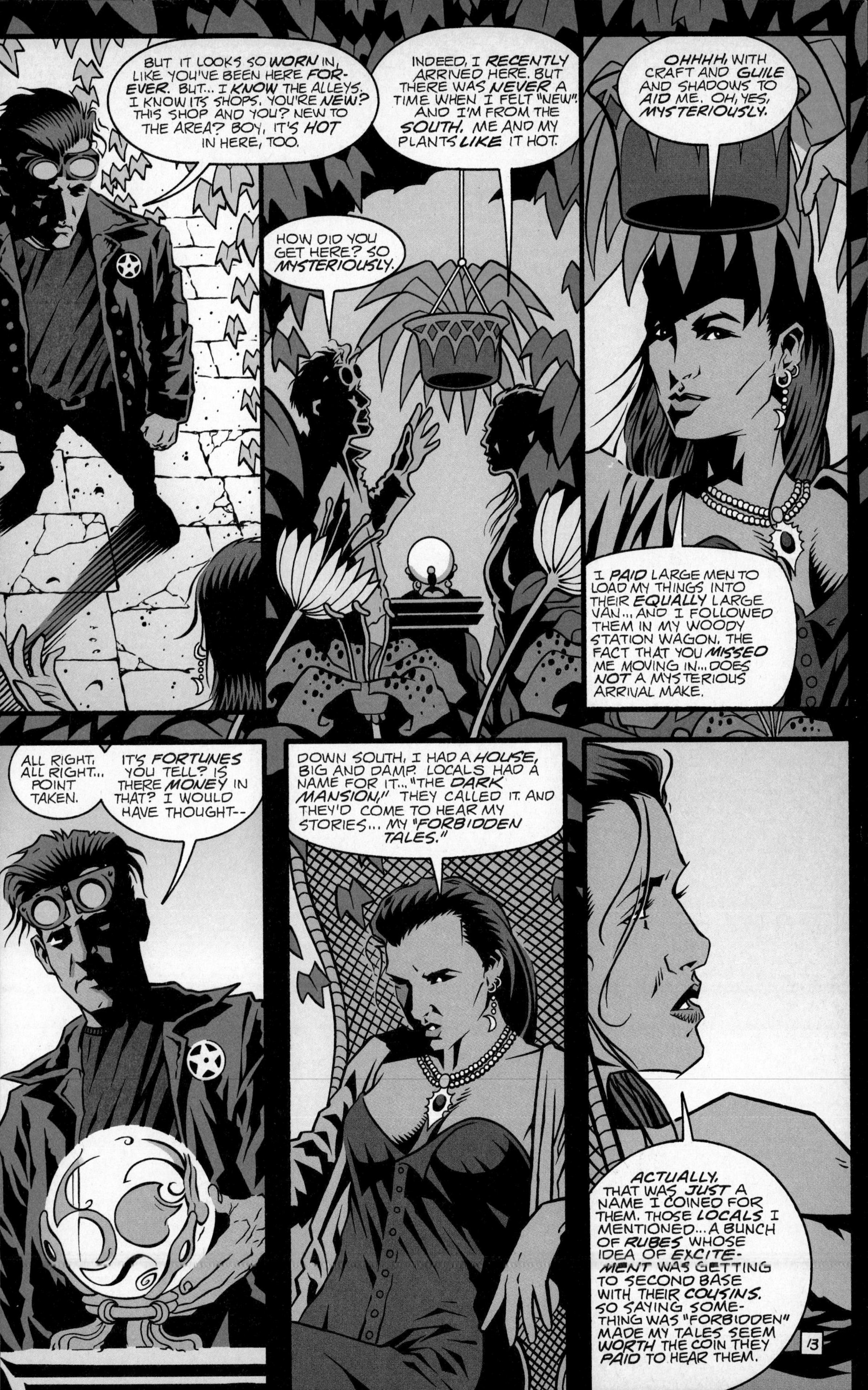
BUT IT LOOKS SO WORN IN, LIKE YOU'VE BEEN HERE FOR-EVER. BUT... I KNOW THE ALLEYS. I KNOW ITS SHOPS. YOU'RE NEW? THIS SHOP AND YOU? NEW TO THE AREA? BOY, IT'S HOT IN HERE, TOO.
INDEED, I RECENTLY ARRIVED HERE. BUT THERE WAS NEVER A TIME WHEN I FELT "NEW". AND I'M FROM THE SOUTH. ME AND MY PLANTS LIKE IT HOT.
HOW DID YOU GET HERE? SO MYSTERIOUSLY.
OHHHH, WITH CRAFT AND GUILE AND SHADOWS TO AID ME. OH, YES, MYSTERIOUSLY.
I PAID LARGE MEN TO LOAD MY THINGS INTO THEIR EQUALLY LARGE VAN... AND I FOLLOWED THEM IN MY WOODY STATION WAGON. THE FACT THAT YOU MISSED ME MOVING IN... DOES NOT A MYSTERIOUS ARRIVAL MAKE.
ALL RIGHT. ALL RIGHT... POINT TAKEN.
IT'S FORTUNES YOU TELL? IS THERE MONEY IN THAT? I WOULD HAVE THOUGHT--
DOWN SOUTH, I HAD A HOUSE, BIG AND DAMP. LOCALS HAD A NAME FOR IT... "THE DARK MANSION," THEY CALLED IT. AND THEY'D COME TO HEAR MY STORIES... MY "FORBIDDEN TALES."
ACTUALLY, THAT WAS JUST A NAME I COINED FOR THEM. THOSE LOCALS I MENTIONED... A BUNCH OF RUBES WHOSE IDEA OF EXCITE-MENT WAS GETTING TO SECOND BASE WITH THEIR COUSINS. SO SAYING SOME-THING WAS "FORBIDDEN" MADE MY TALES SEEM WORTH THE COIN THEY PAID TO HEAR THEM.

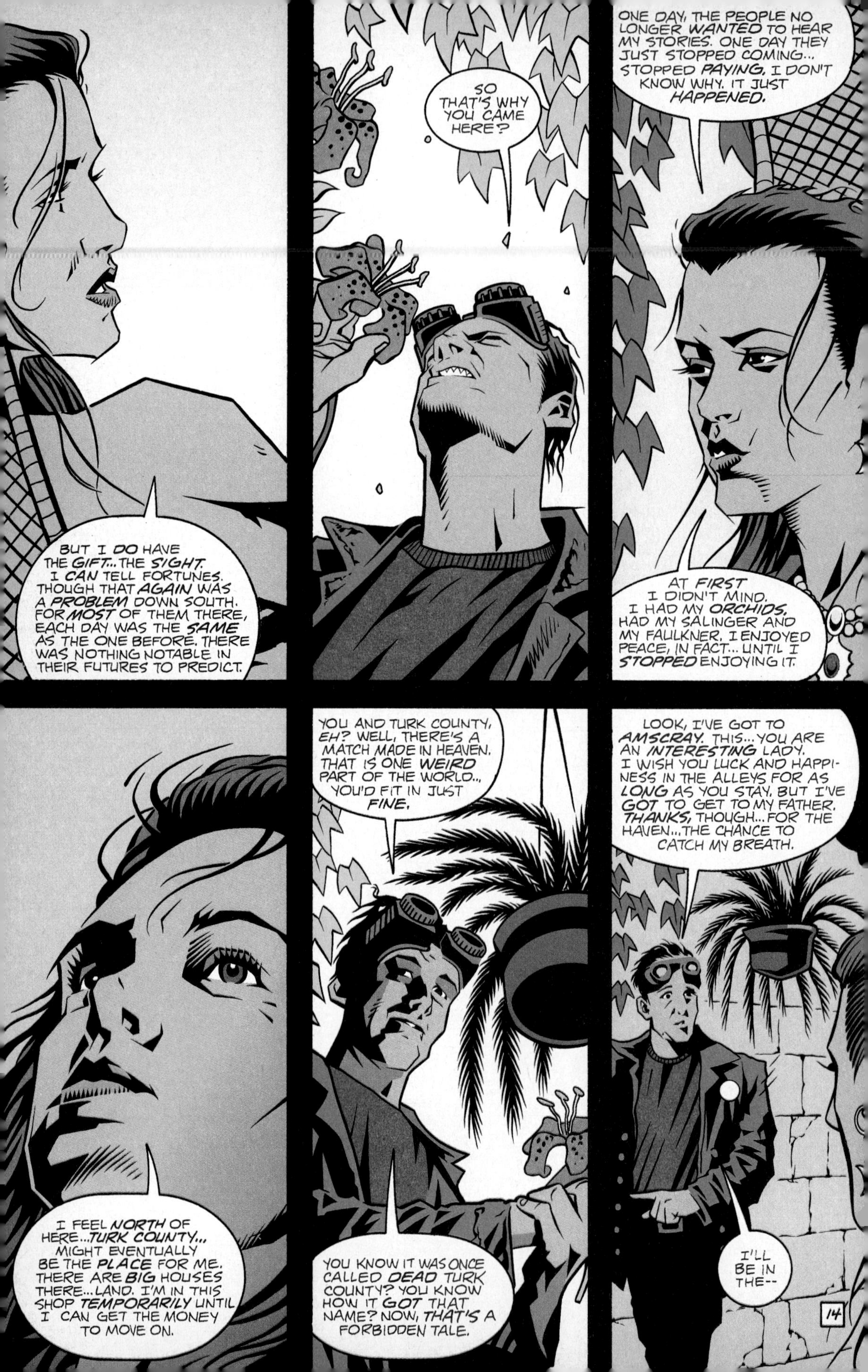
BUT I DO HAVE THE GIFT... THE SIGHT. I CAN TELL FORTUNES. THOUGH THAT AGAIN WAS A PROBLEM DOWN SOUTH. FOR MOST OF THEM THERE, EACH DAY WAS THE SAME AS THE ONE BEFORE. THERE WAS NOTHING NOTABLE IN THEIR FUTURES TO PREDICT.
SO THAT'S WHY YOU CAME HERE?
ONE DAY, THE PEOPLE NO LONGER WANTED TO HEAR MY STORIES. ONE DAY THEY JUST STOPPED COMING... STOPPED PAYING. I DON'T KNOW WHY. IT JUST HAPPENED.
AT FIRST I DIDN'T MIND. I HAD MY ORCHIDS, HAD MY SALINGER AND MY FAULKNER. I ENJOYED PEACE, IN FACT... UNTIL I STOPPED ENJOYING IT.
I FEEL NORTH OF HERE... TURK COUNTY... MIGHT EVENTUALLY BE THE PLACE FOR ME. THERE ARE BIG HOUSES THERE... LAND. I'M IN THIS SHOP TEMPORARILY UNTIL I CAN GET THE MONEY TO MOVE ON.
YOU AND TURK COUNTY, EH? WELL, THERE'S A MATCH MADE IN HEAVEN. THAT IS ONE WEIRD PART OF THE WORLD... YOU'D FIT IN JUST FINE.
YOU KNOW IT WAS ONCE CALLED DEAD TURK COUNTY? YOU KNOW HOW IT GOT THAT NAME? NOW, THAT'S A FORBIDDEN TALE.
LOOK, I'VE GOT TO AMSCRAY. THIS... YOU ARE AN INTERESTING LADY. I WISH YOU LUCK AND HAPPINESS IN THE ALLEYS FOR AS LONG AS YOU STAY, BUT I'VE GOT TO GET TO MY FATHER. THANKS, THOUGH... FOR THE HAVEN... THE CHANCE TO CATCH MY BREATH.
I'LL BE IN THE--

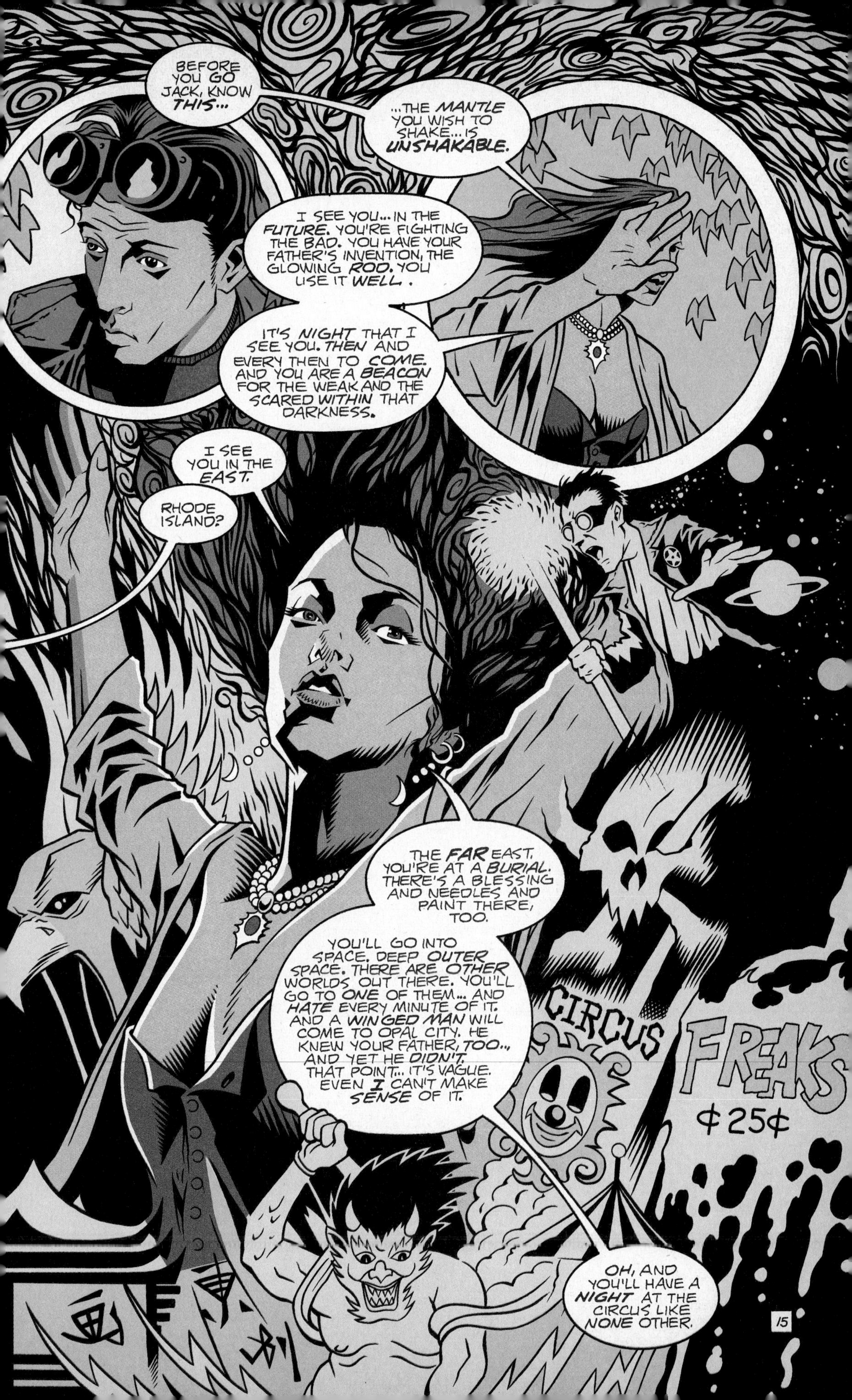
BEFORE YOU GO JACK, KNOW THIS...
...THE MANTLE YOU WISH TO SHAKE... IS UNSHAKABLE.
I SEE YOU... IN THE FUTURE. YOU'RE FIGHTING THE BAD. YOU HAVE YOUR FATHER'S INVENTION, THE GLOWING ROD. YOU USE IT WELL.
IT'S NIGHT THAT I SEE YOU. THEN AND EVERY THEN TO COME. AND YOU ARE A BEACON FOR THE WEAK AND THE SCARED WITHIN THAT DARKNESS.
I SEE YOU IN THE EAST.
RHODE ISLAND?
THE FAR EAST. YOU'RE AT A BURIAL. THERE'S A BLESSING AND NEEDLES AND PAINT THERE, TOO.
YOU'LL GO INTO SPACE. DEEP OUTER SPACE. THERE ARE OTHER WORLDS OUT THERE. YOU'LL GO TO ONE OF THEM... AND HATE EVERY MINUTE OF IT. AND A WINGED MAN WILL COME TO OPAL CITY. HE KNEW YOUR FATHER, TOO... AND YET HE DIDN'T. THAT POINT... IT'S VAGUE. EVEN I CAN'T MAKE SENSE OF IT.
CIRCUS
FREAKS
¢25¢
OH, AND YOU'LL HAVE A NIGHT AT THE CIRCUS LIKE NONE OTHER.

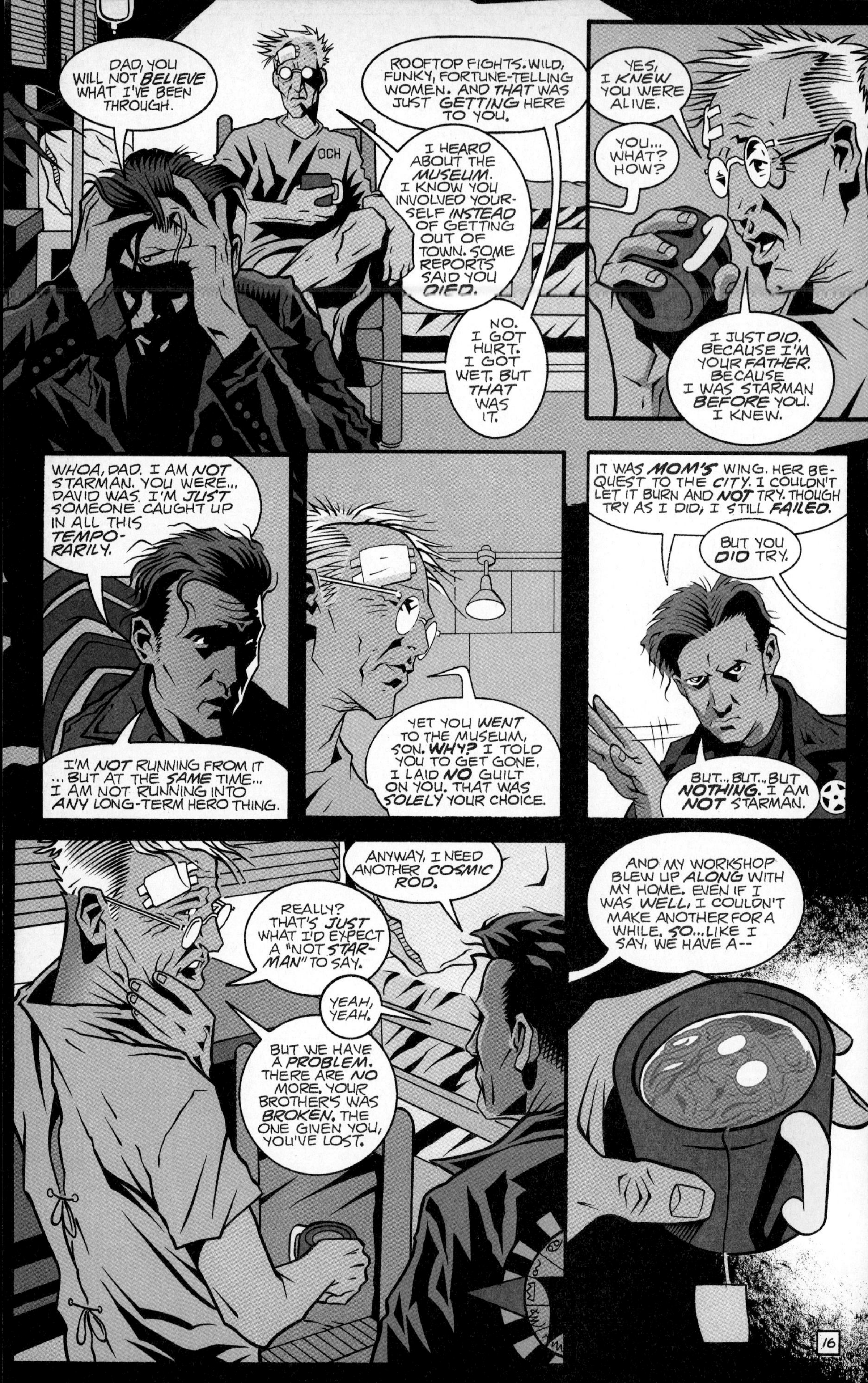
DAD, YOU WILL NOT BELIEVE WHAT I'VE BEEN THROUGH.
ROOFTOP FIGHTS. WILD, FUNKY, FORTUNE-TELLING WOMEN. AND THAT WAS JUST GETTING HERE TO YOU.
I HEARD ABOUT THE MUSEUM. I KNOW YOU INVOLVED YOURSELF INSTEAD OF GETTING OUT OF TOWN. SOME REPORTS SAID YOU DIED.
NO. I GOT HURT. I GOT WET. BUT THAT WAS IT.
YES, I KNEW YOU WERE ALIVE.
YOU... WHAT? HOW?
I JUST DID. BECAUSE I'M YOUR FATHER. BECAUSE I WAS STARMAN BEFORE YOU. I KNEW.
WHOA, DAD. I AM NOT STARMAN. YOU WERE... DAVID WAS. I'M JUST SOMEONE CAUGHT UP IN ALL THIS TEMPORARILY.
I'M NOT RUNNING FROM IT ... BUT AT THE SAME TIME... I AM NOT RUNNING INTO ANY LONG-TERM HERO THING.
YET YOU WENT TO THE MUSEUM, SON. WHY? I TOLD YOU TO GET GONE. I LAID NO GUILT ON YOU. THAT WAS SOLELY YOUR CHOICE.
IT WAS MOM'S WING. HER BEQUEST TO THE CITY. I COULDN'T LET IT BURN AND NOT TRY. THOUGH TRY AS I DID, I STILL FAILED.
BUT YOU DID TRY.
BUT...BUT...BUT NOTHING. I AM NOT STARMAN.
ANYWAY, I NEED ANOTHER COSMIC ROD.
REALLY? THAT'S JUST WHAT I'D EXPECT A "NOT STARMAN" TO SAY.
YEAH, YEAH.
BUT WE HAVE A PROBLEM. THERE ARE NO MORE. YOUR BROTHER'S WAS BROKEN. THE ONE GIVEN YOU, YOU'VE LOST.
AND MY WORKSHOP BLEW UP ALONG WITH MY HOME. EVEN IF I WAS WELL, I COULDN'T MAKE ANOTHER FOR A WHILE. SO...LIKE I SAY, WE HAVE A--

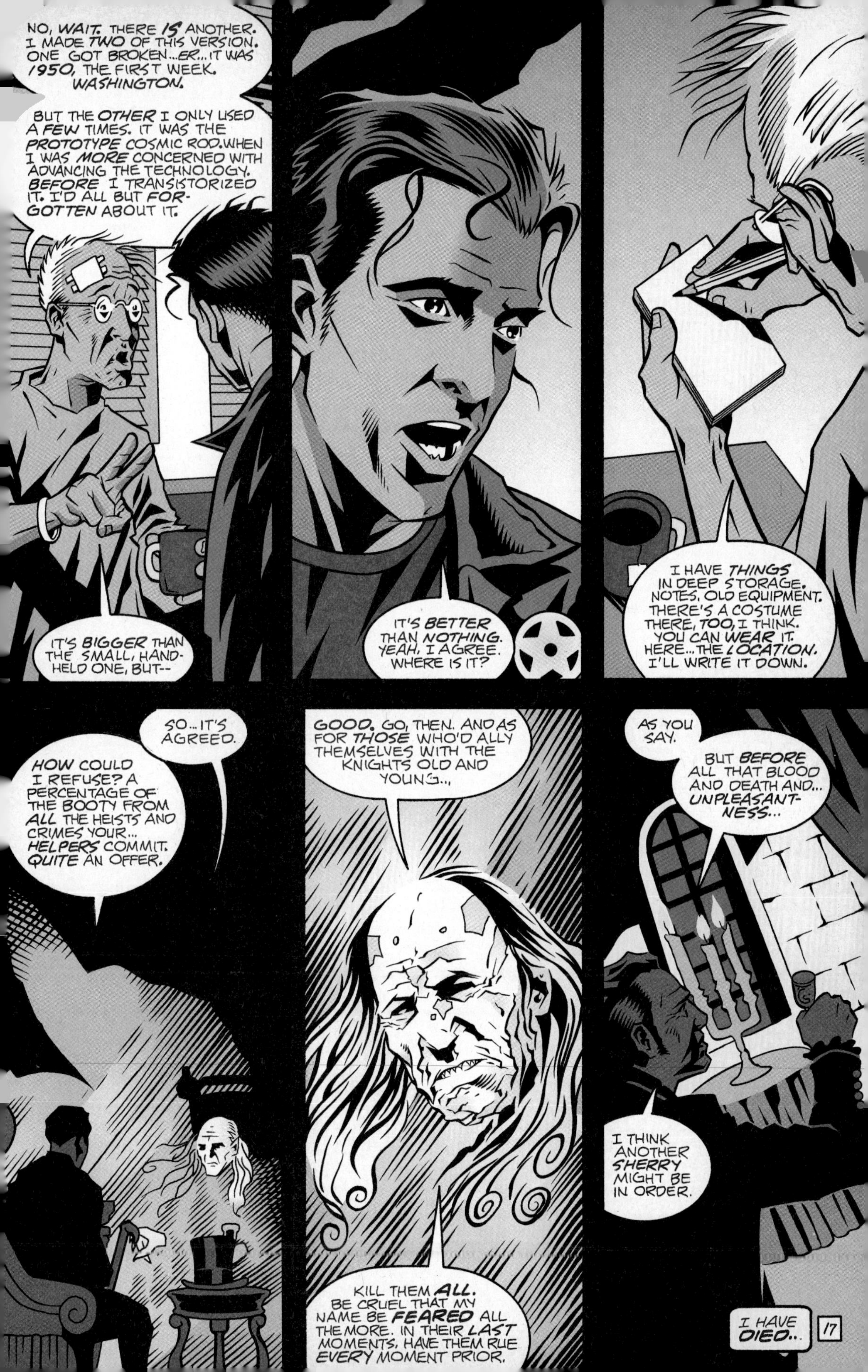
NO, WAIT. THERE IS ANOTHER. I MADE TWO OF THIS VERSION. ONE GOT BROKEN...ER...IT WAS 1950, THE FIRST WEEK. WASHINGTON.
BUT THE OTHER I ONLY USED A FEW TIMES. IT WAS THE PROTOTYPE COSMIC ROD. WHEN I WAS MORE CONCERNED WITH ADVANCING THE TECHNOLOGY. BEFORE I TRANSISTORIZED IT. I'D ALL BUT FORGOTTEN ABOUT IT.
IT'S BIGGER THAN THE SMALL, HAND-HELD ONE, BUT--
IT'S BETTER THAN NOTHING. YEAH, I AGREE. WHERE IS IT?
I HAVE THINGS IN DEEP STORAGE. NOTES, OLD EQUIPMENT. THERE'S A COSTUME THERE, TOO, I THINK. YOU CAN WEAR IT. HERE...THE LOCATION. I'LL WRITE IT DOWN.
SO...IT'S AGREED.
HOW COULD I REFUSE? A PERCENTAGE OF THE BOOTY FROM ALL THE HEISTS AND CRIMES YOUR... HELPERS COMMIT. QUITE AN OFFER.
GOOD. GO, THEN. AND AS FOR THOSE WHO'D ALLY THEMSELVES WITH THE KNIGHTS OLD AND YOUNG...
KILL THEM ALL. BE CRUEL THAT MY NAME BE FEARED ALL THE MORE. IN THEIR LAST MOMENTS, HAVE THEM RUE EVERY MOMENT PRIOR.
AS YOU SAY.
BUT BEFORE ALL THAT BLOOD AND DEATH AND... UNPLEASANTNESS...
I THINK ANOTHER SHERRY MIGHT BE IN ORDER.
I HAVE DIED...

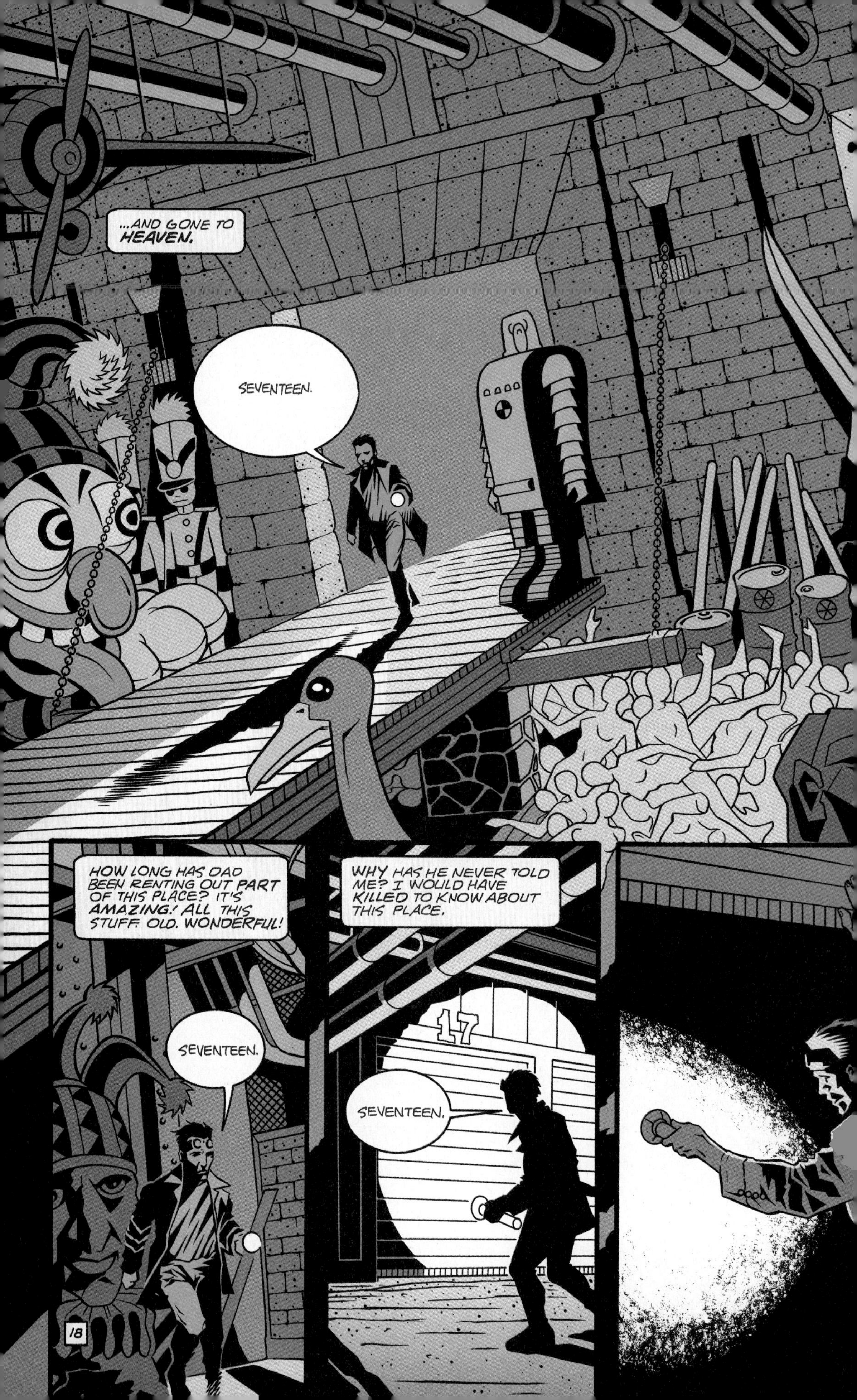
...AND GONE TO HEAVEN.
SEVENTEEN.
HOW LONG HAS DAD BEEN RENTING OUT PART OF THIS PLACE? IT'S AMAZING! ALL THIS STUFF. OLD. WONDERFUL!
SEVENTEEN.
WHY HAS HE NEVER TOLD ME? I WOULD HAVE KILLED TO KNOW ABOUT THIS PLACE.
17
SEVENTEEN.

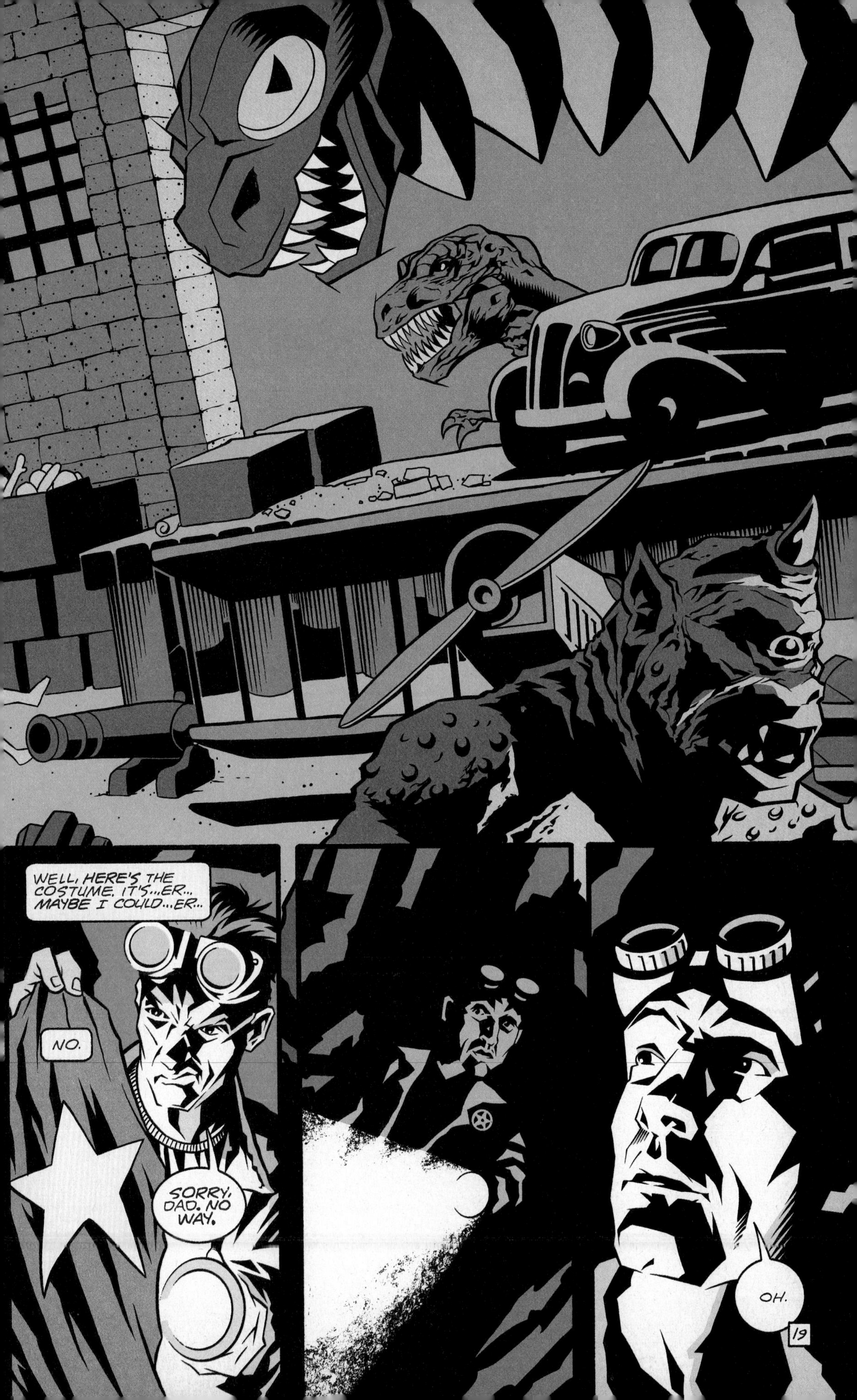
WELL, HERE'S THE COSTUME. IT'S...ER... MAYBE I COULD...ER...
NO.
SORRY, DAD. NO WAY.
OH.
19

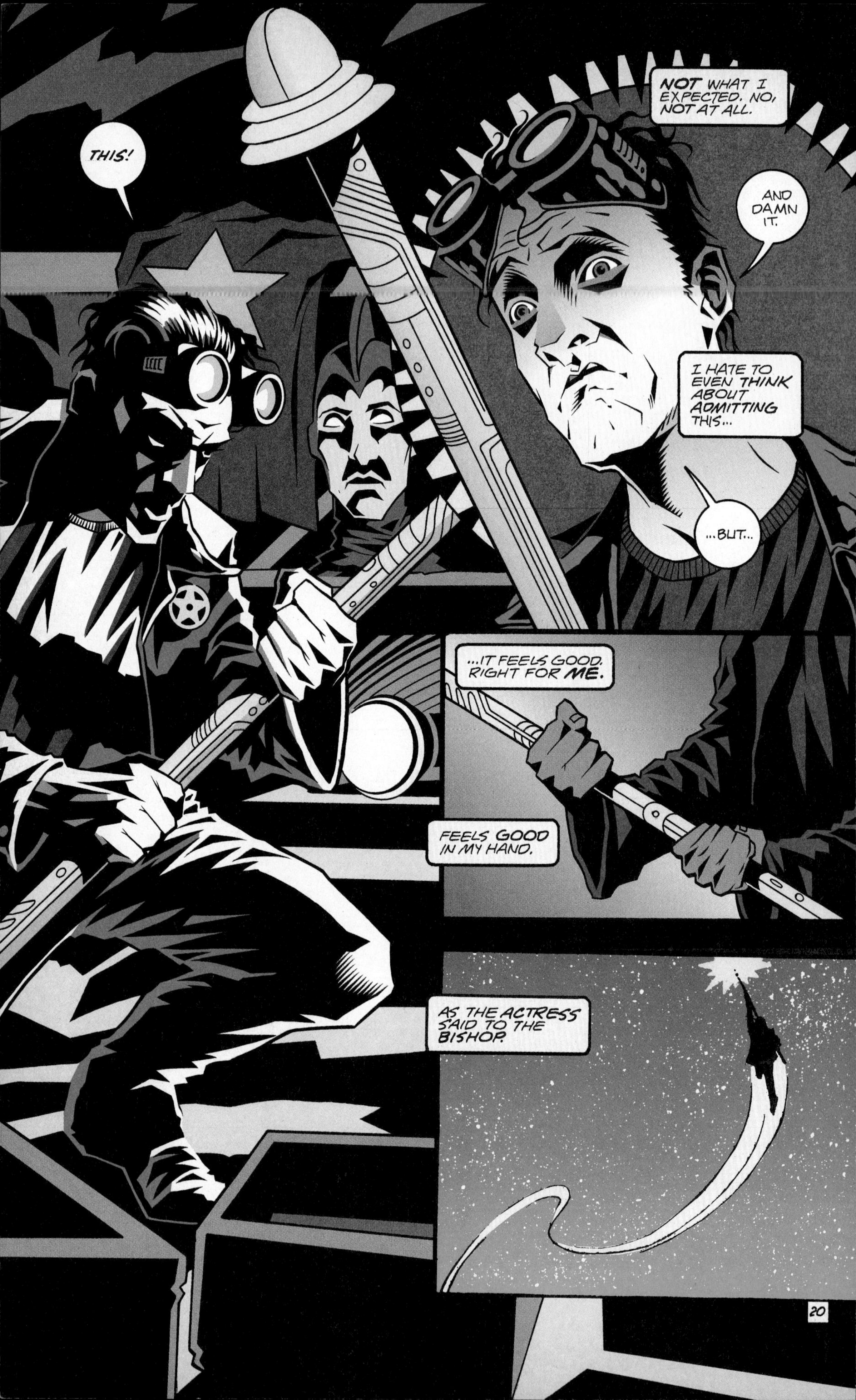
THIS!
NOT WHAT I EXPECTED. NO, NOT AT ALL.
AND DAMN IT.
I HATE TO EVEN THINK ABOUT ADMITTING THIS...
...BUT...
...IT FEELS GOOD. RIGHT FOR ME.
FEELS GOOD IN MY HAND.
AS THE ACTRESS SAID TO THE BISHOP.

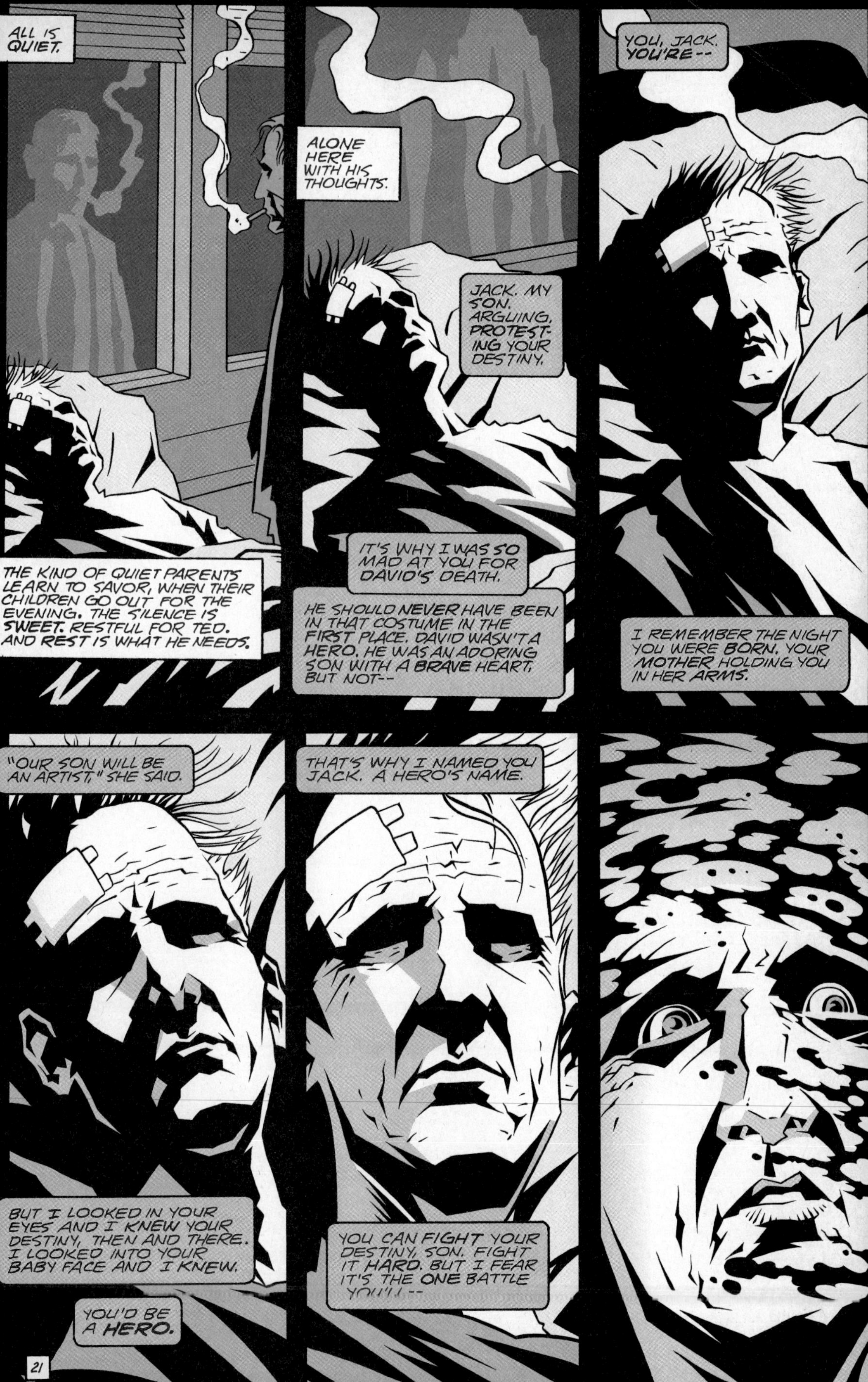
ALL IS QUIET.
THE KIND OF QUIET PARENTS LEARN TO SAVOR, WHEN THEIR CHILDREN GO OUT FOR THE EVENING. THE SILENCE IS SWEET. RESTFUL FOR TED. AND REST IS WHAT HE NEEDS.
ALONE HERE WITH HIS THOUGHTS.
JACK. MY SON. ARGUING, PROTESTING YOUR DESTINY.
IT'S WHY I WAS SO MAD AT YOU FOR DAVID'S DEATH.
HE SHOULD NEVER HAVE BEEN IN THAT COSTUME IN THE FIRST PLACE. DAVID WASN'T A HERO. HE WAS AN ADORING SON WITH A BRAVE HEART, BUT NOT--
YOU, JACK. YOU'RE--
I REMEMBER THE NIGHT YOU WERE BORN. YOUR MOTHER HOLDING YOU IN HER ARMS.
"OUR SON WILL BE AN ARTIST," SHE SAID.
BUT I LOOKED IN YOUR EYES AND I KNEW YOUR DESTINY, THEN AND THERE. I LOOKED INTO YOUR BABY FACE AND I KNEW.
YOU'D BE A HERO.
THAT'S WHY I NAMED YOU JACK. A HERO'S NAME.
YOU CAN FIGHT YOUR DESTINY, SON. FIGHT IT HARD. BUT I FEAR IT'S THE ONE BATTLE YOU'LL--

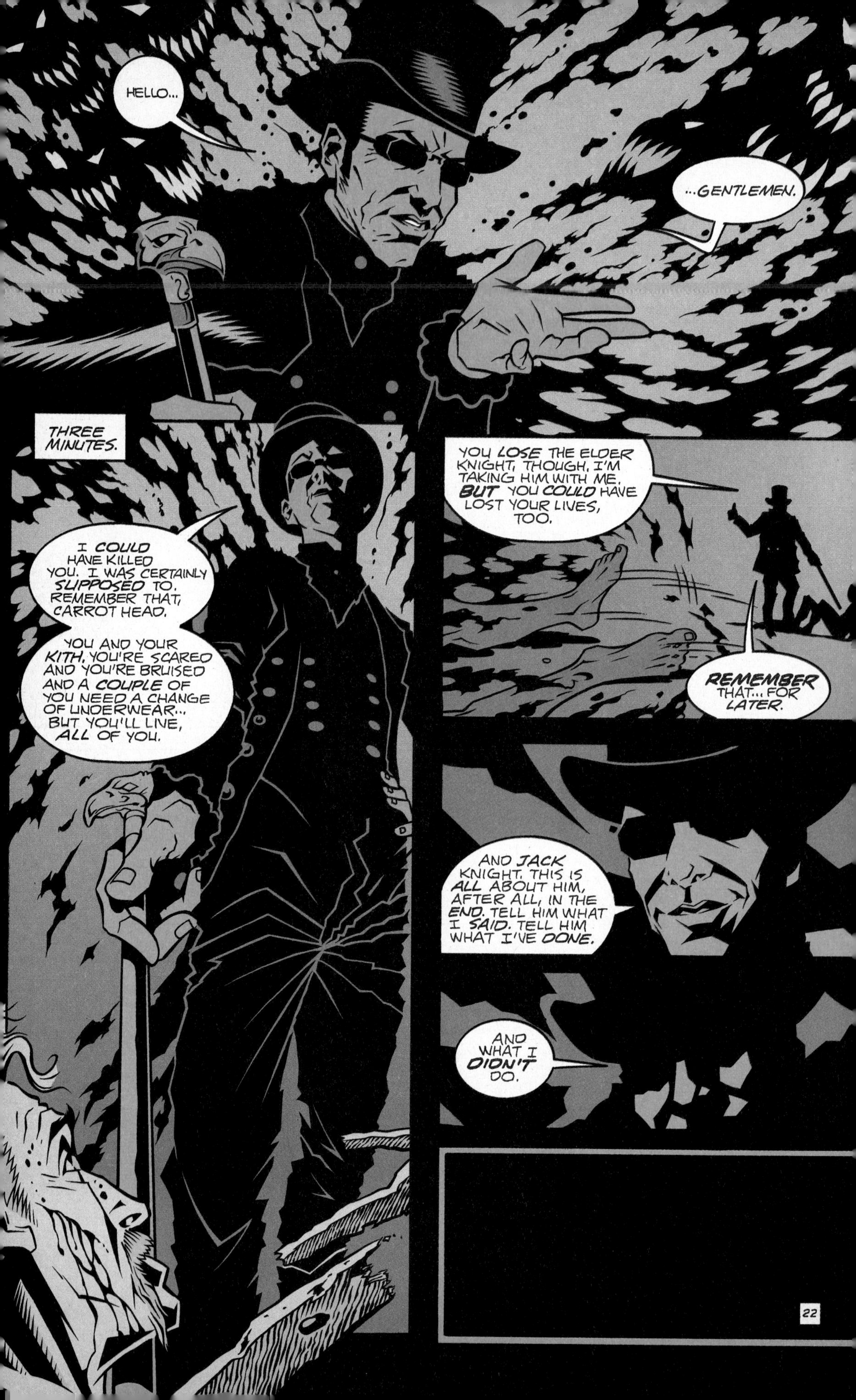
HELLO...
...GENTLEMEN.
THREE MINUTES.
I COULD HAVE KILLED YOU. I WAS CERTAINLY SUPPOSED TO. REMEMBER THAT, CARROT HEAD.
YOU AND YOUR KITH, YOU'RE SCARED AND YOU'RE BRUISED AND A COUPLE OF YOU NEED A CHANGE OF UNDERWEAR... BUT YOU'LL LIVE, ALL OF YOU.
YOU LOSE THE ELDER KNIGHT, THOUGH, I'M TAKING HIM WITH ME. BUT YOU COULD HAVE LOST YOUR LIVES, TOO.
REMEMBER THAT... FOR LATER.
AND JACK KNIGHT. THIS IS ALL ABOUT HIM, AFTER ALL, IN THE END. TELL HIM WHAT I SAID. TELL HIM WHAT I'VE DONE.
AND WHAT I DIDN'T DO.
22

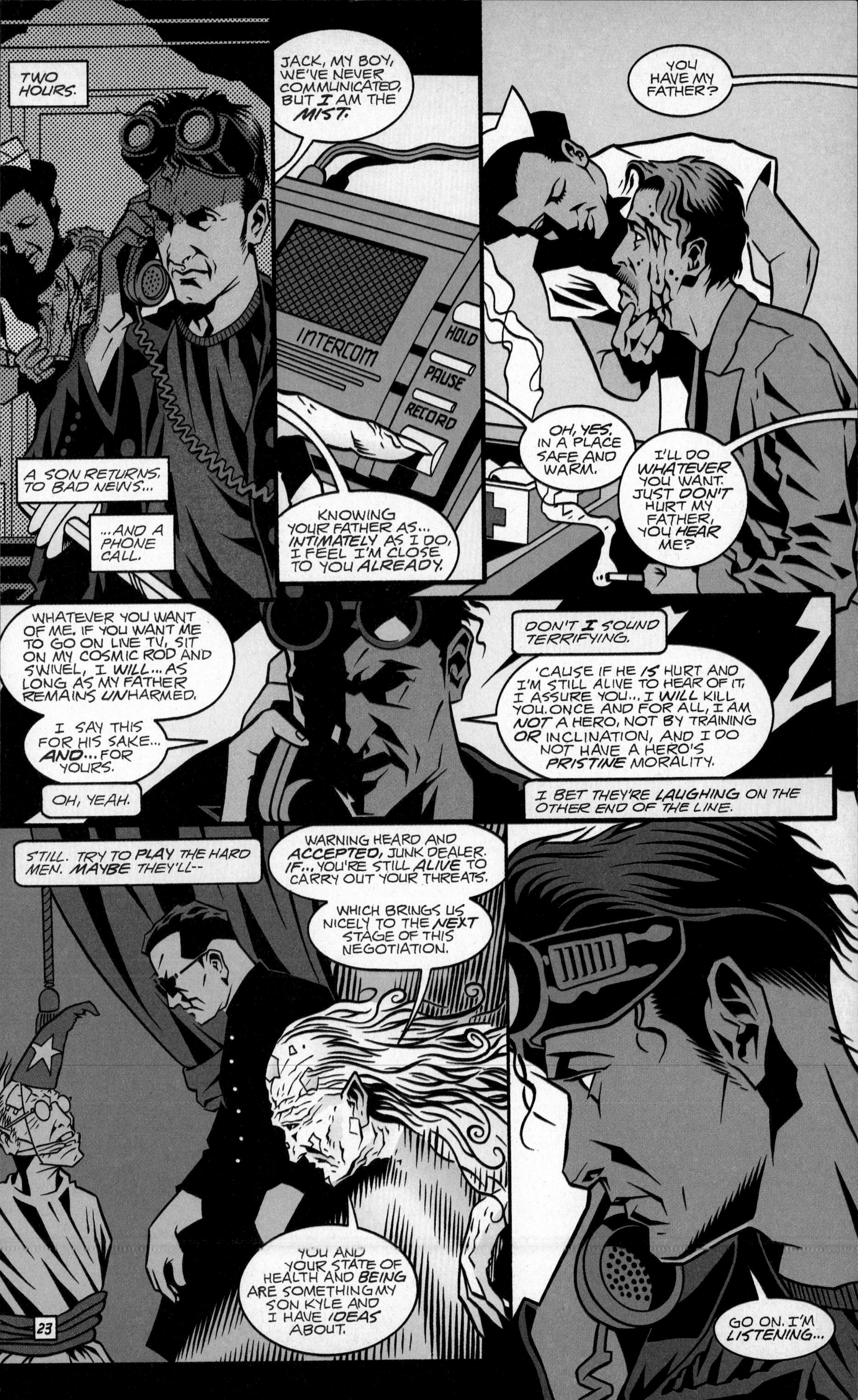
TWO HOURS.
A SON RETURNS, TO BAD NEWS...
...AND A PHONE CALL.
JACK, MY BOY, WE'VE NEVER COMMUNICATED, BUT I AM THE MIST.
KNOWING YOUR FATHER AS... INTIMATELY AS I DO, I FEEL I'M CLOSE TO YOU ALREADY.
INTERCOM
HOLD
PAUSE
RECORD
YOU HAVE MY FATHER?
OH, YES. IN A PLACE SAFE AND WARM.
I'LL DO WHATEVER YOU WANT. JUST DON'T HURT MY FATHER, YOU HEAR ME?
WHATEVER YOU WANT OF ME. IF YOU WANT ME TO GO ON LIVE TV, SIT ON MY COSMIC ROD AND SWIVEL, I WILL... AS LONG AS MY FATHER REMAINS UNHARMED.
I SAY THIS FOR HIS SAKE... AND... FOR YOURS.
OH, YEAH.
DON'T I SOUND TERRIFYING.
'CAUSE IF HE IS HURT AND I'M STILL ALIVE TO HEAR OF IT, I ASSURE YOU... I WILL KILL YOU. ONCE AND FOR ALL, I AM NOT A HERO, NOT BY TRAINING OR INCLINATION, AND I DO NOT HAVE A HERO'S PRISTINE MORALITY.
I BET THEY'RE LAUGHING ON THE OTHER END OF THE LINE.
STILL. TRY TO PLAY THE HARD MEN. MAYBE THEY'LL--
WARNING HEARD AND ACCEPTED, JUNK DEALER. IF... YOU'RE STILL ALIVE TO CARRY OUT YOUR THREATS.
WHICH BRINGS US NICELY TO THE NEXT STAGE OF THIS NEGOTIATION.
YOU AND YOUR STATE OF HEALTH AND BEING ARE SOMETHING MY SON KYLE AND I HAVE IDEAS ABOUT.
GO ON. I'M LISTENING...

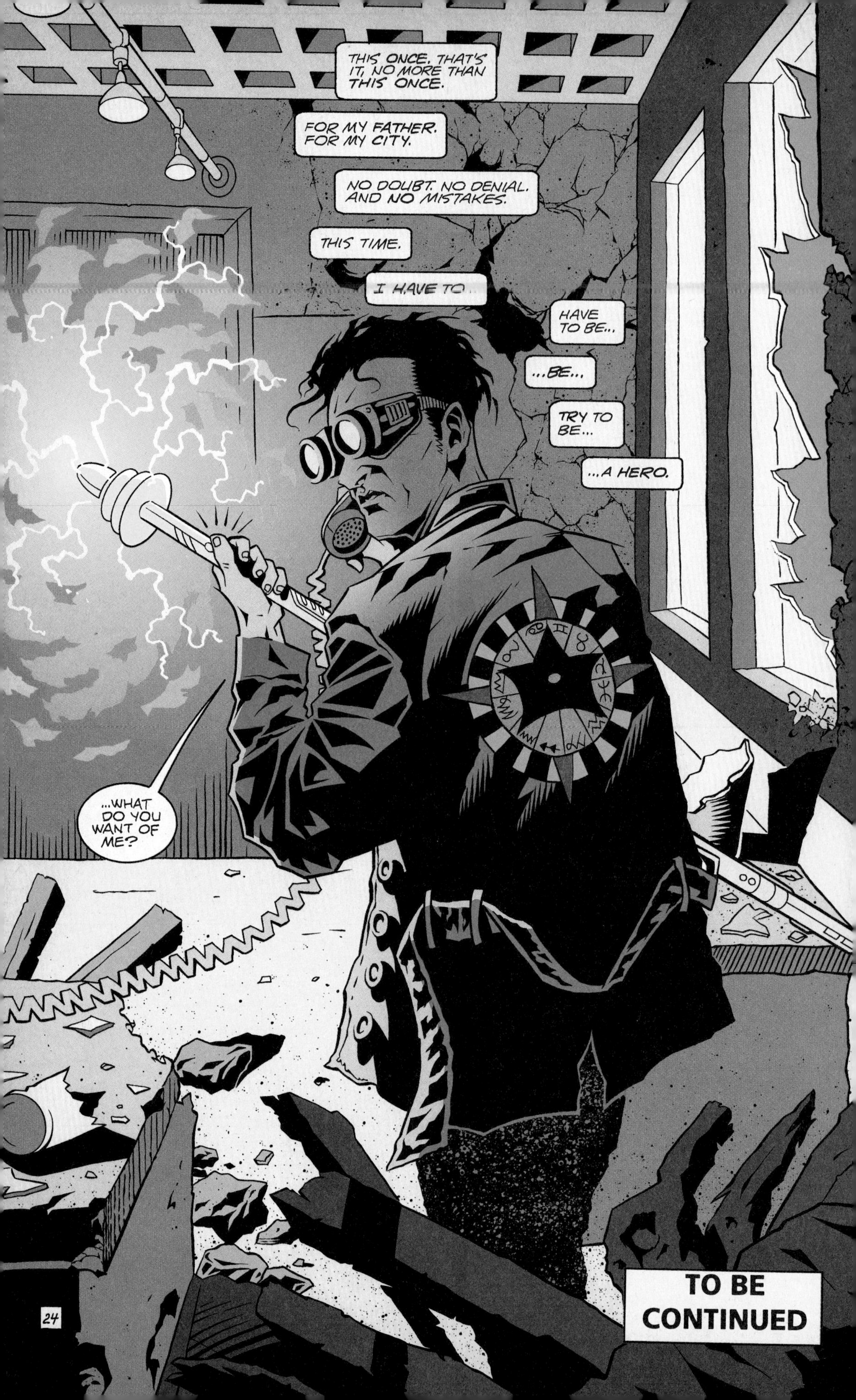

THIS ONCE. THAT'S IT, NO MORE THAN THIS ONCE.
FOR MY FATHER. FOR MY CITY.
NO DOUBT. NO DENIAL. AND NO MISTAKES.
THIS TIME.
I HAVE TO...
HAVE TO BE...
...BE...
TRY TO BE...
...A HERO.
...WHAT DO YOU WANT OF ME?
TO BE CONTINUED

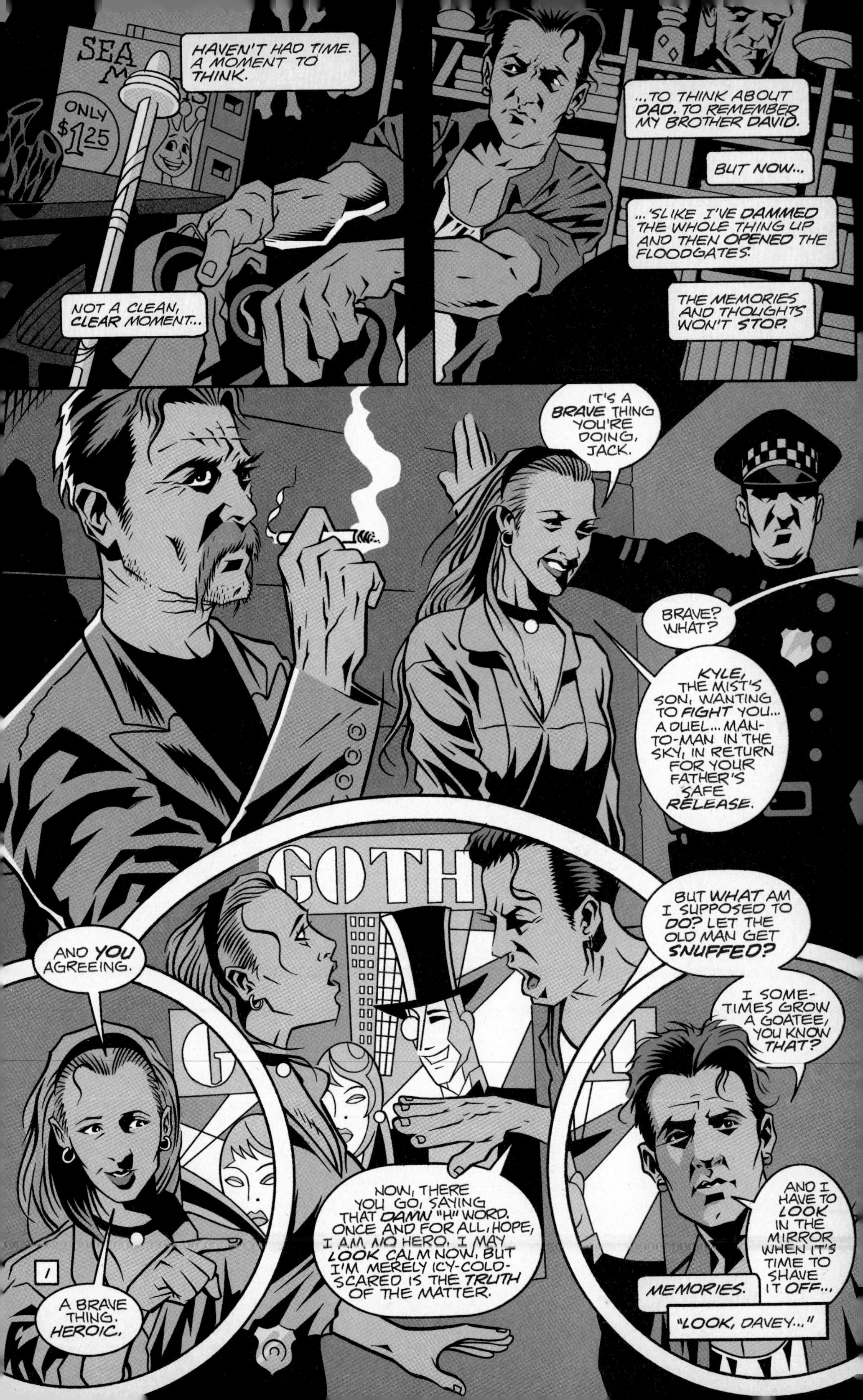
SEA
ONLY $1.25
HAVEN'T HAD TIME. A MOMENT TO THINK.
NOT A CLEAN, CLEAR MOMENT...
...TO THINK ABOUT DAD. TO REMEMBER MY BROTHER DAVID.
BUT NOW...
...'SLIKE I'VE DAMMED THE WHOLE THING UP AND THEN OPENED THE FLOODGATES.
THE MEMORIES AND THOUGHTS WON'T STOP.
IT'S A BRAVE THING YOU'RE DOING, JACK.
BRAVE? WHAT?
KYLE, THE MIST'S SON, WANTING TO FIGHT YOU... A DUEL... MAN-TO-MAN IN THE SKY, IN RETURN FOR YOUR FATHER'S SAFE RELEASE.
GOTH
AND YOU AGREEING.
BUT WHAT AM I SUPPOSED TO DO? LET THE OLD MAN GET SNUFFED?
I SOMETIMES GROW A GOATEE, YOU KNOW THAT?
NOW, THERE YOU GO, SAYING THAT DAMN "H" WORD. ONCE AND FOR ALL, HOPE, I AM NO HERO. I MAY LOOK CALM NOW, BUT I'M MERELY ICY-COLD-SCARED IS THE TRUTH OF THE MATTER.
A BRAVE THING. HEROIC.
1
AND I HAVE TO LOOK IN THE MIRROR WHEN IT'S TIME TO SHAVE IT OFF...
MEMORIES.
"LOOK, DAVEY..."

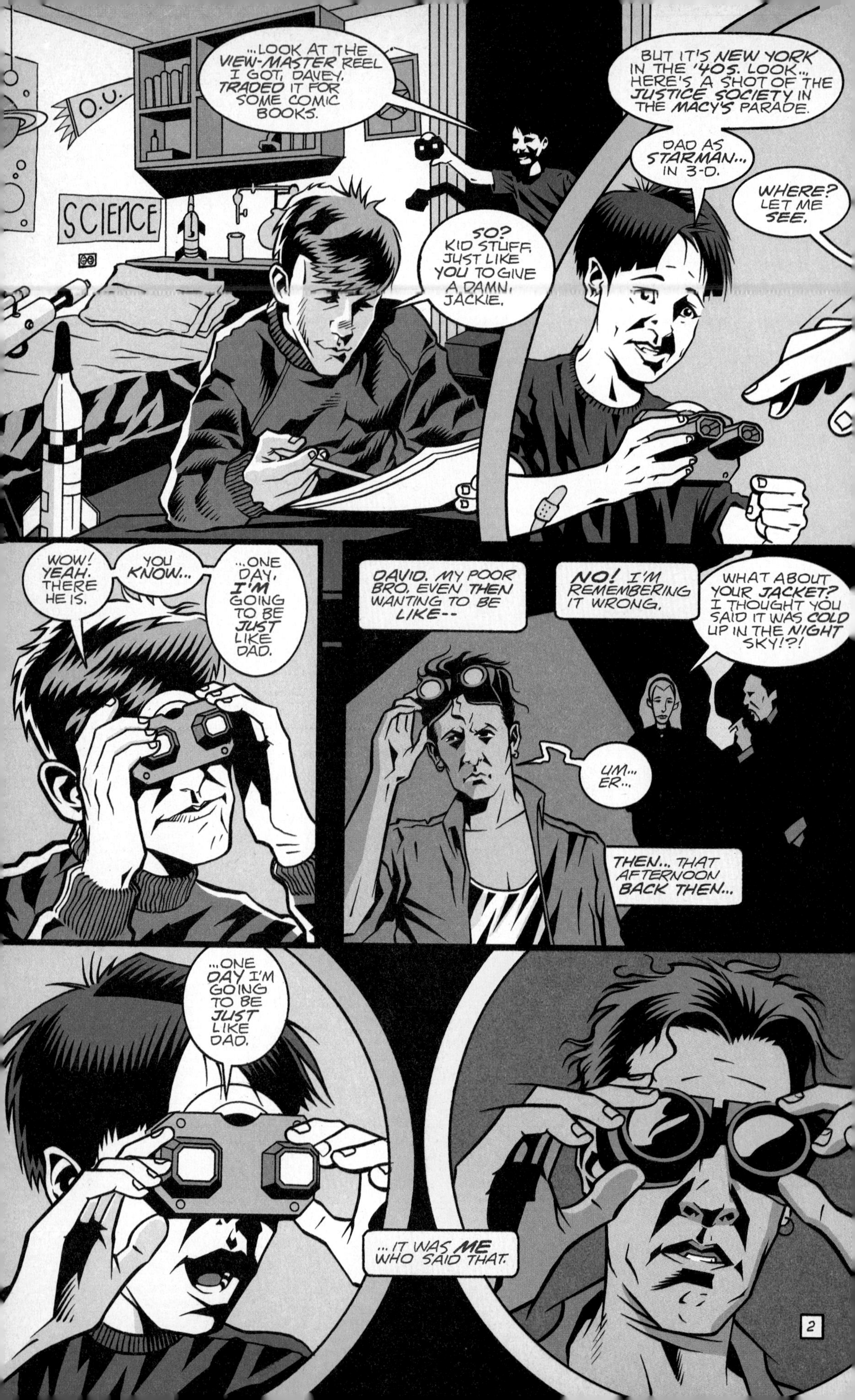

...LOOK AT THE VIEW-MASTER REEL I GOT, DAVEY. TRADED IT FOR SOME COMIC BOOKS.
SO? KID STUFF. JUST LIKE YOU TO GIVE A DAMN, JACKIE.
BUT IT'S NEW YORK IN THE '40S. LOOK... HERE'S A SHOT OF THE JUSTICE SOCIETY IN THE MACY'S PARADE.
DAD AS STARMAN... IN 3-D.
WHERE? LET ME SEE.
SCIENCE
O.U.
WOW! YEAH. THERE HE IS.
YOU KNOW...
...ONE DAY, I'M GOING TO BE JUST LIKE DAD.
DAVID. MY POOR BRO. EVEN THEN WANTING TO BE LIKE--
NO! I'M REMEMBERING IT WRONG.
WHAT ABOUT YOUR JACKET? I THOUGHT YOU SAID IT WAS COLD UP IN THE NIGHT SKY!?!
UM... ER...
THEN... THAT AFTERNOON BACK THEN...
...ONE DAY I'M GOING TO BE JUST LIKE DAD.
...IT WAS ME WHO SAID THAT.

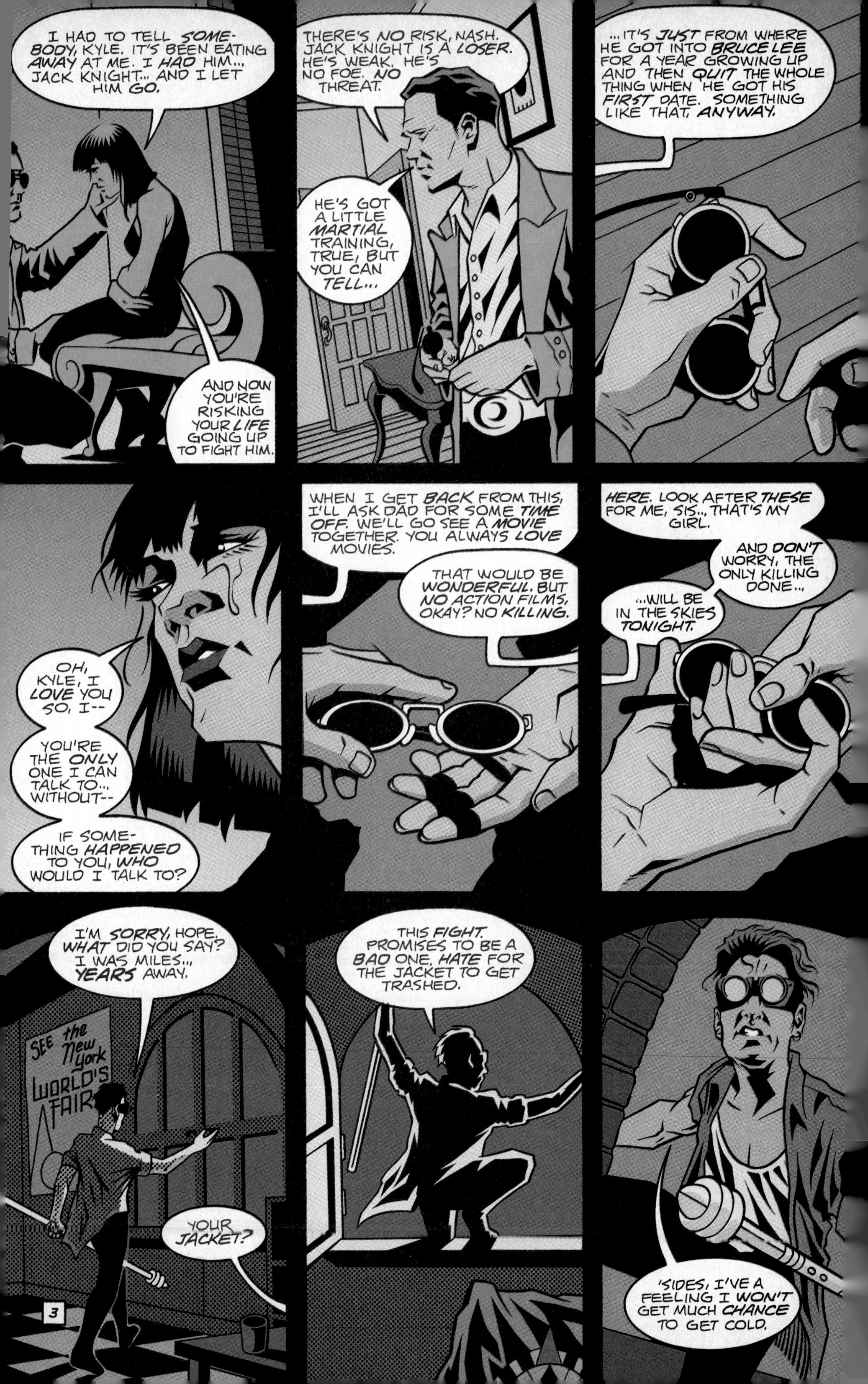
I HAD TO TELL SOMEBODY, KYLE. IT'S BEEN EATING AWAY AT ME. I HAD HIM... JACK KNIGHT... AND I LET HIM GO.
AND NOW YOU'RE RISKING YOUR LIFE GOING UP TO FIGHT HIM.
THERE'S NO RISK, NASH. JACK KNIGHT IS A LOSER. HE'S WEAK. HE'S NO FOE. NO THREAT.
HE'S GOT A LITTLE MARTIAL TRAINING, TRUE, BUT YOU CAN TELL...
...IT'S JUST FROM WHERE HE GOT INTO BRUCE LEE FOR A YEAR GROWING UP AND THEN QUIT THE WHOLE THING WHEN HE GOT HIS FIRST DATE. SOMETHING LIKE THAT, ANYWAY.
OH, KYLE, I LOVE YOU SO, I--
YOU'RE THE ONLY ONE I CAN TALK TO... WITHOUT--
IF SOMETHING HAPPENED TO YOU, WHO WOULD I TALK TO?
WHEN I GET BACK FROM THIS, I'LL ASK DAD FOR SOME TIME OFF. WE'LL GO SEE A MOVIE TOGETHER. YOU ALWAYS LOVE MOVIES.
THAT WOULD BE WONDERFUL. BUT NO ACTION FILMS, OKAY? NO KILLING.
HERE. LOOK AFTER THESE FOR ME, SIS... THAT'S MY GIRL.
AND DON'T WORRY, THE ONLY KILLING DONE...
...WILL BE IN THE SKIES TONIGHT.
I'M SORRY, HOPE. WHAT DID YOU SAY? I WAS MILES... YEARS AWAY.
SEE the New York WORLD'S FAIR
YOUR JACKET?
3
THIS FIGHT. PROMISES TO BE A BAD ONE. HATE FOR THE JACKET TO GET TRASHED.
'SIDES, I'VE A FEELING I WON'T GET MUCH CHANCE TO GET COLD.

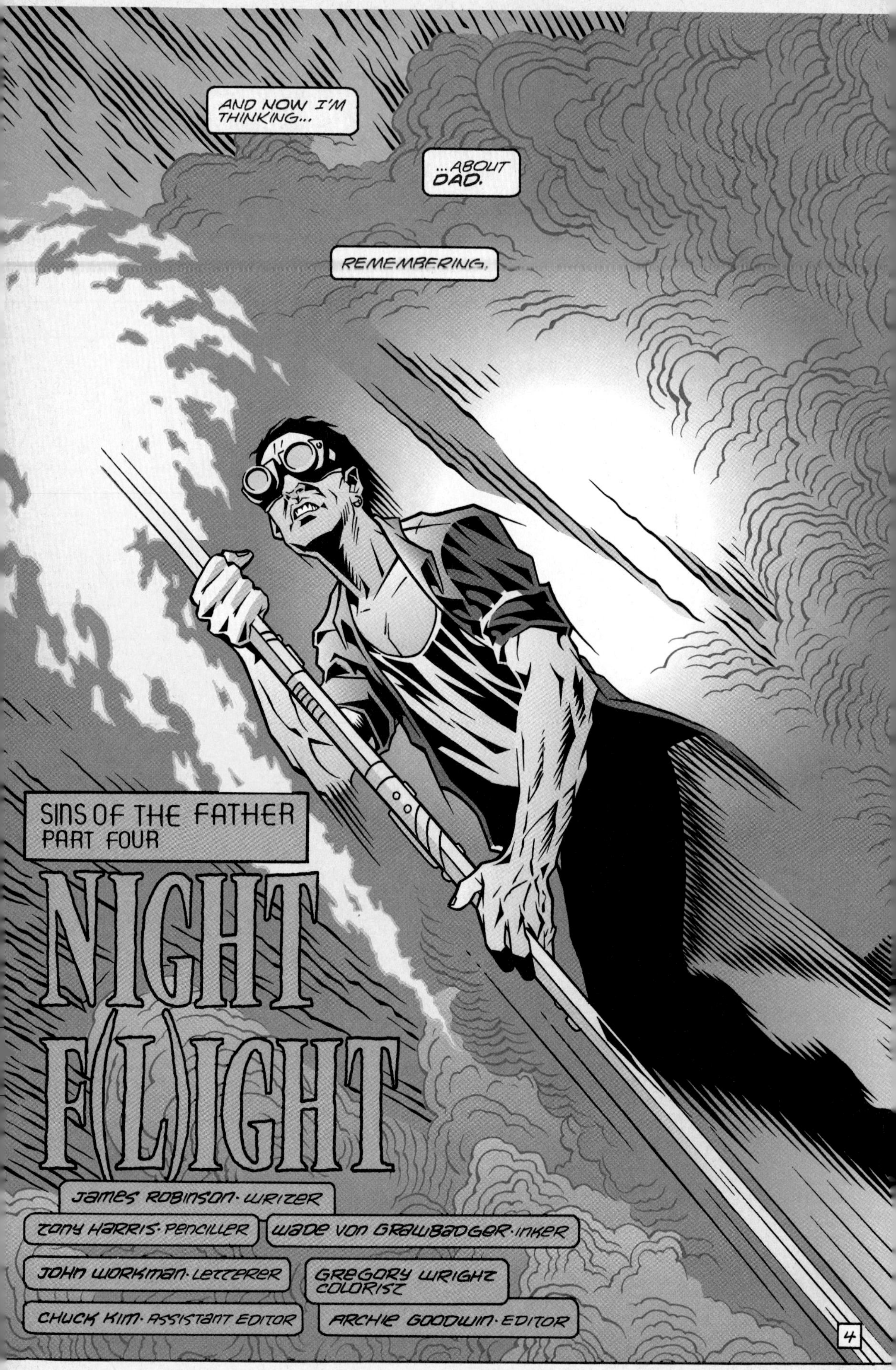
AND NOW I'M THINKING...
...ABOUT DAD.
REMEMBERING.
SINS OF THE FATHER PART FOUR
NIGHT F(L)IGHT
JAMES ROBINSON · WRITER
TONY HARRIS · PENCILLER
WADE VON GRAWBADGER · INKER
JOHN WORKMAN · LETTERER
GREGORY WRIGHT COLORIST
CHUCK KIM · ASSISTANT EDITOR
ARCHIE GOODWIN · EDITOR
4

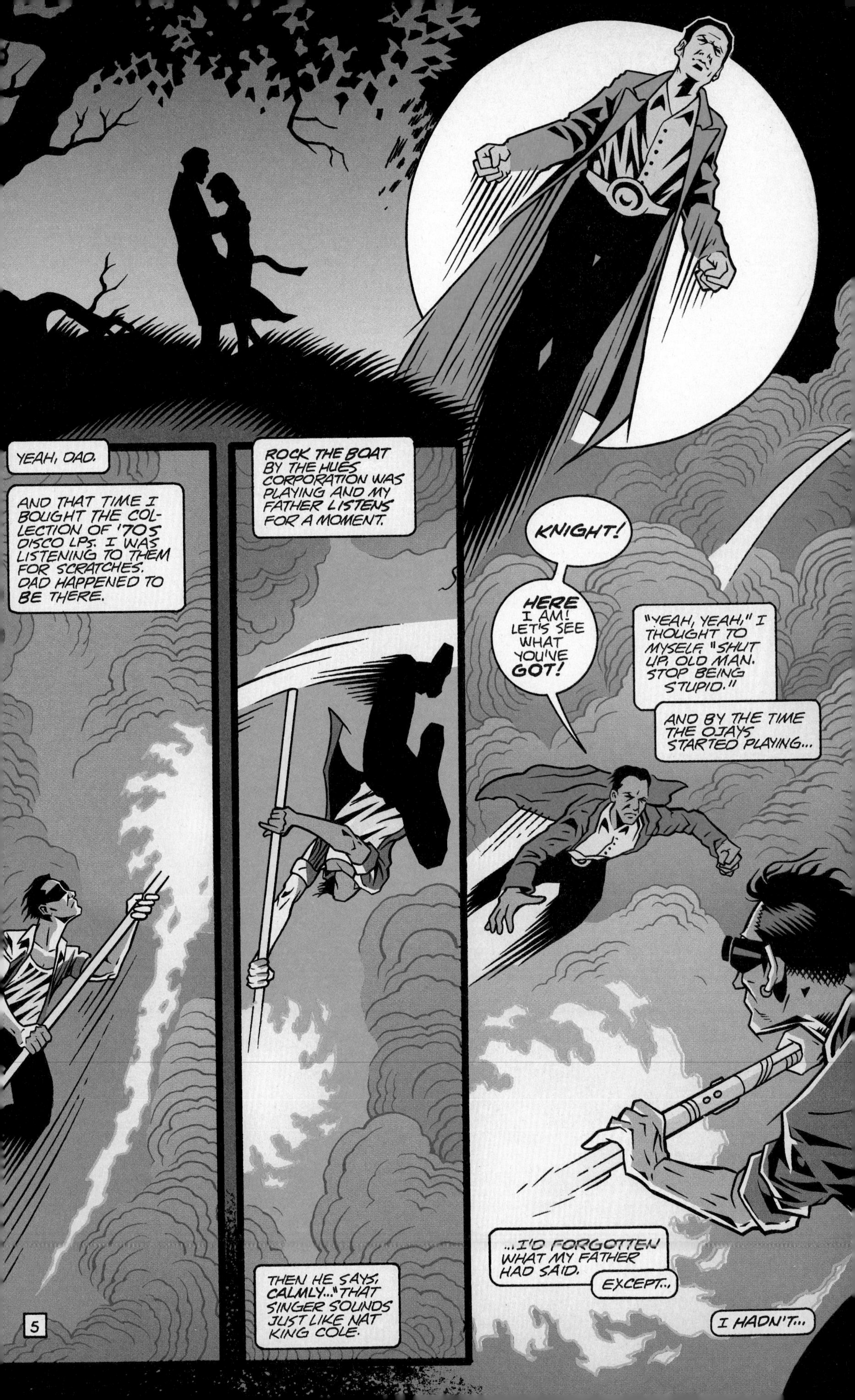

YEAH, DAD.
AND THAT TIME I BOUGHT THE COL-LECTION OF '70S DISCO LPs. I WAS LISTENING TO THEM FOR SCRATCHES. DAD HAPPENED TO BE THERE.
ROCK THE BOAT BY THE HUES CORPORATION WAS PLAYING AND MY FATHER LISTENS FOR A MOMENT.
THEN HE SAYS, CALMLY..."THAT SINGER SOUNDS JUST LIKE NAT KING COLE.
KNIGHT!
HERE I AM! LET'S SEE WHAT YOU'VE GOT!
"YEAH, YEAH," I THOUGHT TO MYSELF. "SHUT UP, OLD MAN. STOP BEING STUPID."
AND BY THE TIME THE OJAYS STARTED PLAYING...
...I'D FORGOTTEN WHAT MY FATHER HAD SAID.
EXCEPT...
I HADN'T...

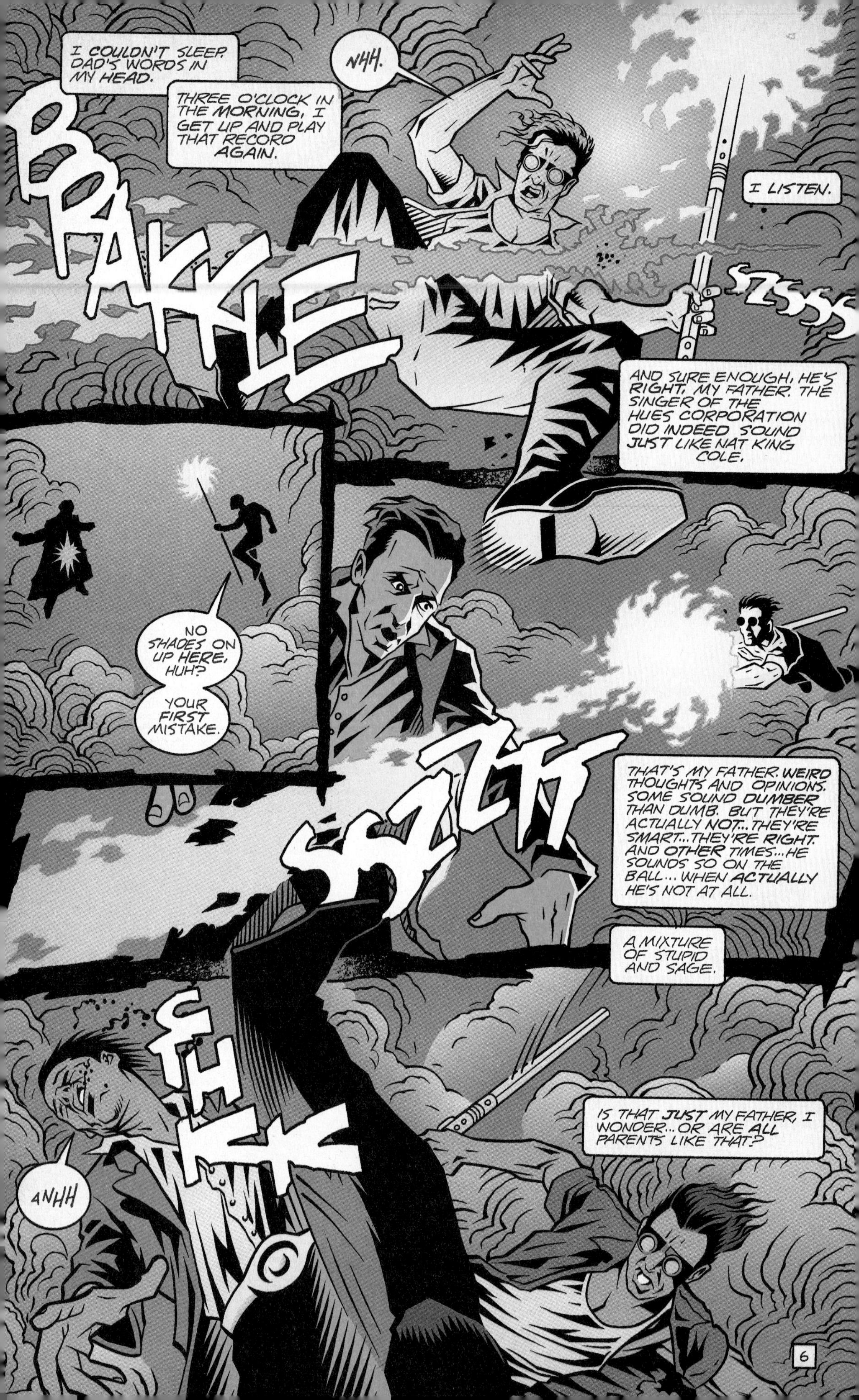
I COULDN'T SLEEP. DAD'S WORDS IN MY HEAD.
NHH.
THREE O'CLOCK IN THE MORNING, I GET UP AND PLAY THAT RECORD AGAIN.
BRAKKLE
I LISTEN.
SZSSS
AND SURE ENOUGH, HE'S RIGHT, MY FATHER. THE SINGER OF THE HUES CORPORATION DID INDEED SOUND JUST LIKE NAT KING COLE.
NO SHADES ON UP HERE, HUH?
YOUR FIRST MISTAKE.
THAT'S MY FATHER. WEIRD THOUGHTS AND OPINIONS. SOME SOUND DUMBER THAN DUMB. BUT THEY'RE ACTUALLY NOT...THEY'RE SMART...THEY'RE RIGHT. AND OTHER TIMES...HE SOUNDS SO ON THE BALL... WHEN ACTUALLY HE'S NOT AT ALL.
A MIXTURE OF STUPID AND SAGE.
IS THAT JUST MY FATHER, I WONDER...OR ARE ALL PARENTS LIKE THAT?
ANHH
6

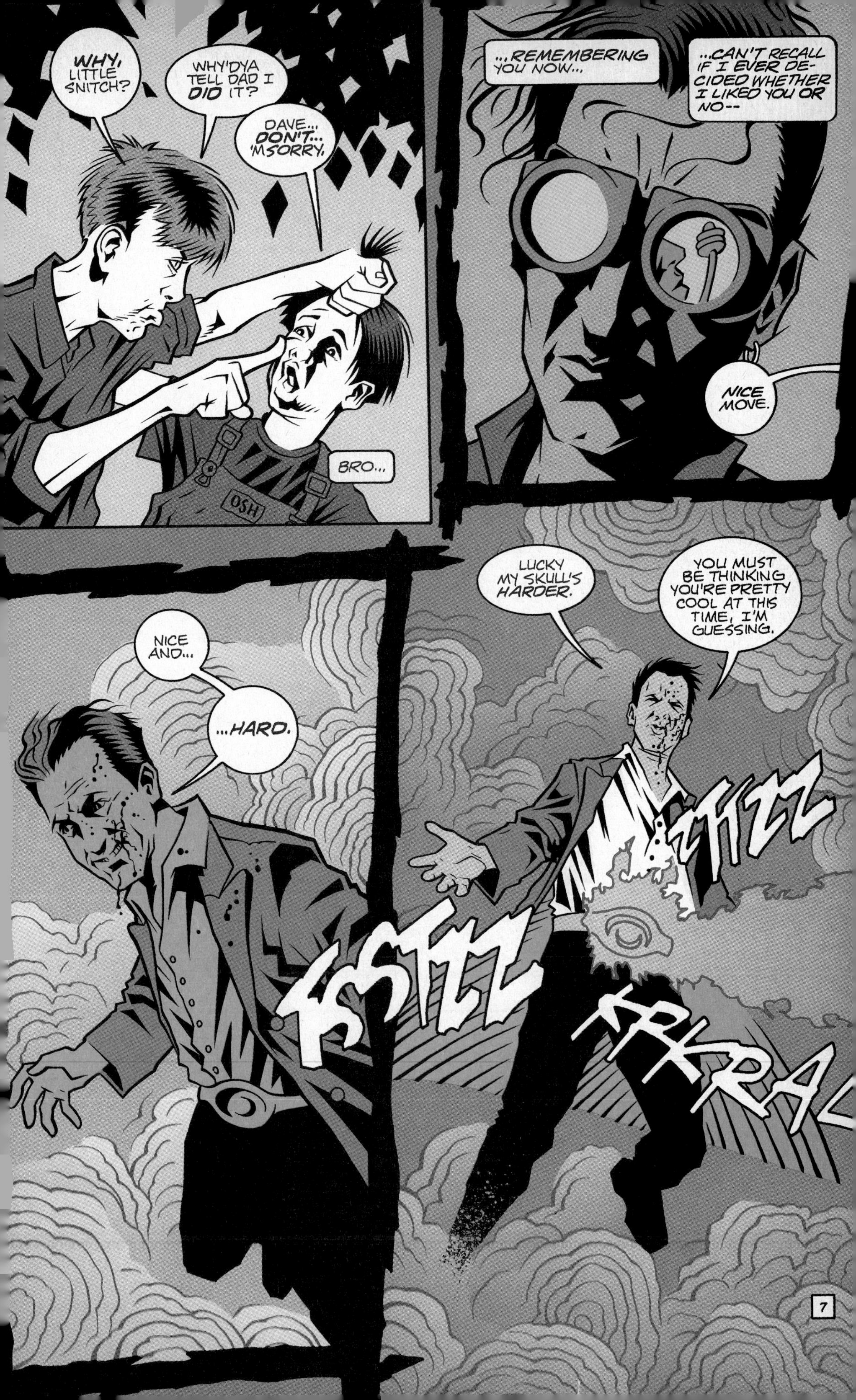
WHY, LITTLE SNITCH?
WHY'DYA TELL DAD I DID IT?
DAVE... DON'T... 'M SORRY.
BRO...
...REMEMBERING YOU NOW...
...CAN'T RECALL IF I EVER DE-CIDED WHETHER I LIKED YOU OR NO--
NICE MOVE.
NICE AND...
...HARD.
LUCKY MY SKULL'S HARDER.
YOU MUST BE THINKING YOU'RE PRETTY COOL AT THIS TIME, I'M GUESSING.
ZZHHZZ
KSSTZZ
KRKRAK

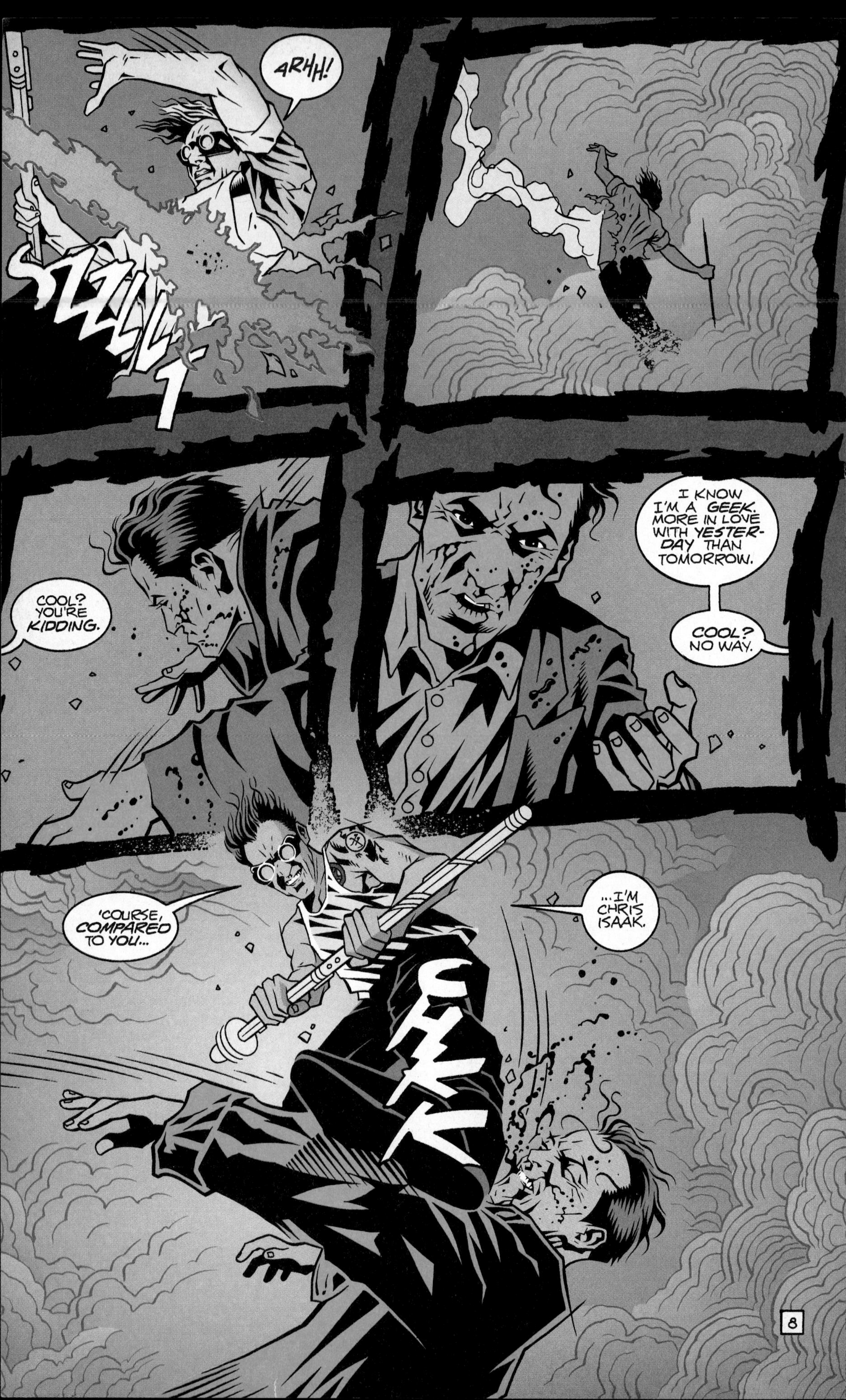
ARHH!
SZZLLL-T
COOL? YOU'RE KIDDING.
I KNOW I'M A GEEK. MORE IN LOVE WITH YESTER-DAY THAN TOMORROW.
COOL? NO WAY.
'COURSE, COMPARED TO YOU...
...I'M CHRIS ISAAK.
CHNK

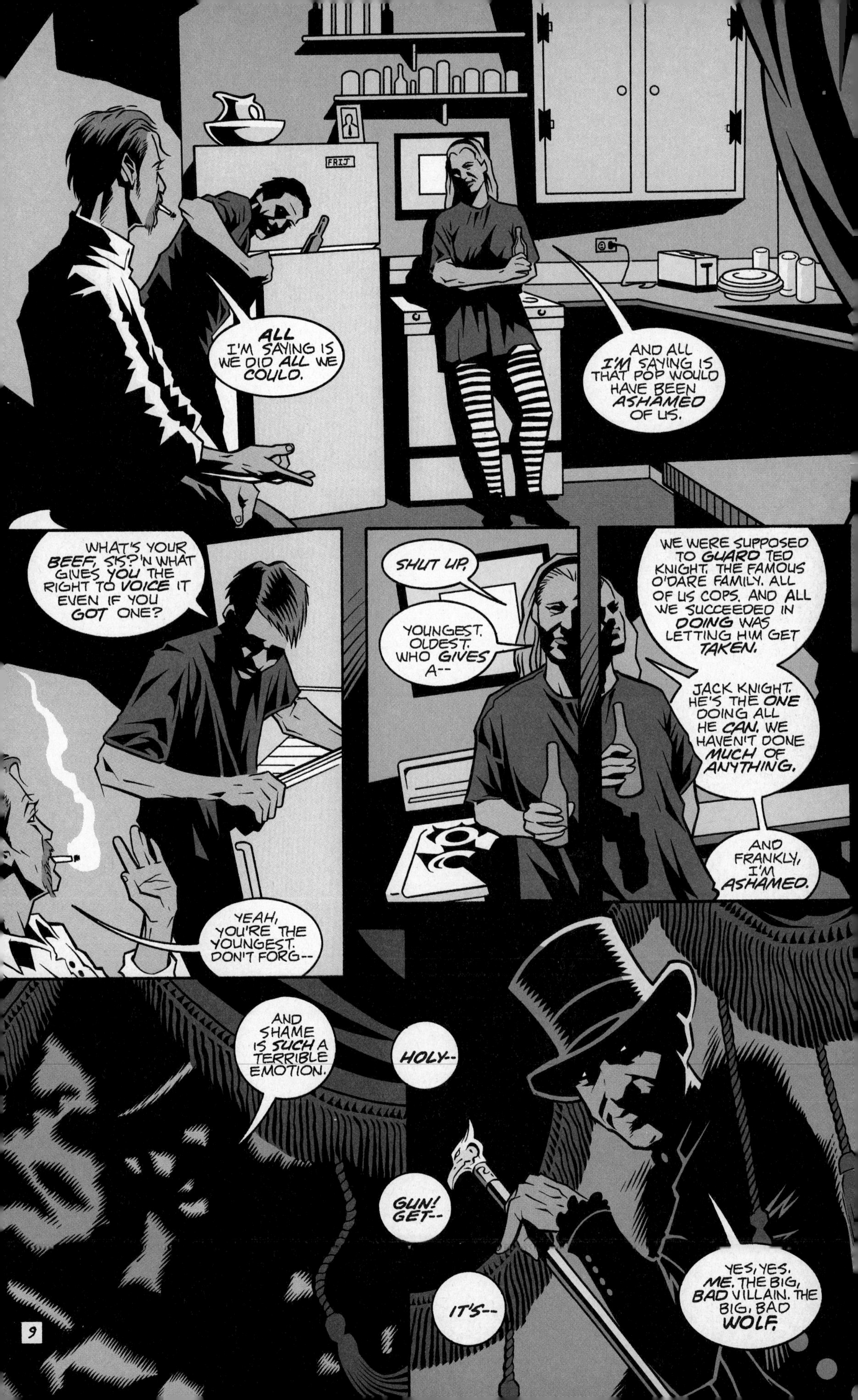
ALL I'M SAYING IS WE DID ALL WE COULD.
AND ALL I'M SAYING IS THAT POP WOULD HAVE BEEN ASHAMED OF US.
FRIJ
WHAT'S YOUR BEEF, SIS? 'N WHAT GIVES YOU THE RIGHT TO VOICE IT EVEN IF YOU GOT ONE?
YEAH, YOU'RE THE YOUNGEST. DON'T FORG--
SHUT UP.
YOUNGEST. OLDEST. WHO GIVES A--
WE WERE SUPPOSED TO GUARD TED KNIGHT. THE FAMOUS O'DARE FAMILY. ALL OF US COPS. AND ALL WE SUCCEEDED IN DOING WAS LETTING HIM GET TAKEN.
JACK KNIGHT. HE'S THE ONE DOING ALL HE CAN. WE HAVEN'T DONE MUCH OF ANYTHING.
AND FRANKLY, I'M ASHAMED.
AND SHAME IS SUCH A TERRIBLE EMOTION.
HOLY--
GUN! GET--
IT'S--
YES, YES. ME. THE BIG, BAD VILLAIN. THE BIG, BAD WOLF.

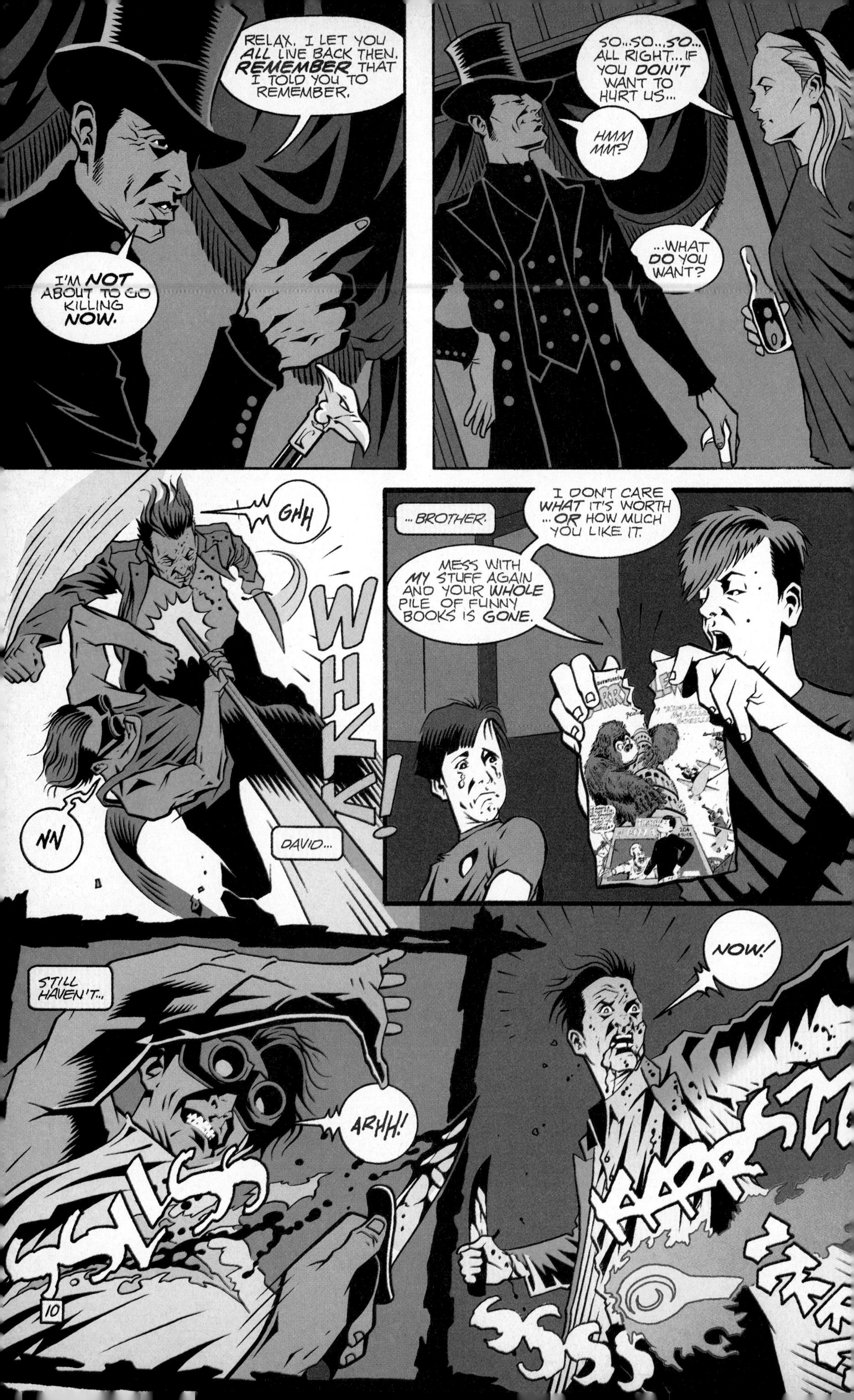

RELAX, I LET YOU ALL LIVE BACK THEN. REMEMBER THAT I TOLD YOU TO REMEMBER.
I'M NOT ABOUT TO GO KILLING NOW.
SO...SO...SO... ALL RIGHT...IF YOU DON'T WANT TO HURT US...
HMM MM?
...WHAT DO YOU WANT?
GHH
WHAK!
NN
DAVID...
...BROTHER.
I DON'T CARE WHAT IT'S WORTH ...OR HOW MUCH YOU LIKE IT.
MESS WITH MY STUFF AGAIN AND YOUR WHOLE PILE OF FUNNY BOOKS IS GONE.
STILL HAVEN'T...
ARHH!
NOW!

YEAH?

NOW WHAT?

...IN OPAL CITY.

ALL THE LOOTING AND KILLING AND ROBBING. THAT SORT OF THING *MIGHT* BE FINE FOR GOTHAM CITY OR METROPOLIS. BUT *NOT* HERE.

WHAT DO I WANT?

I WANT *QUIET* SUNDAY AFTERNOONS. I WANT A GOOD MEAL AND GOOD WINE. I WANT *PEACE...*

I TOOK THE *OLDER* KNIGHT, BEING CAREFUL *NOT* TO HURT HIM, *AND* BEING CAREFUL NO ONE *ELSE* HURT HIM WHEN HE GOT TO THE MIST'S *HIDE-AWAY*.

YEAH, BUT WHY'D YOU TAKE HIM *AT ALL?*

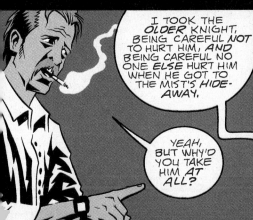

I WAS *JUST* GETTING TO THAT. I TOOK TED KNIGHT AS A SHOW OF MY *ALLEGIANCE* TO THE MIST. I WANTED TO GET *IN* WITH HIM. TO *KNOW* HIS PLANS AND STRENGTHS AND FLAWS, *AND* I HAD TO WAIT FOR THE *BEST* MOMENT.

THE BEST MOMENT?

TO *STORM* HIS LAIR. *ARM* YOURSELVES, GENTLEMEN, AND *LADY*, OH, AND ANY FRIENDS ON THE FORCE YOU MIGHT *HAVE* WHO YOU'D *TRUST* WITH THIS TASK.

REMEMBER A FULL-SCALE POLICE MANEUVER, ALL SIRENS AND SWAT, MIGHT LEAD TO TED KNIGHT'S DEATH, SO YOUR FRIENDS *SHOULD* BE...

...SUBTLE.

THE MIST'S *HIDEOUT!* YOU KNOW WHERE IT *IS?*

NO, WE MET ON PARK BENCHES, LIKE SPIES IN A LEN DEIGHTON NOVEL.

OF COURSE I KNOW WHERE HIS HIDEOUT IS. THE *LAST* PLACE YOU'D THINK TO LOOK, TOO...

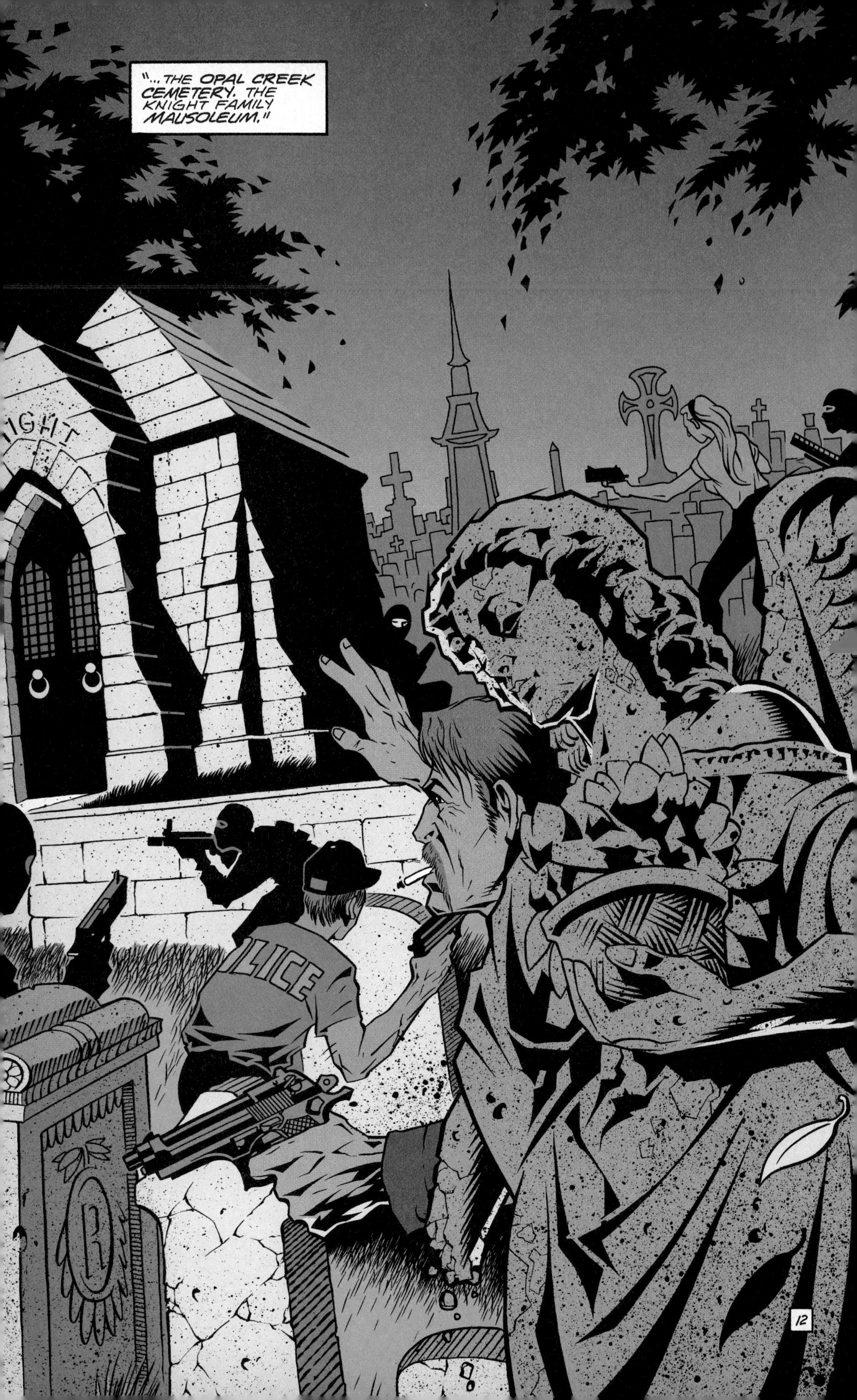
"...THE OPAL CREEK CEMETERY. THE KNIGHT FAMILY MAUSOLEUM."
IGHT
OLICE

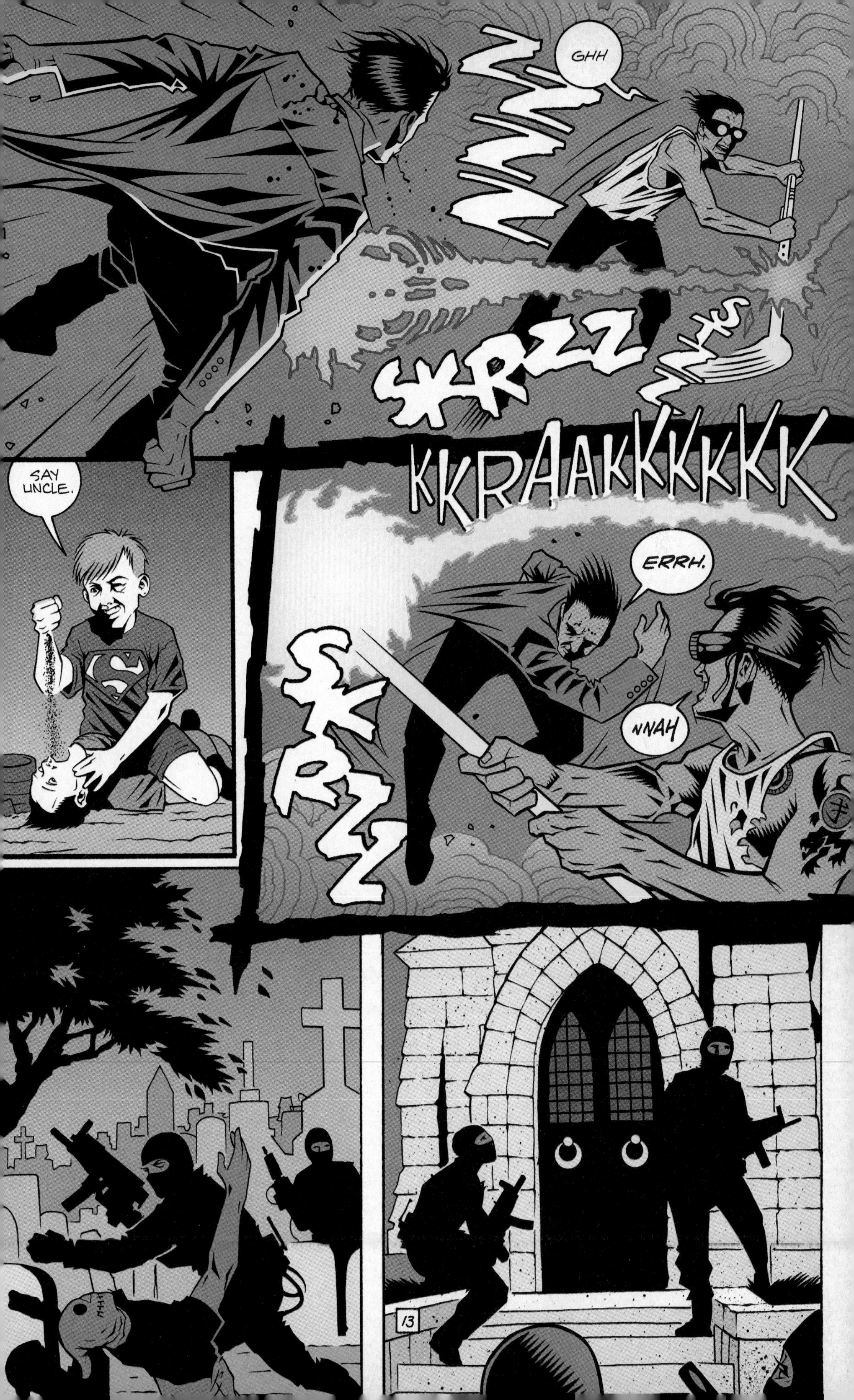
NNNN
GHH
SKRZZ
SHHK
KKRAAKKKKKK
SAY UNCLE.
ERRH.
SKRZZ
NNAH
13

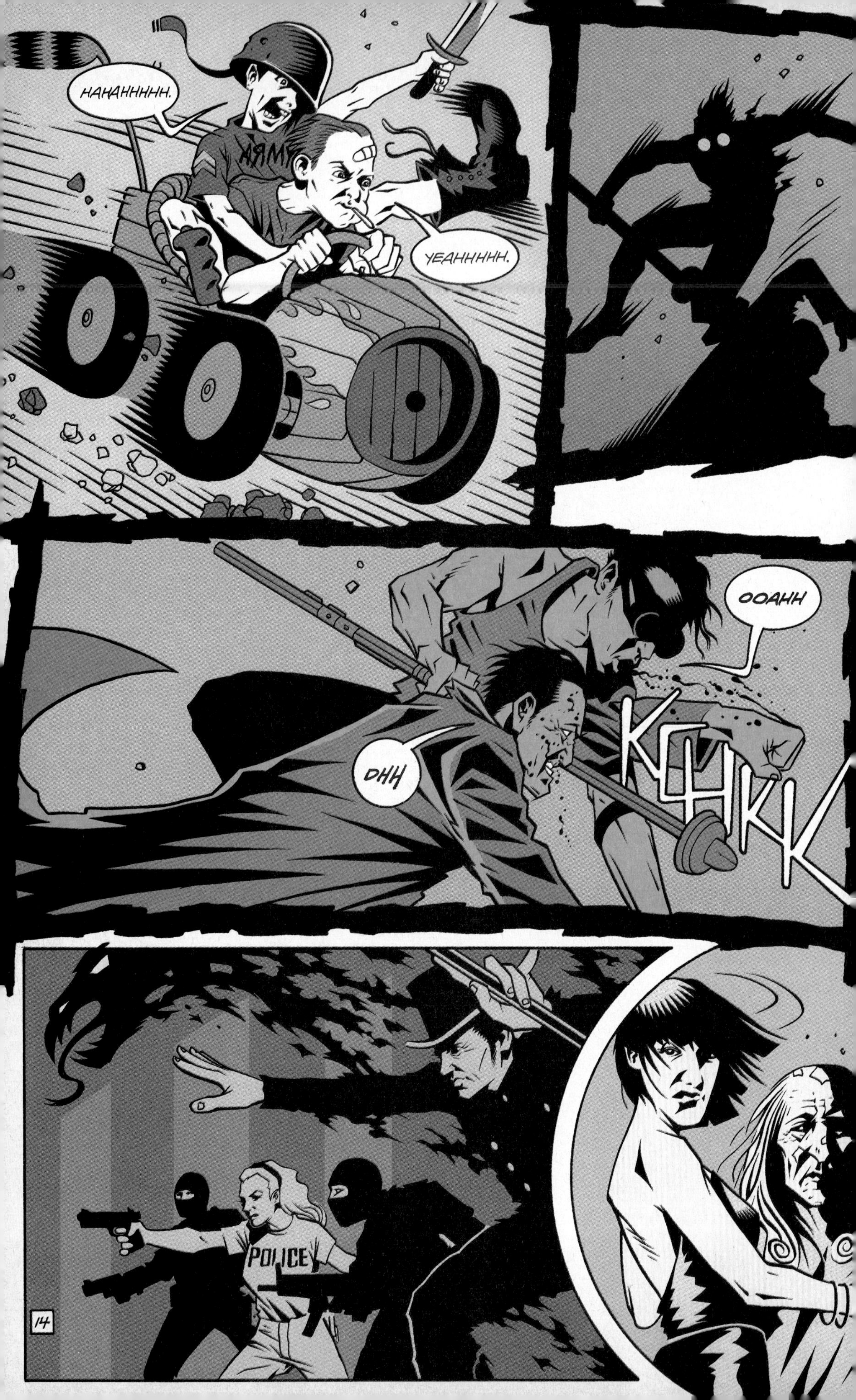
HAHAHHHHH.
YEAHHHHH.
OOAHH
DHH
KCHKK
POLICE
ARMY
14

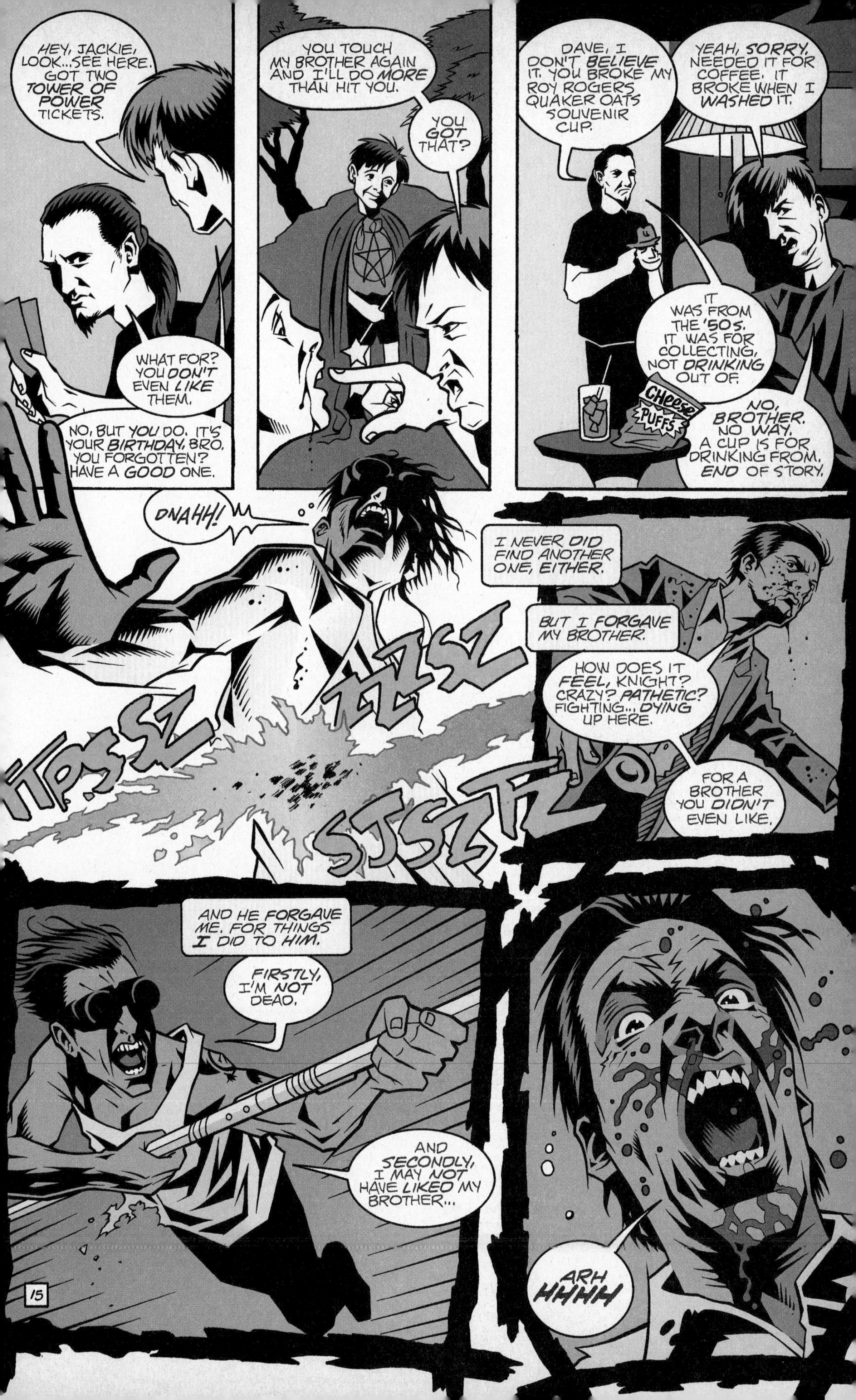

HEY, JACKIE, LOOK...SEE HERE. GOT TWO TOWER OF POWER TICKETS.
WHAT FOR? YOU DON'T EVEN LIKE THEM.
NO, BUT YOU DO. IT'S YOUR BIRTHDAY, BRO. YOU FORGOTTEN? HAVE A GOOD ONE.
YOU TOUCH MY BROTHER AGAIN AND I'LL DO MORE THAN HIT YOU.
YOU GOT THAT?
DAVE, I DON'T BELIEVE IT. YOU BROKE MY ROY ROGERS QUAKER OATS SOUVENIR CUP.
YEAH, SORRY. NEEDED IT FOR COFFEE. IT BROKE WHEN I WASHED IT.
IT WAS FROM THE '50s. IT WAS FOR COLLECTING, NOT DRINKING OUT OF.
CHEESE PUFFS
NO, BROTHER. NO WAY. A CUP IS FOR DRINKING FROM. END OF STORY.
DNAHH!
I NEVER DID FIND ANOTHER ONE, EITHER.
BUT I FORGAVE MY BROTHER.
HOW DOES IT FEEL, KNIGHT? CRAZY? PATHETIC? FIGHTING... DYING UP HERE.
FOR A BROTHER YOU DIDN'T EVEN LIKE.
ITPSSZ
ZZZSZ
SJSZFZ
AND HE FORGAVE ME. FOR THINGS I DID TO HIM.
FIRSTLY, I'M NOT DEAD.
AND SECONDLY, I MAY NOT HAVE LIKED MY BROTHER...
ARH HHHH

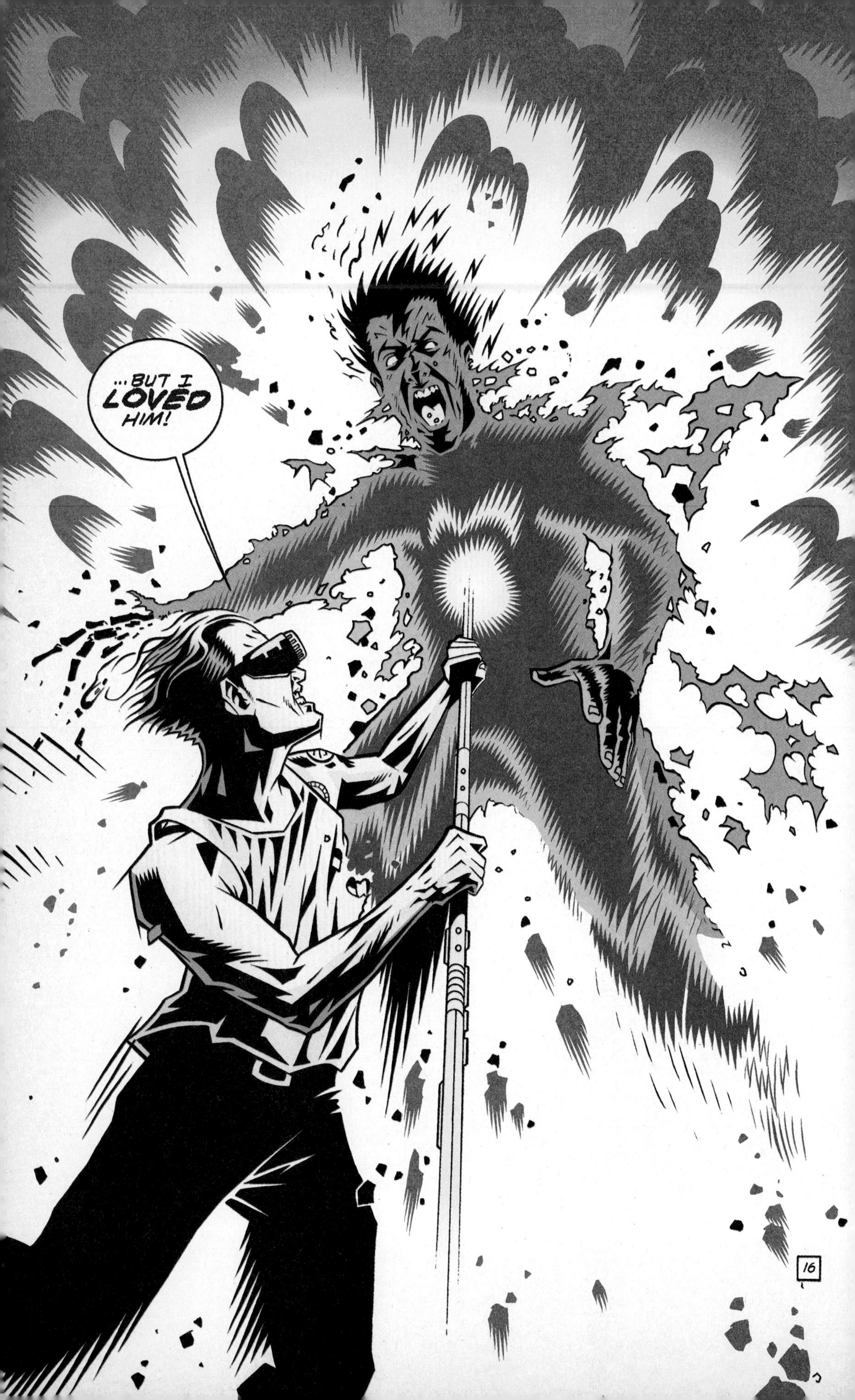
...BUT I LOVED HIM!
16

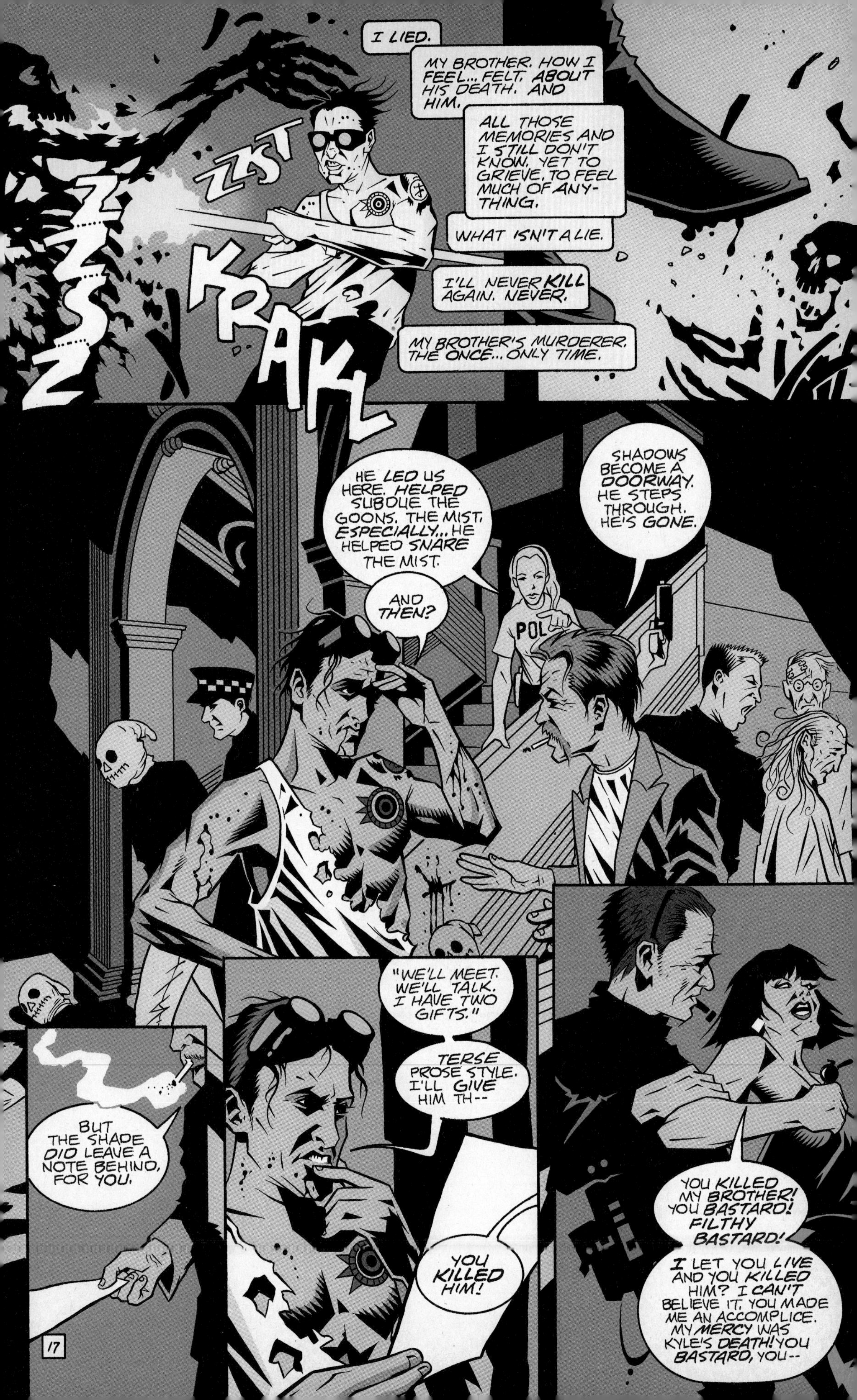
I LIED.
MY BROTHER. HOW I FEEL... FELT, ABOUT HIS DEATH. AND HIM.
ALL THOSE MEMORIES AND I STILL DON'T KNOW. YET TO GRIEVE, TO FEEL MUCH OF ANY-THING.
WHAT ISN'T A LIE.
I'LL NEVER KILL AGAIN. NEVER.
MY BROTHER'S MURDERER. THE ONCE... ONLY TIME.
ZZZT
ZZZZ
KRAKL
HE LED US HERE. HELPED SUBDUE THE GOONS. THE MIST, ESPECIALLY... HE HELPED SNARE THE MIST.
AND THEN?
SHADOWS BECOME A DOORWAY. HE STEPS THROUGH. HE'S GONE.
POL
BUT THE SHADE DID LEAVE A NOTE BEHIND, FOR YOU.
"WE'LL MEET. WE'LL TALK. I HAVE TWO GIFTS."
TERSE PROSE STYLE. I'LL GIVE HIM TH--
YOU KILLED HIM!
YOU KILLED MY BROTHER! YOU BASTARD! FILTHY BASTARD!
I LET YOU LIVE AND YOU KILLED HIM? I CAN'T BELIEVE IT. YOU MADE ME AN ACCOMPLICE. MY MERCY WAS KYLE'S DEATH! YOU BASTARD, YOU--

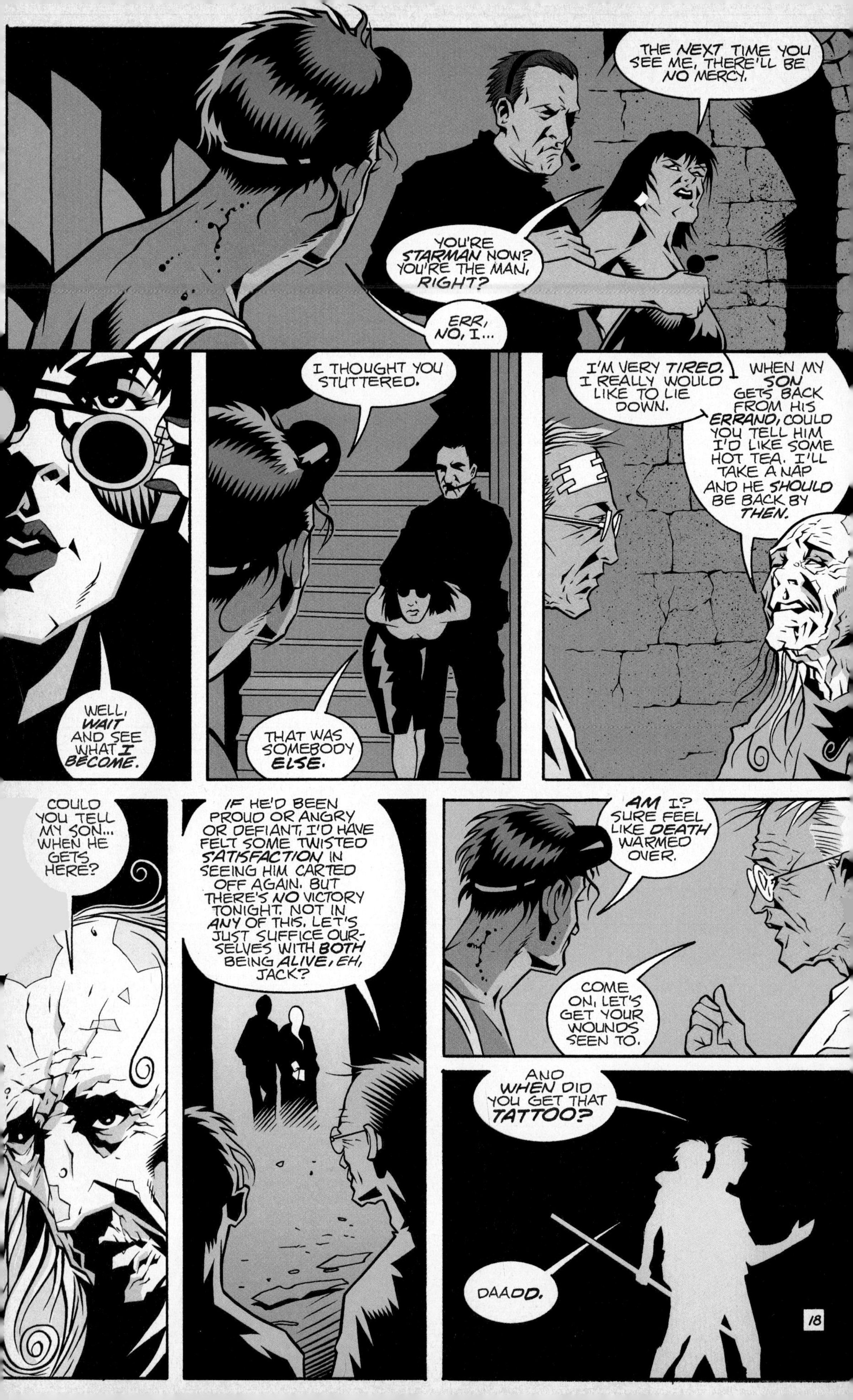
THE NEXT TIME YOU SEE ME, THERE'LL BE NO MERCY.
YOU'RE STARMAN NOW? YOU'RE THE MAN, RIGHT?
ERR, NO, I...
WELL, WAIT AND SEE WHAT I BECOME.
I THOUGHT YOU STUTTERED.
THAT WAS SOMEBODY ELSE.
I'M VERY TIRED. I REALLY WOULD LIKE TO LIE DOWN.
WHEN MY SON GETS BACK FROM HIS ERRAND, COULD YOU TELL HIM I'D LIKE SOME HOT TEA. I'LL TAKE A NAP AND HE SHOULD BE BACK BY THEN.
COULD YOU TELL MY SON... WHEN HE GETS HERE?
IF HE'D BEEN PROUD OR ANGRY OR DEFIANT, I'D HAVE FELT SOME TWISTED SATISFACTION IN SEEING HIM CARTED OFF AGAIN. BUT THERE'S NO VICTORY TONIGHT. NOT IN ANY OF THIS. LET'S JUST SUFFICE OURSELVES WITH BOTH BEING ALIVE, EH, JACK?
AM I? SURE FEEL LIKE DEATH WARMED OVER.
COME ON, LET'S GET YOUR WOUNDS SEEN TO.
AND WHEN DID YOU GET THAT TATTOO?
DAAADD.

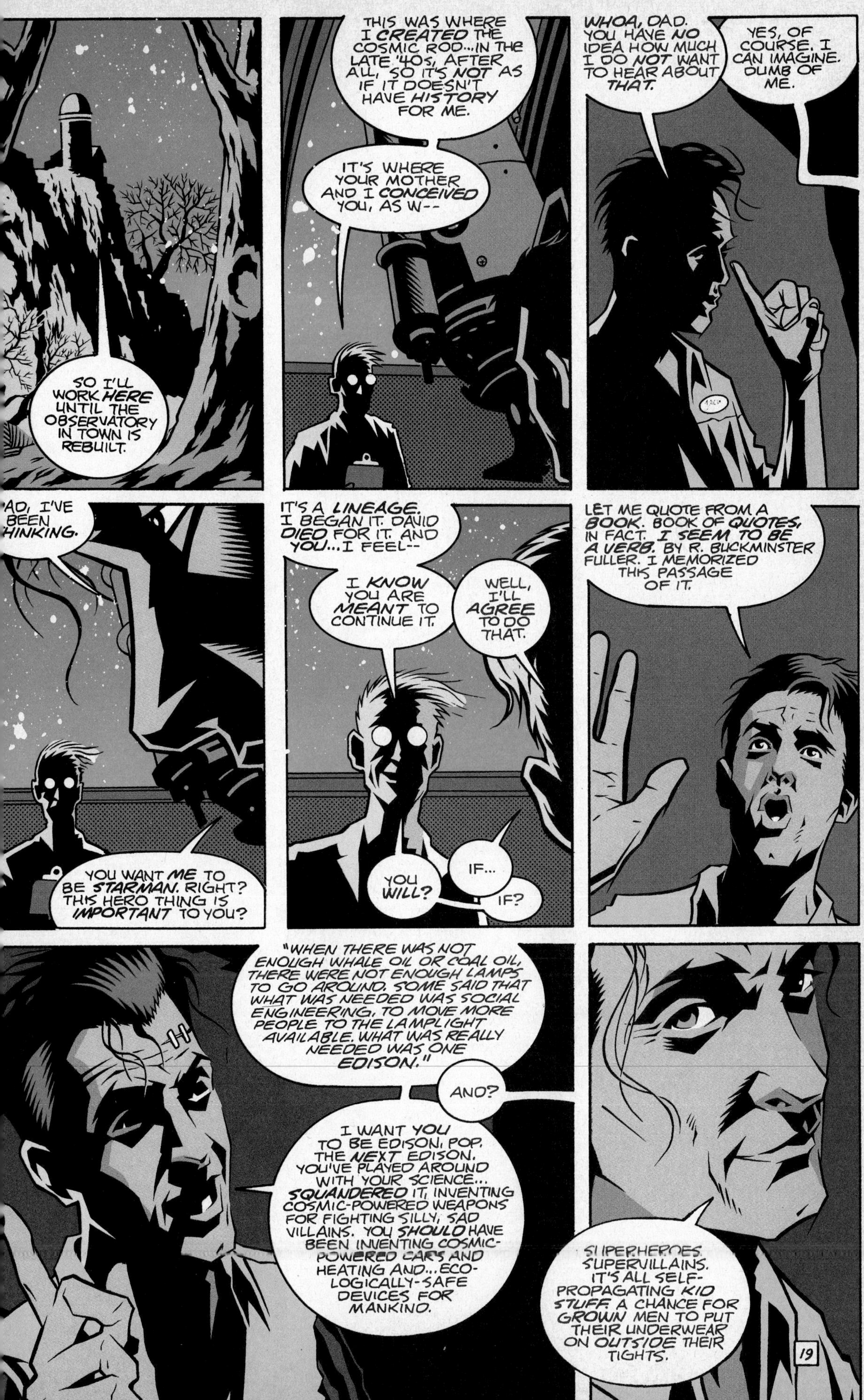
SO I'LL WORK HERE UNTIL THE OBSERVATORY IN TOWN IS REBUILT.
THIS WAS WHERE I CREATED THE COSMIC ROD...IN THE LATE '40s, AFTER ALL, SO IT'S NOT AS IF IT DOESN'T HAVE HISTORY FOR ME.
IT'S WHERE YOUR MOTHER AND I CONCEIVED YOU, AS W--
WHOA, DAD. YOU HAVE NO IDEA HOW MUCH I DO NOT WANT TO HEAR ABOUT THAT.
YES, OF COURSE. I CAN IMAGINE. DUMB OF ME.
AD, I'VE BEEN HINKING.
YOU WANT ME TO BE STARMAN. RIGHT? THIS HERO THING IS IMPORTANT TO YOU?
IT'S A LINEAGE. I BEGAN IT. DAVID DIED FOR IT. AND YOU...I FEEL--
I KNOW YOU ARE MEANT TO CONTINUE IT.
WELL, I'LL AGREE TO DO THAT.
IF...
YOU WILL?
IF?
LET ME QUOTE FROM A BOOK. BOOK OF QUOTES, IN FACT. I SEEM TO BE A VERB. BY R. BUCKMINSTER FULLER. I MEMORIZED THIS PASSAGE OF IT.
"WHEN THERE WAS NOT ENOUGH WHALE OIL OR COAL OIL, THERE WERE NOT ENOUGH LAMPS TO GO AROUND. SOME SAID THAT WHAT WAS NEEDED WAS SOCIAL ENGINEERING, TO MOVE MORE PEOPLE TO THE LAMPLIGHT AVAILABLE. WHAT WAS REALLY NEEDED WAS ONE EDISON."
AND?
I WANT YOU TO BE EDISON, POP. THE NEXT EDISON. YOU'VE PLAYED AROUND WITH YOUR SCIENCE... SQUANDERED IT, INVENTING COSMIC-POWERED WEAPONS FOR FIGHTING SILLY, SAD VILLAINS. YOU SHOULD HAVE BEEN INVENTING COSMIC-POWERED CARS AND HEATING AND... ECO-LOGICALLY-SAFE DEVICES FOR MANKIND.
SUPERHEROES. SUPERVILLAINS. IT'S ALL SELF-PROPAGATING KID STUFF. A CHANCE FOR GROWN MEN TO PUT THEIR UNDERWEAR ON OUTSIDE THEIR TIGHTS.

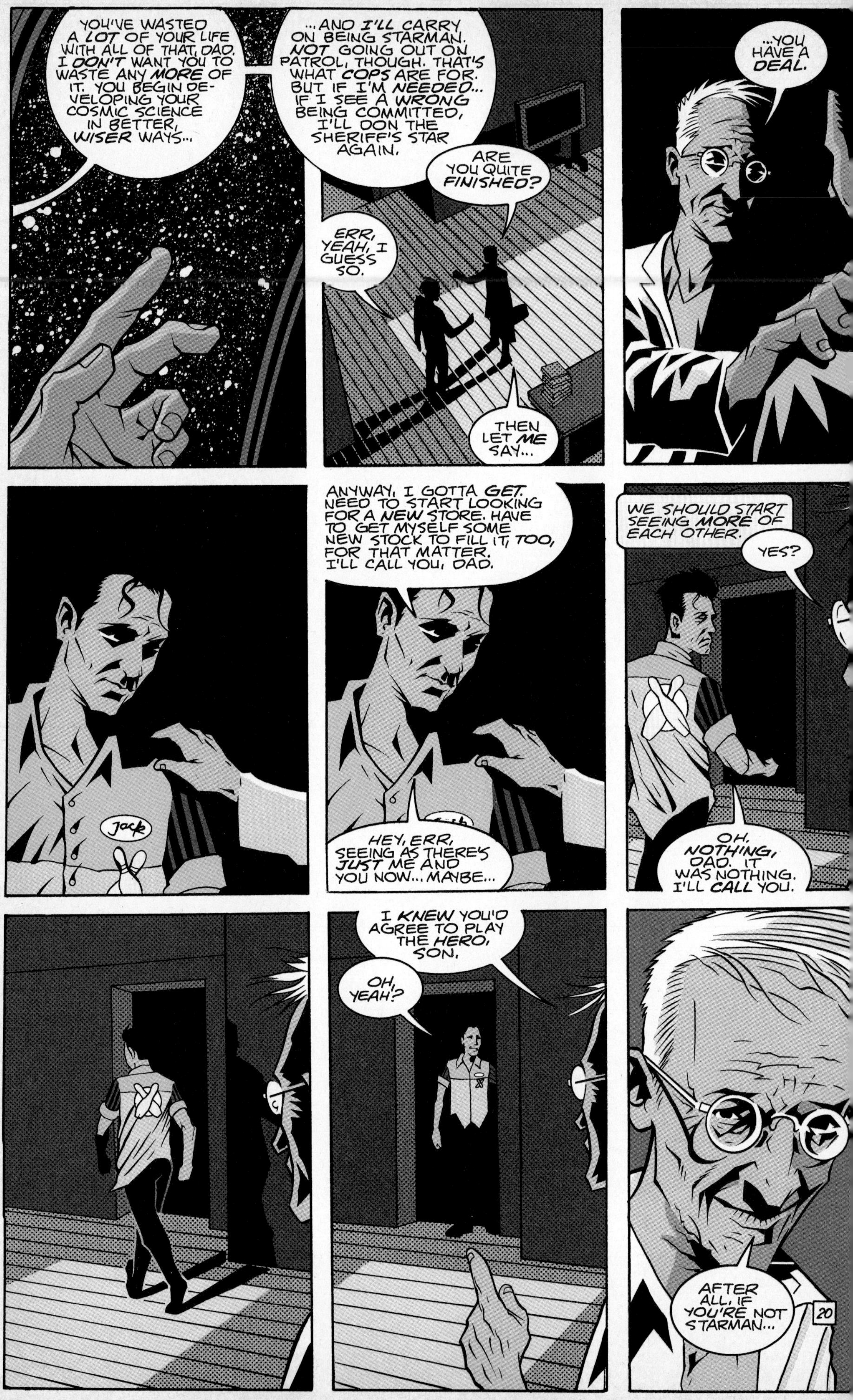
YOU'VE WASTED A LOT OF YOUR LIFE WITH ALL OF THAT, DAD. I DON'T WANT YOU TO WASTE ANY MORE OF IT. YOU BEGIN DE-VELOPING YOUR COSMIC SCIENCE IN BETTER, WISER WAYS...
...AND I'LL CARRY ON BEING STARMAN. NOT GOING OUT ON PATROL, THOUGH. THAT'S WHAT COPS ARE FOR. BUT IF I'M NEEDED... IF I SEE A WRONG BEING COMMITTED, I'LL DON THE SHERIFF'S STAR AGAIN.
ARE YOU QUITE FINISHED?
ERR, YEAH, I GUESS SO.
THEN LET ME SAY...
...YOU HAVE A DEAL.
ANYWAY, I GOTTA GET. NEED TO START LOOKING FOR A NEW STORE. HAVE TO GET MYSELF SOME NEW STOCK TO FILL IT, TOO, FOR THAT MATTER. I'LL CALL YOU, DAD.
Jack
HEY, ERR, SEEING AS THERE'S JUST ME AND YOU NOW... MAYBE...
WE SHOULD START SEEING MORE OF EACH OTHER.
YES?
OH. NOTHING, DAD. IT WAS NOTHING. I'LL CALL YOU.
I KNEW YOU'D AGREE TO PLAY THE HERO, SON.
OH, YEAH?
AFTER ALL, IF YOU'RE NOT STARMAN...
20

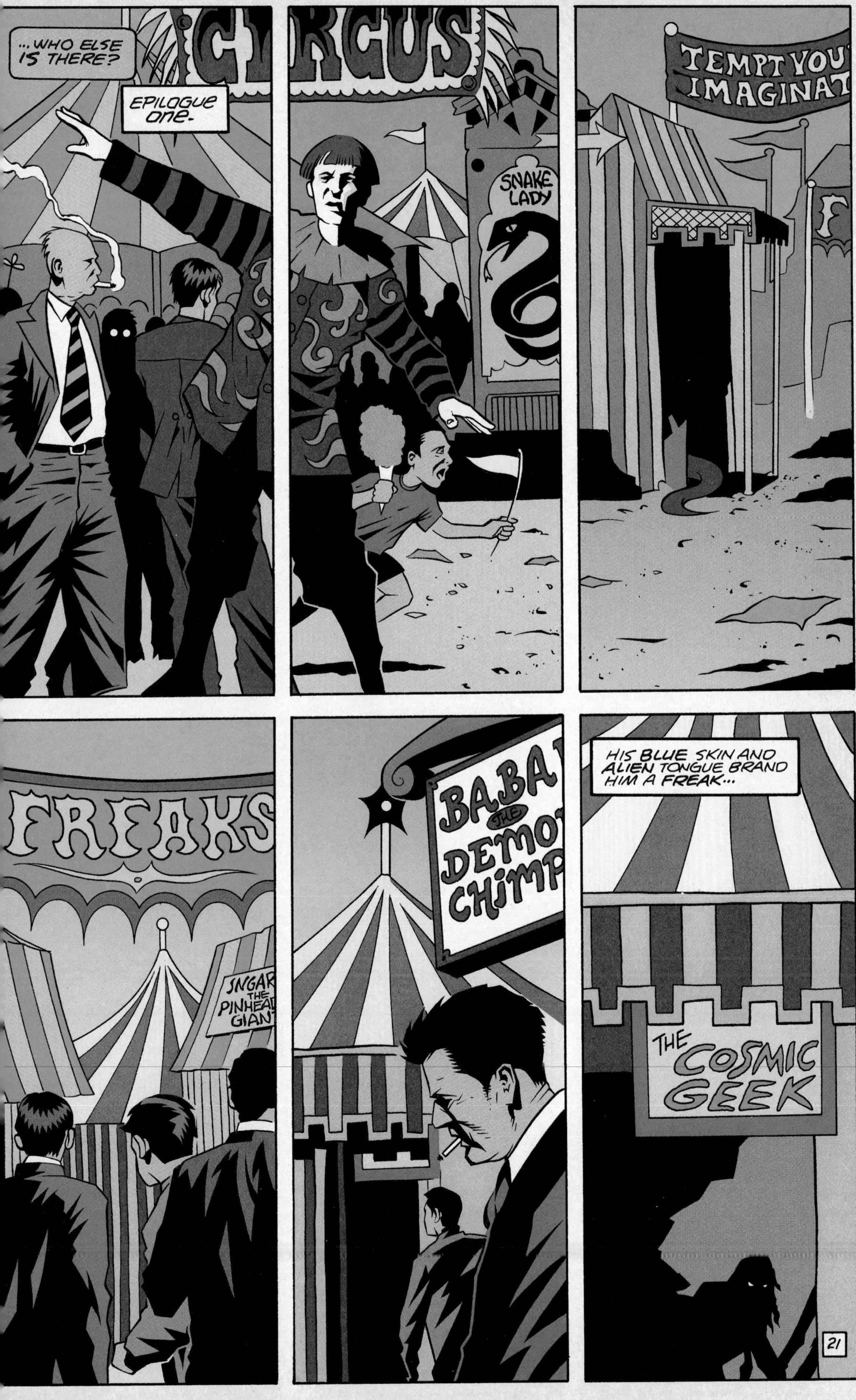

...WHO ELSE IS THERE?
EPILOGUE ONE-
SNAKE LADY
TEMPT YOU
IMAGINAT
FREAKS
SNGAR THE PINHEAD GIANT
BABA THE DEMO CHIMP
HIS BLUE SKIN AND ALIEN TONGUE BRAND HIM A FREAK...
THE COSMIC GEEK
21

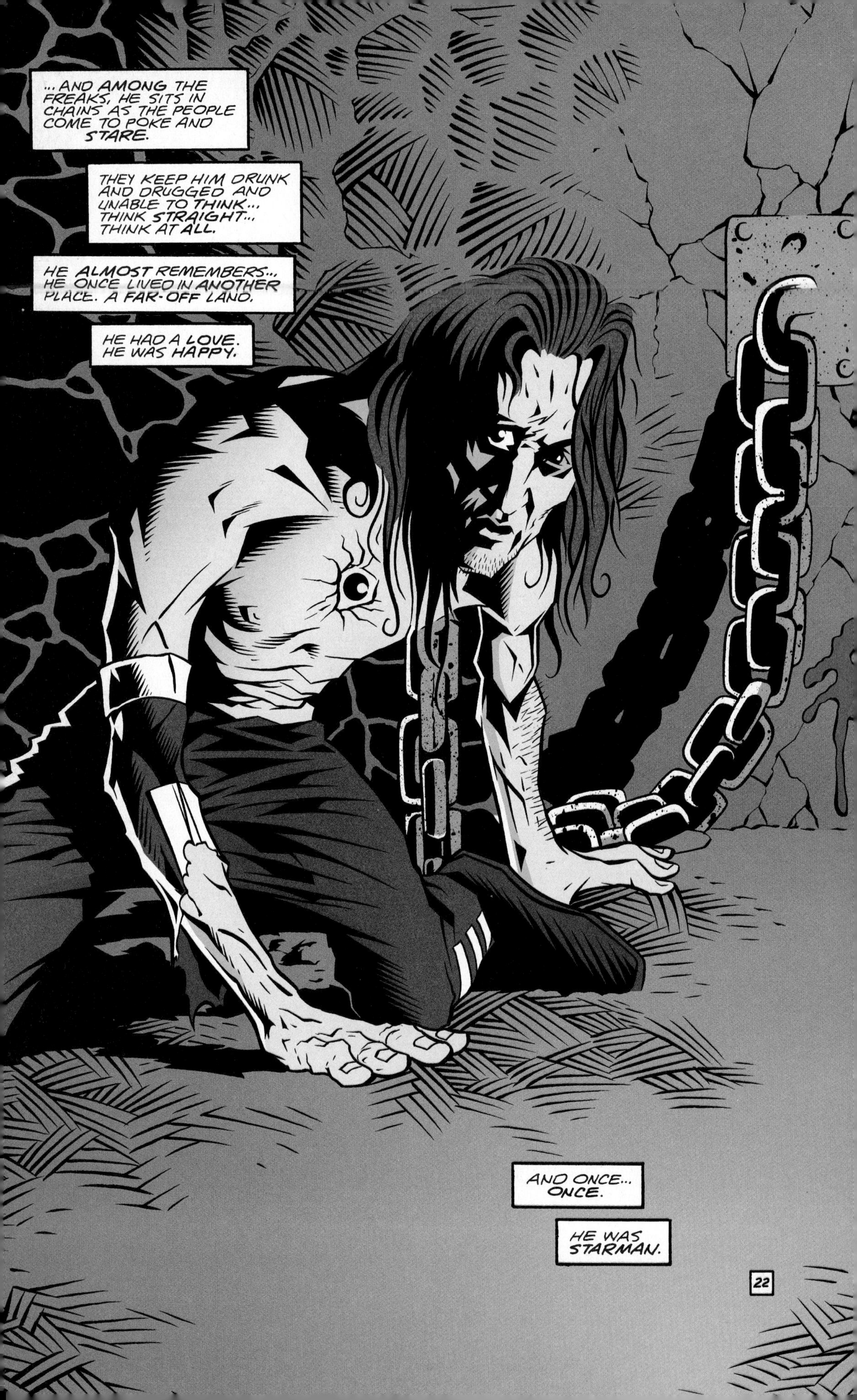
...AND AMONG THE FREAKS, HE SITS IN CHAINS AS THE PEOPLE COME TO POKE AND STARE.
THEY KEEP HIM DRUNK AND DRUGGED AND UNABLE TO THINK... THINK STRAIGHT... THINK AT ALL.
HE ALMOST REMEMBERS... HE ONCE LIVED IN ANOTHER PLACE. A FAR-OFF LAND.
HE HAD A LOVE. HE WAS HAPPY.
AND ONCE... ONCE.
HE WAS STARMAN.

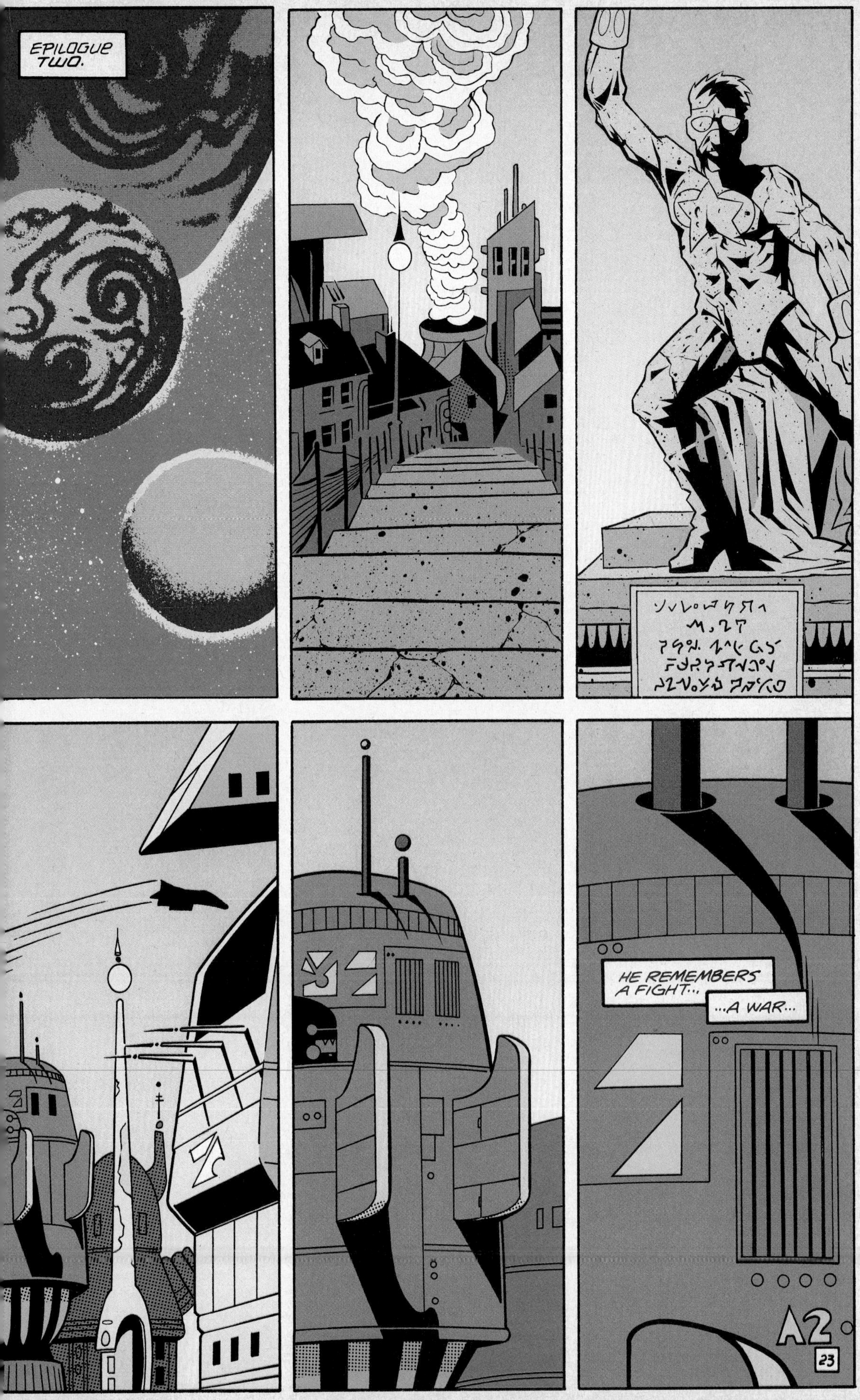
EPILOGUE TWO.
HE REMEMBERS A FIGHT...
...A WAR...
A2

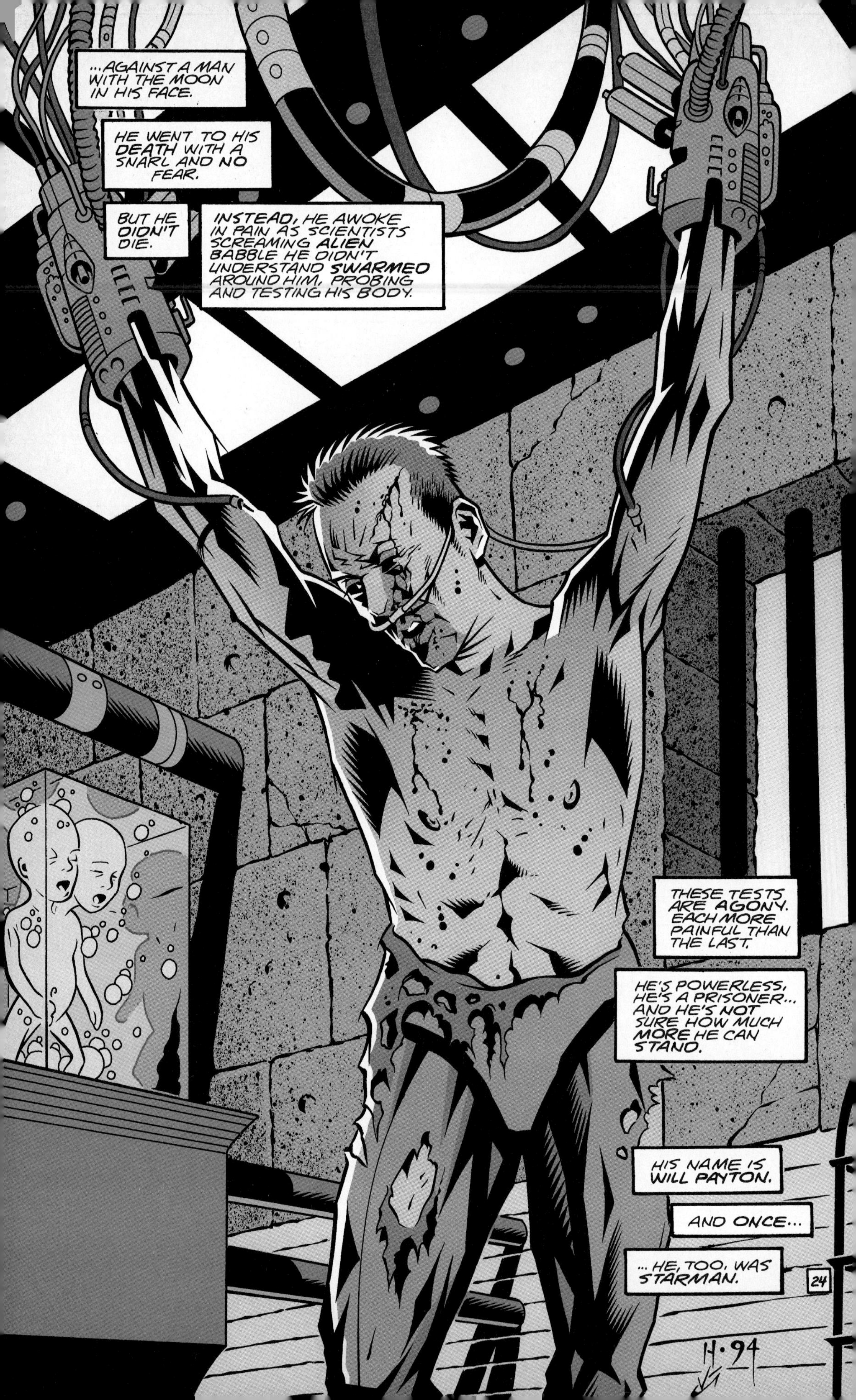
...AGAINST A MAN WITH THE MOON IN HIS FACE.
HE WENT TO HIS DEATH WITH A SNARL AND NO FEAR.
BUT HE DIDN'T DIE.
INSTEAD, HE AWOKE IN PAIN AS SCIENTISTS SCREAMING ALIEN BABBLE HE DIDN'T UNDERSTAND SWARMED AROUND HIM, PROBING AND TESTING HIS BODY.
THESE TESTS ARE AGONY. EACH MORE PAINFUL THAN THE LAST.
HE'S POWERLESS, HE'S A PRISONER... AND HE'S NOT SURE HOW MUCH MORE HE CAN STAND.
HIS NAME IS WILL PAYTON.
AND ONCE...
...HE, TOO, WAS STARMAN.
24
H·94

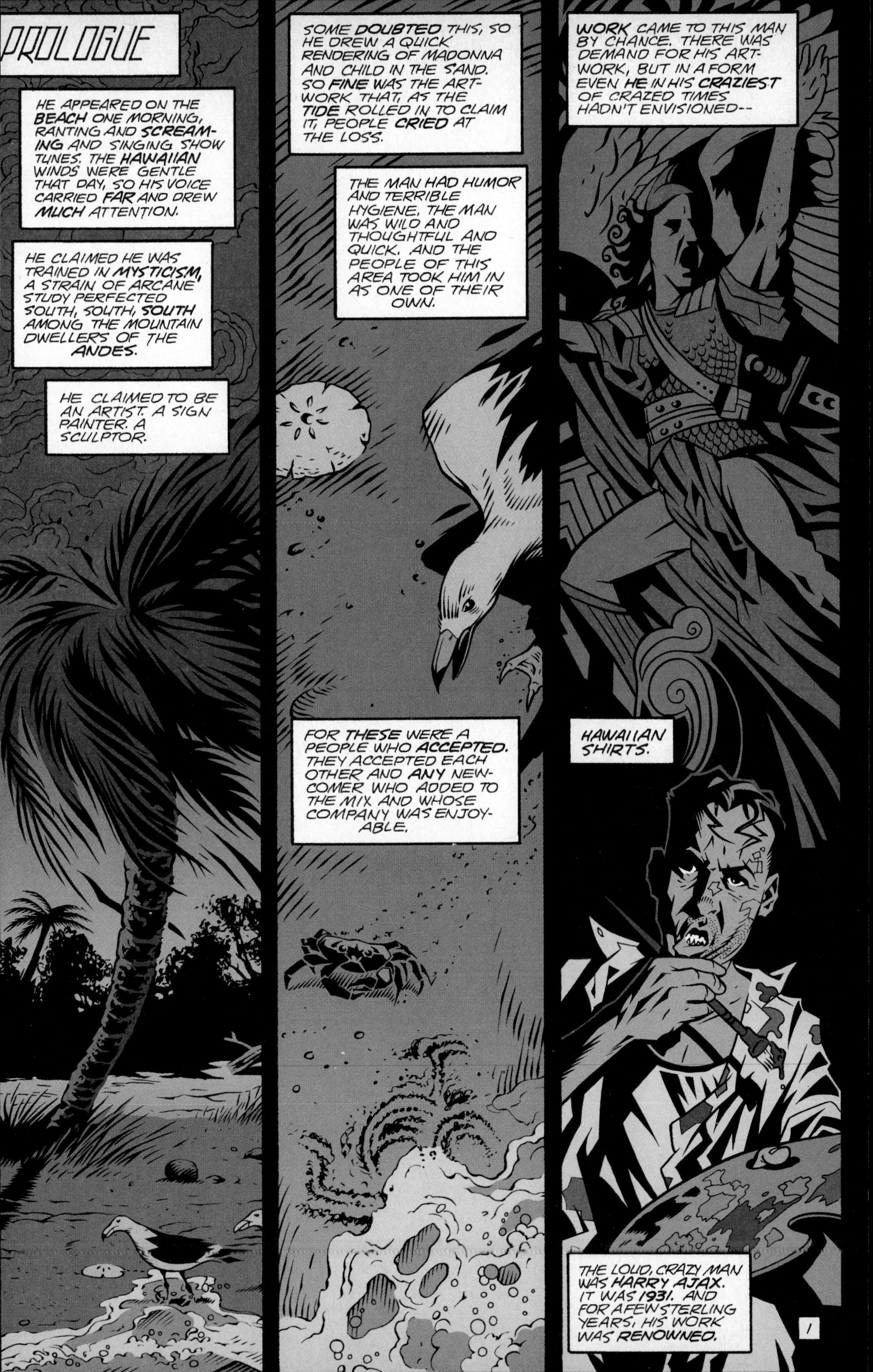
PROLOGUE
HE APPEARED ON THE BEACH ONE MORNING, RANTING AND SCREAMING AND SINGING SHOW TUNES. THE HAWAIIAN WINDS WERE GENTLE THAT DAY, SO HIS VOICE CARRIED FAR AND DREW MUCH ATTENTION.
HE CLAIMED HE WAS TRAINED IN MYSTICISM, A STRAIN OF ARCANE STUDY PERFECTED SOUTH, SOUTH, SOUTH AMONG THE MOUNTAIN DWELLERS OF THE ANDES.
HE CLAIMED TO BE AN ARTIST. A SIGN PAINTER. A SCULPTOR.
SOME DOUBTED THIS, SO HE DREW A QUICK RENDERING OF MADONNA AND CHILD IN THE SAND. SO FINE WAS THE ART-WORK THAT, AS THE TIDE ROLLED IN TO CLAIM IT, PEOPLE CRIED AT THE LOSS.
THE MAN HAD HUMOR AND TERRIBLE HYGIENE. THE MAN WAS WILD AND THOUGHTFUL AND QUICK, AND THE PEOPLE OF THIS AREA TOOK HIM IN AS ONE OF THEIR OWN.
FOR THESE WERE A PEOPLE WHO ACCEPTED. THEY ACCEPTED EACH OTHER AND ANY NEW-COMER WHO ADDED TO THE MIX AND WHOSE COMPANY WAS ENJOY-ABLE.
WORK CAME TO THIS MAN BY CHANCE. THERE WAS DEMAND FOR HIS ART-WORK, BUT IN A FORM EVEN HE IN HIS CRAZIEST OF CRAZED TIMES HADN'T ENVISIONED--
HAWAIIAN SHIRTS.
THE LOUD, CRAZY MAN WAS HARRY AJAX. IT WAS 1931. AND FOR A FEW STERLING YEARS, HIS WORK WAS RENOWNED.
1

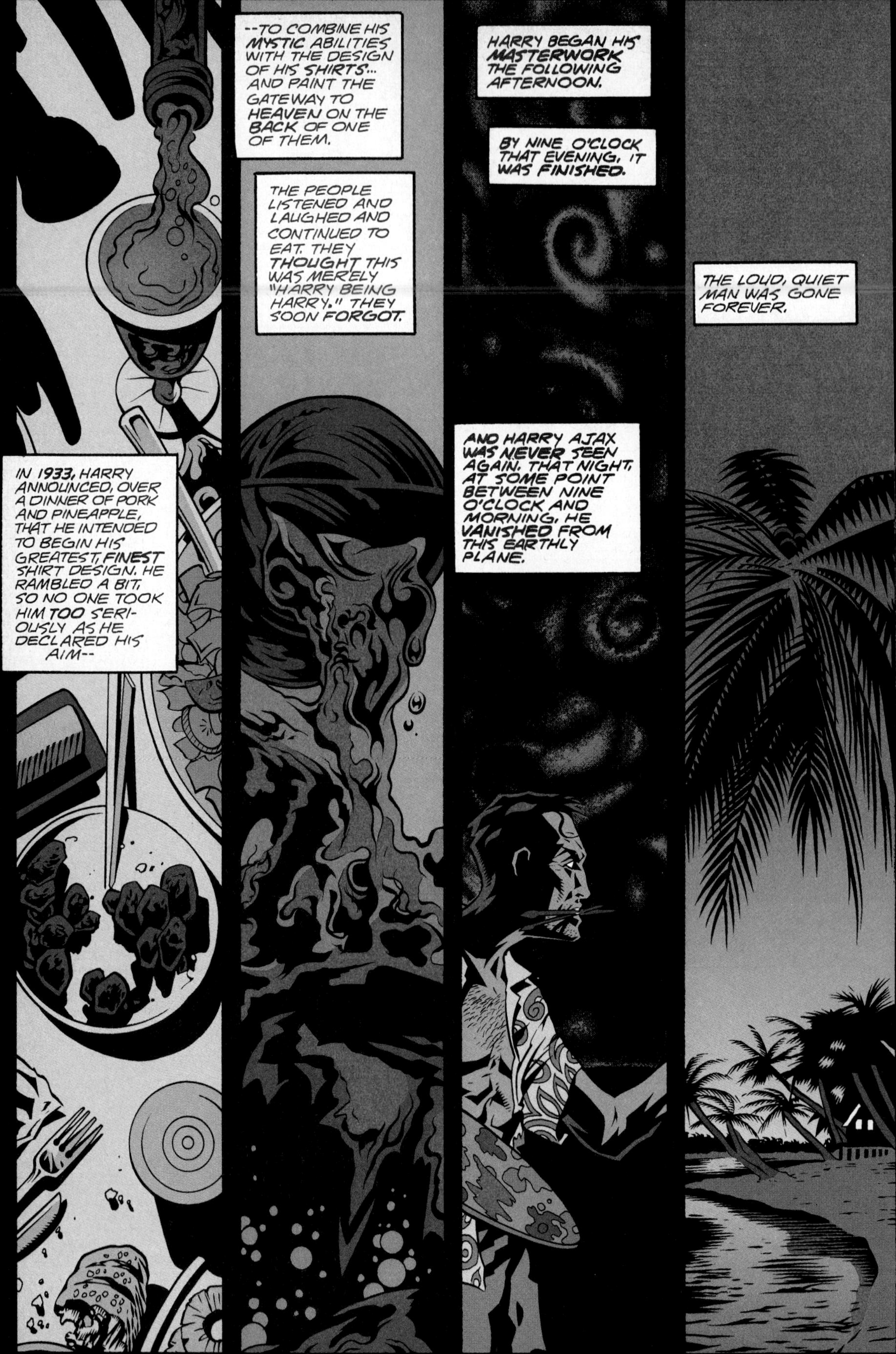
IN 1933, HARRY ANNOUNCED, OVER A DINNER OF PORK AND PINEAPPLE, THAT HE INTENDED TO BEGIN HIS GREATEST, FINEST SHIRT DESIGN. HE RAMBLED A BIT, SO NO ONE TOOK HIM TOO SERIOUSLY AS HE DECLARED HIS AIM--
--TO COMBINE HIS MYSTIC ABILITIES WITH THE DESIGN OF HIS SHIRTS... AND PAINT THE GATEWAY TO HEAVEN ON THE BACK OF ONE OF THEM.
THE PEOPLE LISTENED AND LAUGHED AND CONTINUED TO EAT. THEY THOUGHT THIS WAS MERELY "HARRY BEING HARRY." THEY SOON FORGOT.
HARRY BEGAN HIS MASTERWORK THE FOLLOWING AFTERNOON.
BY NINE O'CLOCK THAT EVENING, IT WAS FINISHED.
AND HARRY AJAX WAS NEVER SEEN AGAIN. THAT NIGHT, AT SOME POINT BETWEEN NINE O'CLOCK AND MORNING, HE VANISHED FROM THIS EARTHLY PLANE.
THE LOUD, QUIET MAN WAS GONE FOREVER.

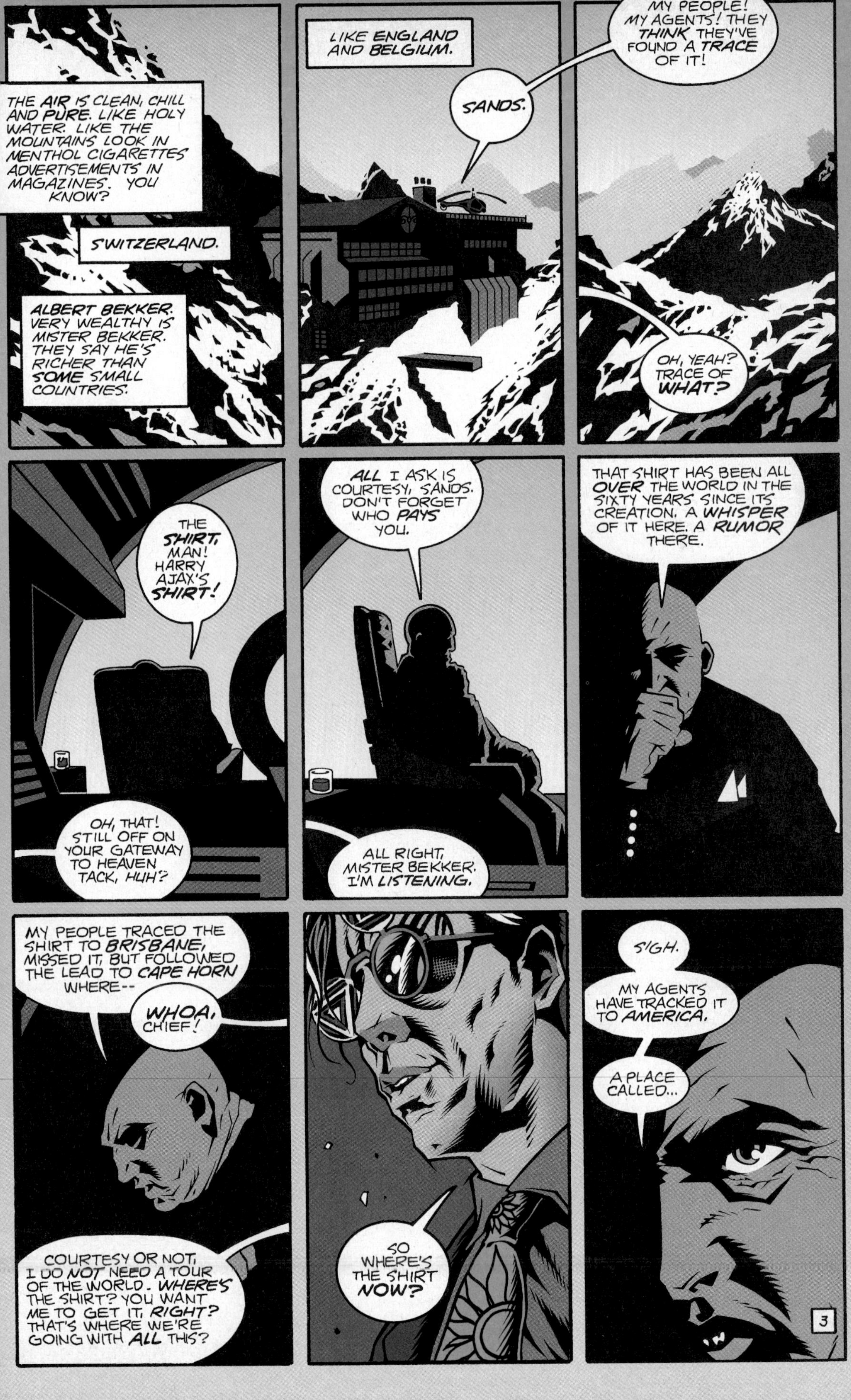
THE AIR IS CLEAN, CHILL AND PURE. LIKE HOLY WATER. LIKE THE MOUNTAINS LOOK IN MENTHOL CIGARETTES' ADVERTISEMENTS IN MAGAZINES. YOU KNOW?
SWITZERLAND.
ALBERT BEKKER. VERY WEALTHY IS MISTER BEKKER. THEY SAY HE'S RICHER THAN SOME SMALL COUNTRIES.
LIKE ENGLAND AND BELGIUM.
SANDS.
MY PEOPLE! MY AGENTS! THEY THINK THEY'VE FOUND A TRACE OF IT!
OH, YEAH? TRACE OF WHAT?
THE SHIRT, MAN! HARRY AJAX'S SHIRT!
OH, THAT! STILL OFF ON YOUR GATEWAY TO HEAVEN TACK, HUH?
ALL I ASK IS COURTESY, SANDS. DON'T FORGET WHO PAYS YOU.
ALL RIGHT, MISTER BEKKER. I'M LISTENING.
THAT SHIRT HAS BEEN ALL OVER THE WORLD IN THE SIXTY YEARS SINCE ITS CREATION. A WHISPER OF IT HERE. A RUMOR THERE.
MY PEOPLE TRACED THE SHIRT TO BRISBANE, MISSED IT, BUT FOLLOWED THE LEAD TO CAPE HORN WHERE--
WHOA, CHIEF!
COURTESY OR NOT, I DO NOT NEED A TOUR OF THE WORLD. WHERE'S THE SHIRT? YOU WANT ME TO GET IT, RIGHT? THAT'S WHERE WE'RE GOING WITH ALL THIS?
SO WHERE'S THE SHIRT NOW?
SIGH.
MY AGENTS HAVE TRACKED IT TO AMERICA.
A PLACE CALLED...
3

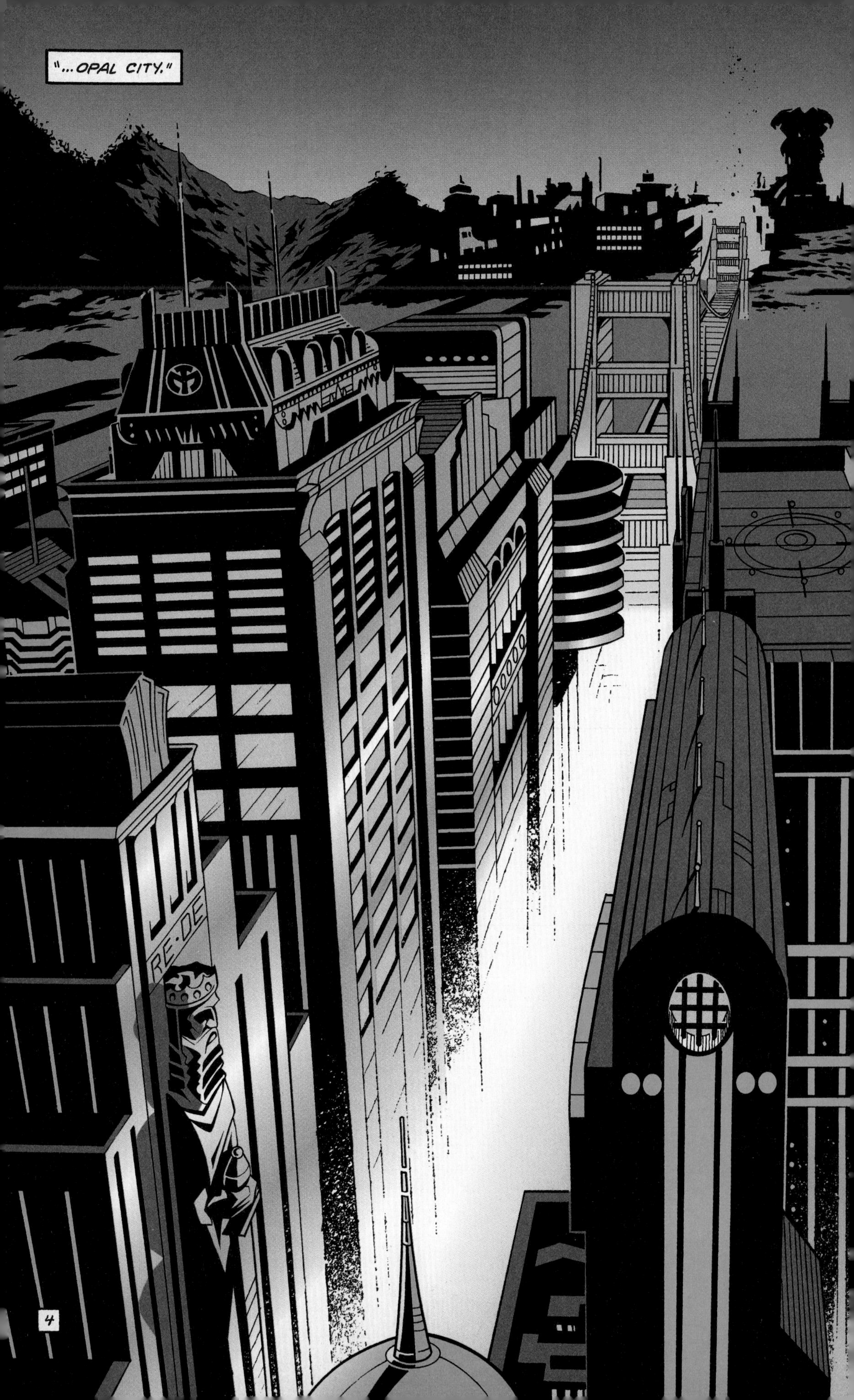
"...OPAL CITY."
RE·DE

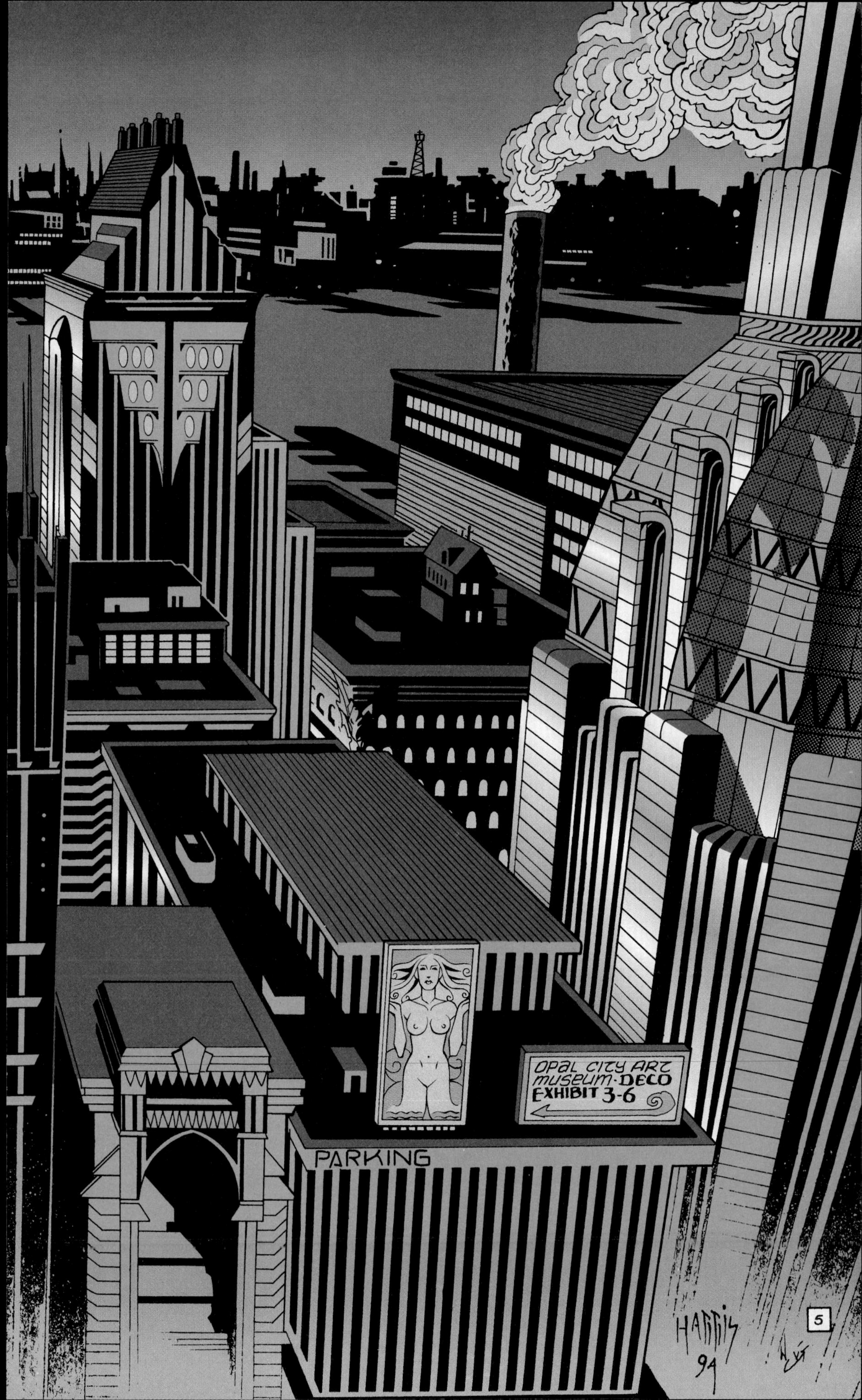
OPAL CITY ART
MUSEUM·DECO
EXHIBIT 3-6
PARKING
HARRIS
94

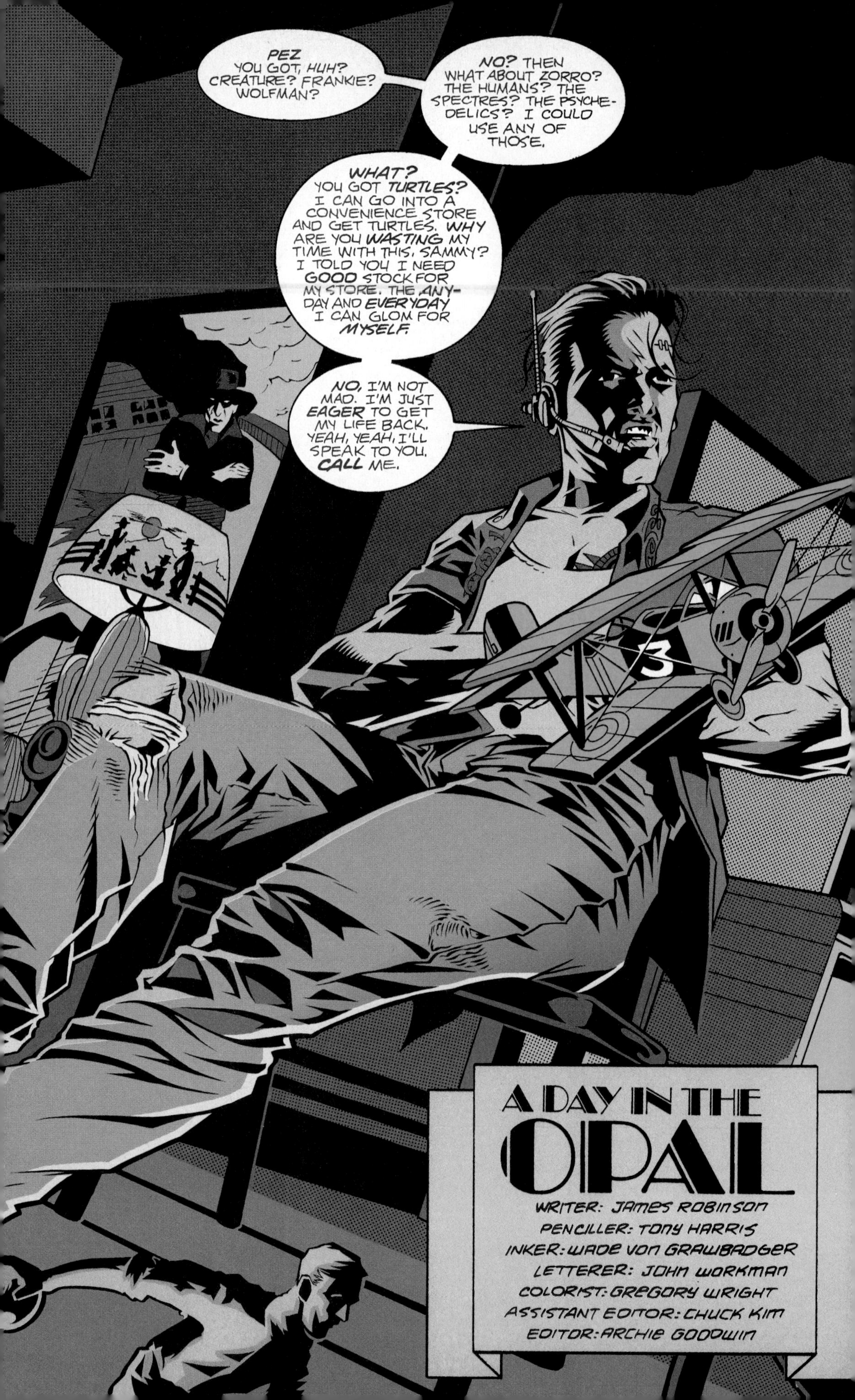
PEZ YOU GOT, HUH? CREATURE? FRANKIE? WOLFMAN?
NO? THEN WHAT ABOUT ZORRO? THE HUMANS? THE SPECTRES? THE PSYCHE-DELICS? I COULD USE ANY OF THOSE.
WHAT? YOU GOT TURTLES? I CAN GO INTO A CONVENIENCE STORE AND GET TURTLES. WHY ARE YOU WASTING MY TIME WITH THIS, SAMMY? I TOLD YOU I NEED GOOD STOCK FOR MY STORE. THE ANY-DAY AND EVERYDAY I CAN GLOM FOR MYSELF.
NO, I'M NOT MAD. I'M JUST EAGER TO GET MY LIFE BACK. YEAH, YEAH, I'LL SPEAK TO YOU. CALL ME.
A DAY IN THE OPAL
WRITER: JAMES ROBINSON
PENCILLER: TONY HARRIS
INKER: WADE VON GRAWBADGER
LETTERER: JOHN WORKMAN
COLORIST: GREGORY WRIGHT
ASSISTANT EDITOR: CHUCK KIM
EDITOR: ARCHIE GOODWIN

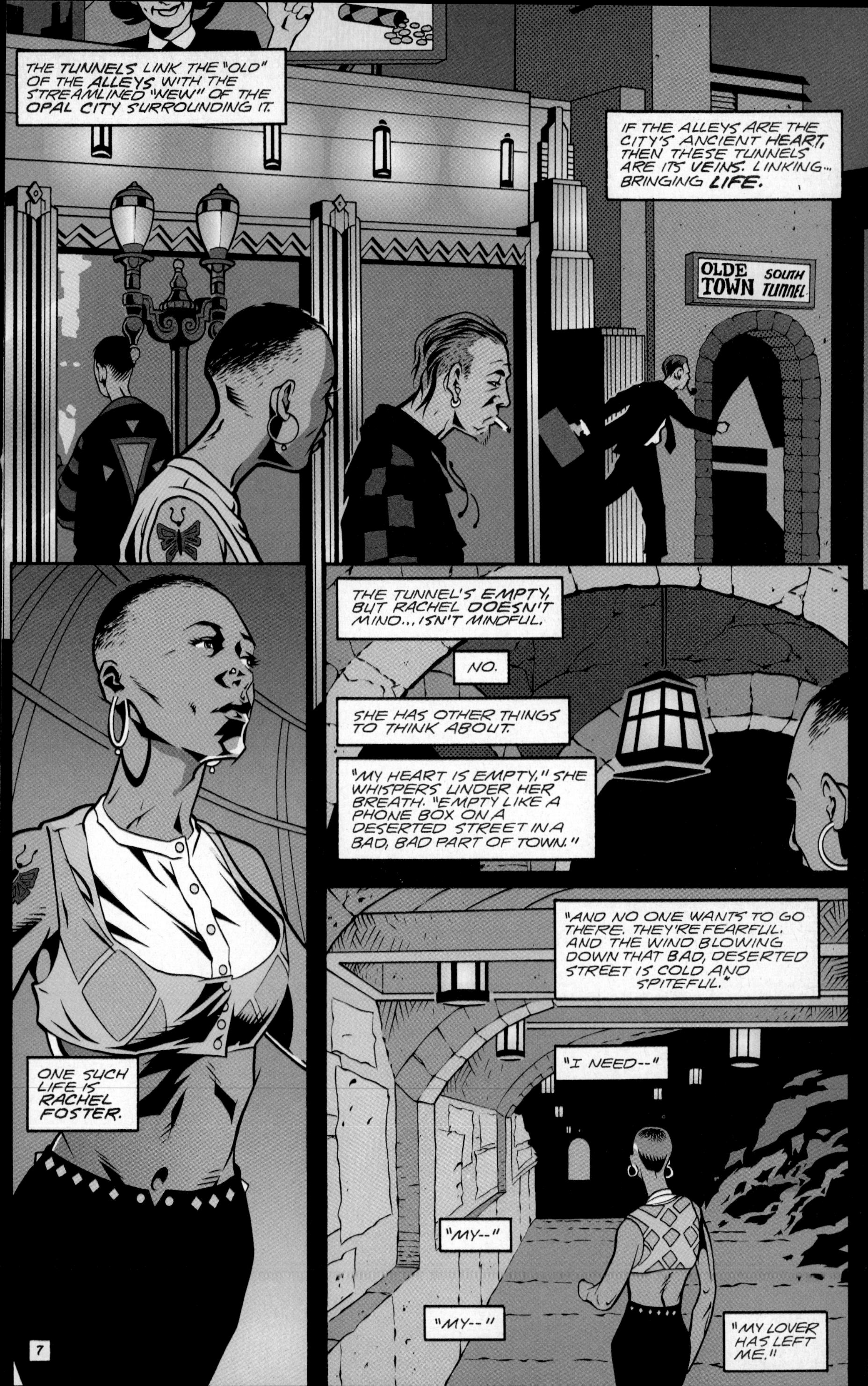
THE TUNNELS LINK THE "OLD" OF THE ALLEYS WITH THE STREAMLINED "NEW" OF THE OPAL CITY SURROUNDING IT.
IF THE ALLEYS ARE THE CITY'S ANCIENT HEART, THEN THESE TUNNELS ARE ITS VEINS. LINKING... BRINGING LIFE.
OLDE TOWN SOUTH TUNNEL
ONE SUCH LIFE IS RACHEL FOSTER.
THE TUNNEL'S EMPTY, BUT RACHEL DOESN'T MIND... ISN'T MINDFUL.
NO.
SHE HAS OTHER THINGS TO THINK ABOUT.
"MY HEART IS EMPTY," SHE WHISPERS UNDER HER BREATH. "EMPTY LIKE A PHONE BOX ON A DESERTED STREET IN A BAD, BAD PART OF TOWN."
"AND NO ONE WANTS TO GO THERE. THEY'RE FEARFUL. AND THE WIND BLOWING DOWN THAT BAD, DESERTED STREET IS COLD AND SPITEFUL."
"I NEED--"
"MY--"
"MY--"
"MY LOVER HAS LEFT ME."

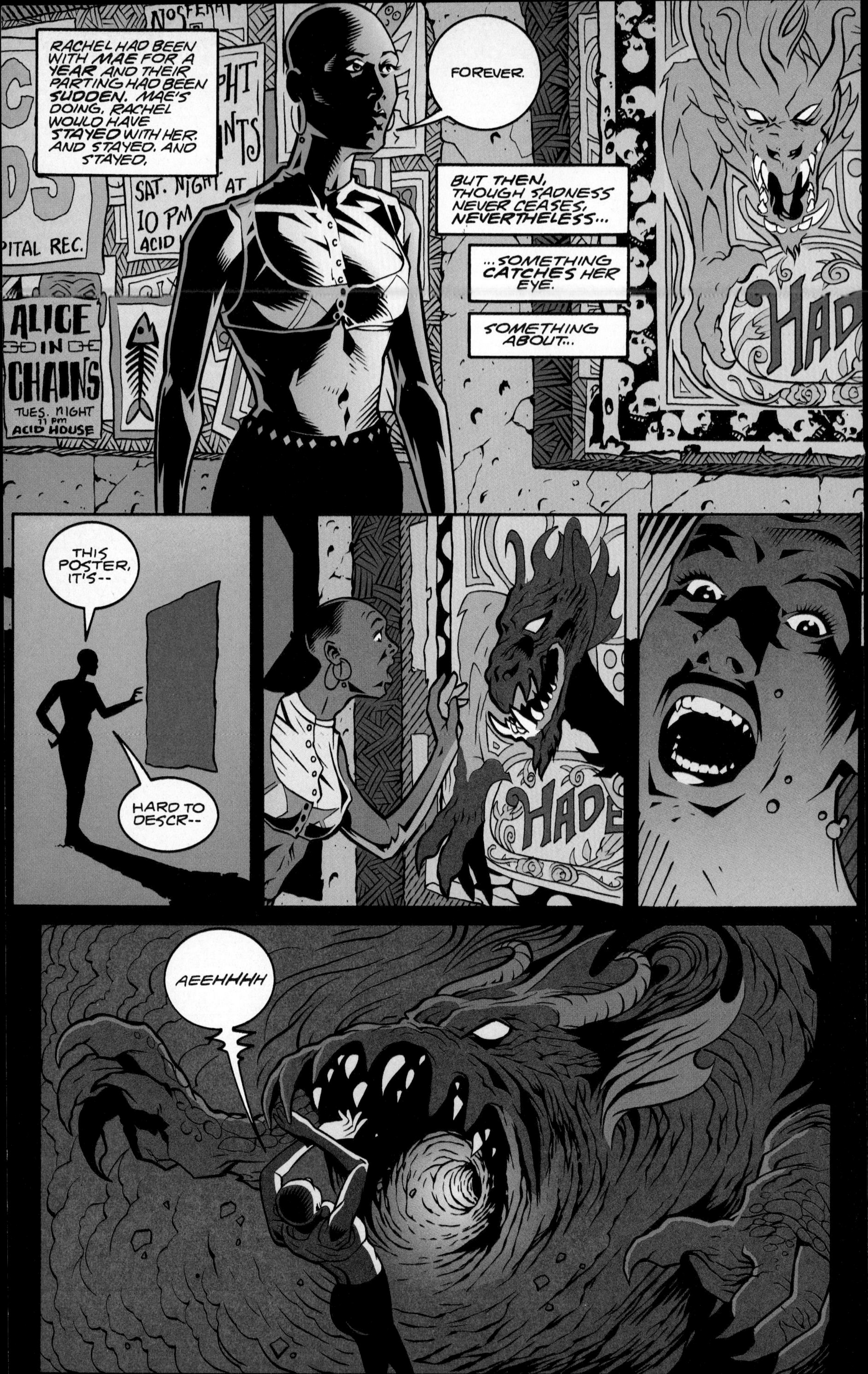
RACHEL HAD BEEN WITH MAE FOR A YEAR AND THEIR PARTING HAD BEEN SUDDEN. MAE'S DOING. RACHEL WOULD HAVE STAYED WITH HER. AND STAYED. AND STAYED.
FOREVER.
BUT THEN, THOUGH SADNESS NEVER CEASES, NEVERTHELESS...
...SOMETHING CATCHES HER EYE.
SOMETHING ABOUT...
NOSFERATU
SAT. NIGHT AT 10 PM ACID
PITAL REC.
ALICE IN CHAINS TUES. NIGHT 11 pm ACID HOUSE
HADE
THIS POSTER, IT'S--
HARD TO DESCR--
HADE
AEEHHHH

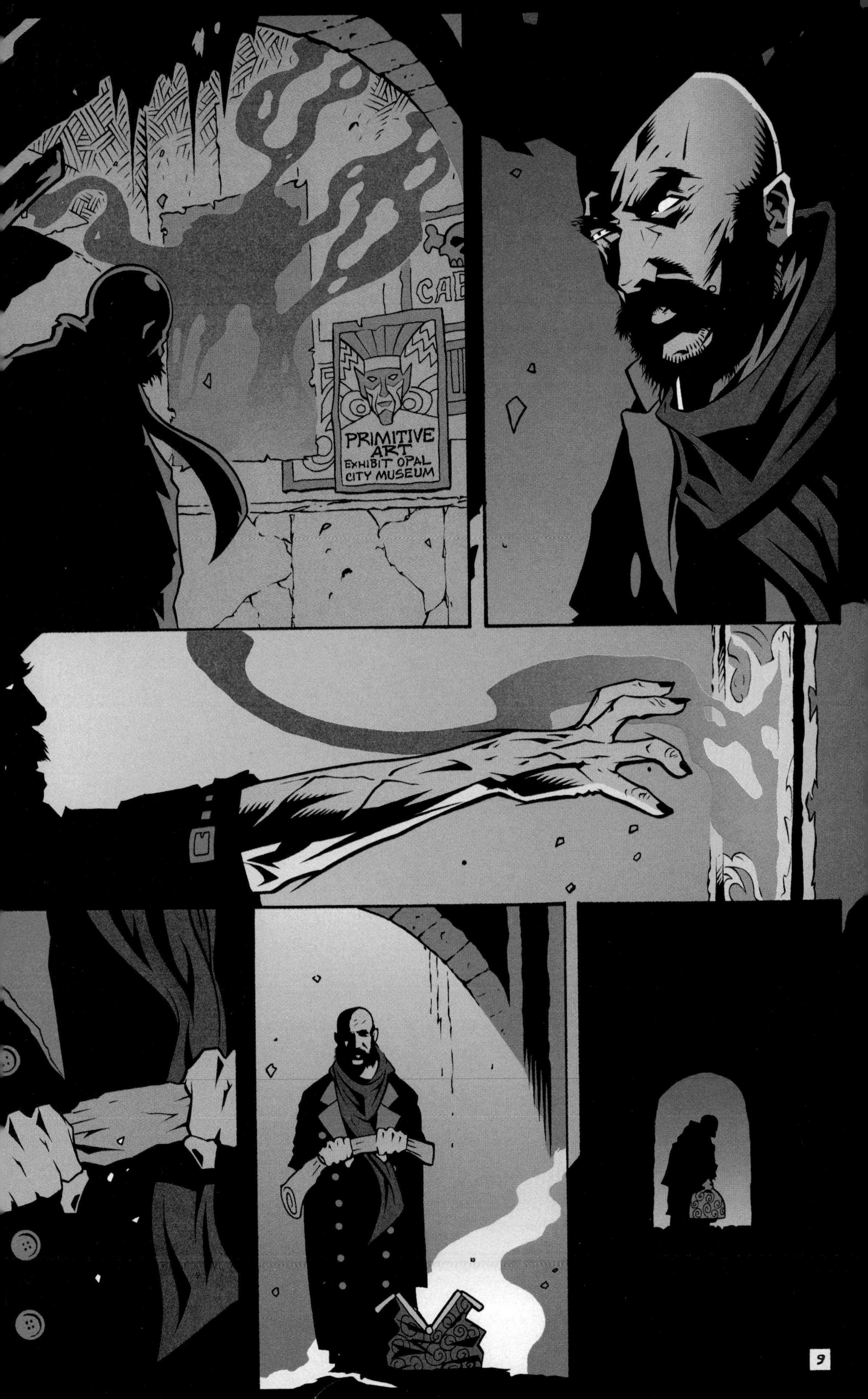
CAB
PRIMITIVE ART
EXHIBIT OPAL CITY MUSEUM

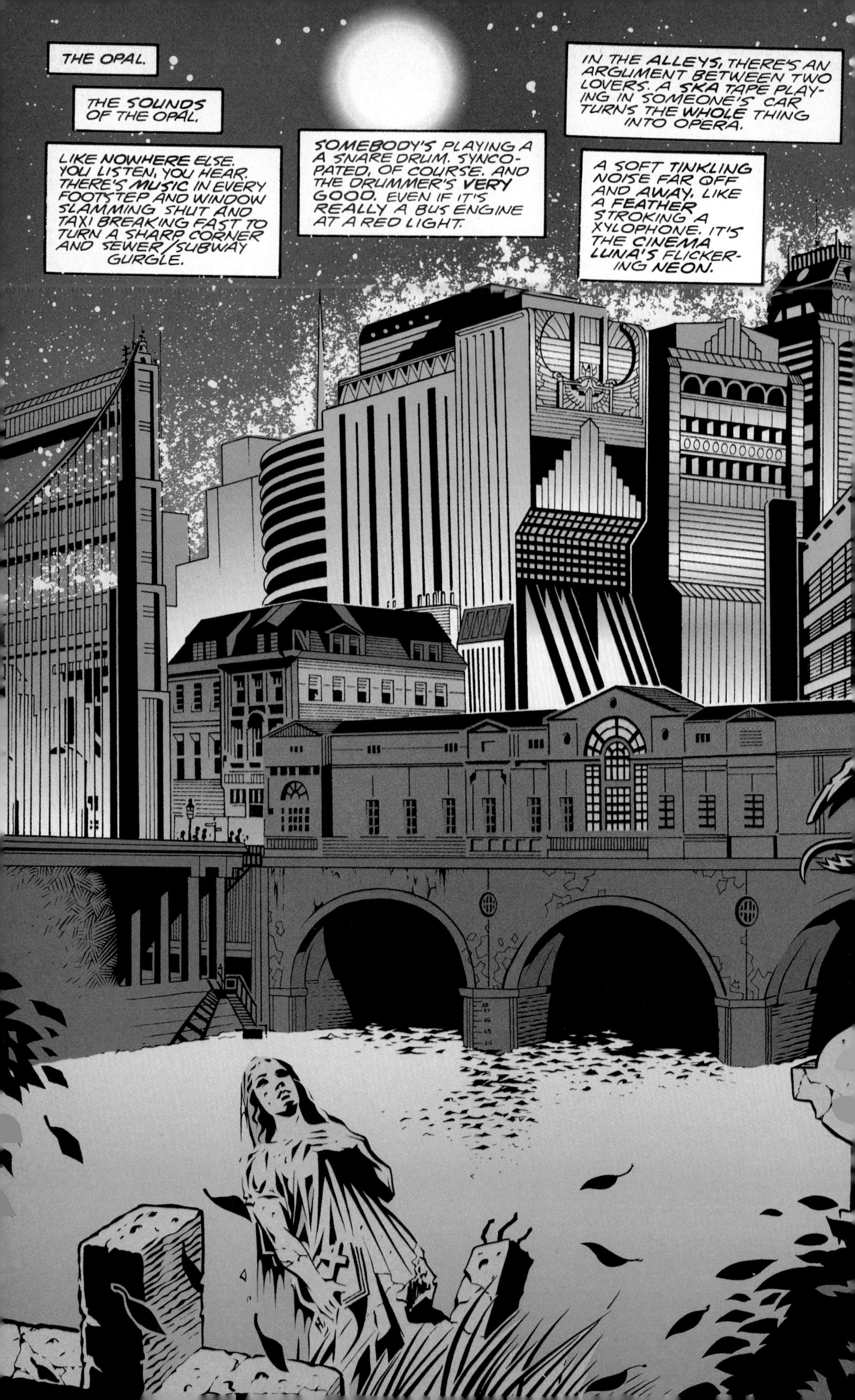
THE OPAL.
THE SOUNDS OF THE OPAL.
LIKE NOWHERE ELSE. YOU LISTEN, YOU HEAR. THERE'S MUSIC IN EVERY FOOTSTEP AND WINDOW SLAMMING SHUT AND TAXI BREAKING FAST TO TURN A SHARP CORNER AND SEWER/SUBWAY GURGLE.
SOMEBODY'S PLAYING A A SNARE DRUM. SYNCOPATED, OF COURSE. AND THE DRUMMER'S VERY GOOD. EVEN IF IT'S REALLY A BUS ENGINE AT A RED LIGHT.
IN THE ALLEYS, THERE'S AN ARGUMENT BETWEEN TWO LOVERS. A SKA TAPE PLAYING IN SOMEONE'S CAR TURNS THE WHOLE THING INTO OPERA.
A SOFT TINKLING NOISE FAR OFF AND AWAY, LIKE A FEATHER STROKING A XYLOPHONE. IT'S THE CINEMA LUNA'S FLICKERING NEON.

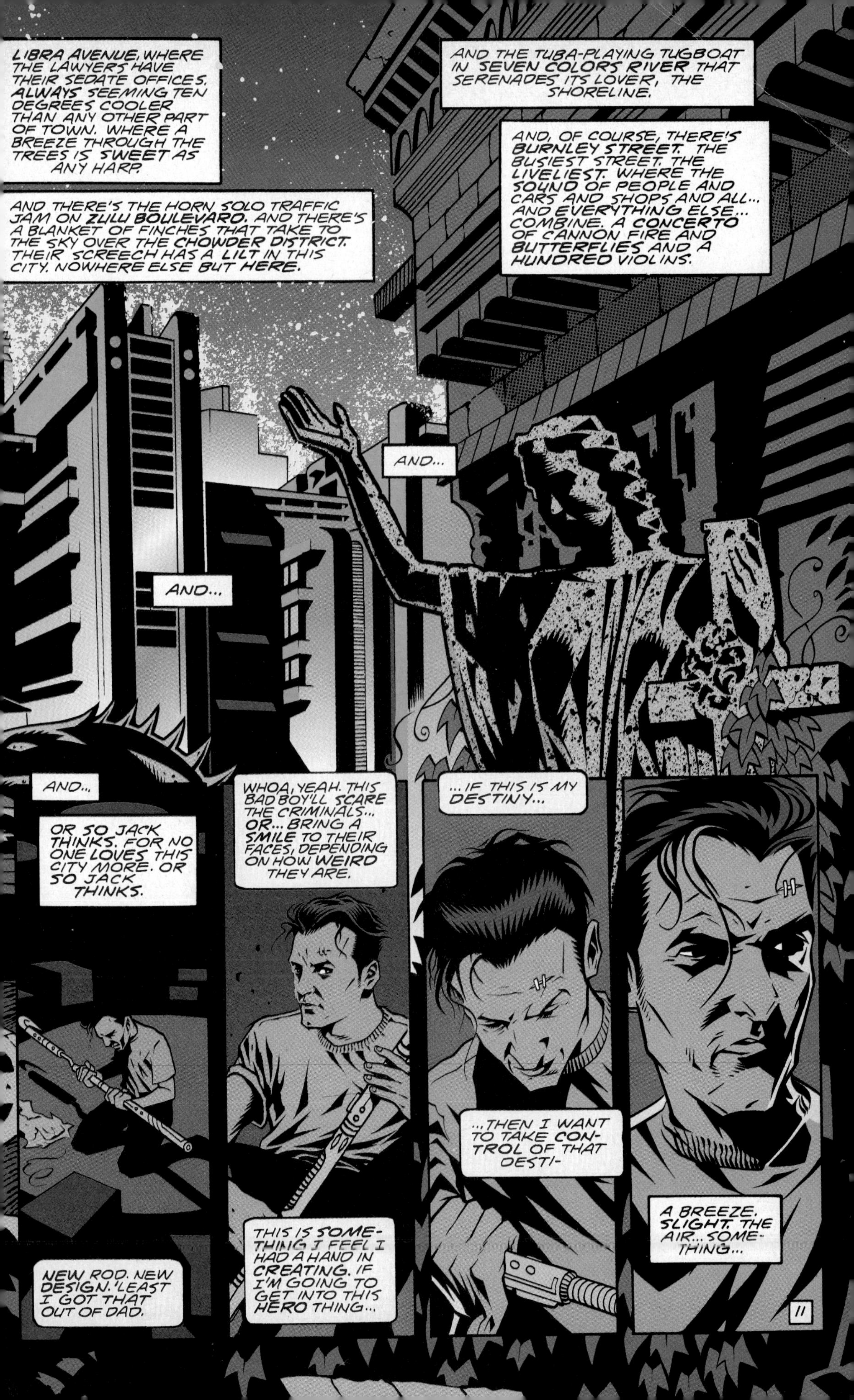
LIBRA AVENUE, WHERE THE LAWYERS HAVE THEIR SEDATE OFFICES. ALWAYS SEEMING TEN DEGREES COOLER THAN ANY OTHER PART OF TOWN. WHERE A BREEZE THROUGH THE TREES IS SWEET AS ANY HARP.
AND THERE'S THE HORN SOLO TRAFFIC JAM ON ZULU BOULEVARD. AND THERE'S A BLANKET OF FINCHES THAT TAKE TO THE SKY OVER THE CHOWDER DISTRICT. THEIR SCREECH HAS A LILT IN THIS CITY. NOWHERE ELSE BUT HERE.
AND THE TUBA-PLAYING TUGBOAT IN SEVEN COLORS RIVER THAT SERENADES ITS LOVER, THE SHORELINE.
AND, OF COURSE, THERE'S BURNLEY STREET. THE BUSIEST STREET. THE LIVELIEST. WHERE THE SOUND OF PEOPLE AND CARS AND SHOPS AND ALL... AND EVERYTHING ELSE... COMBINE. A CONCERTO OF CANNON FIRE AND BUTTERFLIES AND A HUNDRED VIOLINS.
AND...
AND...
AND...
OR SO JACK THINKS. FOR NO ONE LOVES THIS CITY MORE. OR SO JACK THINKS.
NEW ROD. NEW DESIGN. 'LEAST I GOT THAT OUT OF DAD.
WHOA, YEAH. THIS BAD BOY'LL SCARE THE CRIMINALS... OR... BRING A SMILE TO THEIR FACES, DEPENDING ON HOW WEIRD THEY ARE.
THIS IS SOMETHING I FEEL I HAD A HAND IN CREATING. IF I'M GOING TO GET INTO THIS HERO THING...
...IF THIS IS MY DESTINY...
...THEN I WANT TO TAKE CONTROL OF THAT DESTI-
A BREEZE. SLIGHT. THE AIR... SOMETHING...

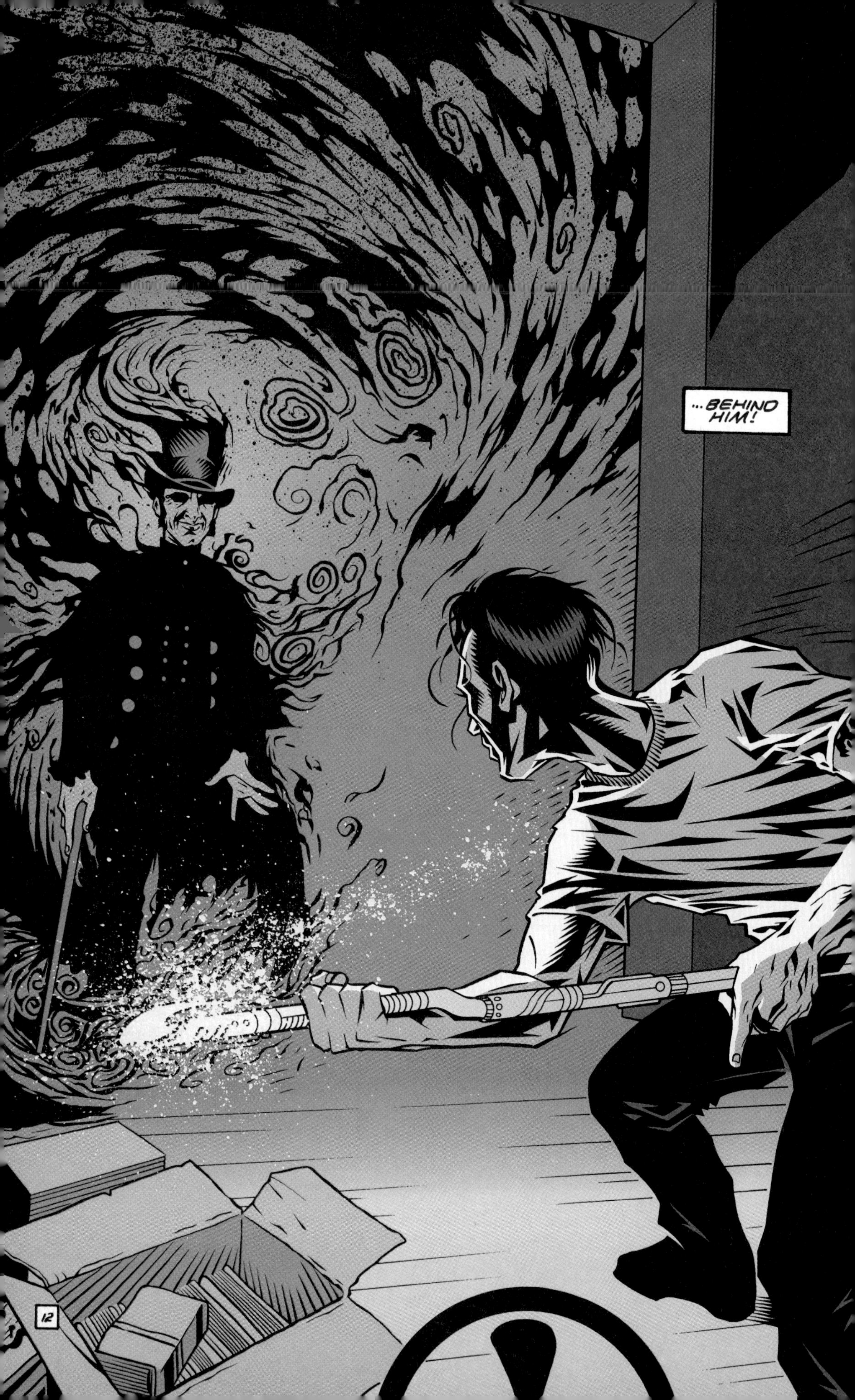
...BEHIND HIM!
12

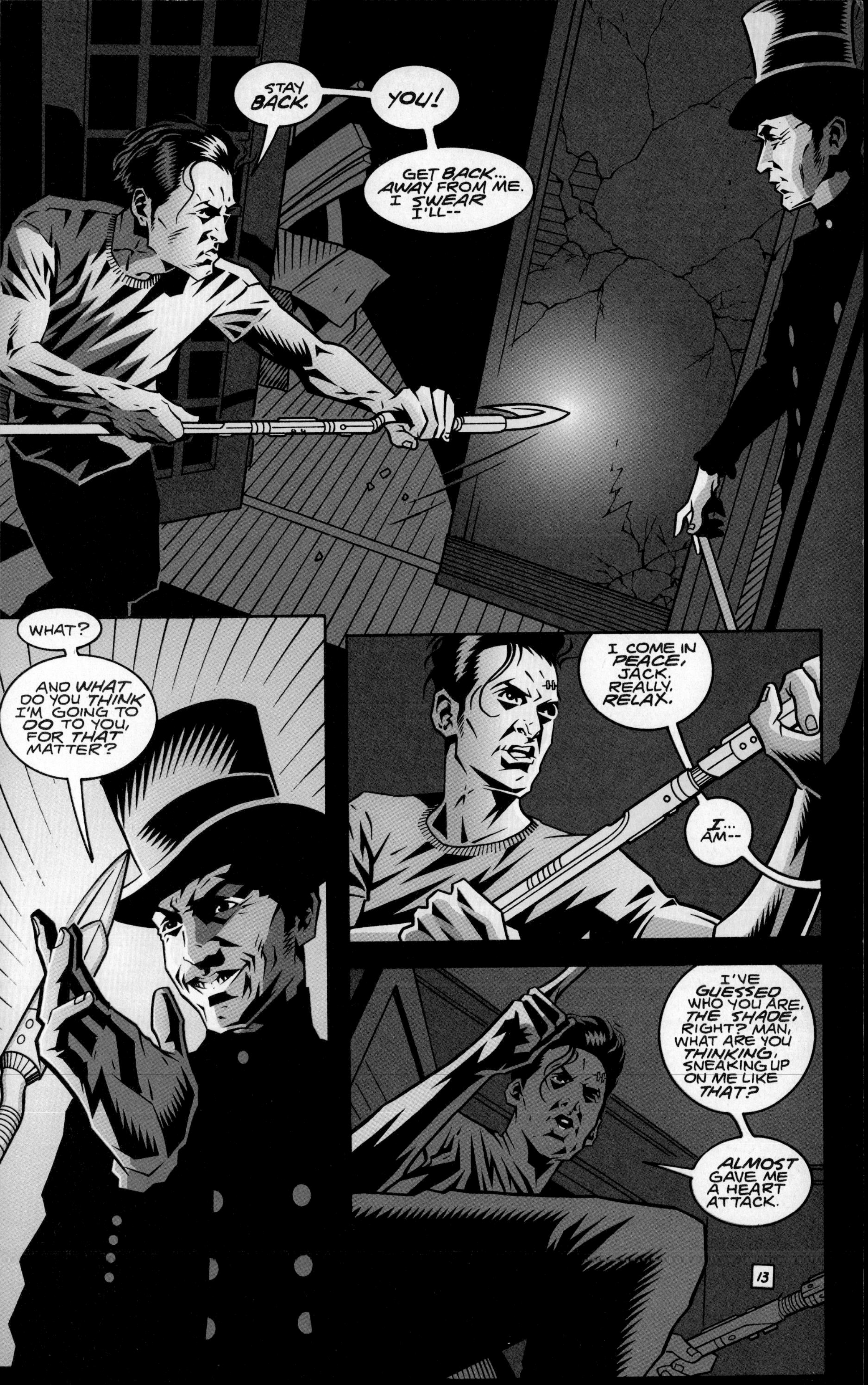
STAY BACK.
YOU!
GET BACK... AWAY FROM ME. I SWEAR I'LL--
WHAT?
AND WHAT DO YOU THINK I'M GOING TO DO TO YOU, FOR THAT MATTER?
I COME IN PEACE, JACK. REALLY. RELAX.
I... AM--
I'VE GUESSED WHO YOU ARE. THE SHADE, RIGHT? MAN, WHAT ARE YOU THINKING, SNEAKING UP ON ME LIKE THAT?
ALMOST GAVE ME A HEART ATTACK.

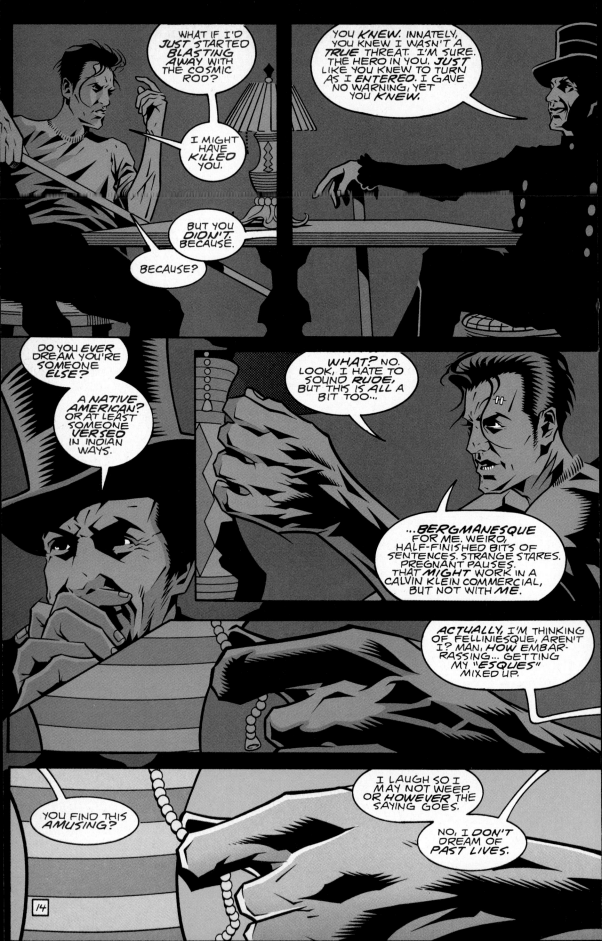

WHAT IF I'D *JUST* STARTED *BLASTING* AWAY WITH THE COSMIC ROD?

I MIGHT HAVE *KILLED* YOU.

BUT YOU *DIDN'T.* BECAUSE.

BECAUSE?

YOU *KNEW.* INNATELY, YOU KNEW I WASN'T A *TRUE* THREAT. I'M SURE. THE HERO IN YOU. *JUST* LIKE YOU KNEW TO TURN AS I *ENTERED.* I GAVE NO WARNING, YET YOU *KNEW.*

DO YOU *EVER* DREAM YOU'RE SOMEONE *ELSE?*

A NATIVE AMERICAN? OR AT LEAST SOMEONE *VERSED* IN INDIAN WAYS.

WHAT? NO. LOOK, I HATE TO SOUND *RUDE,* BUT THIS IS ALL A BIT TOO...

...*BERGMANESQUE* FOR ME. WEIRD, HALF-FINISHED BITS OF SENTENCES. STRANGE STARES. PREGNANT PAUSES. THAT *MIGHT* WORK IN A CALVIN KLEIN COMMERCIAL, BUT NOT WITH *ME.*

ACTUALLY, I'M THINKING OF FELLINIESQUE, AREN'T I? MAN, HOW EMBAR-RASSING... GETTING MY *"ESQUES"* MIXED UP.

YOU FIND THIS *AMUSING?*

I LAUGH SO I MAY NOT WEEP OR *HOWEVER* THE SAYING GOES.

NO, I *DON'T* DREAM OF *PAST LIVES.*

14

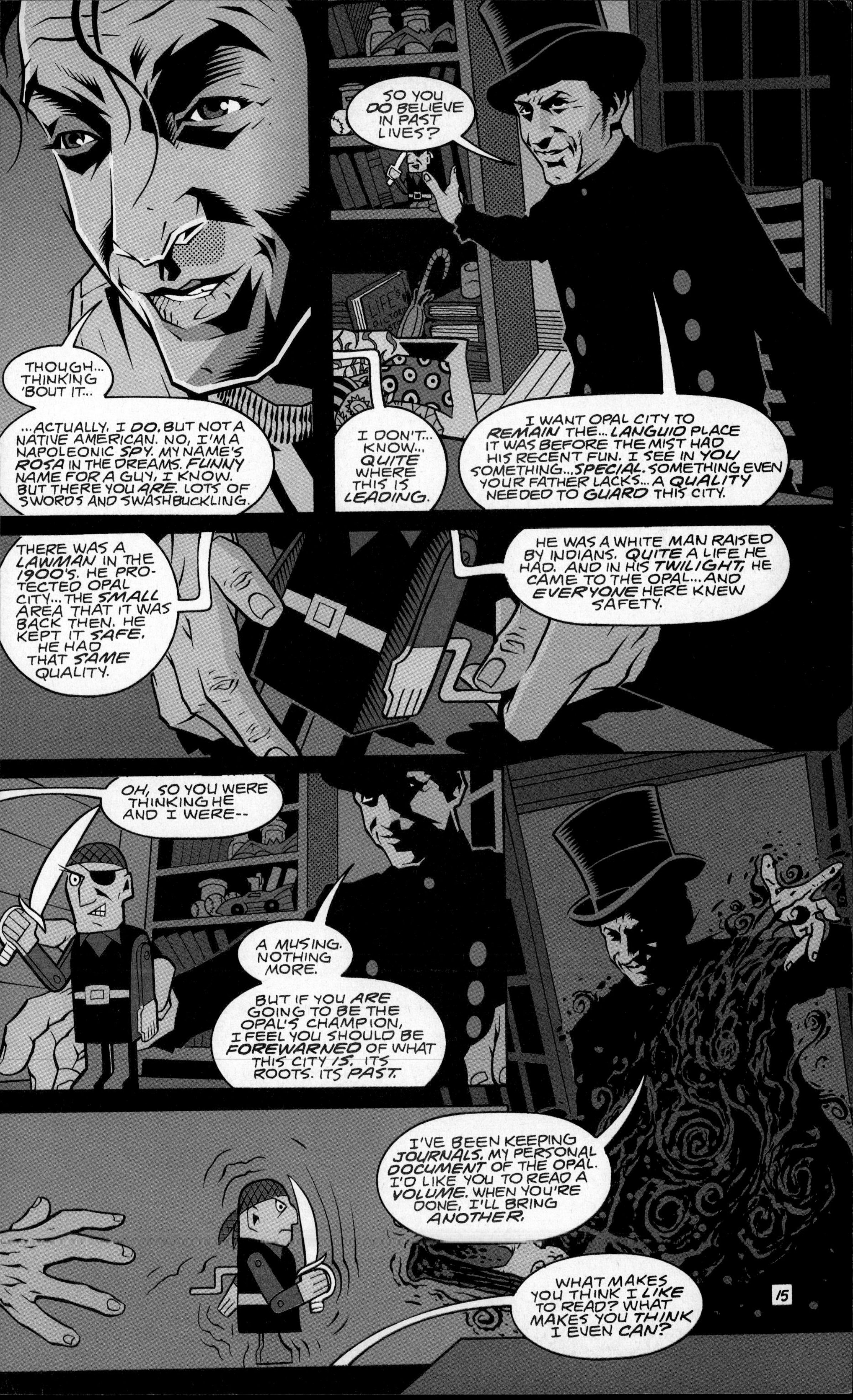

SO YOU DO BELIEVE IN PAST LIVES?
THOUGH... THINKING 'BOUT IT...
...ACTUALLY, I DO, BUT NOT A NATIVE AMERICAN. NO, I'M A NAPOLEONIC SPY. MY NAME'S ROSA IN THE DREAMS. FUNNY NAME FOR A GUY, I KNOW. BUT THERE YOU ARE. LOTS OF SWORDS AND SWASHBUCKLING.
I DON'T... KNOW... QUITE WHERE THIS IS LEADING.
I WANT OPAL CITY TO REMAIN THE... LANGUID PLACE IT WAS BEFORE THE MIST HAD HIS RECENT FUN. I SEE IN YOU SOMETHING... SPECIAL. SOMETHING EVEN YOUR FATHER LACKS... A QUALITY NEEDED TO GUARD THIS CITY.
THERE WAS A LAWMAN IN THE 1900'S. HE PROTECTED OPAL CITY... THE SMALL AREA THAT IT WAS BACK THEN. HE KEPT IT SAFE. HE HAD THAT SAME QUALITY.
HE WAS A WHITE MAN RAISED BY INDIANS. QUITE A LIFE HE HAD. AND IN HIS TWILIGHT, HE CAME TO THE OPAL... AND EVERYONE HERE KNEW SAFETY.
OH, SO YOU WERE THINKING HE AND I WERE--
A MUSING. NOTHING MORE.
BUT IF YOU ARE GOING TO BE THE OPAL'S CHAMPION, I FEEL YOU SHOULD BE FOREWARNED OF WHAT THIS CITY IS. ITS ROOTS. ITS PAST.
I'VE BEEN KEEPING JOURNALS. MY PERSONAL DOCUMENT OF THE OPAL. I'D LIKE YOU TO READ A VOLUME. WHEN YOU'RE DONE, I'LL BRING ANOTHER.
WHAT MAKES YOU THINK I LIKE TO READ? WHAT MAKES YOU THINK I EVEN CAN?

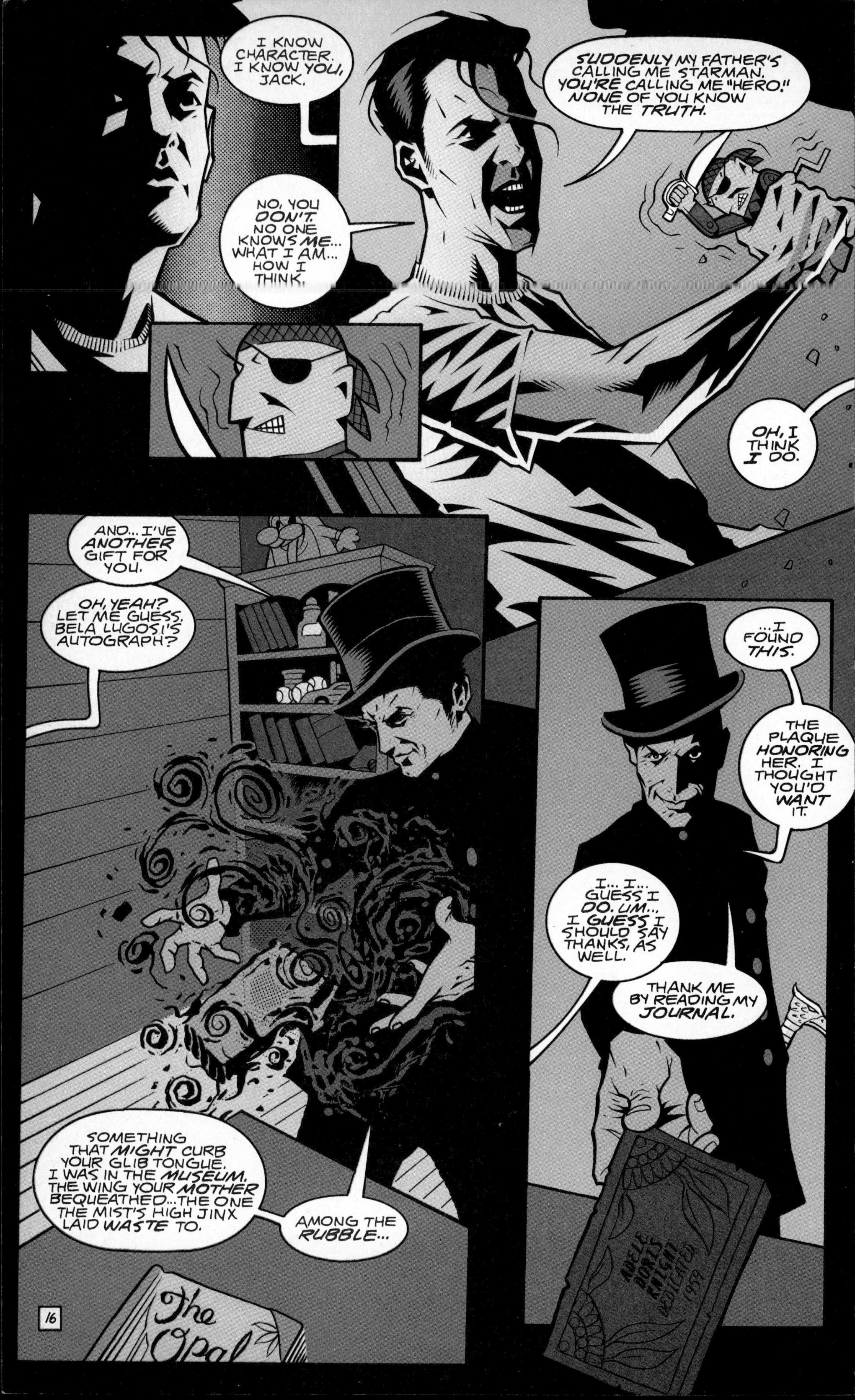

I KNOW CHARACTER. I KNOW YOU, JACK.
SUDDENLY MY FATHER'S CALLING ME STARMAN. YOU'RE CALLING ME "HERO." NONE OF YOU KNOW THE TRUTH.
NO, YOU DON'T. NO ONE KNOWS ME... WHAT I AM... HOW I THINK.
OH, I THINK I DO.
AND... I'VE ANOTHER GIFT FOR YOU.
OH, YEAH? LET ME GUESS. BELA LUGOSI'S AUTOGRAPH?
SOMETHING THAT MIGHT CURB YOUR GLIB TONGUE. I WAS IN THE MUSEUM. THE WING YOUR MOTHER BEQUEATHED... THE ONE THE MIST'S HIGH JINX LAID WASTE TO.
AMONG THE RUBBLE...
...I FOUND THIS.
THE PLAQUE HONORING HER. I THOUGHT YOU'D WANT IT.
I... I... GUESS I DO. UM... I GUESS I SHOULD SAY THANKS, AS WELL.
THANK ME BY READING MY JOURNAL.
The Opal
ADELE DORIS KNIGHT DEDICATED 1959

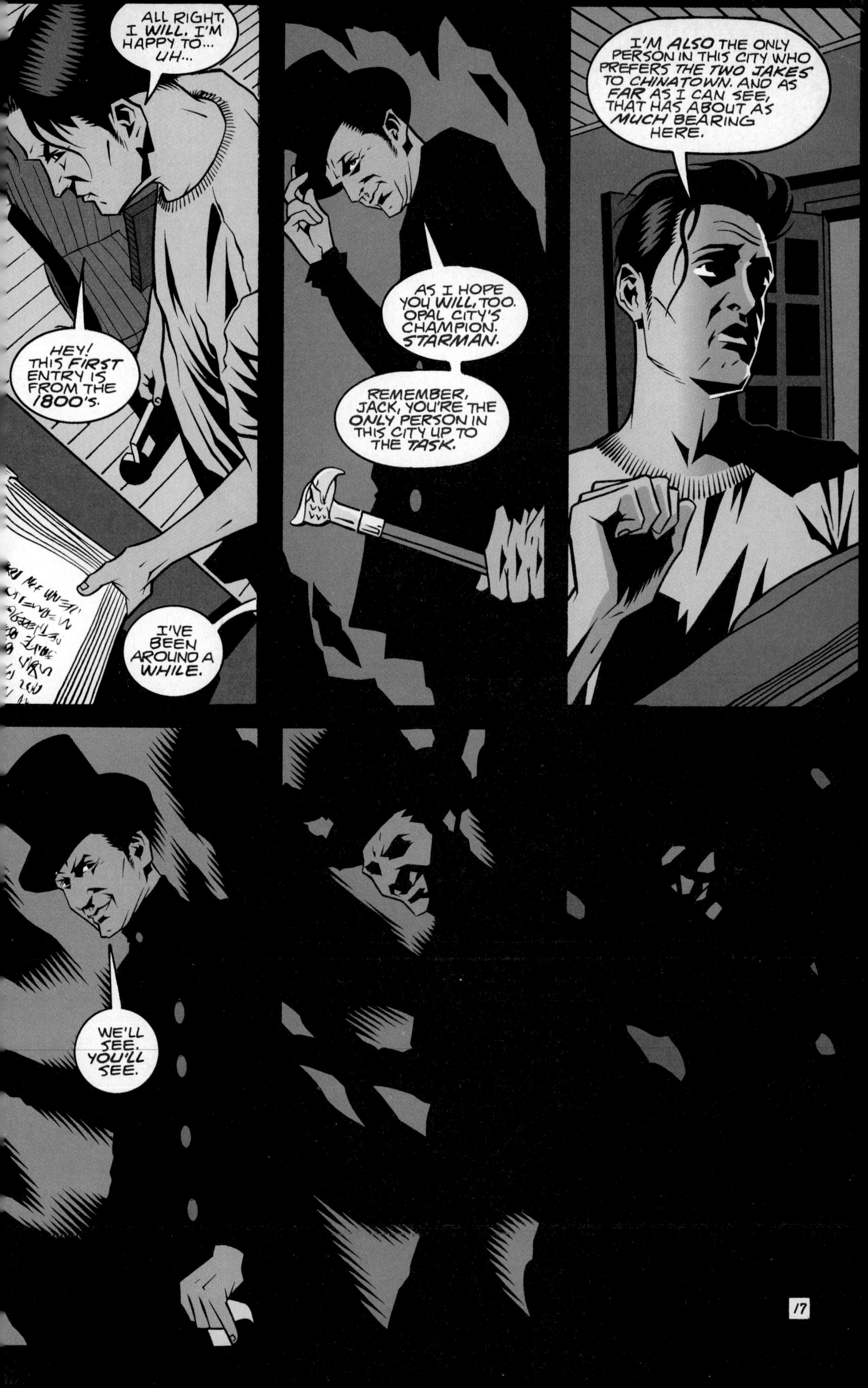
ALL RIGHT, I WILL. I'M HAPPY TO... UH...
HEY! THIS FIRST ENTRY IS FROM THE 1800'S.
I'VE BEEN AROUND A WHILE.
AS I HOPE YOU WILL, TOO. OPAL CITY'S CHAMPION. STARMAN.
REMEMBER, JACK, YOU'RE THE ONLY PERSON IN THIS CITY UP TO THE TASK.
I'M ALSO THE ONLY PERSON IN THIS CITY WHO PREFERS THE TWO JAKES TO CHINATOWN. AND AS FAR AS I CAN SEE, THAT HAS ABOUT AS MUCH BEARING HERE.
WE'LL SEE. YOU'LL SEE.

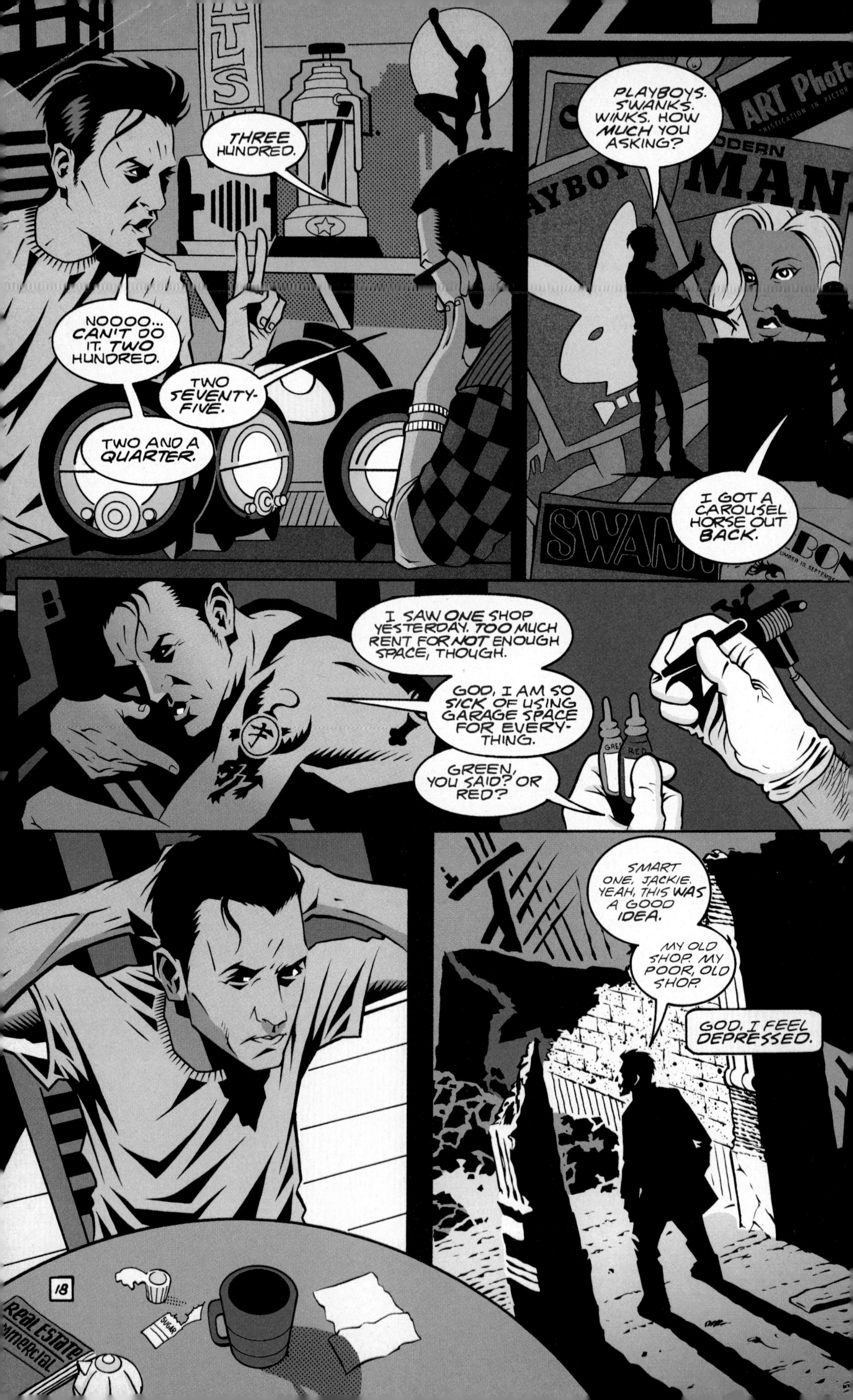
THREE HUNDRED.
NOOOO... CAN'T DO IT. TWO HUNDRED.
TWO SEVENTY-FIVE.
TWO AND A QUARTER.
PLAYBOYS. SWANKS. WINKS. HOW MUCH YOU ASKING?
I GOT A CAROUSEL HORSE OUT BACK.
I SAW ONE SHOP YESTERDAY. TOO MUCH RENT FOR NOT ENOUGH SPACE, THOUGH.
GOD, I AM SO SICK OF USING GARAGE SPACE FOR EVERY-THING.
GREEN, YOU SAID? OR RED?
SMART ONE, JACKIE. YEAH, THIS WAS A GOOD IDEA.
MY OLD SHOP. MY POOR, OLD SHOP.
GOD, I FEEL DEPRESSED.
REAL ESTATE
18

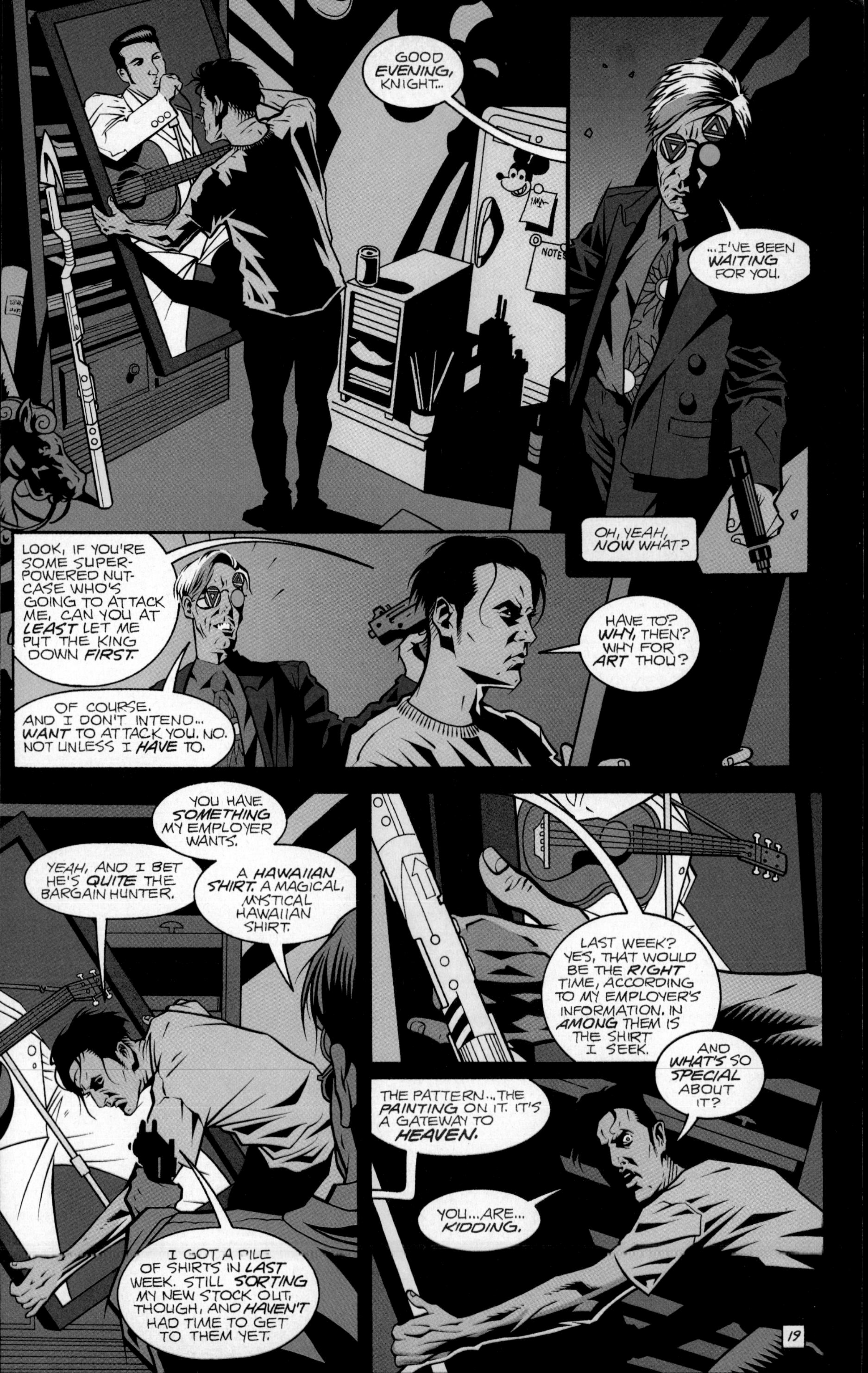
GOOD EVENING, KNIGHT...
...I'VE BEEN WAITING FOR YOU.
OH, YEAH, NOW WHAT?
LOOK, IF YOU'RE SOME SUPER-POWERED NUT-CASE WHO'S GOING TO ATTACK ME, CAN YOU AT LEAST LET ME PUT THE KING DOWN FIRST.
OF COURSE. AND I DON'T INTEND... WANT TO ATTACK YOU. NO. NOT UNLESS I HAVE TO.
HAVE TO? WHY, THEN? WHY FOR ART THOU?
YOU HAVE SOMETHING MY EMPLOYER WANTS.
YEAH, AND I BET HE'S QUITE THE BARGAIN HUNTER.
A HAWAIIAN SHIRT. A MAGICAL, MYSTICAL HAWAIIAN SHIRT.
I GOT A PILE OF SHIRTS IN LAST WEEK. STILL SORTING MY NEW STOCK OUT, THOUGH, AND HAVEN'T HAD TIME TO GET TO THEM YET.
LAST WEEK? YES, THAT WOULD BE THE RIGHT TIME, ACCORDING TO MY EMPLOYER'S INFORMATION. IN AMONG THEM IS THE SHIRT I SEEK.
AND WHAT'S SO SPECIAL ABOUT IT?
THE PATTERN... THE PAINTING ON IT. IT'S A GATEWAY TO HEAVEN.
YOU... ARE... KIDDING.
NOTES

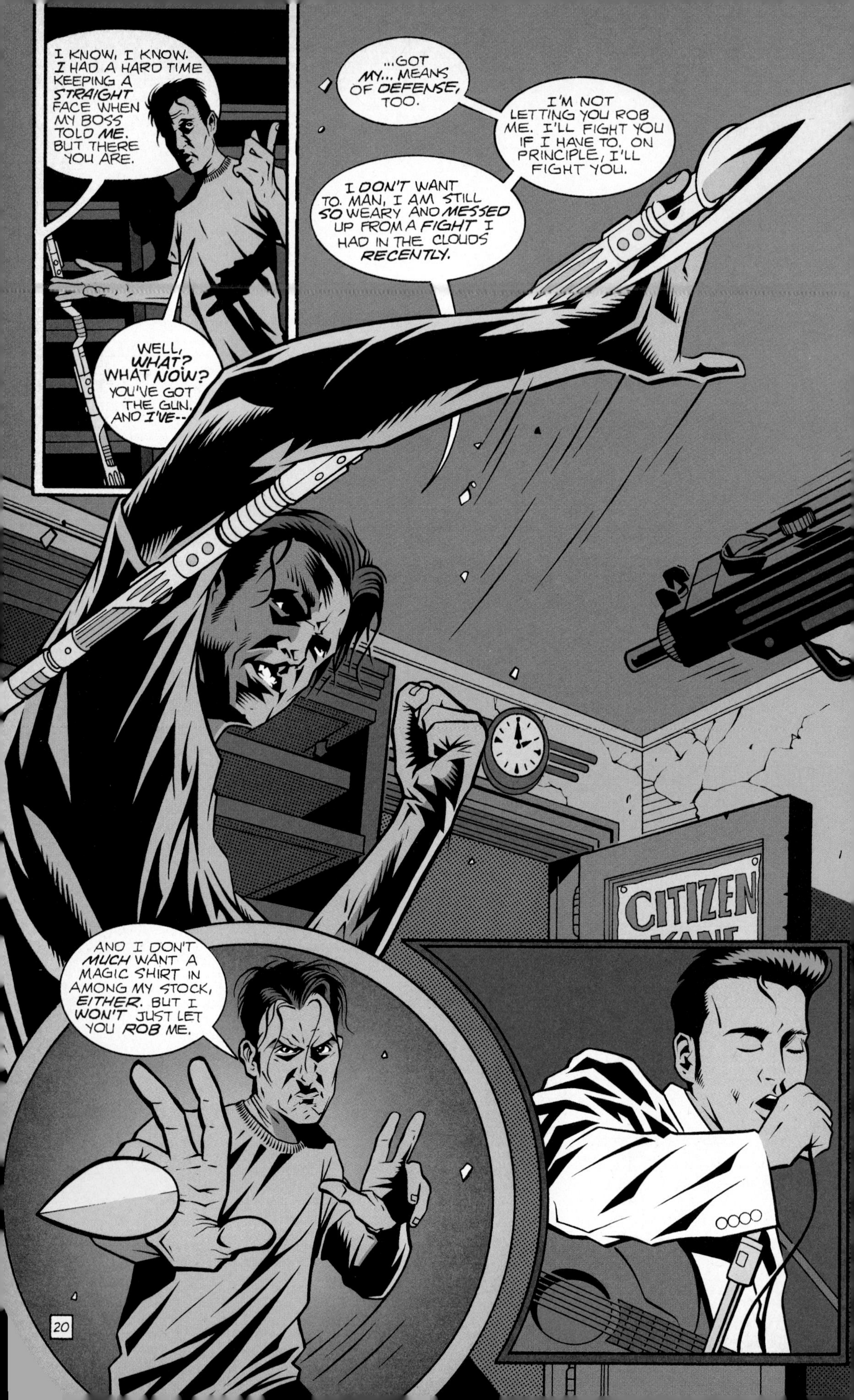
I KNOW, I KNOW. I HAD A HARD TIME KEEPING A STRAIGHT FACE WHEN MY BOSS TOLD ME. BUT THERE YOU ARE.
WELL, WHAT? WHAT NOW? YOU'VE GOT THE GUN, AND I'VE--
...GOT MY... MEANS OF DEFENSE, TOO.
I'M NOT LETTING YOU ROB ME. I'LL FIGHT YOU IF I HAVE TO. ON PRINCIPLE, I'LL FIGHT YOU.
I DON'T WANT TO. MAN, I AM STILL SO WEARY AND MESSED UP FROM A FIGHT I HAD IN THE CLOUDS RECENTLY.
CITIZEN
AND I DON'T MUCH WANT A MAGIC SHIRT IN AMONG MY STOCK, EITHER. BUT I WON'T JUST LET YOU ROB ME.

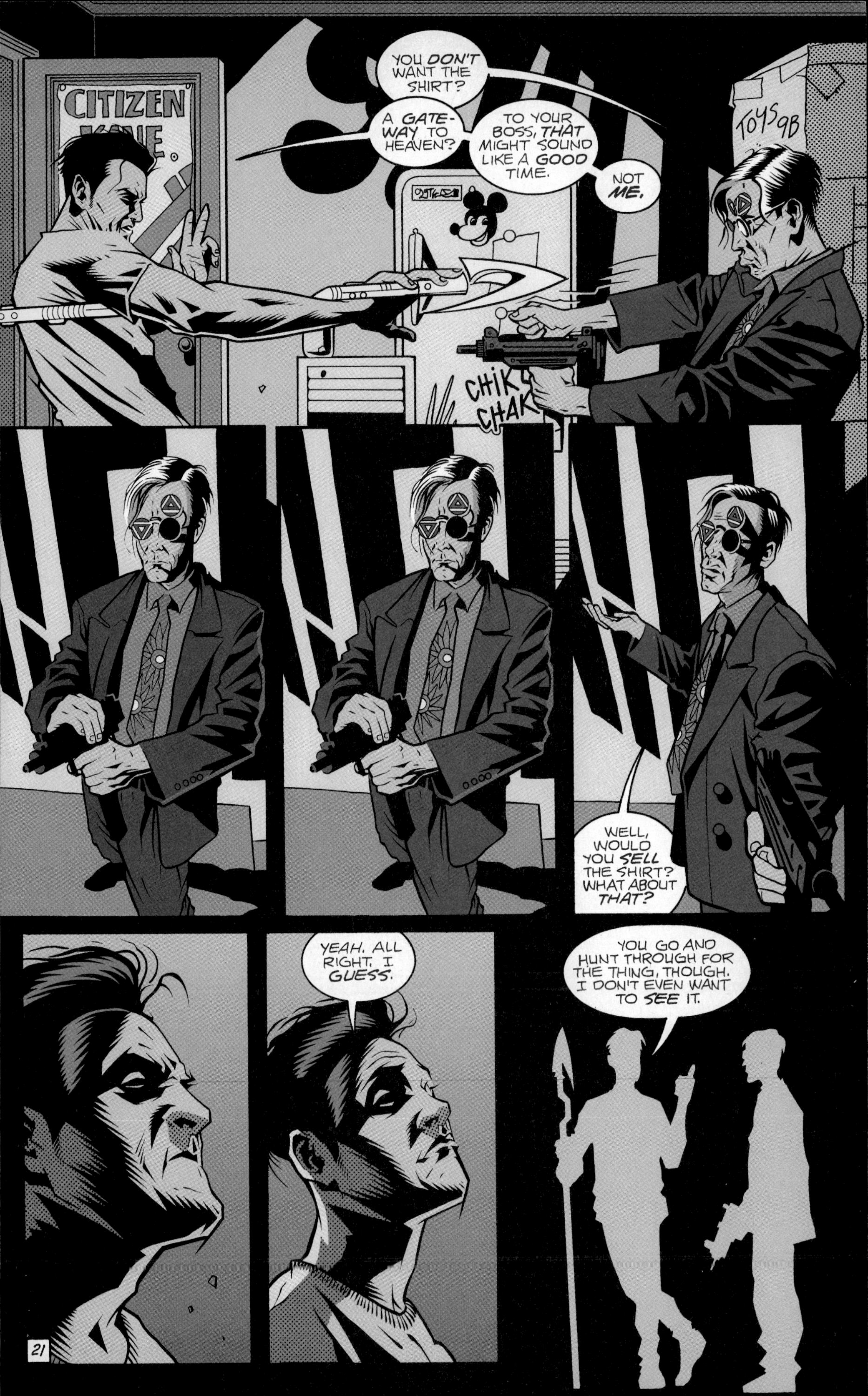
CITIZEN KANE
YOU DON'T WANT THE SHIRT?
A GATE-WAY TO HEAVEN?
TO YOUR BOSS, THAT MIGHT SOUND LIKE A GOOD TIME.
NOT ME.
TOYS 9B
CHIK CHAK
WELL, WOULD YOU SELL THE SHIRT? WHAT ABOUT THAT?
YEAH. ALL RIGHT. I GUESS.
YOU GO AND HUNT THROUGH FOR THE THING, THOUGH. I DON'T EVEN WANT TO SEE IT.

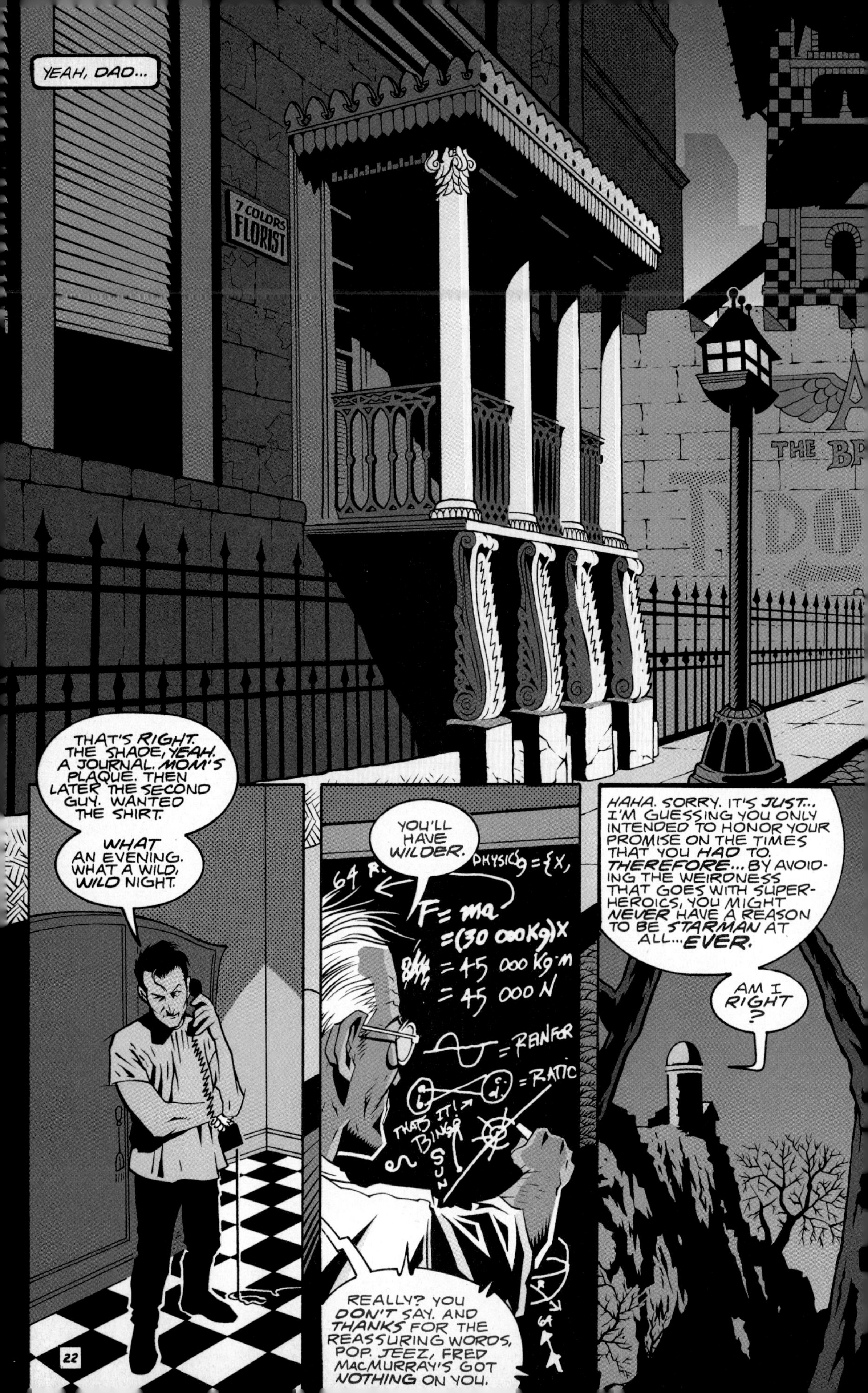
YEAH, DAD...
7 COLORS FLORIST
THAT'S RIGHT. THE SHADE, YEAH. A JOURNAL. MOM'S PLAQUE. THEN LATER THE SECOND GUY. WANTED THE SHIRT.
WHAT AN EVENING. WHAT A WILD, WILD NIGHT.
YOU'LL HAVE WILDER.
REALLY? YOU DON'T SAY. AND THANKS FOR THE REASSURING WORDS, POP. JEEZ, FRED MACMURRAY'S GOT NOTHING ON YOU.
HAHA. SORRY. IT'S JUST... I'M GUESSING YOU ONLY INTENDED TO HONOR YOUR PROMISE ON THE TIMES THAT YOU HAD TO. THEREFORE... BY AVOIDING THE WEIRDNESS THAT GOES WITH SUPER-HEROICS, YOU MIGHT NEVER HAVE A REASON TO BE STARMAN AT ALL... EVER.
AM I RIGHT?

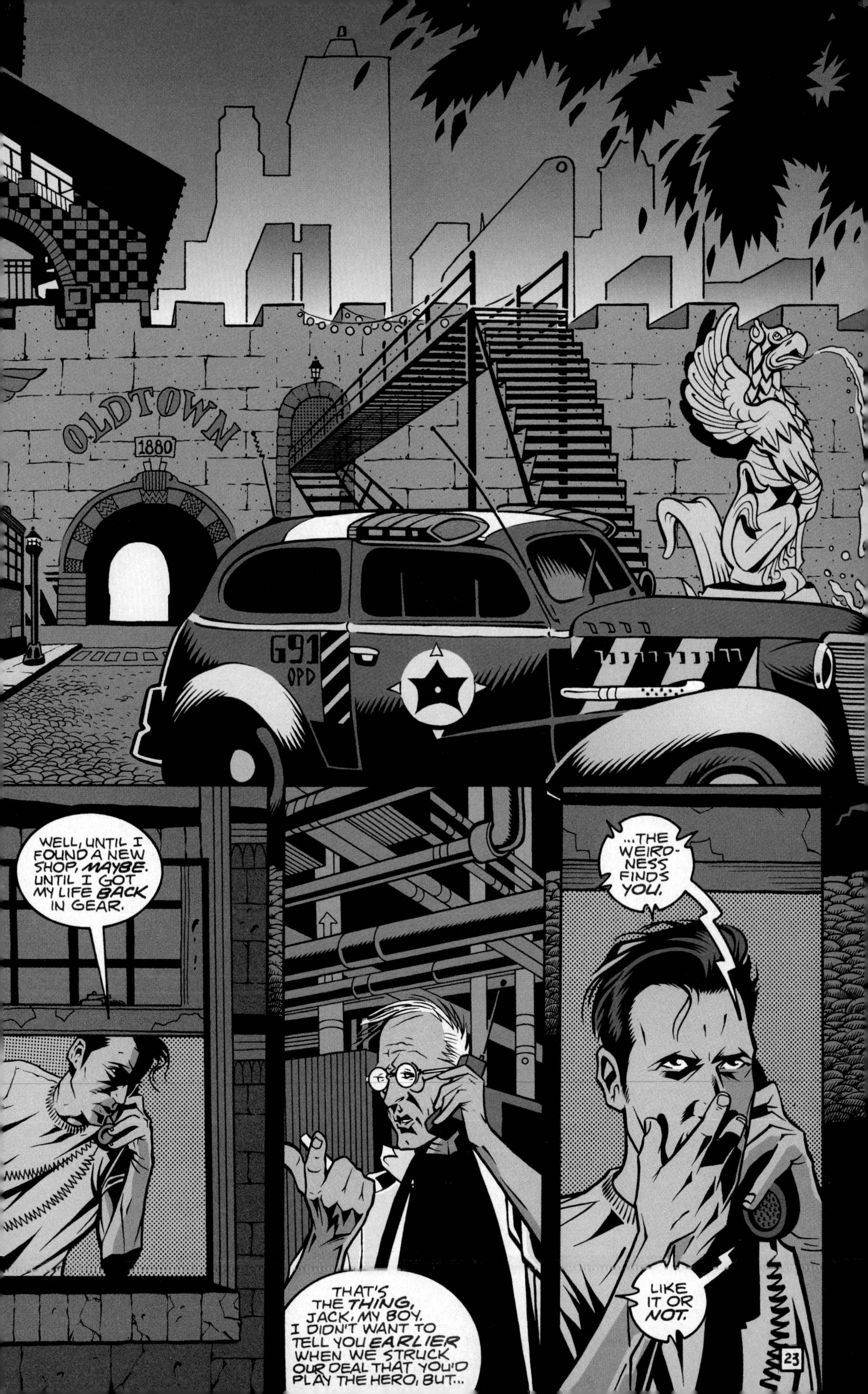
OLDTOWN
1880
G91
OPD
WELL, UNTIL I FOUND A NEW SHOP, MAYBE. UNTIL I GOT MY LIFE BACK IN GEAR.
THAT'S THE THING, JACK, MY BOY. I DIDN'T WANT TO TELL YOU EARLIER WHEN WE STRUCK OUR DEAL THAT YOU'D PLAY THE HERO, BUT...
...THE WEIRDNESS FINDS YOU.
LIKE IT OR NOT.

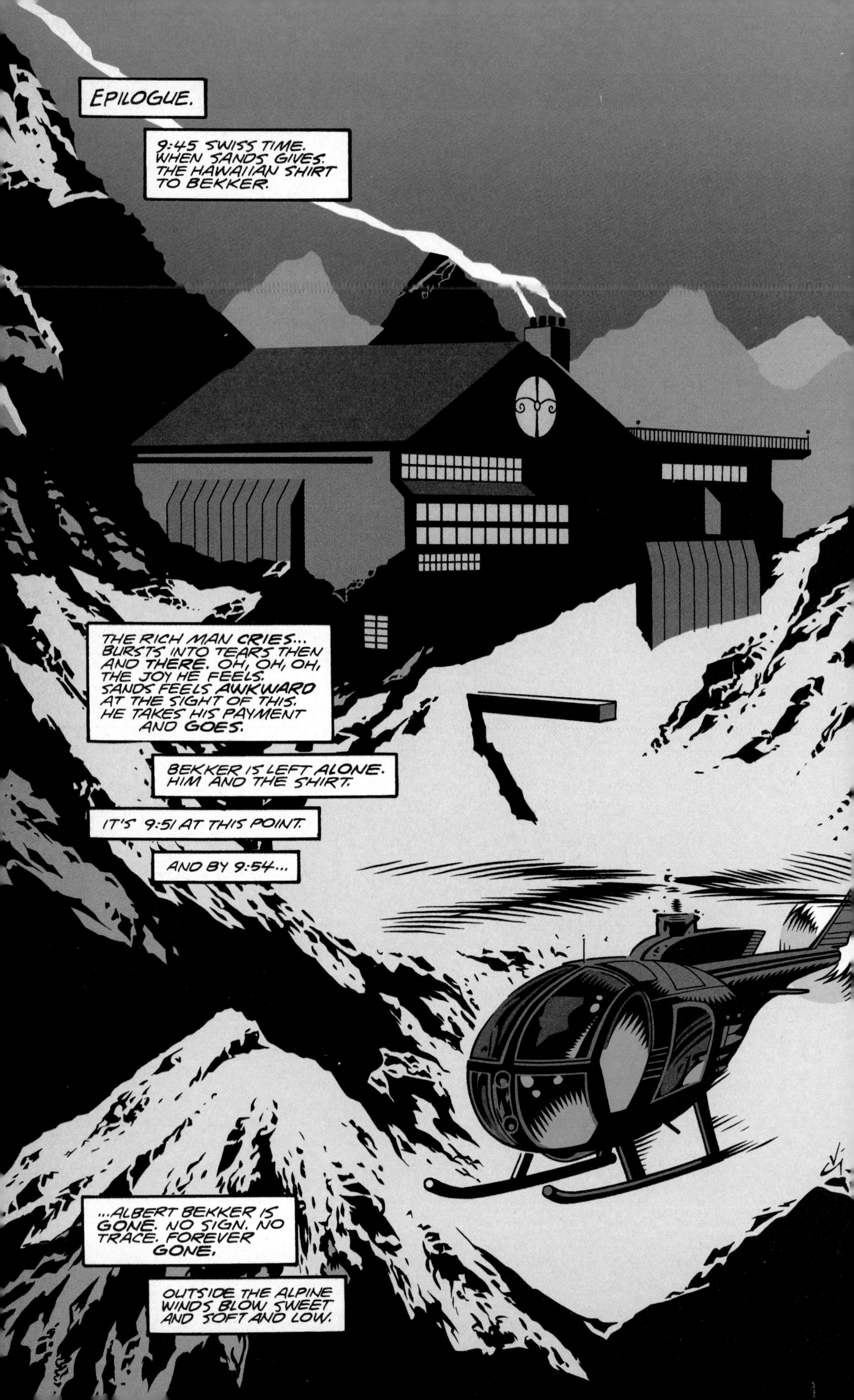
EPILOGUE.
9:45 SWISS TIME. WHEN SANDS GIVES. THE HAWAIIAN SHIRT TO BEKKER.
THE RICH MAN CRIES... BURSTS INTO TEARS THEN AND THERE. OH, OH, OH, THE JOY HE FEELS. SANDS FEELS AWKWARD AT THE SIGHT OF THIS. HE TAKES HIS PAYMENT AND GOES.
BEKKER IS LEFT ALONE. HIM AND THE SHIRT.
IT'S 9:51 AT THIS POINT.
AND BY 9:54...
...ALBERT BEKKER IS GONE. NO SIGN. NO TRACE. FOREVER GONE.
OUTSIDE THE ALPINE WINDS BLOW SWEET AND SOFT AND LOW.

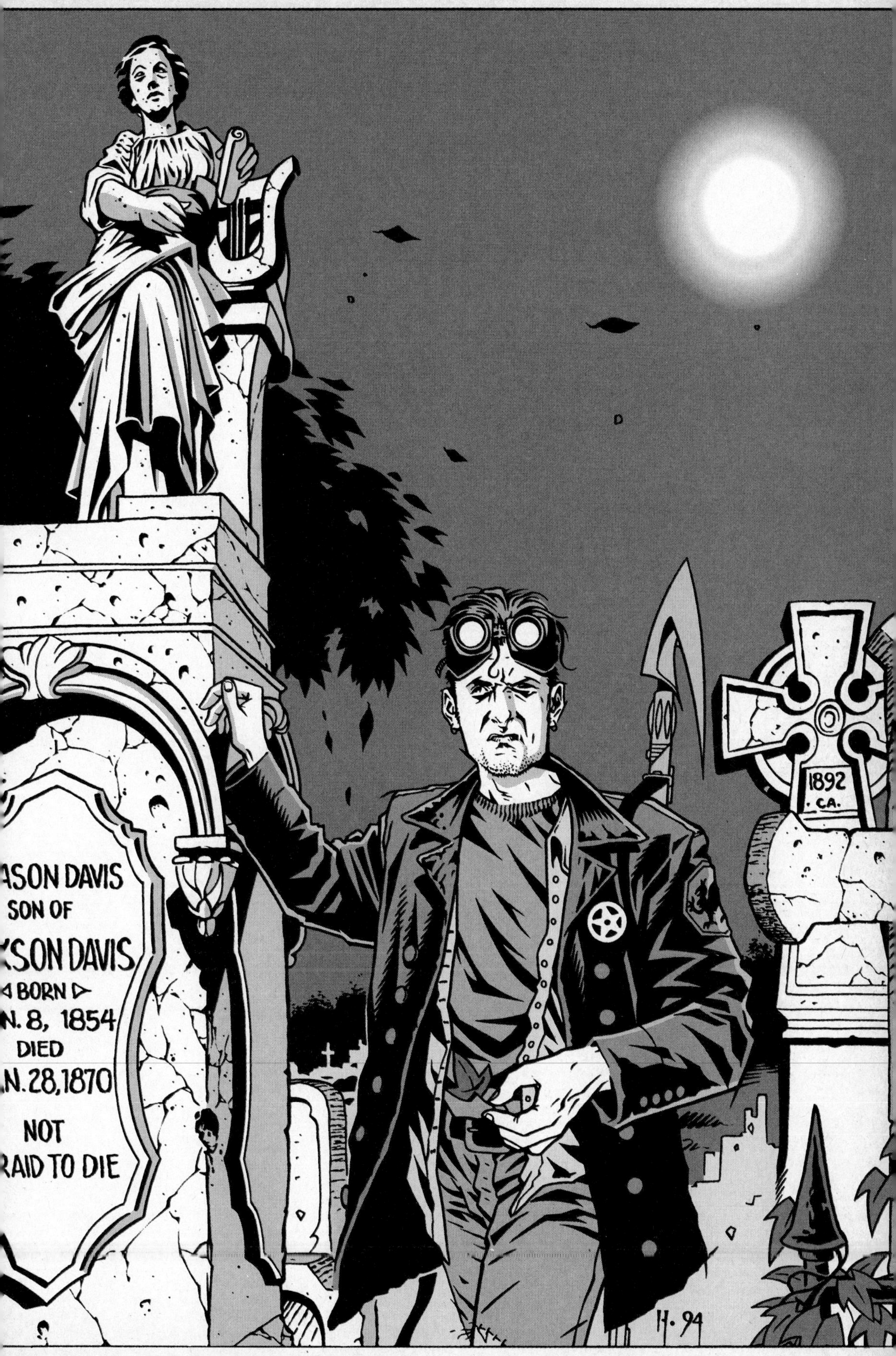
ASON DAVIS
SON OF
KSON DAVIS
BORN
N. 8, 1854
DIED
N. 28, 1870
NOT
RAID TO DIE
1892
CA.

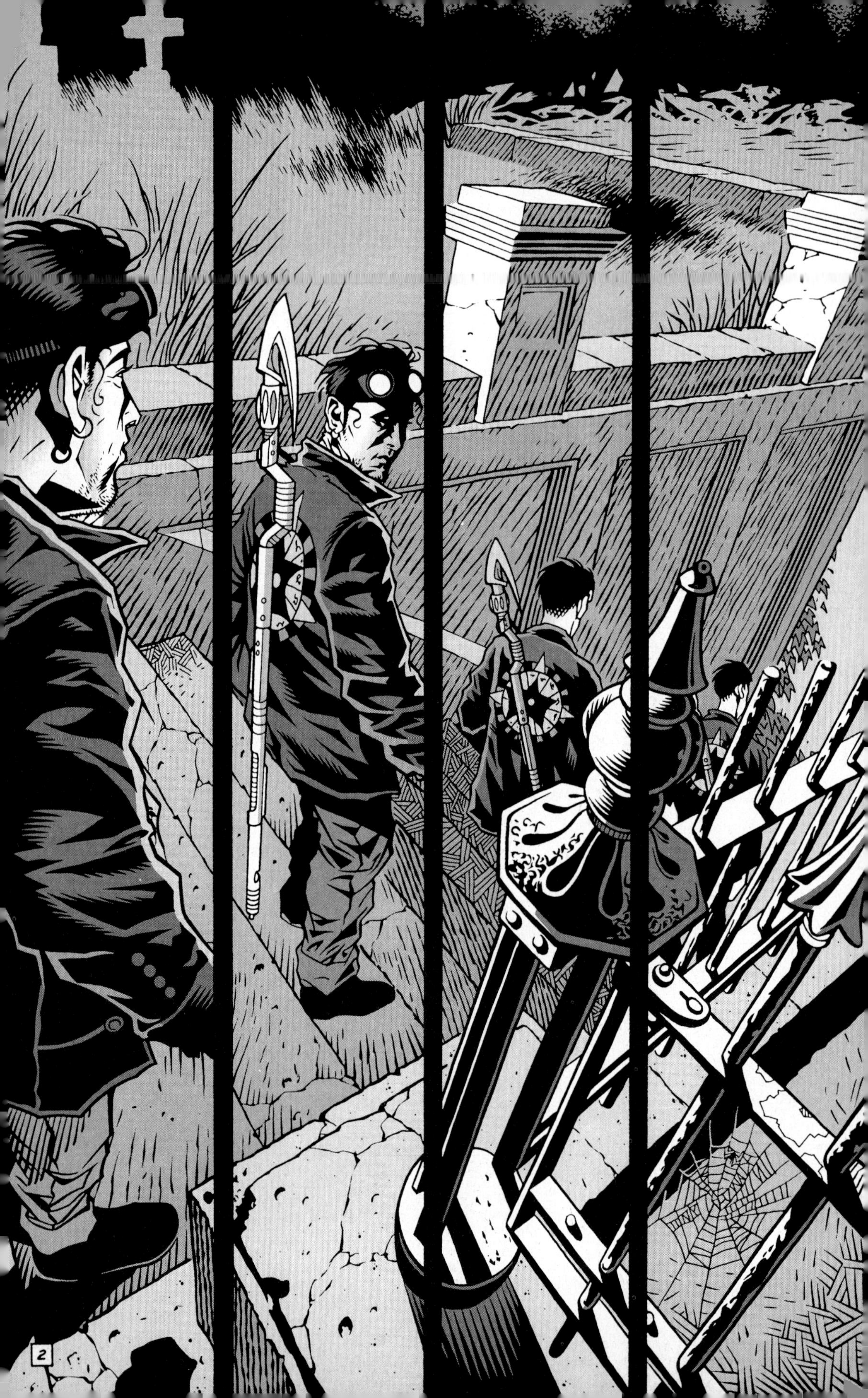

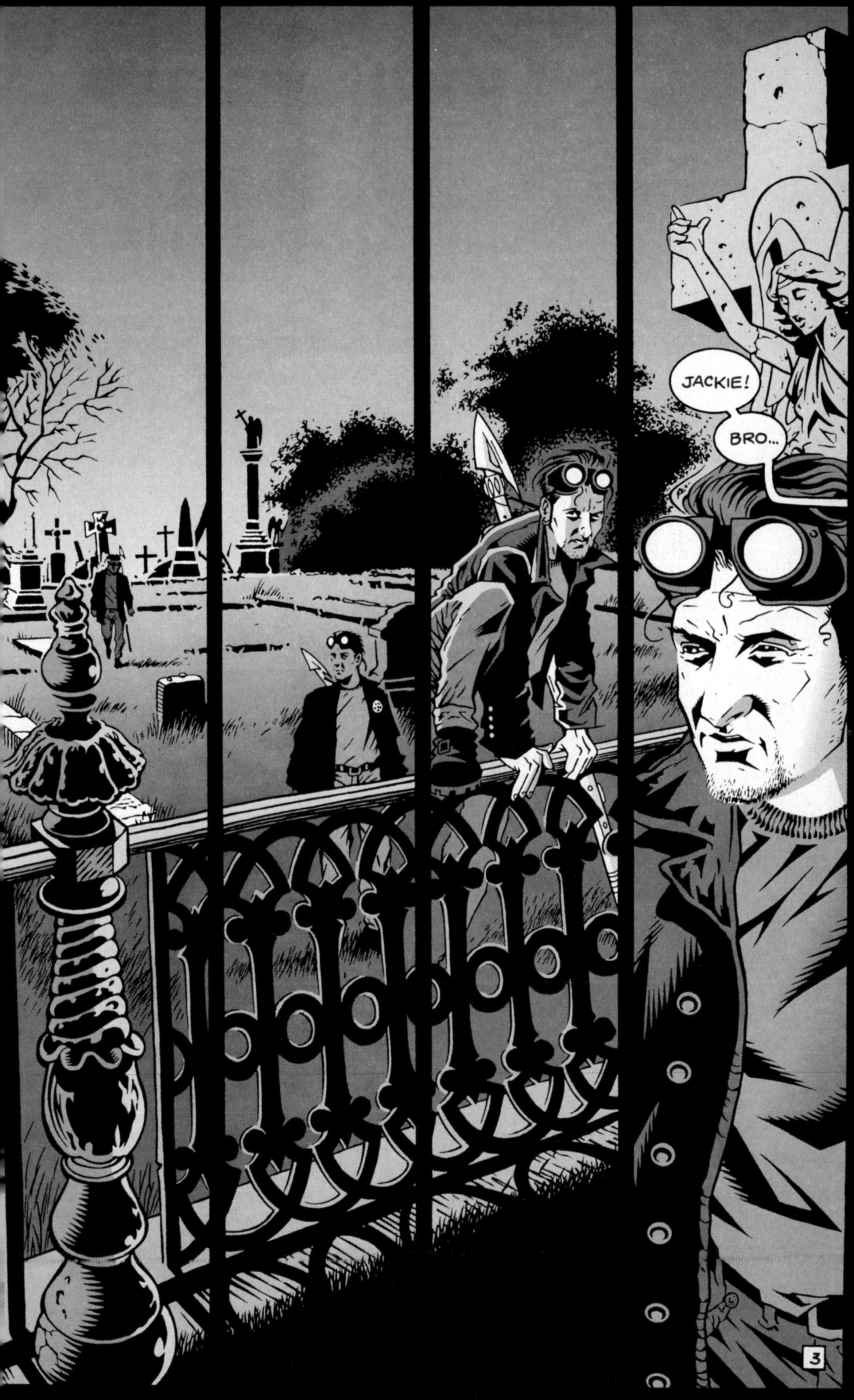
JACKIE!
BRO...

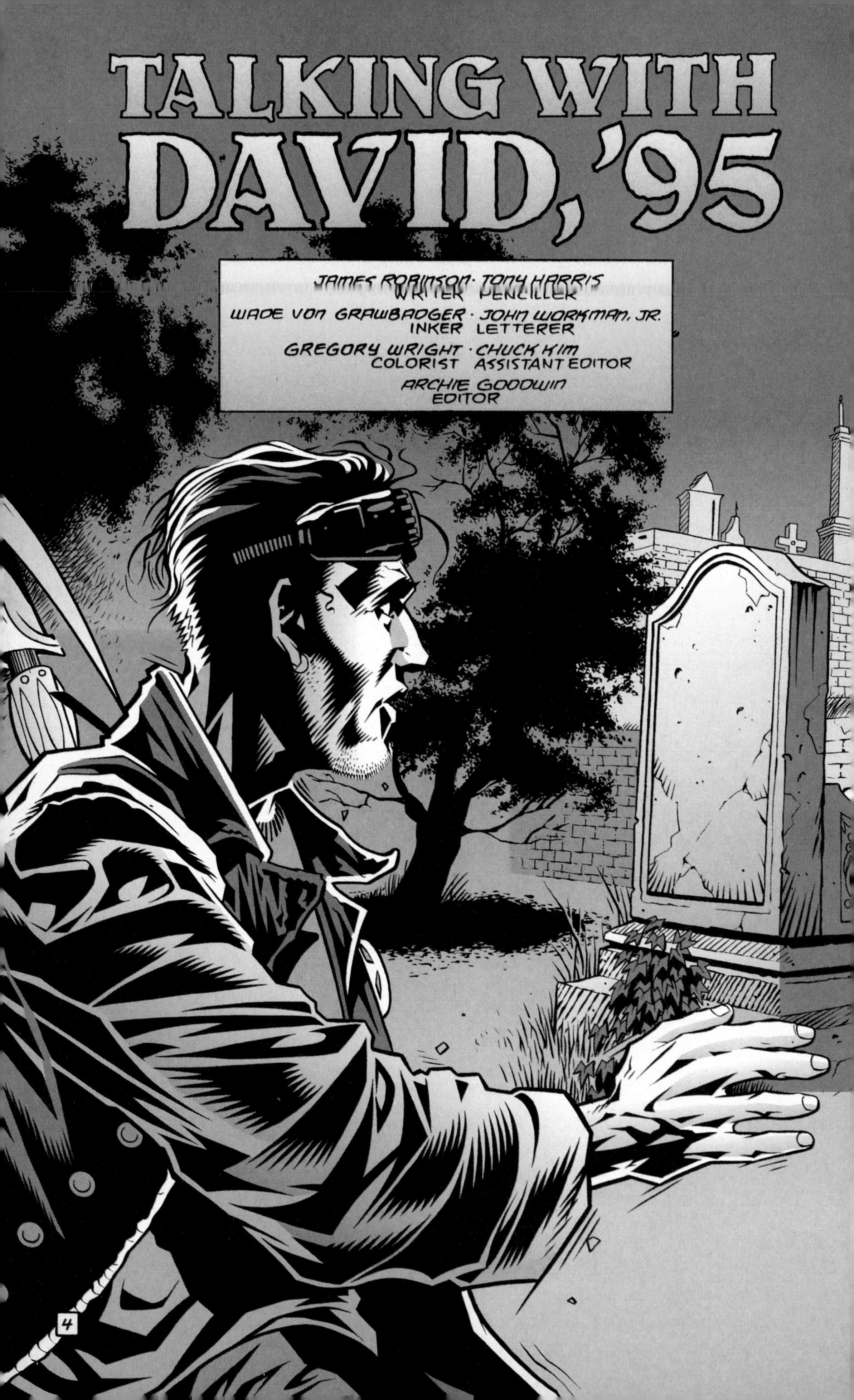
TALKING WITH DAVID, '95
JAMES ROBINSON · TONY HARRIS
WRITER PENCILLER
WADE VON GRAWBADGER · JOHN WORKMAN, JR.
INKER LETTERER
GREGORY WRIGHT · CHUCK KIM
COLORIST ASSISTANT EDITOR
ARCHIE GOODWIN
EDITOR

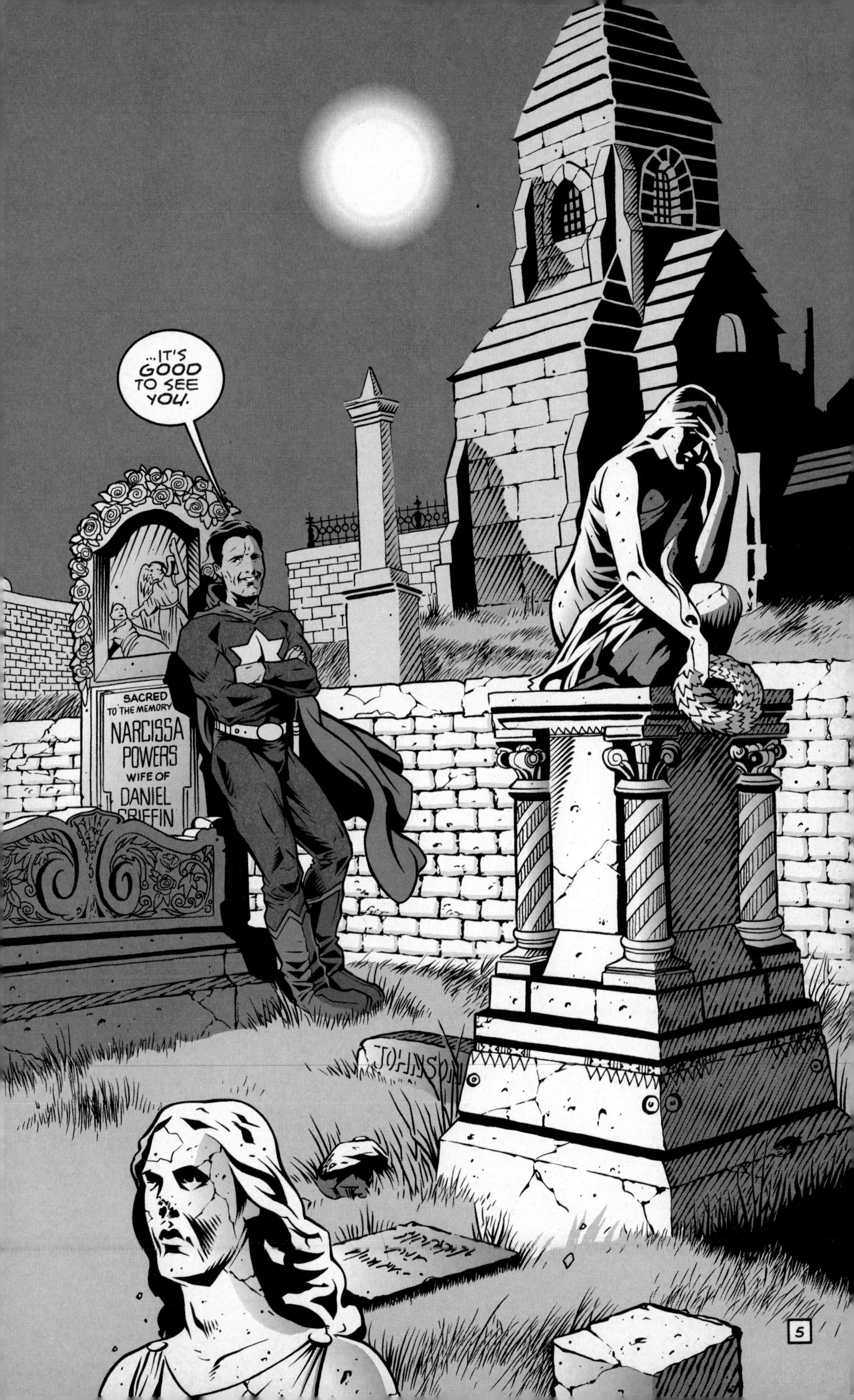
...IT'S GOOD TO SEE YOU.
SACRED TO THE MEMORY NARCISSA POWERS WIFE OF DANIEL GRIFFIN
JOHNSON

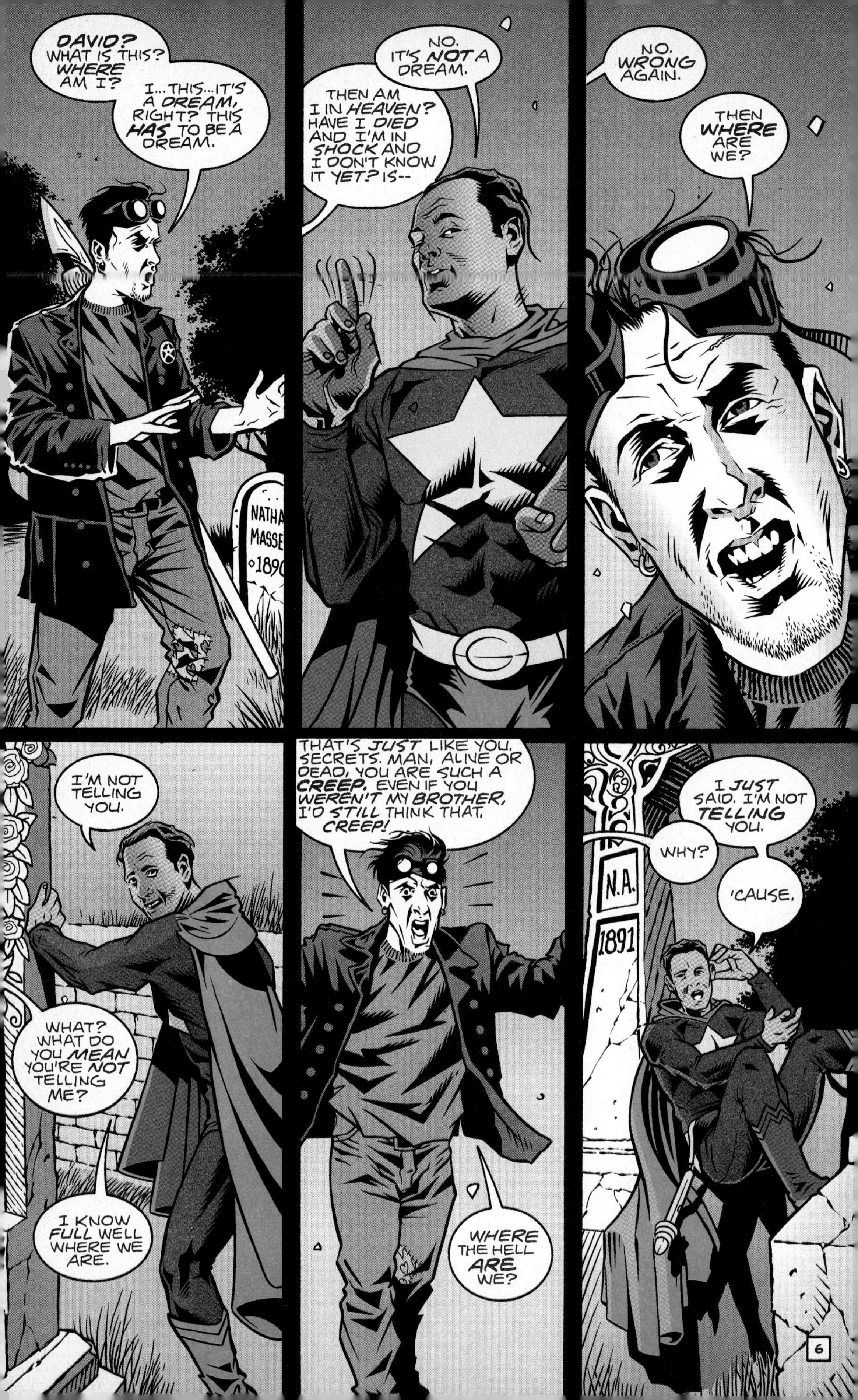
DAVID? WHAT IS THIS? WHERE AM I?
I... THIS...IT'S A DREAM, RIGHT? THIS HAS TO BE A DREAM.
NATHA
MASSE
1890
NO. IT'S NOT A DREAM.
THEN AM I IN HEAVEN? HAVE I DIED AND I'M IN SHOCK AND I DON'T KNOW IT YET? IS--
NO. WRONG AGAIN.
THEN WHERE ARE WE?
I'M NOT TELLING YOU.
WHAT? WHAT DO YOU MEAN YOU'RE NOT TELLING ME?
I KNOW FULL WELL WHERE WE ARE.
THAT'S JUST LIKE YOU. SECRETS. MAN, ALIVE OR DEAD, YOU ARE SUCH A CREEP. EVEN IF YOU WEREN'T MY BROTHER, I'D STILL THINK THAT. CREEP!
WHERE THE HELL ARE WE?
I JUST SAID. I'M NOT TELLING YOU.
WHY?
'CAUSE.
N.A.
1891

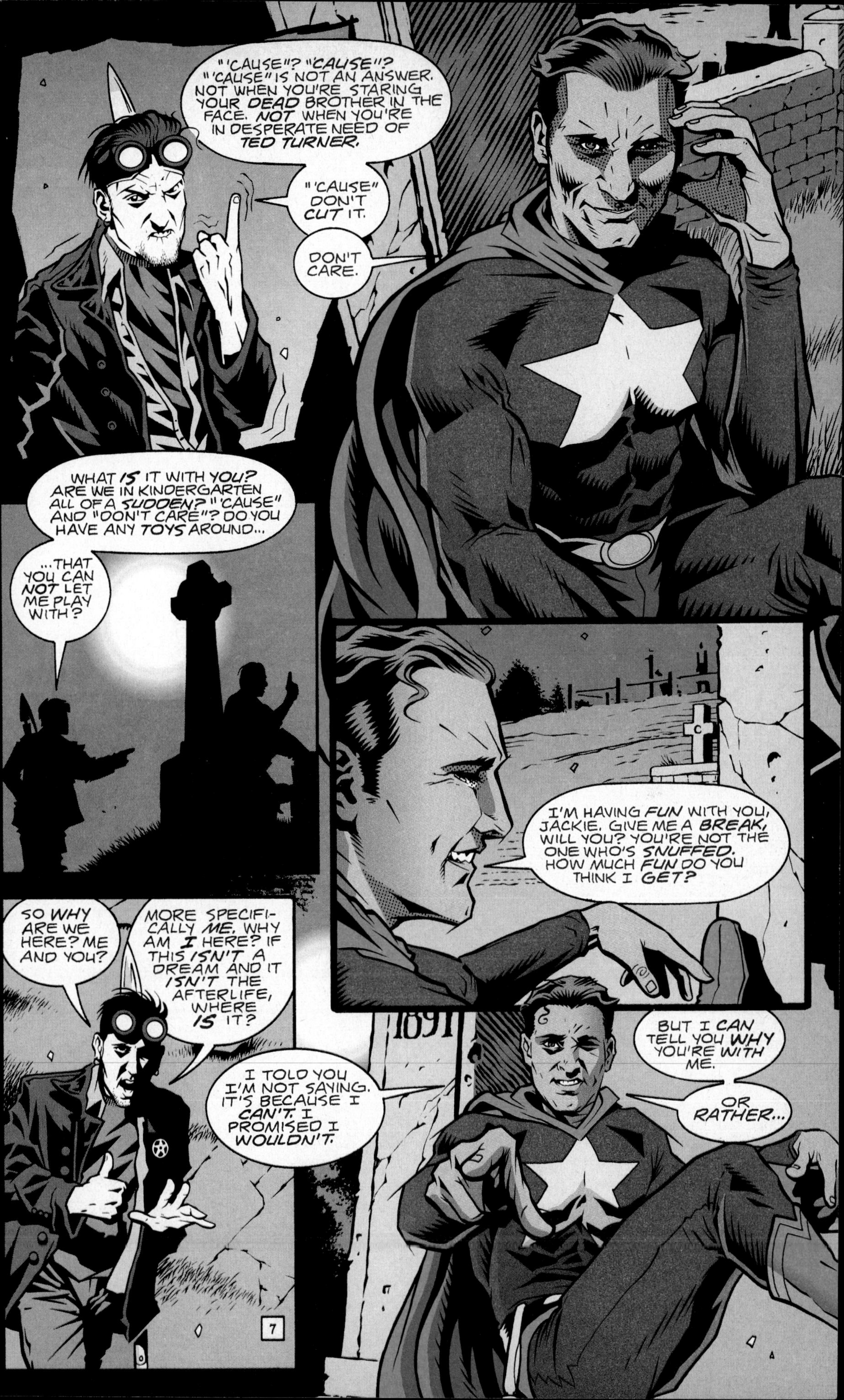
"'CAUSE"? "CAUSE"? "'CAUSE" IS NOT AN ANSWER. NOT WHEN YOU'RE STARING YOUR DEAD BROTHER IN THE FACE. NOT WHEN YOU'RE IN DESPERATE NEED OF TED TURNER.
"'CAUSE" DON'T CUT IT.
DON'T CARE.
WHAT IS IT WITH YOU? ARE WE IN KINDERGARTEN ALL OF A SUDDEN? "'CAUSE" AND "DON'T CARE"? DO YOU HAVE ANY TOYS AROUND...
...THAT YOU CAN NOT LET ME PLAY WITH?
I'M HAVING FUN WITH YOU, JACKIE. GIVE ME A BREAK, WILL YOU? YOU'RE NOT THE ONE WHO'S SNUFFED. HOW MUCH FUN DO YOU THINK I GET?
SO WHY ARE WE HERE? ME AND YOU?
MORE SPECIFICALLY ME. WHY AM I HERE? IF THIS ISN'T A DREAM AND IT ISN'T THE AFTERLIFE, WHERE IS IT?
1891
I TOLD YOU I'M NOT SAYING. IT'S BECAUSE I CAN'T. I PROMISED I WOULDN'T.
BUT I CAN TELL YOU WHY YOU'RE WITH ME.
OR RATHER...

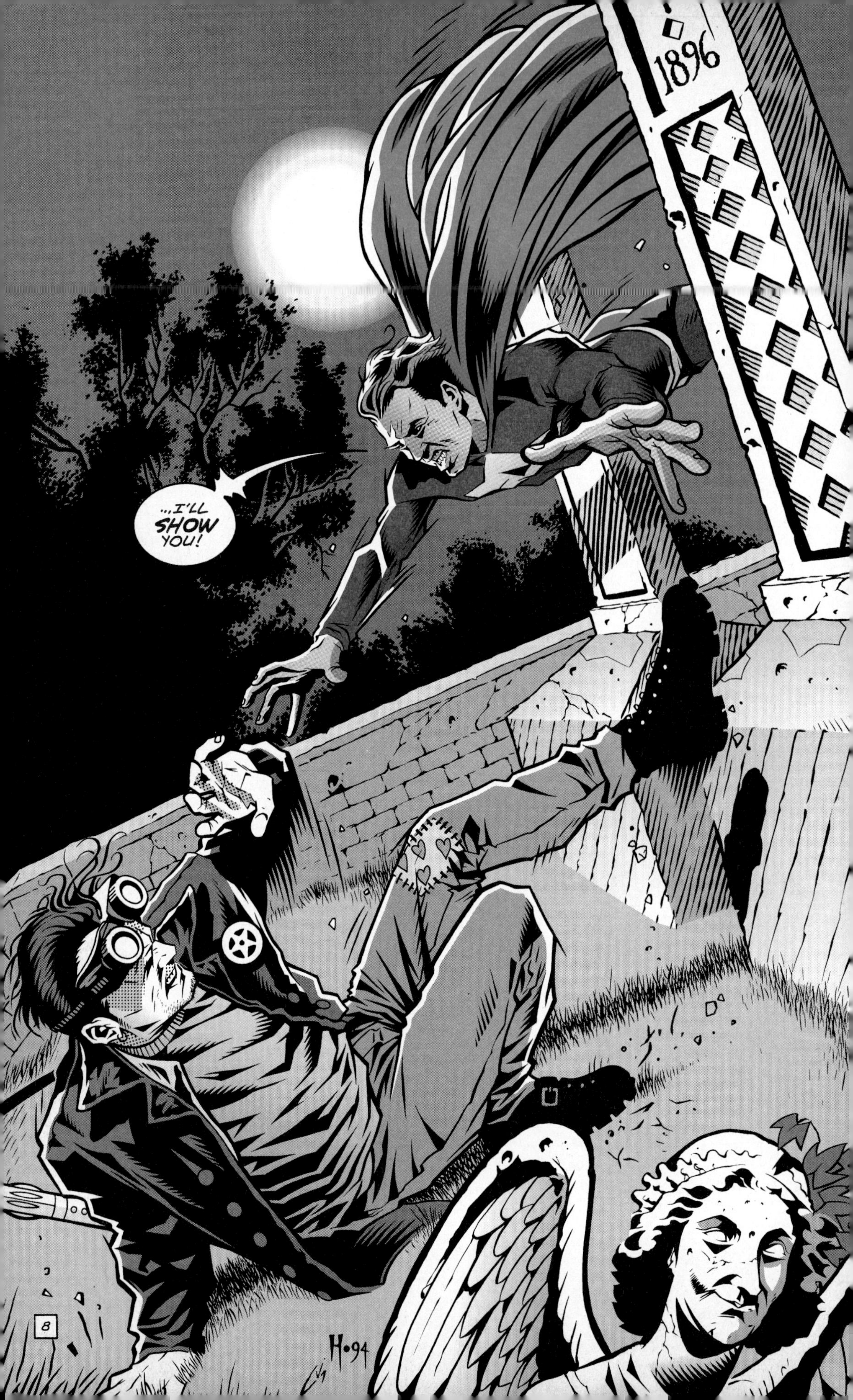
1896
...I'LL SHOW YOU!
H•94

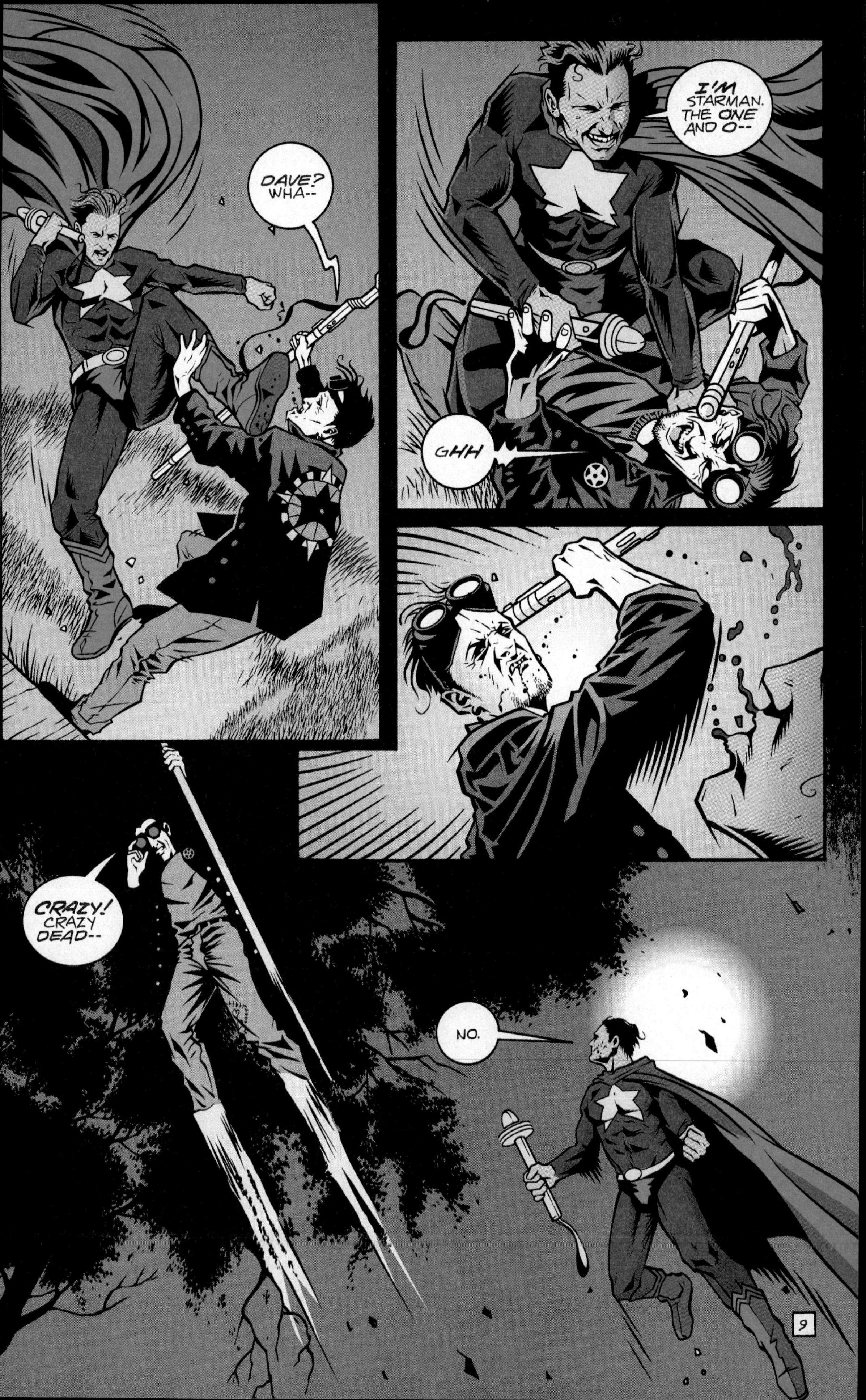
DAVE? WHA--
I'M STARMAN. THE ONE AND O--
GHH
CRAZY! CRAZY DEAD--
NO.

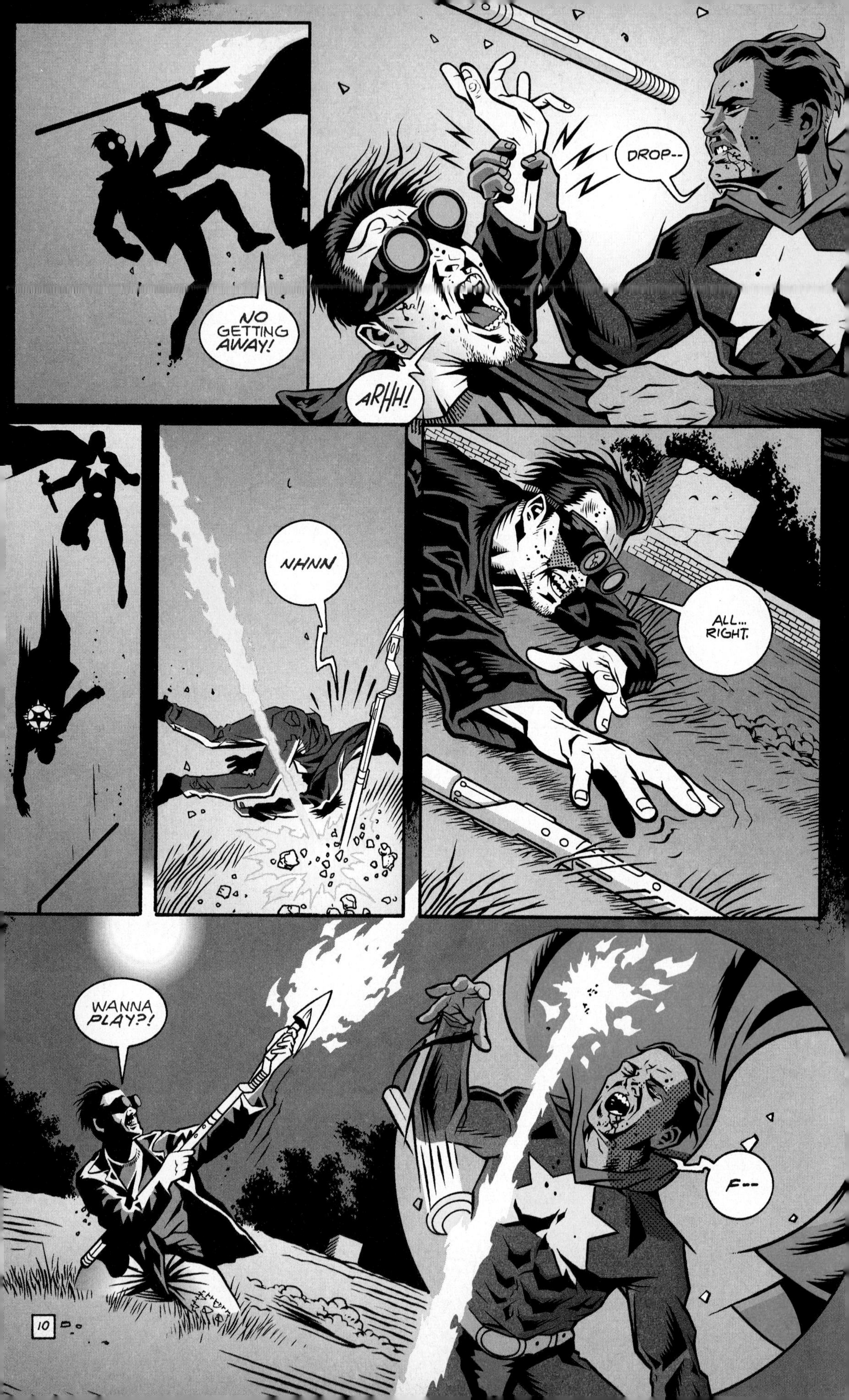
DROP--
NO GETTING AWAY!
ARHH!
NHNN
ALL... RIGHT.
WANNA PLAY?!
F--

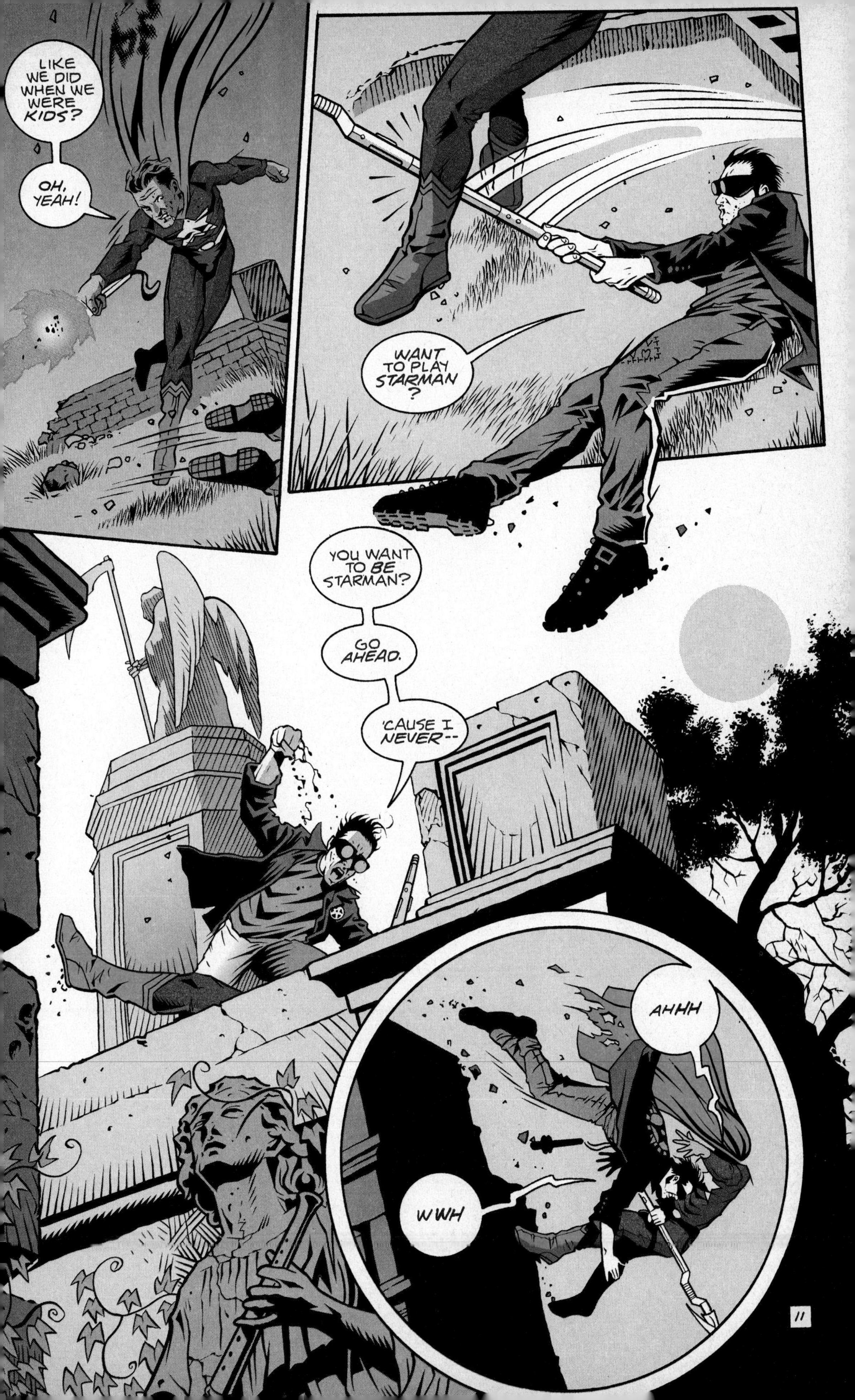
LIKE WE DID WHEN WE WERE KIDS?
OH, YEAH!
WANT TO PLAY STARMAN?
YOU WANT TO BE STARMAN?
GO AHEAD.
'CAUSE I NEVER--
AHHH
WWH
11

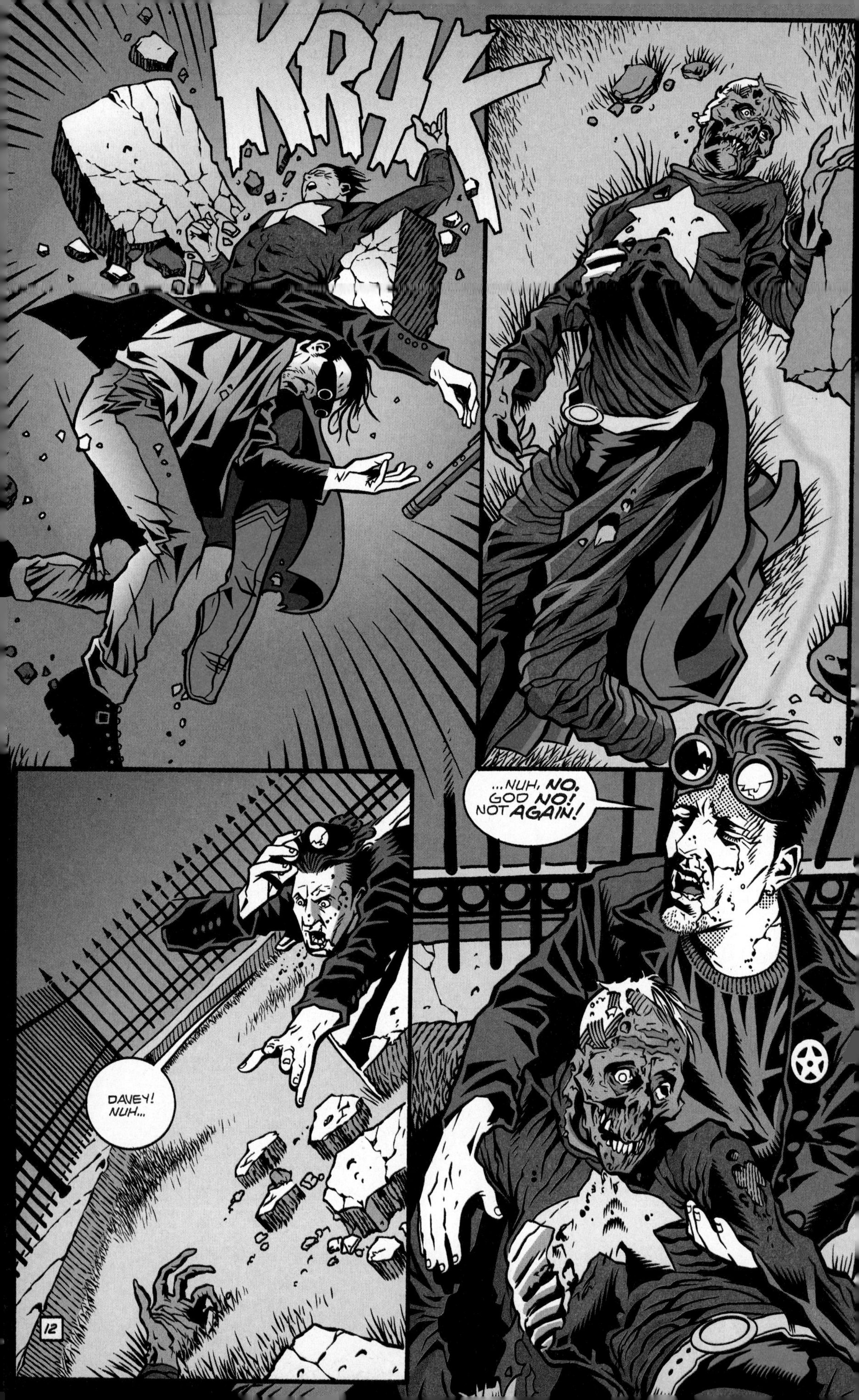
KRAK
DAVEY! NUH...
...NUH, NO. GOD NO! NOT AGAIN!
12

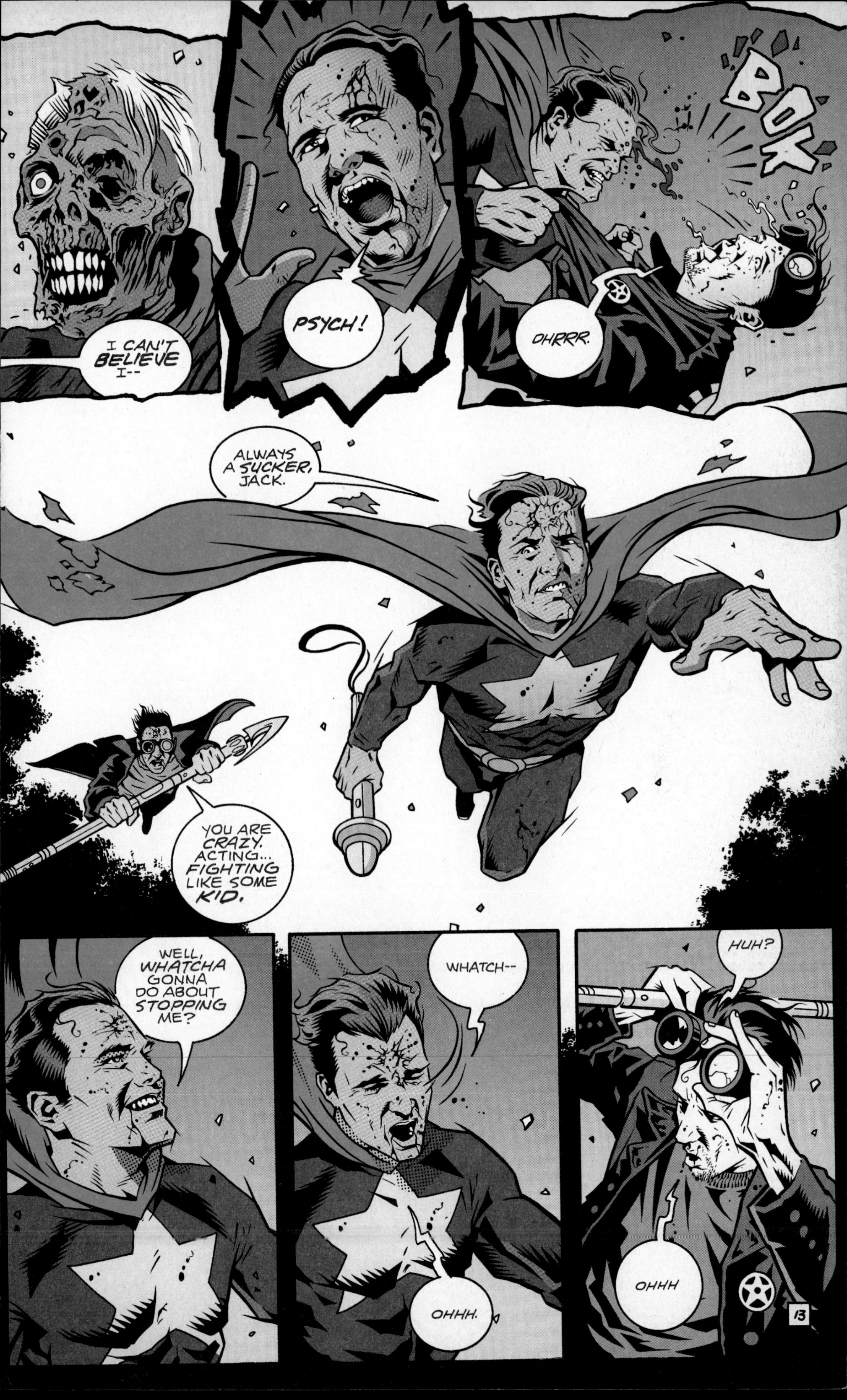
I CAN'T BELIEVE I--
PSYCH!
BOK
OHRRR.
ALWAYS A SUCKER, JACK.
YOU ARE CRAZY. ACTING... FIGHTING LIKE SOME KID.
WELL, WHATCHA GONNA DO ABOUT STOPPING ME?
WHATCH--
OHHH.
HUH?
OHHH
13

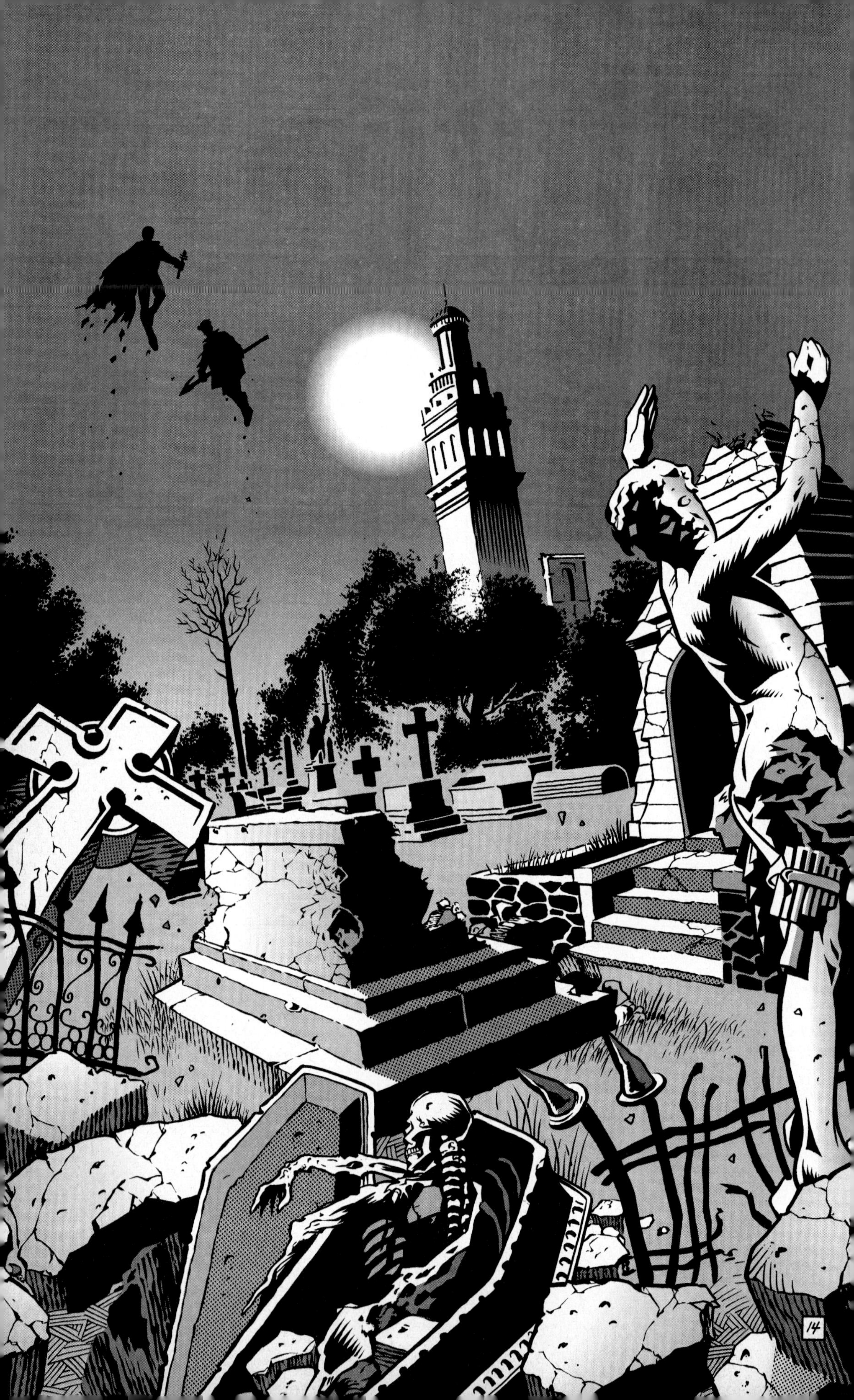
14

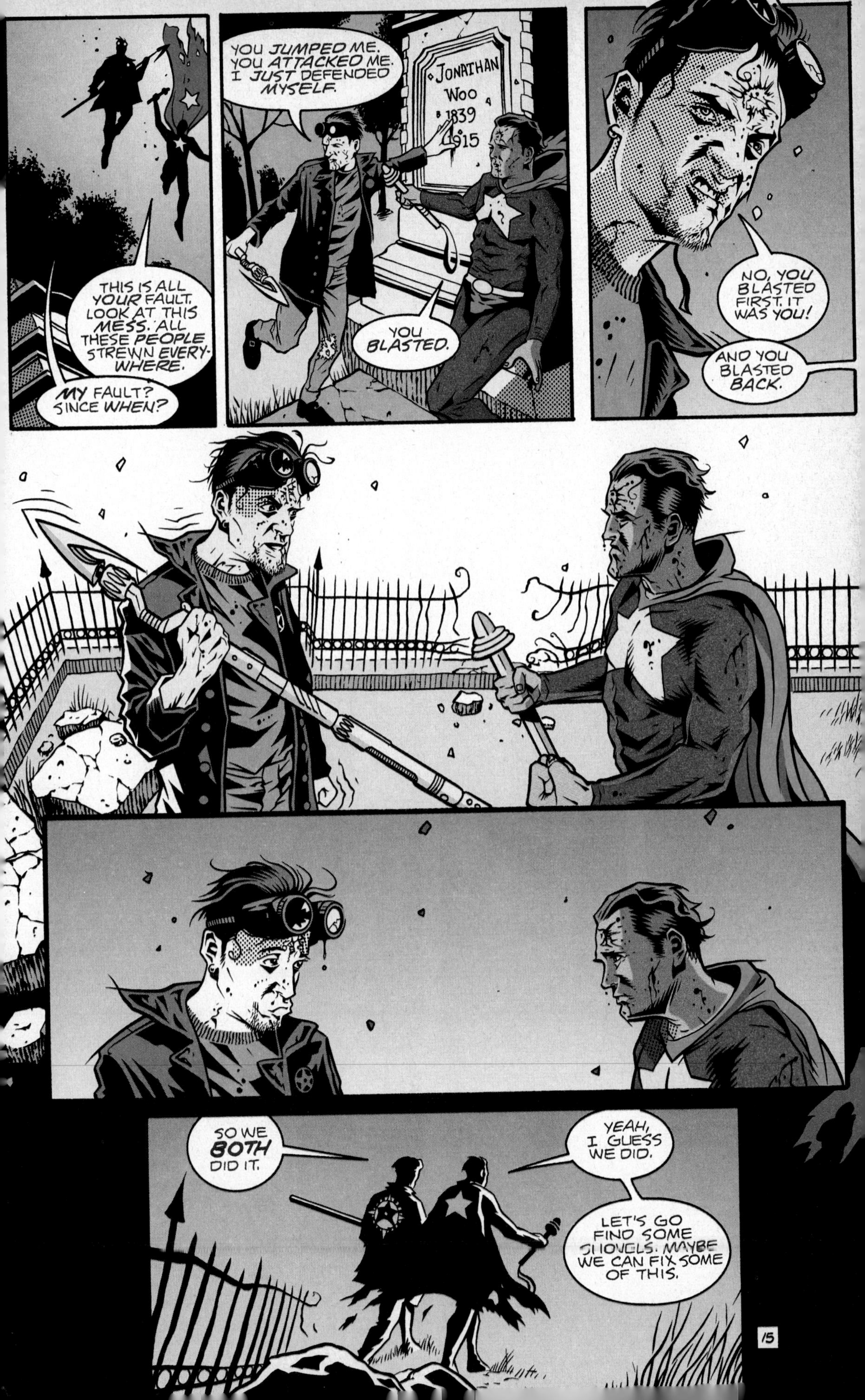

THIS IS ALL YOUR FAULT. LOOK AT THIS MESS. ALL THESE PEOPLE STREWN EVERYWHERE.
MY FAULT? SINCE WHEN?
YOU JUMPED ME. YOU ATTACKED ME. I JUST DEFENDED MYSELF.
JONATHAN WOO 1839 1915
YOU BLASTED.
NO, YOU BLASTED FIRST. IT WAS YOU!
AND YOU BLASTED BACK.
SO WE BOTH DID IT.
YEAH, I GUESS WE DID.
LET'S GO FIND SOME SHOVELS. MAYBE WE CAN FIX SOME OF THIS.

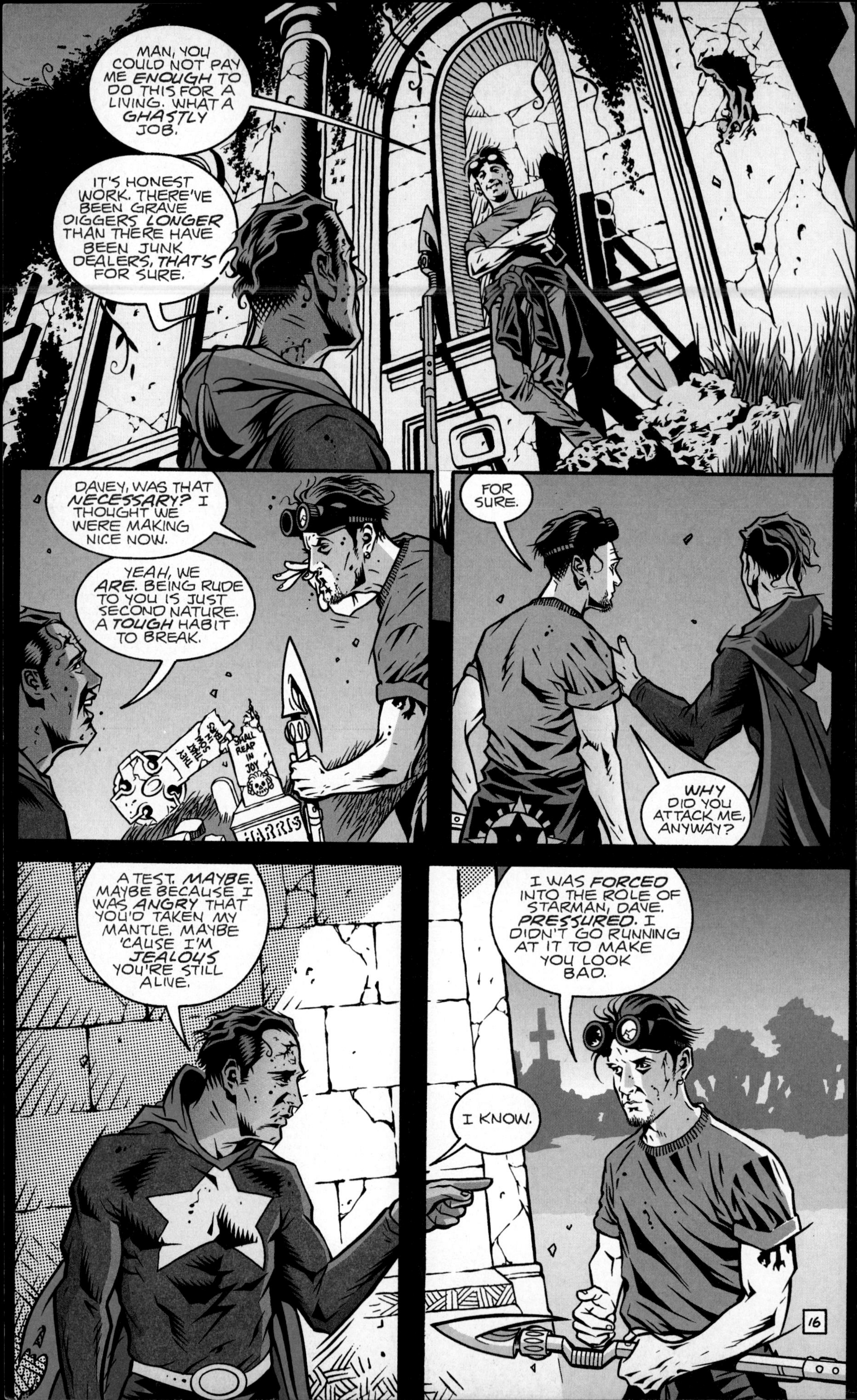
MAN, YOU COULD NOT PAY ME ENOUGH TO DO THIS FOR A LIVING. WHAT A GHASTLY JOB.
IT'S HONEST WORK. THERE'VE BEEN GRAVE DIGGERS LONGER THAN THERE HAVE BEEN JUNK DEALERS, THAT'S FOR SURE.
DAVEY, WAS THAT NECESSARY? I THOUGHT WE WERE MAKING NICE NOW.
YEAH, WE ARE. BEING RUDE TO YOU IS JUST SECOND NATURE. A TOUGH HABIT TO BREAK.
THEY THAT SOW IN TEARS
SHALL REAP IN JOY
HARRIS
FOR SURE.
WHY DID YOU ATTACK ME, ANYWAY?
A TEST. MAYBE. MAYBE BECAUSE I WAS ANGRY THAT YOU'D TAKEN MY MANTLE, MAYBE 'CAUSE I'M JEALOUS YOU'RE STILL ALIVE.
I WAS FORCED INTO THE ROLE OF STARMAN, DAVE. PRESSURED. I DIDN'T GO RUNNING AT IT TO MAKE YOU LOOK BAD.
I KNOW.
16

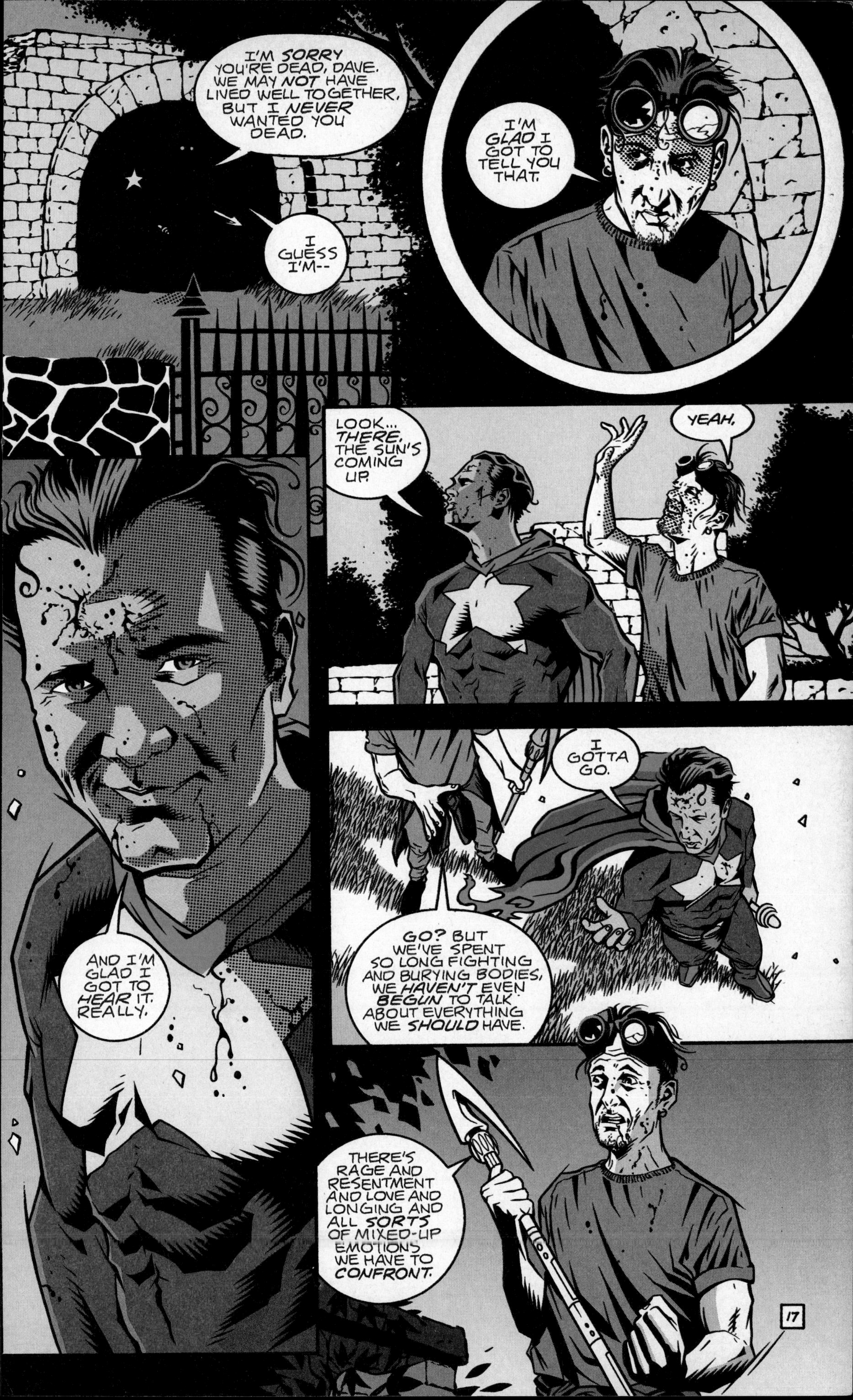
I'M SORRY YOU'RE DEAD, DAVE. WE MAY NOT HAVE LIVED WELL TOGETHER, BUT I NEVER WANTED YOU DEAD.
I GUESS I'M--
I'M GLAD I GOT TO TELL YOU THAT.
AND I'M GLAD I GOT TO HEAR IT. REALLY.
LOOK... THERE. THE SUN'S COMING UP.
YEAH.
I GOTTA GO.
GO? BUT WE'VE SPENT SO LONG FIGHTING AND BURYING BODIES, WE HAVEN'T EVEN BEGUN TO TALK ABOUT EVERYTHING WE SHOULD HAVE.
THERE'S RAGE AND RESENTMENT AND LOVE AND LONGING AND ALL SORTS OF MIXED-UP EMOTIONS WE HAVE TO CONFRONT.

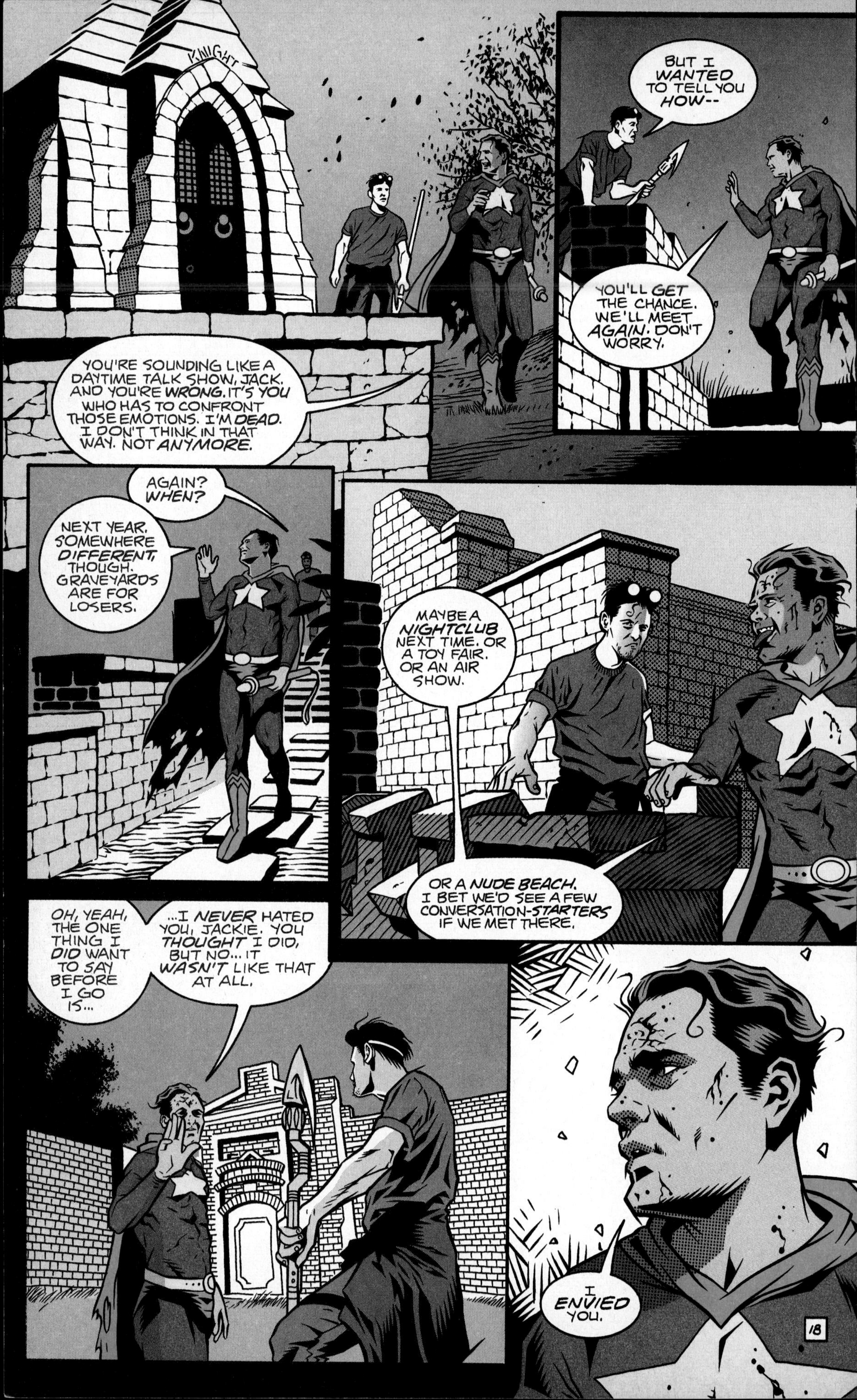
KNIGHT
YOU'RE SOUNDING LIKE A DAYTIME TALK SHOW, JACK. AND YOU'RE WRONG. IT'S YOU WHO HAS TO CONFRONT THOSE EMOTIONS. I'M DEAD. I DON'T THINK IN THAT WAY. NOT ANYMORE.
BUT I WANTED TO TELL YOU HOW--
YOU'LL GET THE CHANCE. WE'LL MEET AGAIN. DON'T WORRY.
AGAIN? WHEN?
NEXT YEAR. SOMEWHERE DIFFERENT, THOUGH. GRAVEYARDS ARE FOR LOSERS.
MAYBE A NIGHTCLUB NEXT TIME. OR A TOY FAIR. OR AN AIR SHOW.
OR A NUDE BEACH. I BET WE'D SEE A FEW CONVERSATION-STARTERS IF WE MET THERE.
OH, YEAH, THE ONE THING I DID WANT TO SAY BEFORE I GO IS...
...I NEVER HATED YOU, JACKIE. YOU THOUGHT I DID, BUT NO... IT WASN'T LIKE THAT AT ALL.
I ENVIED YOU.
18

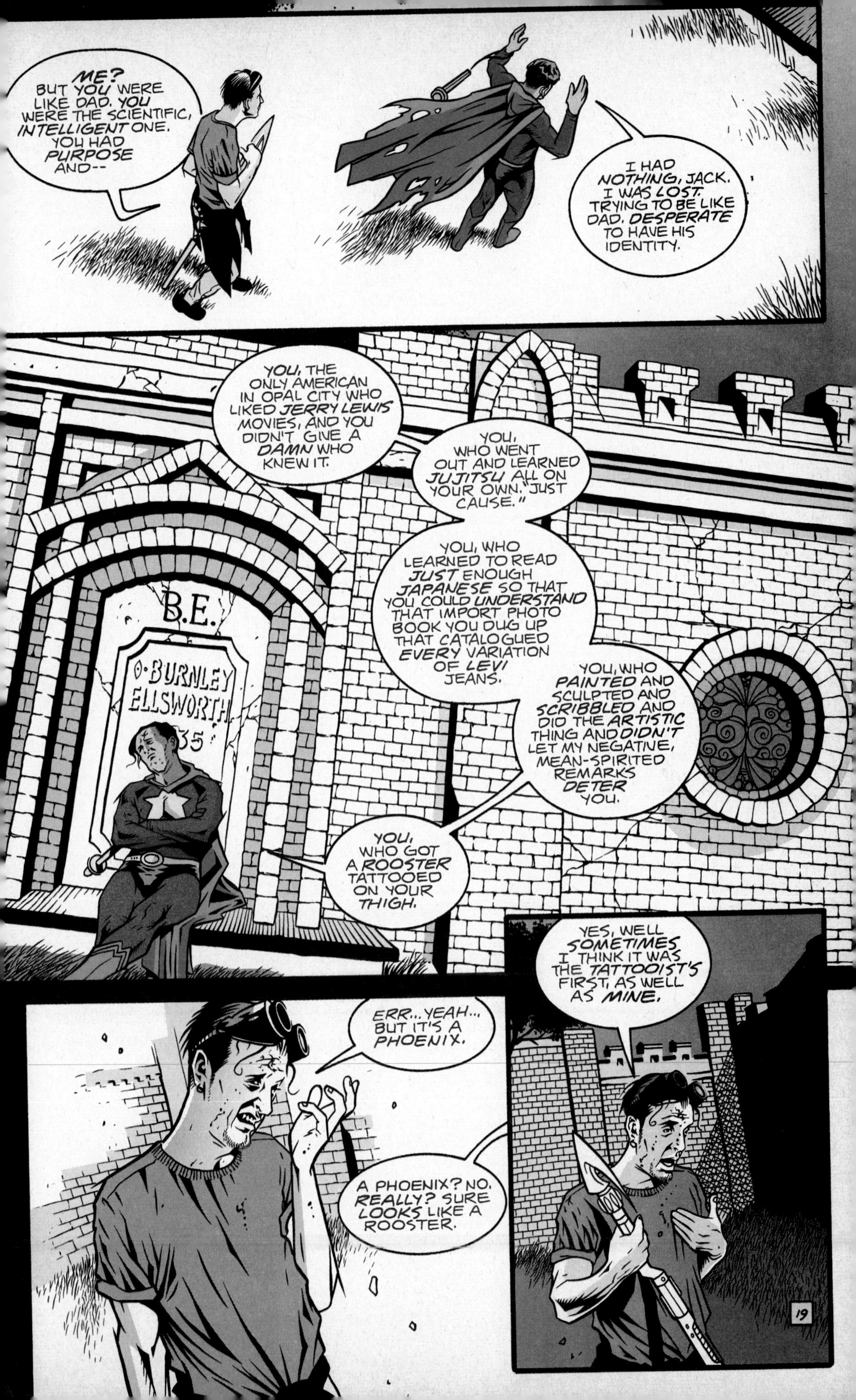
ME? BUT YOU WERE LIKE DAD. YOU WERE THE SCIENTIFIC, INTELLIGENT ONE. YOU HAD PURPOSE AND--
I HAD NOTHING, JACK. I WAS LOST. TRYING TO BE LIKE DAD. DESPERATE TO HAVE HIS IDENTITY.
YOU, THE ONLY AMERICAN IN OPAL CITY WHO LIKED JERRY LEWIS MOVIES, AND YOU DIDN'T GIVE A DAMN WHO KNEW IT.
YOU, WHO WENT OUT AND LEARNED JUJITSU ALL ON YOUR OWN. "JUST CAUSE."
YOU, WHO LEARNED TO READ JUST ENOUGH JAPANESE SO THAT YOU COULD UNDERSTAND THAT IMPORT PHOTO BOOK YOU DUG UP THAT CATALOGUED EVERY VARIATION OF LEVI JEANS.
YOU, WHO PAINTED AND SCULPTED AND SCRIBBLED AND DID THE ARTISTIC THING AND DIDN'T LET MY NEGATIVE, MEAN-SPIRITED REMARKS DETER YOU.
YOU, WHO GOT A ROOSTER TATTOOED ON YOUR THIGH.
B.E.
BURNLEY ELLSWORTH
YES, WELL SOMETIMES I THINK IT WAS THE TATTOOIST'S FIRST, AS WELL AS MINE.
ERR... YEAH... BUT IT'S A PHOENIX.
A PHOENIX? NO. REALLY? SURE LOOKS LIKE A ROOSTER.
19

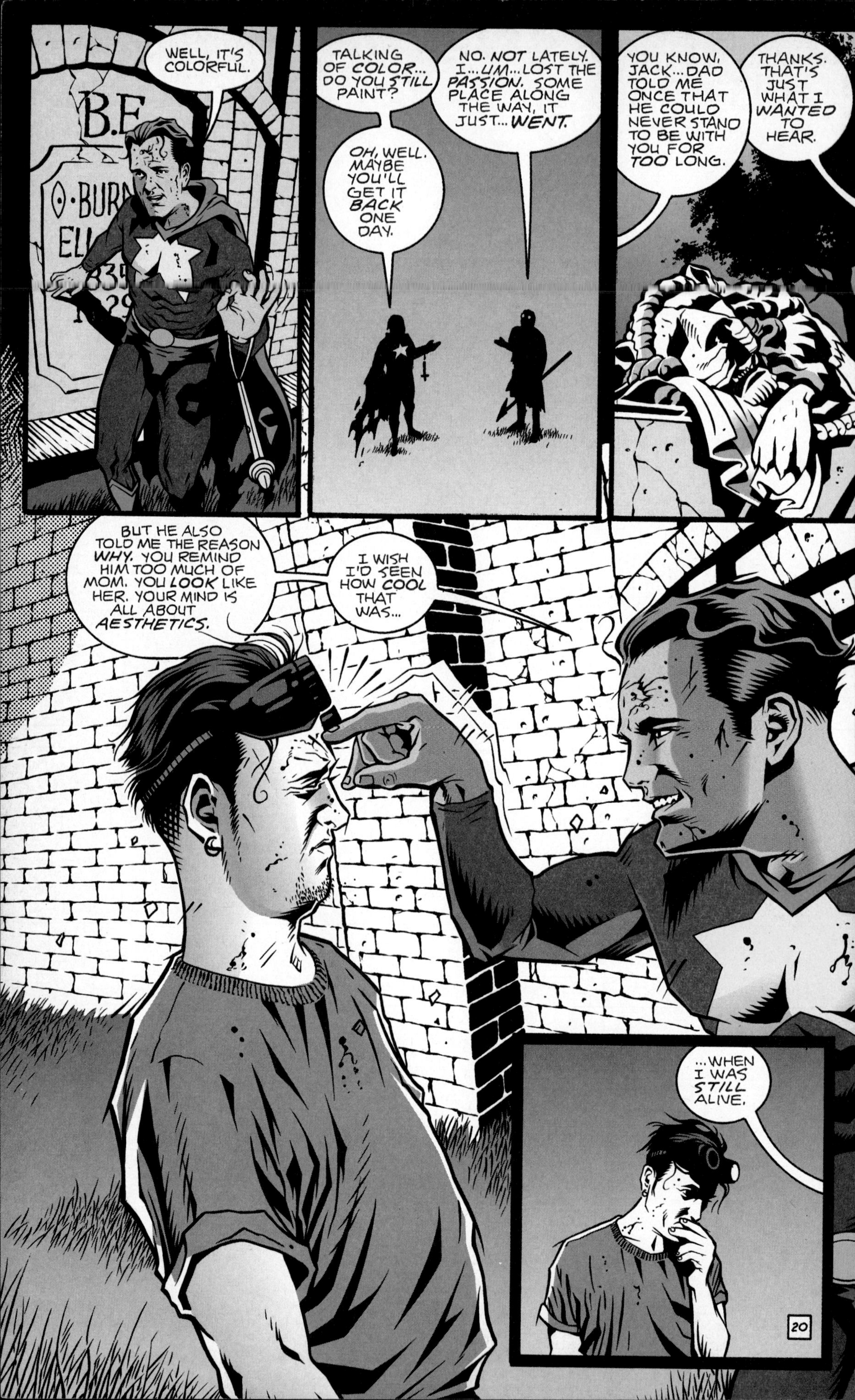
WELL, IT'S COLORFUL.
TALKING OF COLOR... DO YOU STILL PAINT?
NO. NOT LATELY. I...UM...LOST THE PASSION. SOME PLACE ALONG THE WAY, IT JUST...WENT.
OH, WELL. MAYBE YOU'LL GET IT BACK ONE DAY.
YOU KNOW, JACK...DAD TOLD ME ONCE THAT HE COULD NEVER STAND TO BE WITH YOU FOR TOO LONG.
THANKS. THAT'S JUST WHAT I WANTED TO HEAR.
BUT HE ALSO TOLD ME THE REASON WHY. YOU REMIND HIM TOO MUCH OF MOM. YOU LOOK LIKE HER. YOUR MIND IS ALL ABOUT AESTHETICS.
I WISH I'D SEEN HOW COOL THAT WAS...
...WHEN I WAS STILL ALIVE.

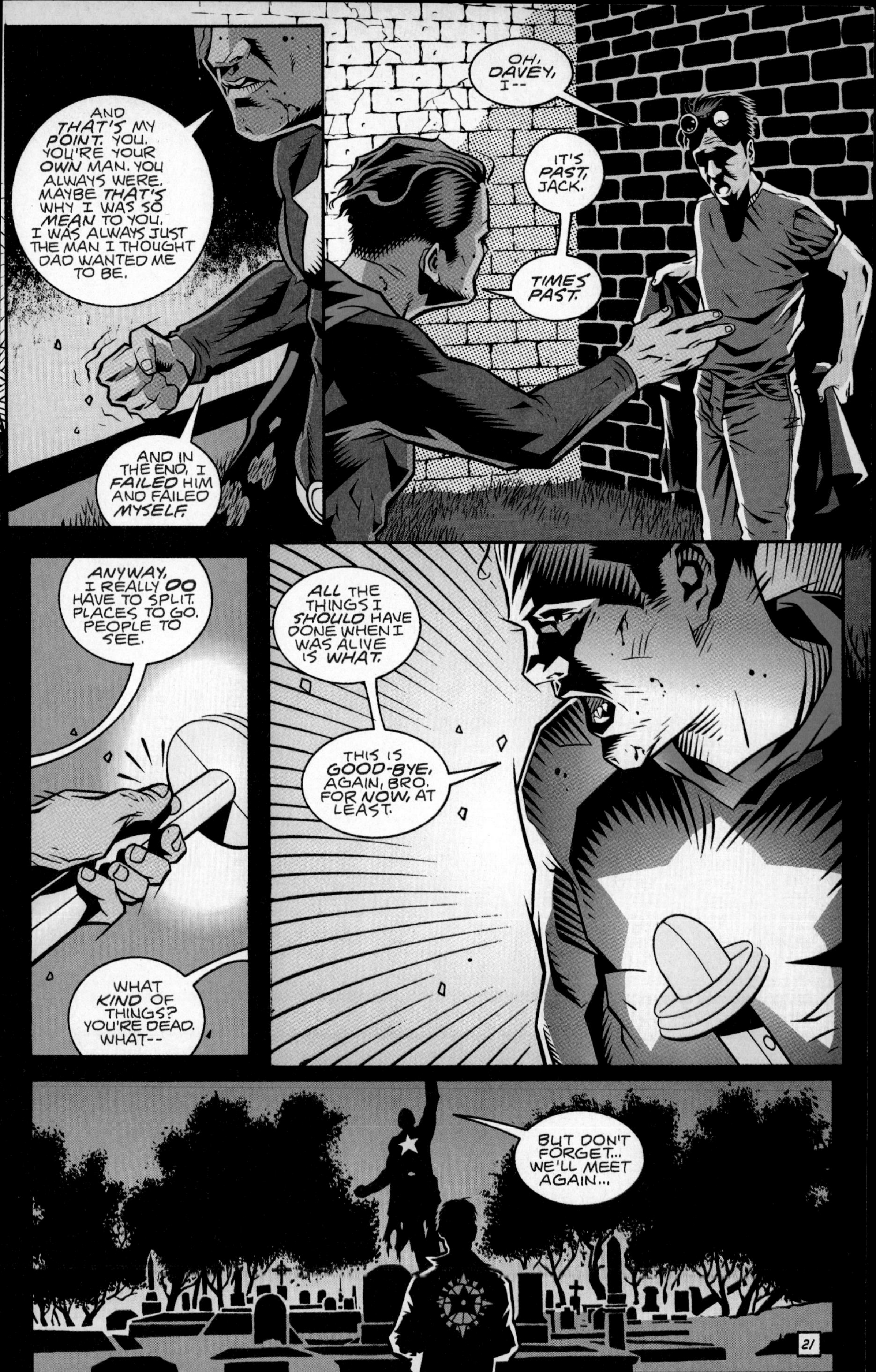
AND THAT'S MY POINT. YOU. YOU'RE YOUR OWN MAN. YOU ALWAYS WERE. MAYBE THAT'S WHY I WAS SO MEAN TO YOU. I WAS ALWAYS JUST THE MAN I THOUGHT DAD WANTED ME TO BE.
AND IN THE END, I FAILED HIM AND FAILED MYSELF.
OH, DAVEY, I--
IT'S PAST, JACK.
TIMES PAST.
ANYWAY, I REALLY DO HAVE TO SPLIT. PLACES TO GO. PEOPLE TO SEE.
WHAT KIND OF THINGS? YOU'RE DEAD. WHAT--
ALL THE THINGS I SHOULD HAVE DONE WHEN I WAS ALIVE IS WHAT.
THIS IS GOOD-BYE, AGAIN, BRO. FOR NOW, AT LEAST.
BUT DON'T FORGET... WE'LL MEET AGAIN...

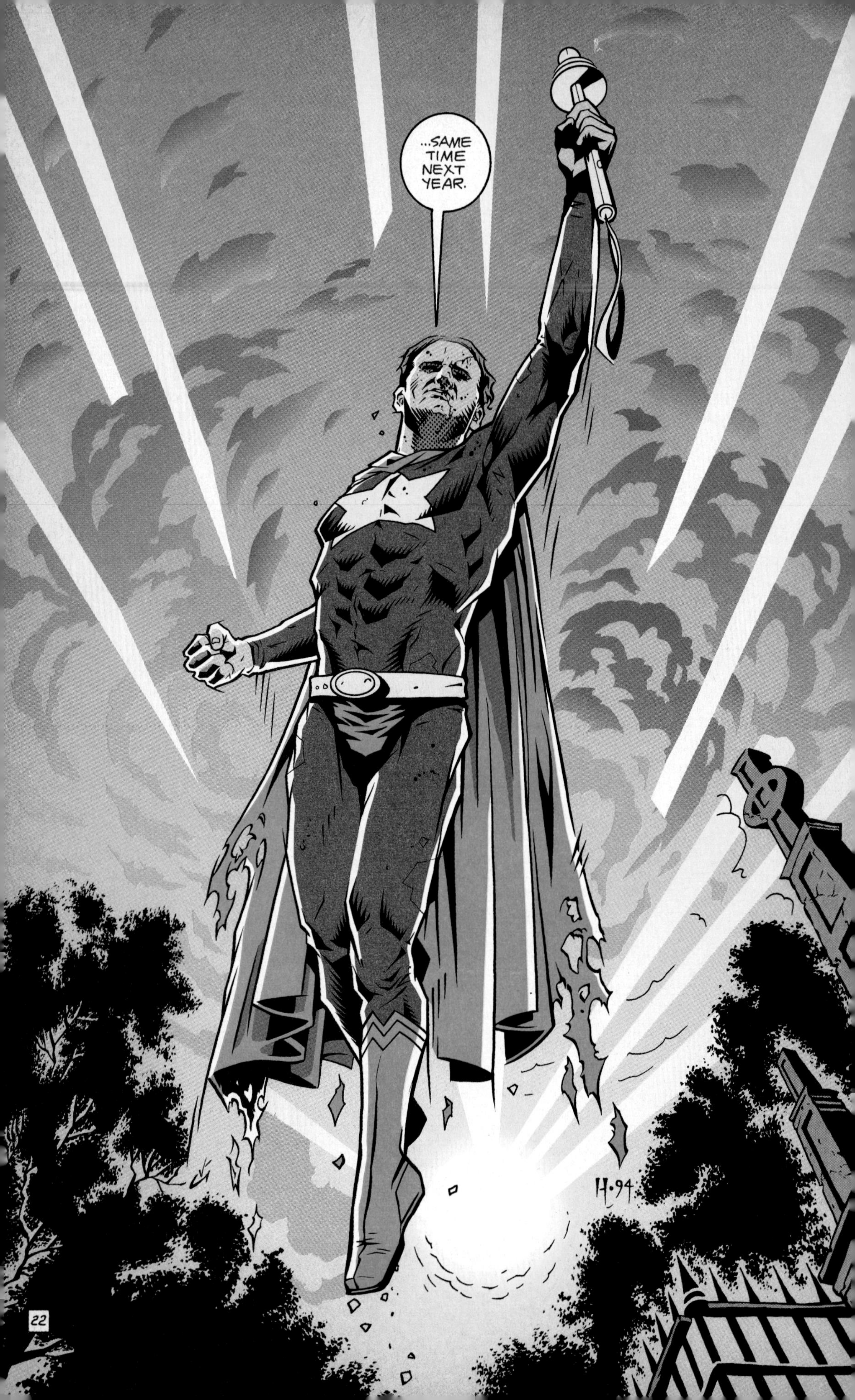
...SAME TIME NEXT YEAR.
H·94

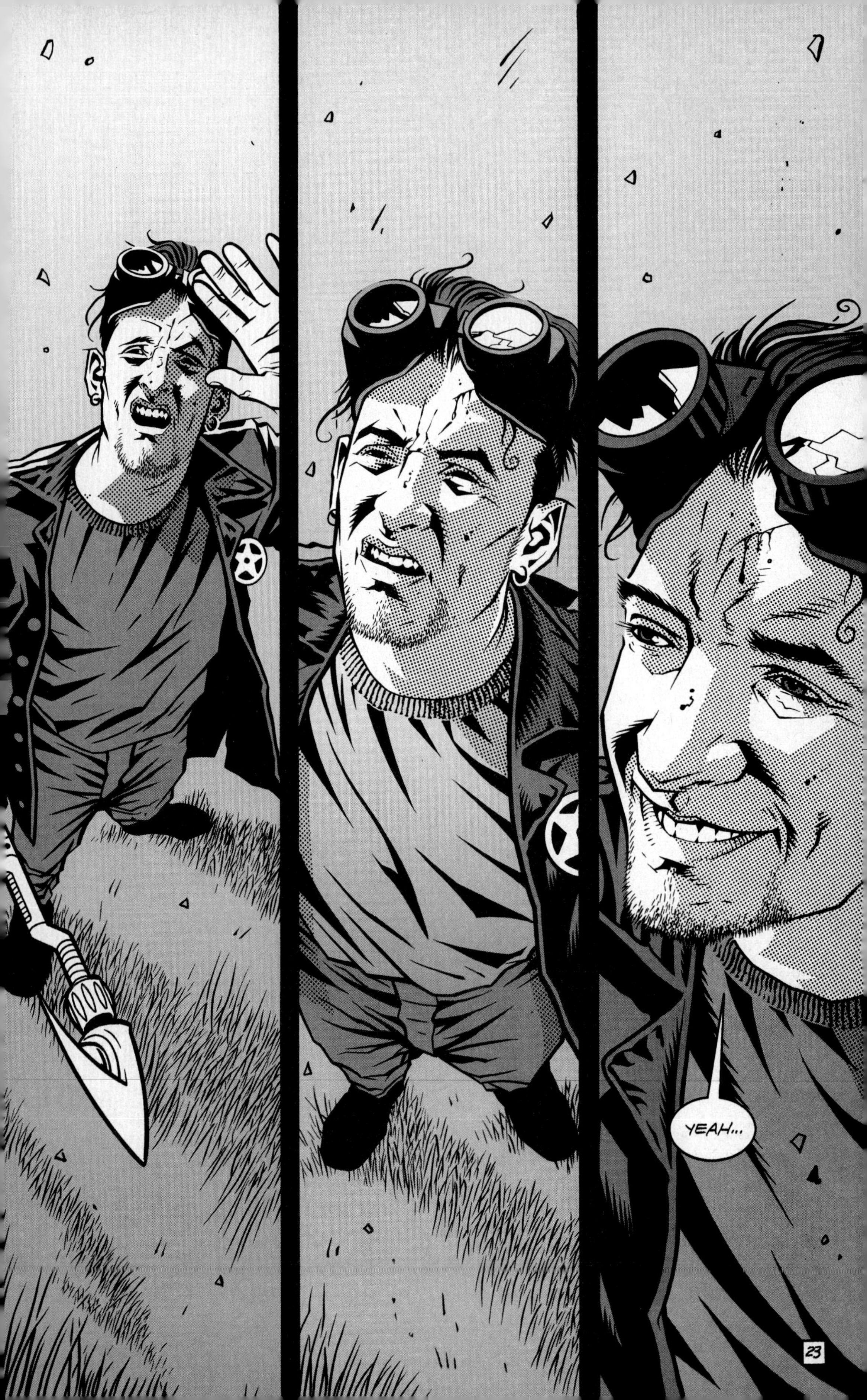
YEAH...

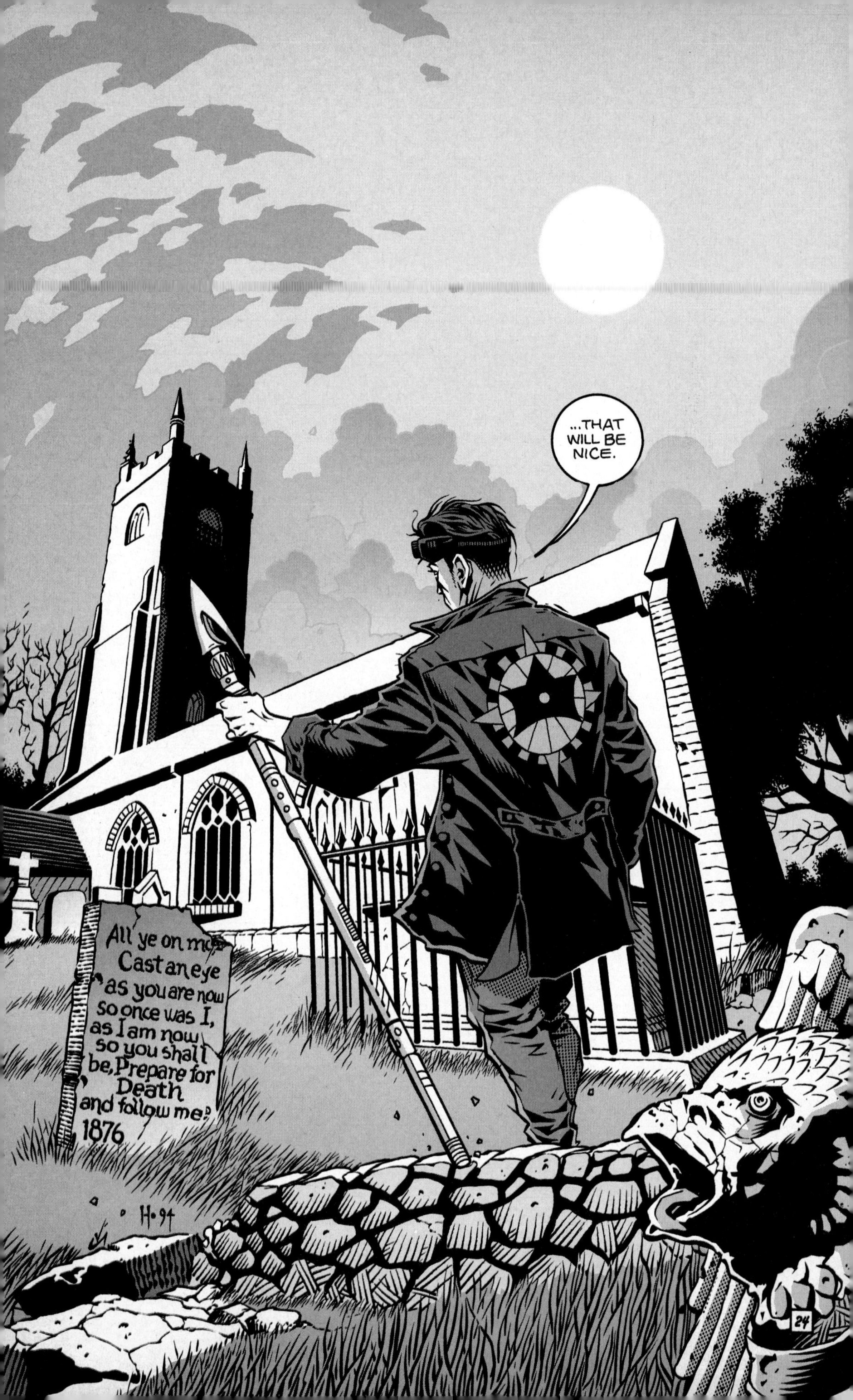
...THAT WILL BE NICE.
All ye on me Cast an eye as you are now so once was I, as I am now so you shall be, Prepare for Death and follow me. 1876
H.94

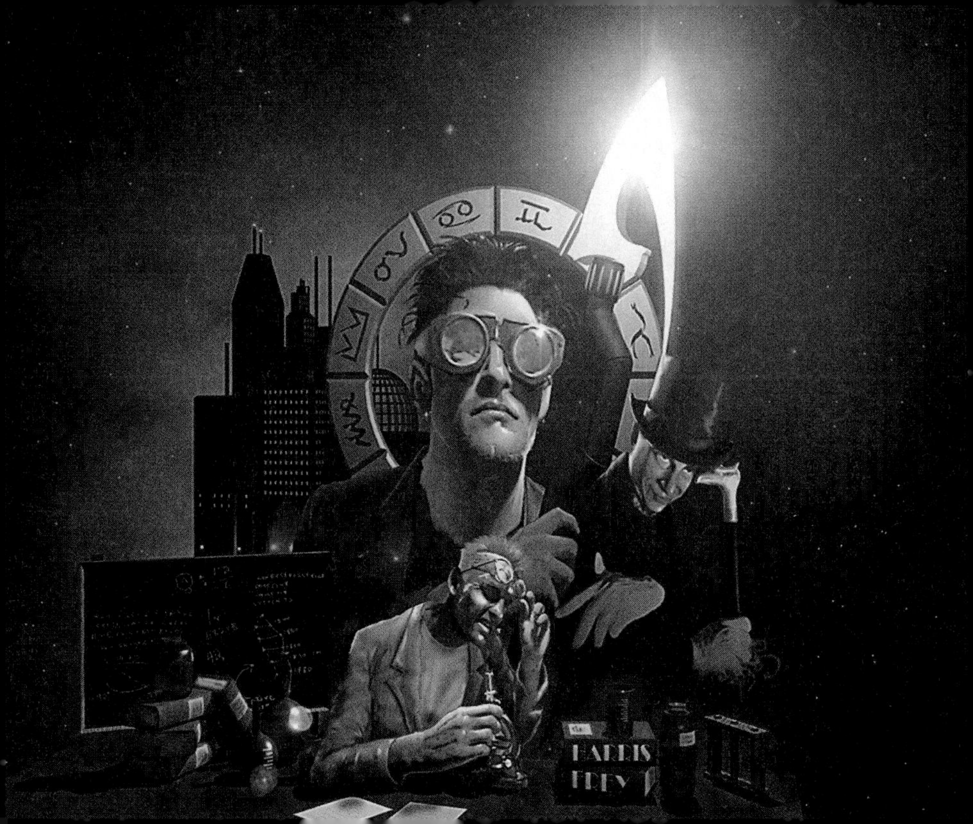
HARRIS
FREY

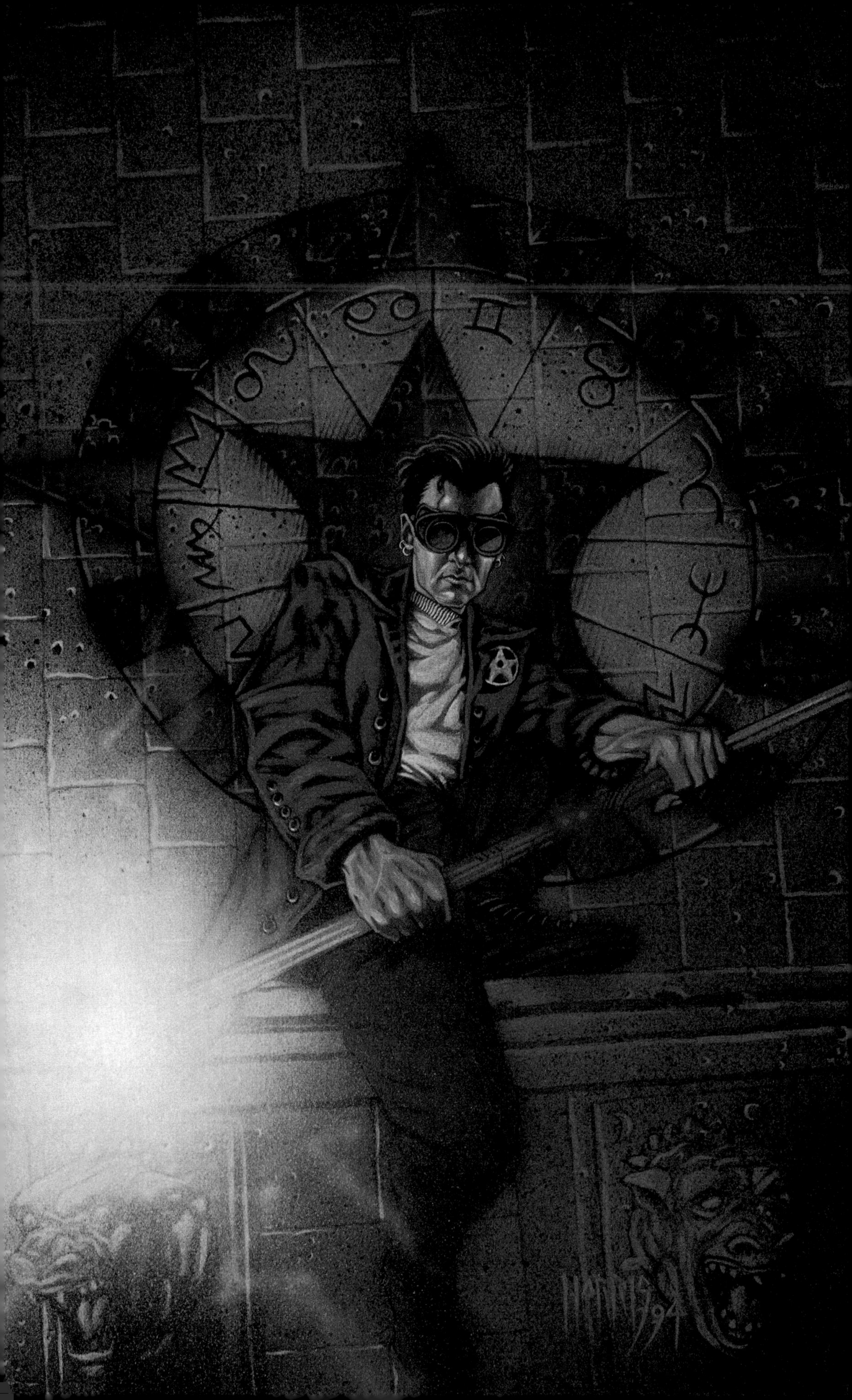

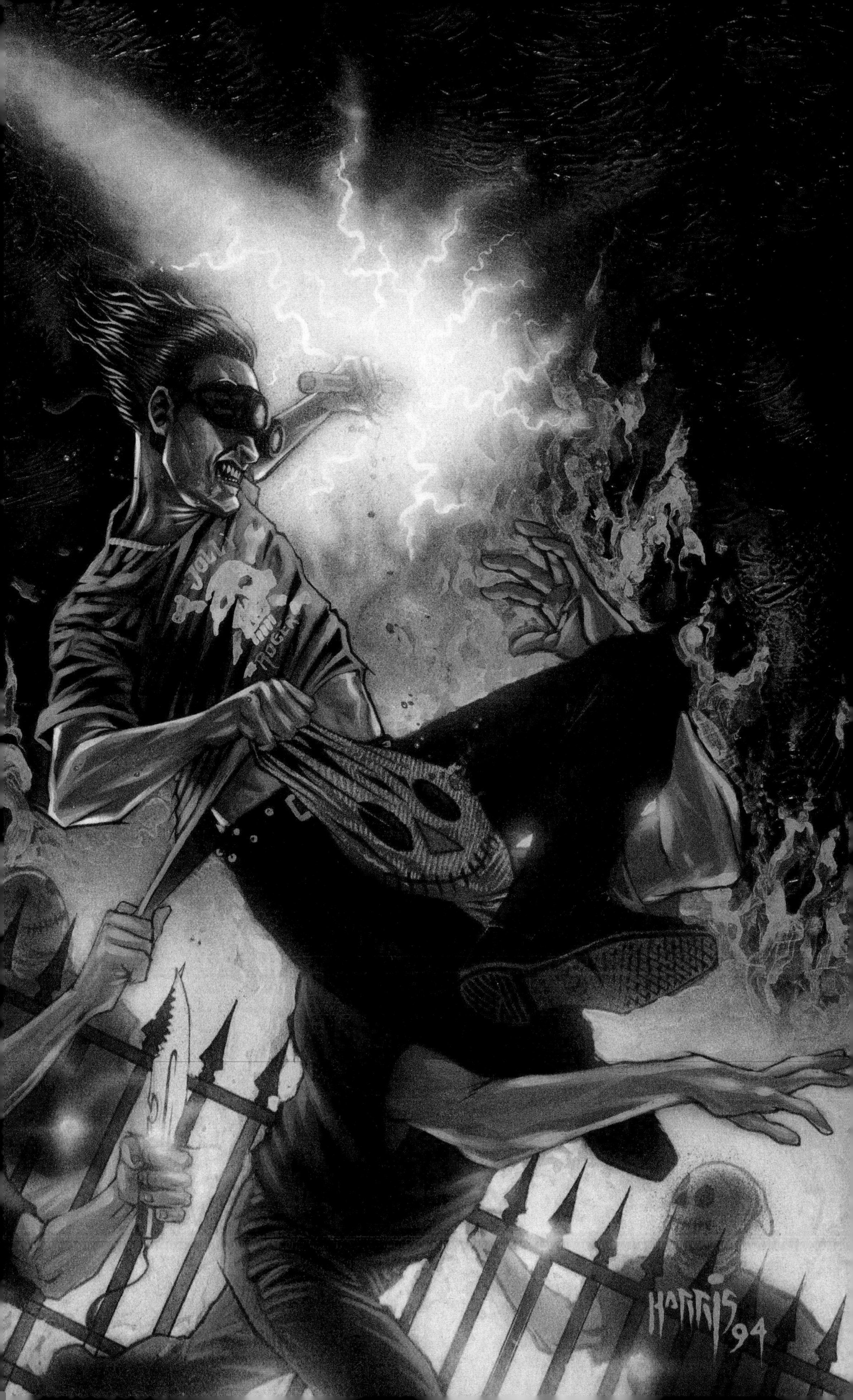

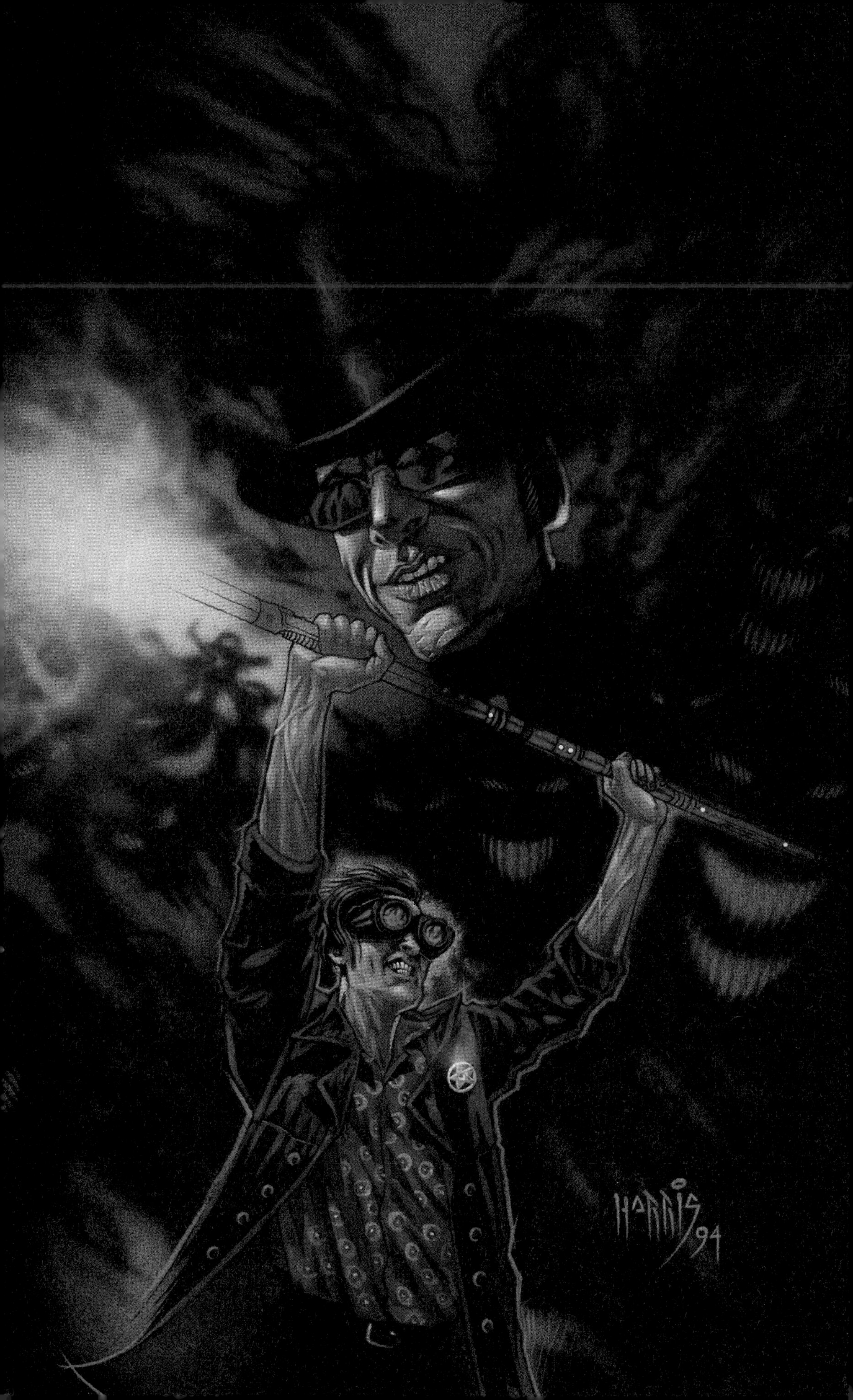
HARRIS 94

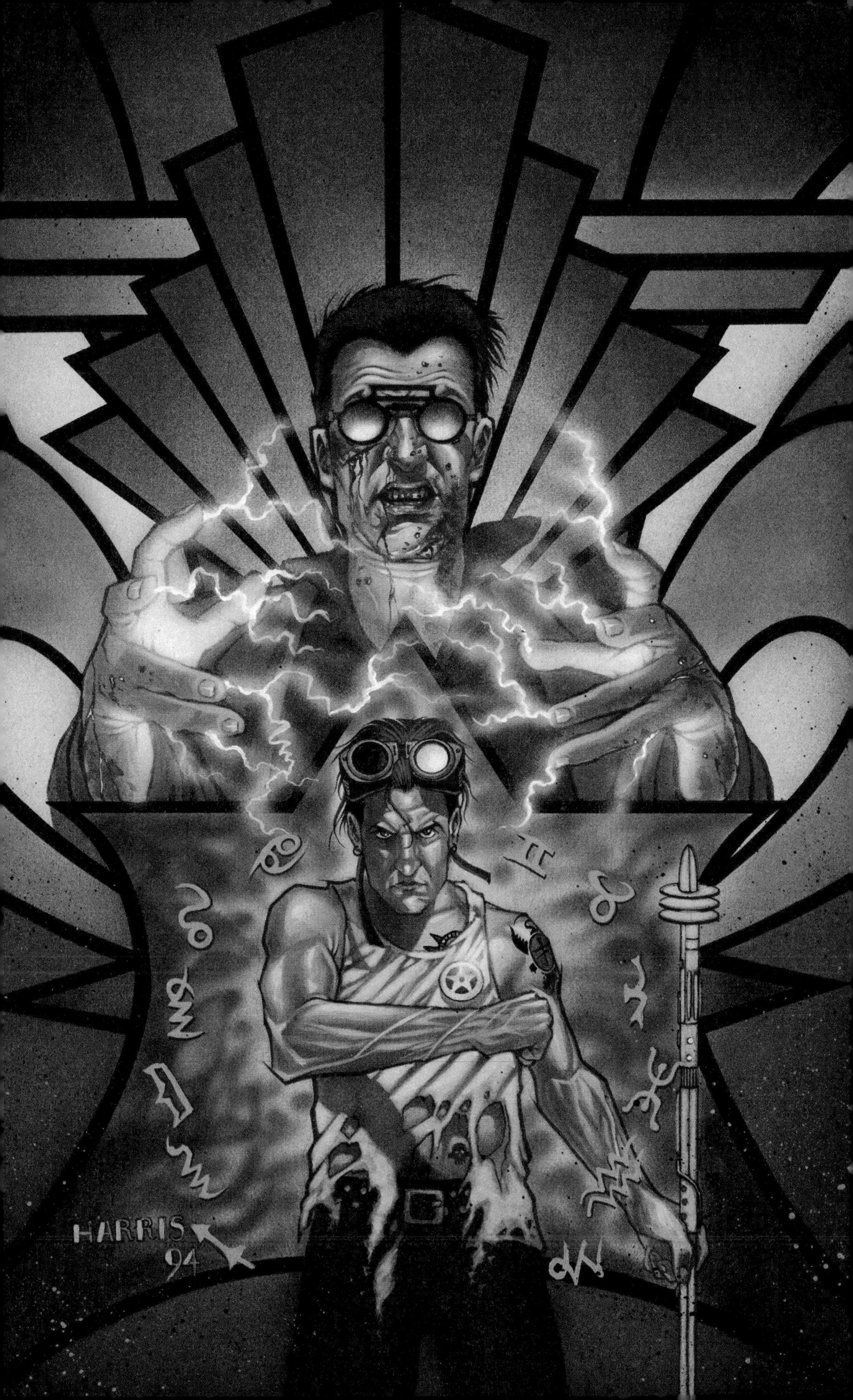
HARRIS
94

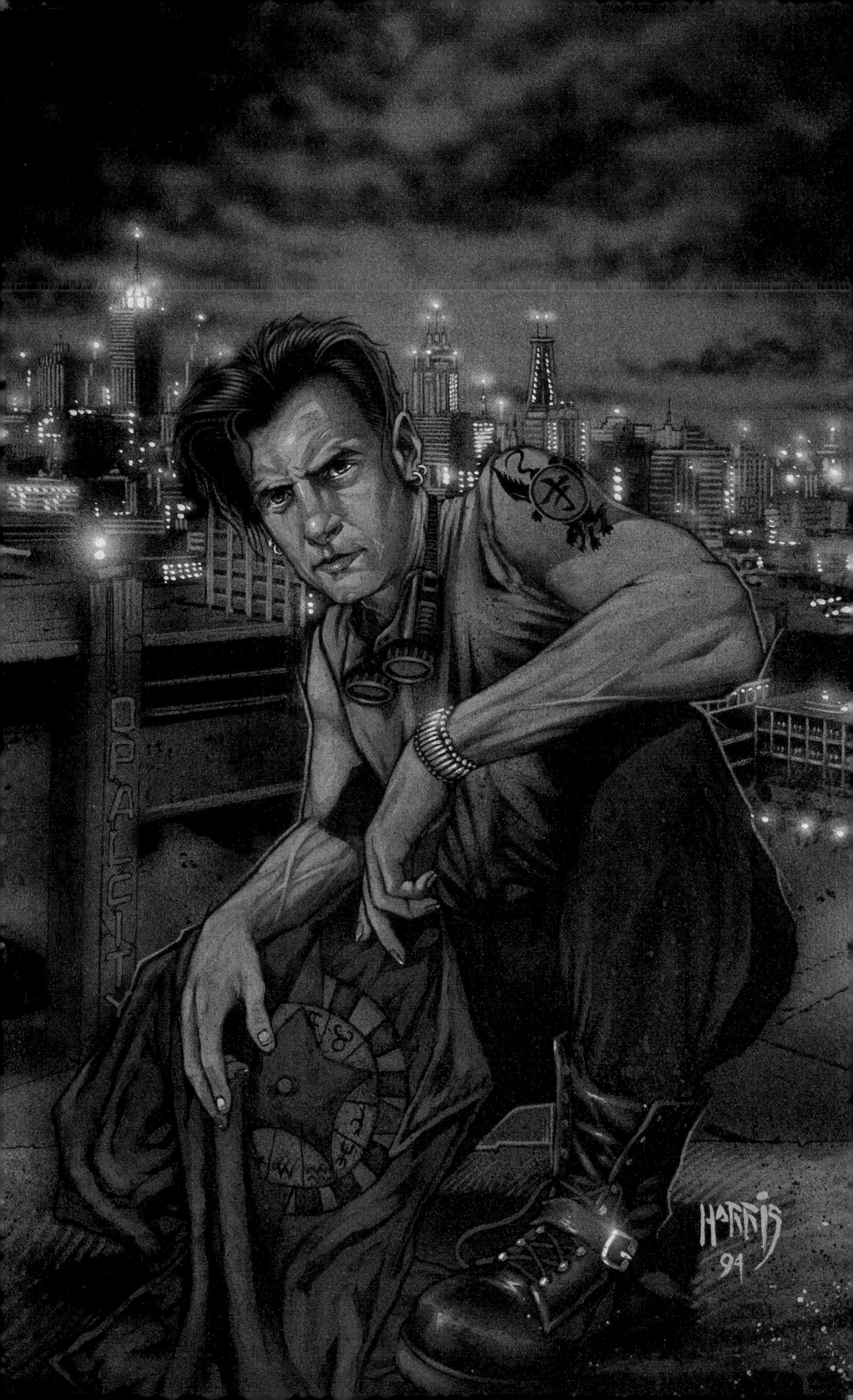
OPALCITY
HARRIS
94

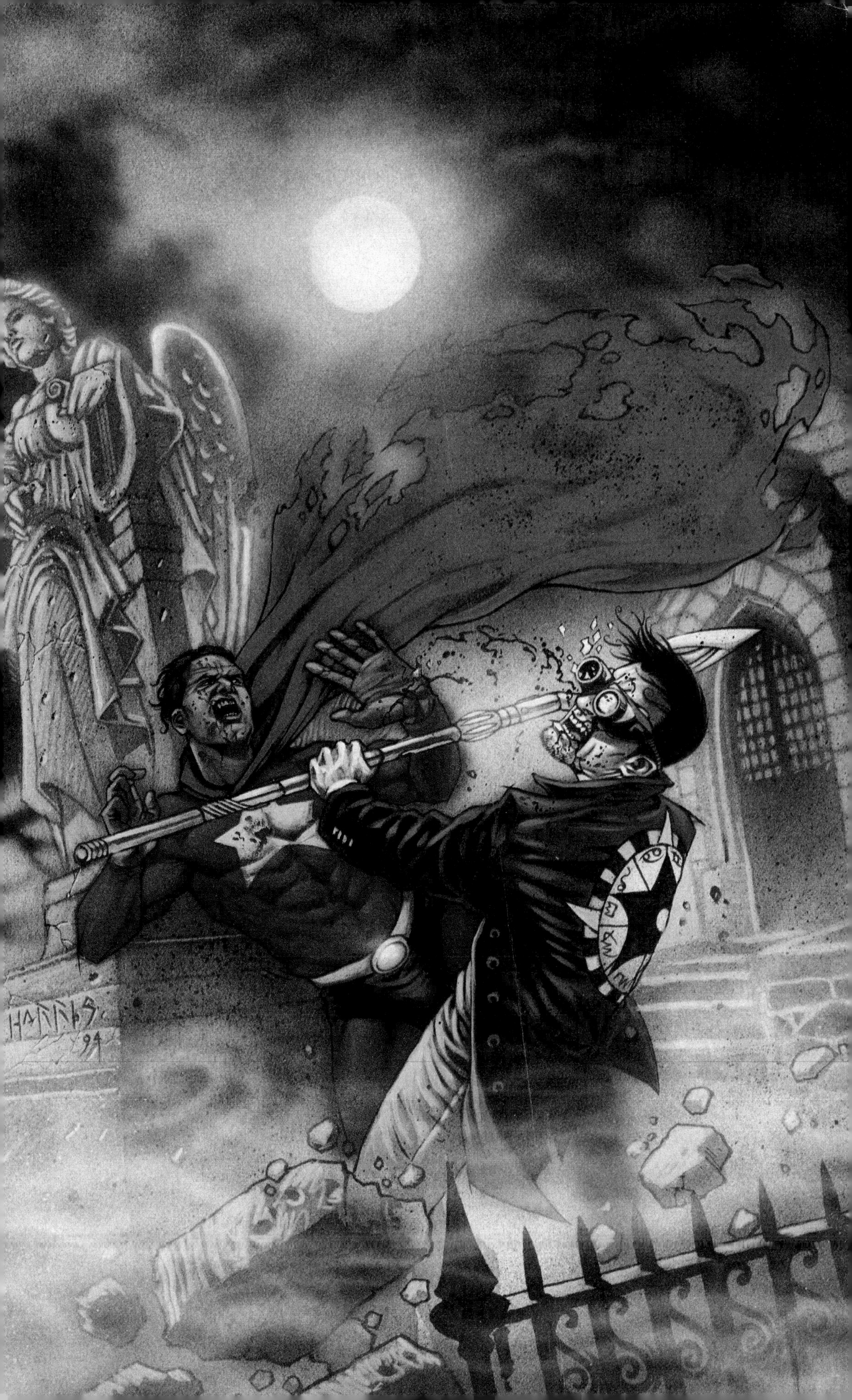

Also by James Robinson

THE GOLDEN AGE
(W) Robinson (A) Smith/Ory

BATMAN: COLLECTED LEGENDS OF THE DARK KNIGHT
(W) James Robinson/various (A) Sale/various

Collections featuring the "Golden Age" Starman

ALL STAR COMICS ARCHIVES Vol. 2
(W) various (A) various

THE GREATEST GOLDEN AGE STORIES EVER TOLD
(W) various (A) various

ZERO HOUR: CRISIS IN TIME
(W) Jurgens (A) Jurgens/Ordway

Other Collections of Interest from DC

DC UNIVERSE

BATMAN VS. PREDATOR: THE COLLECTED EDITION
(W) Gibbons (A) Andy Kubert/Adam Kubert

BATMAN: THE CULT
(W) Starlin (A) Wrightson

BATMAN: THE DARK KNIGHT RETURNS
(W) Miller (A) Miller/Varley/Janson

BATMAN: KNIGHTFALL Part 1: BROKEN BAT
(W) various (A) various

BATMAN: KNIGHTFALL Part 2: WHO RULES THE NIGHT
(W) various (A) various

BATMAN: KNIGHTSEND
(W) various (A) various

BATMAN: PREY
(W) Moench (A) Gulacy/Austin

BATMAN: SHAMAN
(W) O'Neil (A) Hannigan/Beatty

BATMAN: SWORD OF AZRAEL
(W) O'Neil (A) Quesada/Nowlan

BATMAN: TALES OF THE DEMON
(W) O'Neil (A) N. Adams/various

BATMAN: VENOM
(W) O'Neil (A) Von Eeden/various

BATMAN: YEAR ONE
(W) Miller (A) Mazzucchelli

BATMAN: YEAR TWO
(W) Barr (A) A.Davis/McFarlane/various

DEADMAN: LOST SOULS
Suggested for mature readers
(W) Baron (A) K. Jones

THE DEATH OF SUPERMAN Trilogy
THE DEATH OF SUPERMAN
(W) various (A) various

WORLD WITHOUT A SUPERMAN
(W) various (A) various

THE RETURN OF SUPERMAN
(W) various (A) various

GREEN LANTERN/GREEN ARROW:
HARD-TRAVELING HEROES
(W) O'Neil (A) N. Adams

GREEN LANTERN/GREEN ARROW: MORE
HARD-TRAVELING HEROES
(W) O'Neil (A) N. Adams/various

JUSTICE LEAGUE: A NEW BEGINNING
(W) Giffen/DeMatteis (A) Maguire

LEGENDS: THE COLLECTED EDITION
(W) Ostrander/Wein (A) Byrne/K.Kesel

LEGENDS OF THE WORLD'S FINEST
(W) W. Simonson (A) Brereton

THE MAN OF STEEL
(W) Byrne (A) Byrne/Giordano

THE RAY: IN A BLAZE OF POWER
(W) J.C. Harris (A) Quesada/Nichols

THE SPECTRE: CRIMES AND PUNISHMENTS
(W) Ostrander (A) Mandrake

SUPERMAN/DOOMSDAY: HUNTER/PREY
(W) Jurgens (A) Jurgens/Breeding

WONDER WOMAN: THE CONTEST
(W) Messner-Loebs (A) Deodato, Jr.

WORLD'S FINEST
(W) Gibbons (A) Rude/K. Kesel

DC UNIVERSE — ARCHIVES

ALL STAR COMICS ARCHIVES Vol. 1
(W) various (A) various

JUSTICE LEAGUE OF AMERICA ARCHIVES Vol. 1
(W) various (A) various

JUSTICE LEAGUE OF AMERICA ARCHIVES Vol. 2
(W) various (A) various

JUSTICE LEAGUE OF AMERICA ARCHIVES Vol. 3
(W) various (A) various

SHAZAM! ARCHIVES Vol. 1
(W) various (A) various

VERTIGO

All VERTIGO backlist books are suggested for mature readers

JONAH HEX: TWO-GUN MOJO
(W) Lansdale (W) Truman/Glanzman

SANDMAN MYSTERY THEATRE: THE TARANTULA
(W) M. Wagner (A) G. Davis

THE SANDMAN: PRELUDES & NOCTURNES
(W) Gaiman (A) Kieth/Dringenberg/M. Jones, III

THE SANDMAN: THE DOLL'S HOUSE
(W) Gaiman (A) Dringenberg/various

THE SANDMAN: DREAM COUNTRY
(W) Gaiman (A) various

THE SANDMAN: SEASON OF MISTS
(W) Gaiman (A) K. Jones/various

THE SANDMAN: A GAME OF YOU
(W) Gaiman (A) McManus/various

THE SANDMAN: BRIEF LIVES
(W) Gaiman (A) Thompson/Locke

THE SANDMAN: FABLES AND REFLECTIONS
(W) Gaiman (A) various

THE SANDMAN: WORLDS' END
(W) Gaiman (A) various

OTHER

CAMELOT 3000
(W) Barr (A) Bolland

RONIN
(W/A) Miller

WATCHMEN
(W) A. Moore (A) Gibbons